Inventing the Classics

Inventing the Classics

MODERNITY, NATIONAL IDENTITY,
AND JAPANESE LITERATURE

Edited by
Haruo Shirane
and Tomi Suzuki

STANFORD UNIVERSITY PRESS

STANFORD, CALIFORNIA

Stanford University Press
Stanford, California

© 2000 by the Board of Trustees of the
Leland Stanford Junior University

Printed in the United States of America
on acid-free, archival-quality paper

Library of Congress Cataloging-in-Publication Data

Inventing the classics : modernity, national identity, and Japanese
literature / edited by Haruo Shirane and Tomi Suzuki
      p.   cm.
   Includes bibliographical references and index.
   ISBN 0-8047-3990-0 (alk. paper)—ISBN 0-8047-4105-0 (paper :
alk paper)
   1. Japanese literature—History and criticism.   2. Nationalism
and literature—Japan.   3. Ideology and literature.   4. Nationalism and education—Japan.   I. Shirane, Haruo, 1951–
II. Suzuki, Tomi, 1951–

PL714.I58 2001
895.6'09—dc21   00-0058337
                                                         Rev.

Typeset by BookMatters in 11/13 Adobe Garamond

Original Printing 2000

Last figure below indicates year of this printing:
09   08   07   06   05   04   03   02   01   00

Acknowledgments

This book emerged out of an international symposium, "Canon Formation: Gender, Nationalism, and Japanese Literature," held in March 1997 at Columbia University. We are deeply indebted to the presenters and discussants: Ryūichi Abe, Paul Anderer, David Bialock, Linda Chance, Lewis Cook, Horikiri Minoru, Mack Horton, Kawahira Hitoshi, Kōnoshi Takamitsu, Kurozumi Makoto, William Lee, Mitamura Masako, Mitani Kuniaki, Momokawa Takahito, Joshua Mostow, Murai Osamu, Shinada Yoshikazu, Takahashi Tōru, and Tanaki Keiko. Special thanks to the Japanese literature graduate students — Kevin Collins, Anne Commons, Cheryl Crowley, Peter Flueckiger, Naomi Fukumori, Mikiko Iwaya, Iori Jōkō, Masaaki Kinugasa, David Lurie, Herschel Miller, and Jamie Newhard — without whom the conference would not have occurred. Not enough can be said for Yuiko Yampolsky, who was the conference coordinator, and Gina Bookhout, the department administrator. We owe a great debt to the sponsors: Itoh Foundation, Social Science Research Council, All Nippon Airlines, Donald Keene Center of Japanese Culture, and the Department of East Asian Languages and Cultures at Columbia University. As always, our gratitude to the CV Starr East Asian Library, especially Yasuko Makino and Amy Heinrich. Special thanks to David Lurie, who helped to edit the final papers, to Jamie Newhard, Cheryl Crowley, Hershel Miller, and Peter Flueckiger, who labored extensively on translations that ultimately could not be included, and to Anne Commons, for her meticulous work and singular dedication. Torquil Duthie compiled the bibliography. Winifred Olsen was a wonderful editor and insightful advisor. Our thanks to Janet Walker, the reader, and to Helen Tartar for her long-time support, wise guidance, and great patience. It should be noted that a different version of this book, with different authors and papers, appeared earlier in Japanese as Haruo Shirane and Tomi Suzuki, eds., *Sōzōsareta koten: Kanon keisei, Kokumin kokka, Nihon bungaku*, Shin'yōsha, 1999.

Haruo Shirane and Tomi Suzuki
New York City, 1999

Contents

Contributors

DAVID T. BIALOCK is Assistant Professor of Japanese literature at the University of Southern California. His publications include "Voice, Text, and the Question of Poetic Borrowing in Late Classical Japanese Poetry" and several articles on *The Tale of the Heike*. He is currently finishing a book that examines *The Heike* in relationship to Buddhist thought and problems of space, ritual, music, and other aspects of medieval Japanese culture.

LINDA H. CHANCE is Associate Professor of Japanese Language and Literature at the University of Pennsylvania. Her book *Formless in Form: Kenkō, Tsurezuregusa, and the Rhetoric of Japanese Fragmentary Prose* was published in 1997 by Stanford University Press. In addition to her interests in genre, particularly the prose miscellany, she studies aspects of the feminine in Japanese literature.

KŌNOSHI TAKAMITSU is Professor in the Department of Comparative Literature and Culture in the Graduate School of Arts and Sciences at the University of Tokyo. He is a specialist in ancient Japanese literature and is the author of *Kojiki no tassei: sono ronri to hōhō* (Tokyo daigaku shuppankai, 1983), *Kojiki no sekaikan* (Yoshikawa kōbunkan, 1986), *Kakinomoto no Hitomaro kenkyū: kodai waka bungaku no seiritsu* (Hanawa shobō, 1992), *Kojiki—tennō no sekai no monogatari* (Nihon hōsō shuppan kyōkai, 1995), and *Kojiki to Nihon shoki—'tennō shinwa' no rekishi*, Kōdansha gendai shinsho (Kōdansha, 1999), and co-editor of *Kojiki*, Shinpen Nihon koten bungaku zenshū (Shōgakukan, 1997).

KUROZUMI MAKOTO is Professor in the Department of Area Studies in the Graduate School of Arts and Science at the University of Tokyo. He has written widely on Tokugawa intellectual history and ethics, particularly on Confucianism and Ogyū Sorai. His articles include "Jugaku to kinsei Nihon shakai" (Neo-Confucianism and Tokugawa society), *Nihon tsūshi* 13 Kinsei 3 (Iwanami shoten, 1994), and "Tokugawa zenki jukyō no seikaku" (The Nature of Early Tokugawa Confucianism), *Shisō* 792 (June 1990), which has been translated by Herman Ooms in *Journal of Japanese Studies* 20, no. 2 (autumn 1994).

WILLIAM LEE, who wrote his Ph.D. dissertation on historical kabuki, is an Assistant Professor at Minnesota State University–Akita, Akita, Japan. His current research interests include Japanese theater, folk performing arts, and popular culture. He has just completed a translation of the kabuki play *Ishikiri Kajiwara*. Other recent work includes the essay "From Sazae-san to Crayon Shin-chan: Family Anime, Social Change, and Nostalgia in Japan" in *Japan Pop! Inside the World of Japanese Popular Culture*, edited by Tim Craig (Armonk, N.Y.: M. E. Sharpe, 2000).

JOSHUA S. MOSTOW is Associate Professor in the Department of Asian Studies at the University of British Columbia. He is a specialist in both Japanese art and Japanese literature and has written widely on the relationship between painting and poetry, including "Nihon no Bijutsushi Gensetsu to 'Miyabi,'" (Art Historical Discourse in Japan and 'Courtliness'), in *Kataru Genzai, Katarareru kako: Nihon bijutsu hyakunen*, edited by Tokyo Kokuritsu Bunkazai Kenkyūjo (Heibonsha, 1999). He is the author of *Pictures of the Heart: The Hyakunin Isshu in Word and Image* (Honolulu: University of Hawai'i Press, 1996).

SHINADA YOSHIKAZU is Associate Professor at Seishin joshi daigaku (University of the Sacred Heart) in Tokyo. He is a specialist in ancient Japanese literature, particularly the *Man'yōshū*, and has written articles such as "Minzoku no koe—kōshō bungaku no ichimen" (Voice of the Folk—One Aspect of the Concept of Oral Literature) in *Koe to moji* (Hanawa shobō, 1999). He is the author and co-editor of *Uta o yomu, sanjūichi ji no shigaku* (Sanseidō, 1997).

HARUO SHIRANE, Shinchō Professor of Japanese Literature and Culture in the Department of East Asian Languages and Cultures at Columbia University, has written widely on Japanese fiction, poetry, criticism, and cultural history. He is the author of *The Bridge of Dreams: A Poetics of the Tale of Genji* (Stanford: Stanford University Press, 1987), the Japanese translation of which won the Kadokawa Genyoshi Prize in 1993, and *Traces of Dreams: Landscape, Cultural Memory, and the Poetry of Basho* (Stanford: Stanford University Press, 1998), which received the Haiku Society of America Merit

Book Award for Criticism. He is editor of *Early Modern Japanese Literature, An Anthology: 1600–1900* (New York: Columbia University Press, 2001).

TOMI SUZUKI is Associate Professor of Japanese and Comparative Literature in the Department of East Asian Languages and Cultures at Columbia University. A specialist in nineteenth- and twentieth-century narrative fiction and criticism, she is the author of *Narrating the Self: Fictions of Japanese Modernity* (Stanford: Stanford University Press, 1996; Japanese edition published by Iwanami shoten in 2000). She is currently working on a manuscript on gender, genre, and modernity.

Historical Periods

Nara Period	710–784
Heian Period	794–1185
Kamakura Period	1185–1333
Period of North and South Courts	1336–92
Muromachi Period	1392–1573
Warring States Period	1477–1573
Edo (Tokugawa) Period	1600–1867
Meiji Period	1868–1912
Taishō Period	1912–26
Shōwa Period	1926–89
Heisei Period	1989–present

Inventing the Classics

Introduction: Issues in Canon Formation

HARUO SHIRANE

Today when we speak of the Japanese literary classics, we think of texts such as the *Man'yōshū* (Collection of Ten Thousand Leaves, late 8th c.), the *Kojiki* (Record of Ancient Matters, 712), *Genji monogatari* (The Tale of Genji, early 11th c.), *Makura no sōshi* (The Pillow Book, late 10th c.), *Heike monogatari* (The Tale of the Heike, ca. 14th c.), and *Tsurezuregusa* (Essays in Idleness, early 14th c.) and of authors such as Matsuo Bashō, Ihara Saikaku, and Chikamatsu Monzaemon. These texts and authors are repeatedly anthologized in textbooks in Japan and abroad and are widely thought to be the repository of Japanese culture, spirit, and taste. This status, however, is as much a result of reception in the medieval period, when the vernacular canon was first formed, as it is of the radical configuration of notions of literature and learning that occurred in the nineteenth and twentieth centuries. The objective of this volume of essays is to historicize this complex sociopolitical process, particularly as it relates to the emergence of linguistic and cultural nationalism, by which these texts and authors were privileged and became the cultural icons of Japan's "tradition."

I

Today the term "canon" usually refers to authorized texts, particularly those in school curricula, or texts widely perceived to be worthy of interpretation and imitation. Canon in the narrower sense means the standard repertoire, the most highly prized or most frequently read or performed works within a particular genre or institution. By contrast, canon in the broader, more political sense—the way in which it is used in this book—means those texts that are recognized by established or powerful institutions. Historically, Western canon theory can be divided roughly into two approaches. The foundational, which sees a foundation or bedrock in the text, holds that a canonical text embodies some universal, unchanging, or absolute value. A good example is the famous essay, "What is a classic?" written in 1850 by Charles-Augustin Sainte-Beuve, which notes that a true classic is the work of "an author who has enriched the human mind," "who has discovered some unequivocal moral truth, or has once more seized hold of some eternal passion. . . . "[1] The second approach, generally followed today, is antifoundational, and holds that there is no foundation in the text, that works in a canon reflect the interests of a particular group or society at a particular time: here the term canon, which implies conflict and change, deliberately replaces and critiques the notions of the classic and of tradition, both of which suggest something unchanging or given. In this view, traditions, like literary classics, are constructed, particularly by dominant communities or institutions. At the same time, in deference to the foundational position, it would be foolish to imply that the texts are empty boxes ready to be filled by their next owners. Each text implies certain moral or aesthetic values and possesses certain formal characteristics, such as gendered authorship, that have had a significant impact on the manner in which it has been received.

Taking an antifoundational position, John Guillory has argued that the ideological or cultural value of the texts in a canon does not lie in the texts themselves but in the processes and institutions that give the texts value. "Canonicity is not a property of the work itself but of its transmission" and its relation to institutions such as the school.[2] Pierre Bourdieu, upon whom Guillory draws for his central thesis, has pointed to two fundamental forms of production: the production of the work and the production of the value of the work. In fact, for Bourdieu, "The production of discourse (critical, historical, etc.) about the work of art is one of the conditions of production of the work."[3] A canonical text in this sense is constantly *re*-produced. Canon formation is thus concerned not only with the immediate producers of the work—the authors, the scribes, the printers, etc.—but also with those agents and institutions (such as commentators, patrons, temples, schools, museums, publishing houses) that produce or *re*-produce the value of the text and that create the consumers and audiences capable of recognizing and desiring that value. Key questions, then, are how, by whom, and for what purposes this value is generated, maintained, and transmitted.

In contrast to literary canons, which are in constant flux, scriptural canons in Europe have tended to be stable and are often closed, since religious institutions (e.g., the Church) usually control the choice of canonical texts, limit their interpretation, and train those who interpret and teach the texts. The Bible, for example, is no longer open to change or expansion. In Japan, however, the scriptural canons, which were primarily Buddhist but which included Shinto, Confucian, and other syncretic forms, showed considerable diversity and fluidity. The Shinto canon, which emerged in the medieval period and became closely associated with *kokugaku* (nativist learning) in the eighteenth century before being adapted as a form of national religion in the Meiji period, had the remarkable ability to claim various texts—such as the "Age of the Gods" volume of the *Nihon shoki* (Chronicles of Japan, 720), which had earlier been a state history—as scripture (*shinten*). The modern critic Saeki Shōichi has even claimed that vernacular Japanese literature as a whole is the Shinto canon: the *Kojiki*, *The Tale of Genji*, *Ise monogatari* (Tales of Ise, late 10th c.), *nō* drama, and other Japanese literary texts embody and transmit Shinto beliefs (such as worship of the spirit of the dead or the desire for purification) from one generation to the next.[4]

How then were canons established in Japan? In what ways did these texts become canonical? The broad range of overlapping institutional practices examined in the following essays include (1) the preservation, collation, and transmission of a text or its variants, which was critical prior to printing in the seventeenth century; (2) extensive commentary, exegesis, and criticism; (3) the use of a text in a school curriculum; (4) the employment of a text as a model for diction, style, or grammar, or as a source of allusion and reference, both of which were critical to the medieval construction of the poetic canon; (5) the use of a text as a source for knowledge of historical and institutional precedents (*yūsoku kojitsu*), which was of critical importance for both court and warrior administrations; (6) the adoption of a text as the embodiment of a set of religious beliefs; (7) the inclusion of a text in anthologies; (8) the construction of genealogies and lines of descent, an important technique for schools and scholarly families; (9) the writing of literary histories, which occurred from the Meiji period; and (10) the incorporation of a text into institutional discourse, particularly state ideology, as with the *Kojiki*. In many of these instances, there is a prominent stress on genealogy and "origins," which become a frequent source of authority, ranging from the origins of a clan (*uji*), a family house (*ie*), a school (*mon*), to national origins.

GENRE AND COMPETING CANONS

Another key issue in canon formation is that of genre configurations. The history of canon formation, at least in the European tradition, has often been seen as a history of the rise and fall of different genres or modes. The *Genji ippon kyō* (Genji One Volume Sutra, 1176), a Buddhist text written by Priest Chōken in the late twelfth century, reveals that the genre hierarchy as it existed in the late Heian and early medieval periods was, roughly speaking, from top to bottom: (1) Buddhist scriptures; (2) Confucian texts; (3) histories such as the *Records of the Historian* (*Shih chi, Shiki*); (4) Chinese belle lettres (*bun*) such as the *Anthology of Literature* (*Wen hsüan, Monzen*), a collection of Chinese poetry and literary prose; (5) Japanese classical poetry (*waka*); and (6) vernacular tales (*monogatari*) and stories (*sōshi*), as well as diaries (*nikki*) and related writings in the kana syllabary. The genre hierarchy here follows the Chinese model, with religious/philosophical texts, histories, and poetry held in highest regard, while fiction is relegated to the bottom. The most highly regarded canon, at least from the Buddhist priest's point of view, was the Buddhist, followed by the Confucian canon. Next came the two highest Chinese literary genres, history and poetry. At the bottom were the two genres in the Japanese syllabary, waka and monogatari, with waka of much higher status than prose fiction in kana. Cultural identity was also a major element in the genre hierarchy. The top four categories, the most prestigious genres, were of foreign origin, identified primarily with China (Kara). The two bottom genres, by contrast, were identified with native culture, with Japan (Yamato).

In the eighteenth century, the scholars of kokugaku, who attacked what they perceived to be foreign influences and created an alternative sphere of learning based on what they perceived to be purely Japanese texts, attempted to invert the genre hierarchy found in texts such as the *Genji ippon kyō*. They placed waka and monogatari, texts in the Japanese syllabary, at the top, while attempting to decanonize the other four categories, Buddhist and Confucian texts and Chinese poetry and histories. It was not, however, until the mid-Meiji period, with the rise of modern nationalism, the influence of Western phonocentricism, the emphasis on a "national language" (*kokugo*) based on kana, and the defeat of China in the Sino-Japanese War, that this inversion finally became irreversible. Throughout the premodern period, *gakumon*, the Japanese word for learning, meant the study of Chinese texts (*kangaku*), which was the center of various premodern discourses, and it was not until the establishment of *kokubungaku* (national literature studies) in the mid-Meiji period that Japanese literature was conceived largely, though not entirely, as kana-based literature.

The writers or commentators of a genre or text held in low regard frequently attempted to elevate that genre or text by giving it traits borrowed from higher genres or canons. In the kana preface to the *Kokinshū* (Collection of Old and New Japanese Poems, 905), for example, Ki no Tsurayuki (ca. 868–945) attempted to raise the authority of waka, hitherto considered a low "private" form, by drawing on Chinese poetry and poetics. *The Tale of Genji* and *Tales of Ise* rose to the top of the literary canon through their association with waka, which was a more canonical genre than monogatari, and through reconfiguration as history (biography), which was, along with poetry and scripture, considered the highest genre. *Renga*, or linked verse, which began as a marginal, popular genre, attempted to elevate itself by drawing on the authority of the orthodoxy represented by the Nijō school of court waka. Bashō likewise drew heavily on classical poetry as well as Chinese poetry in an effort to make haikai, considered lowly entertainment, part of a high poetic tradition.

The inability of a text to absorb traits of a more highly regarded genre or take on new functions could likewise result in decanonization, as in the case of *Sagoromo monogatari* (The Tale of Sagoromo, 1058–80) and Fujiwara Kintō's *Wakan rōeishū* (Japanese and Chinese Poems to Sing, 1012). *The Tale of Sagoromo*, a vernacular court tale considered by medieval poets as well as Edo kokugaku scholars to be of great importance, second only to *Genji* and *Ise*, was valued by both waka and renga poets as a rich source of poetry and poetic imagery, but it lacked sufficient intrinsic interest to survive as a work of prose fiction in the modern period.[5] A similar fate awaited *Wakan rōeishū*, a collection of waka matched with lines from noted Chinese poems, which served a multiplicity of functions—a collection of "songs" (*kayō*), an elementary textbook for reading, and a calligraphy handbook. With the disappearance of these pedagogical and social functions and the denigration of Chinese poetry (*kanshi*) in the modern period, it lost its wide appeal. By contrast, *Taketori monogatari* (*Tale of the Bamboo Cutter*, 910), which was considered the grandfather of the monogatari in *The Tale of Genji*, was virtually ignored during the medieval period. Unlike *Tales of Ise*, which became

the object of massive commentary, *The Bamboo Cutter* was not closely associated with poetry, history, or scripture, the three most highly valued genres.
In the modern period, however, the fortunes of *The Bamboo Cutter* rose with
those of the novel (*shōsetsu*), and the text has become one of the most popular classics. In *Kokubungaku zenshi: Heianchō hen* (Complete History of
Japanese Literature: The Heian Court, 1905), the first full-length study of
Heian literary history, Fujioka Sakutarō (1870–1910)—referring to the
shōsetsu as "occupying the highest literary position"—praises *The Bamboo
Cutter* as "our country's first novel."[6]

Perhaps the most important genre change occurred in the definition of
literature itself. Prior to the eighteenth century in Europe, literature in the
broadest sense meant anything that was related to reading and writing.[7]
More precisely, it referred to the humanities broadly defined, to writings of
high quality, including those in the fields of history, theology, philosophy,
and even natural science. From around the middle of the eighteenth century,
this notion of literature gradually began to narrow and to include only creative or imaginative literature, with particular stress on the genres of poetry,
the tale (prose fiction), and drama, as opposed to other forms such as rhetorical persuasion, didactic argumentation, and historical narration.[8] The emergence of this new notion of literature was accompanied by the slow rise in
the prestige of the novel, which came to enforce the notion of literature as
imaginative or creative writing.

This nineteenth-century European notion of imaginative literature had a
profound impact on the construction of both the institution and field of
modern kokubungaku, including the construction of "classical Japanese literature." In the Meiji period the term *bungaku* embraced two notions: literature as humanities or belle lettres, a concept that fused earlier Japanese and
Chinese notions of literature and learning with the broader European conception of literature as humanities, and a more narrow notion of creative or
imaginative writing, which derived in large part from Europe.[9] In the latter
half of the Meiji period, there was a rapid shift toward the latter, corresponding to the shift in Europe from the early eighteenth-century notion of
literature as humanities to that of imaginative literature in the nineteenth
century. As Tomi Suzuki has noted, Meiji literary historians sometimes referred to the narrow definition of bungaku as *bibungaku* (elegant literature)
or *junbungaku* (pure literature), stressing in particular imagination (*sōzōryoku*), feeling (*kanjō*), and thought (*shisō*). The earlier notion of literature as
humanities was reflected in the establishment at the University of Tokyo
in 1877 of Bunka daigaku, the College of Bungaku, or the Division of

Humanities, which embraced various disciplines, including the Department of Japanese and Chinese Classics (Wakan bungaku ka), while the nineteenth-century notion of imaginative literature was reflected in the subsequent separation of Japanese literature (eventually called *kokubun*) and Japanese history as distinct disciplines in 1888 and in the institutional breakup of what had once been kangaku (Chinese studies) into the programs of philosophy, history, and literature.[10] The new disciplinary configurations, derived in large part from the German model, radically altered the premodern literary canon, leaving out texts in such fields as history, philosophy, religion, and political science, which had hitherto been an integral part of literary learning.

The nineteenth-century European unitary notion of literature, of various genres belonging to one larger species, and the European stress on drama, poetry, and the novel, genres considered the epitome of imaginative literature, had a significant effect on the generic conception of Japanese literature, which had held poetry in high esteem but not drama and prose fiction. In the Meiji period, the notion of the novel, considered in the Enlightenment, Spencerian scheme as the most advanced genre, was employed to bring together a wide range of texts—such as monogatari, *setsuwa* (folk stories), *otogi-zōshi* (anonymous short tales), *kana-zōshi* (kana books), *ukiyo-zōshi* (books of the floating world), *kibyōshi* (illustrated books)—which had hitherto been treated as separate phenomena and had not been considered, with the exception of the Heian monogatari, to be serious writing.[11] Ihara Saikaku (1642–1693), the Genroku haikai poet and writer of ukiyo-zōshi, had fallen into considerable obscurity by the end of the Edo period, and it was almost impossible during the early Meiji period to obtain copies of his works, which were no longer printed. It was not until the late 1880s, when Japanese writers and intellectuals began to look to their own tradition for the Japanese equivalent of the European "realistic" novelist, that the long-forgotten Genroku writer was exhumed, recognized as the foremost fiction writer of the Edo period, and advertised as "Saikaku, the realist of Japan."

From the late twelfth century to the Meiji period, *The Tale of Genji* had been read, at least in the medieval *wagaku* (Japanese studies) tradition, as a handbook for poetry, a model for poetic diction and imagery. Even Motoori Norinaga (1730–1801), who attempted to assert the value of *The Tale of Genji* as narrative fiction, applied a theory, that of *mono no aware*, which was based on a classical poetic model of cathartic expressionism. Modern literary scholarship on *The Tale of Genji*, by contrast, can be seen as an extended attempt to escape from this long tradition of poetic readings—from the hegemony of waka, which had received a thousand years of attention as the canonical form—and to reread *Genji* first as a realistic novel, and then as a psychological novel. In the early Meiji period, *The Tale of Genji*, which in its opening chapters depicts an ideal period of direct imperial rule (that of Emperors Uda and Daigo), was thought to reflect the "return to imperial rule" movement behind the Meiji Restoration. In the period of heavy Westernization and global nationalism that followed, by contrast, *Genji* was proclaimed to be the world's first realistic novel, and the text was translated into English so that it could become part of "world literature."

[margin note: GENJI AS WORLD LITERATURE THROUGH TRANSLATION]

Whereas poetry, first in the form of *shi* (Chinese-style poetry) and then later in the shape of waka, had long been regarded as the highest of genres in Japan, the new European notion of "poetry" (translated as *shi*), like the new notion of "prose" (*sanbun*), brought together a variety of genres—for example, waka, haikai, and kayō, together with the newly created *shintaishi* (new, free-form verse). Matsuo Bashō (1644–1694), who had been considered a haikai poet (*haijin*), now was thought of also in the new, wider sense of "poet" (*shijin*), and became a source of inspiration for other shijin such as Shimazaki Tōson (1872–1943), the Romantic poet of shintaishi, who saw Bashō as an alienated poet-artist. Thus, while Bashō's reputation as a haijin suffered in the Meiji period, he was resurrected, at least in part, as a shijin.

Until the Meiji period, performing arts such as nō, *kyōgen* (comic drama), *jōruri* (puppet plays), and kabuki were not considered the object of commentary by medieval wagaku or Tokugawa kokugaku scholars. However, under the influence of the Western notion of dramatic literature, particularly Greek tragedy, Shakespeare's plays, and European opera, drama came to be considered an integral, if not key, part of national literature, and was raised to the level of "art" (*geijutsu*) from mere "performance" (*geinō*). Jōruri and kabuki were not regarded as a form of dramatic literature, as the respected works of a specific playwright, until the Meiji period, when kokubungaku scholars and reformers of national theater, led by Tsubouchi Shōyō (1859–1935), transformed Chikamatsu into a central literary figure, "Japan's foremost dramatist," under the heavy influence of Western models, particularly Shakespeare. With the demise of the Tokugawa military government, nō, which had become a form of classical theater in the Edo period, almost disappeared, but it was revived and the name changed from *sarugaku* (monkey music) or nō to the more dignified name of *nōgaku* (nō opera), a shift that reflected the nationalist need to match Europe's operatic tradition.[12]

[margin note: MOVE AWAY FROM PRESENTATION]

The modern notions of literature also drove a wedge between writing and its various material presentations. From as early as the classical period, writing (especially poetry), calligraphy, and painting were often inseparable. In

Meiji institutional discourse, by contrast, writing was separated from its visual or material presentation, which was studied as a new discipline, that of art (*bijutsu*). As Satō Dōshin has shown, in the 1880s the categories of painting exhibits shifted from the term *shoga*, which did not distinguish between calligraphy and painting, to *kaiga*, which referred specifically to painting but excluded calligraphy.[13] Calligraphy, which had been considered one of the three great cultural accomplishments (along with poetry and music), and which had been inseparable from the practice of poetry for a thousand years, was thus lost in the new configuration of disciplines.

GENDER AND CANON FORMATION

Another key issue in canonization, particularly among feminist scholars, has been the androcentric or male-centered nature of the European literary canon.[14] Some critics have argued that women's writing is always "bitextual," in dialogue with *both* masculine and feminine literary traditions, that is to say, women's writing looks back to both a male and female canon, while male writing need only concern itself with the dominant canon.[15] Of particular interest here is the fact that, due to the position of Heian kana literature, much of which was written by women and which stood within a larger Chinese canon, "bitextuality" applied both to women's writing and to men's writing.

In the Heian period (794–1185), for example, it was admirable for a male courtier to be able to master Yamato discourse, which was associated with women's writing and feminine aesthetics, alongside the more masculine Chinese discourse, which was reserved for politics, government, philosophy, and religion. Heian male courtiers used the cursive *hiragana* script, wrote in the genres associated with women, and took on women's roles, as exemplified by Ki no Tsurayuki in *Tosa nikki* (Tosa Diary, 935). In later periods, men similarly relished women's roles, for example, in the *onna-mono* (women plays) in nō drama or the *onnagata* (woman's role) in Edo kabuki. Significantly, however, women almost never entered into the masculine, public, Chinese-related discourse, and they rarely, if ever, played male roles. When a woman attempted to cross into the male sphere, as the scholarly woman with garlic breath in the rainy-night discussion does in the "Broom Tree" (*Hahakigi*) chapter of *The Tale of Genji*, it was looked upon with scorn and aversion, though certain women authors such as Sei Shōnagon and Murasaki Shikibu managed to successfully display their Chinese knowledge as a means of enhancing their own status. As Mitamura Masako has pointed out, men had a strong desire to control not only their own spheres but the female sphere as well, and managed to do so, whereas women were largely confined to their own sphere.[16]

The close association of women with the origins of kana literature created extreme ambivalence among medieval and Edo commentators, who were generally male and inclined to be influenced by Confucian gender constructions. As Linda Chance points out in her essay, one of the reasons that Edo commentators and teachers such as the Neo-Confucian scholar Hayashi Razan (1583–1657) gravitated to Yoshida Kenkō's (1283–1350) *Tsurezuregusa*, which became a major classic in the seventeenth century, was that it was not only in hiragana, a requirement for teaching the new commoner audience, but also that it was written by a man, thus providing a viable alternative to Heian kana texts by women. In another example, Kamo no Mabuchi (1697–1769), one of the major founders of kokugaku, positively associated masculinity (*masuraoburi*) with the *Man'yōshū* and the ancient period, while negatively associating femininity (*taoyameburi*) with the Heian period, and saw a historical deterioration from masculine to feminine as the capital moved from Nara to Heian (Kyoto). Mabuchi's gendered poetic history was a means of revalorizing waka, which had long been associated with Heian women's literature, as originally male and thus a superior form. By contrast, Norinaga, Mabuchi's leading disciple, positively interpreted femininity and weakness, which he valorized as a form of *mono no aware*, of sincerity, of true feeling, as opposed to masculinity, which he associated with China and with superficiality.

The Meiji ambivalence toward the Heian period is also evident in the dissatisfaction that Haga Yaichi (1867–1927) and Tachibana Senzaburō (1867–1901), the editors of *Kokubungaku tokuhon* (Japanese Literature Reader, 1890) and pioneers of national literature study, expressed toward the Heian vernacular, which they felt was too soft and effeminate. Despite their decision to leave out *kanbun* (Chinese prose) texts, they valued Chinese and Buddhist influences, which they felt imbued medieval and Edo literature with "lofty ideas," and preferred *wakan konkō bun* (mixed Japanese-Chinese style), which they felt was "more vigorous and manly" than the Heian hiragana style.[17] By contrast, Fujioka Sakutarō, the first major scholar of Heian literature and the author of *Kokubungaku zenshi: Heianchō hen*, written immediately after the Russo-Japanese War, argued that for the nation to be strong, it must be masculine and based on *bushidō* (the way of the warrior), but for the nation to be cultivated, it must turn to the femininity and culture found in Heian literature. If the Heian period, the Japanese equivalent of the period of Greece and Rome, celebrated letters (*bun*) and the nobility, the Tokugawa period, the equivalent of the European Renaissance, celebrated weapons (*bu*) and the warrior (*bushi*).

Writings in hiragana represented only a minor part of the broad corpus dominated by kangaku, and of all the prose texts written by women in the Heian period, only *The Tale of Genji* was canonized in the early medieval period, and it was canonized by men at court (Fujiwara Shunzei, Fujiwara Teika, and other male poets) as a handbook for poetic composition. The early medieval canonizers, who were men, made no mention of *The Pillow Book, Izumi Shikibu nikki* (Izumi Shikibu Diary, early 11th c.), or *Kagerō nikki* (Gossamer Diary, late 10th c.). Women poets appear in the *Hyakunin isshu* (One Hundred Poets, One Poem Each, edited by Fujiwara Teika) and other prominent poetry collections, but no mention is made of their prose writings except for *Murasaki Shikibu nikki* (Murasaki Shikibu Diary, early 11th c.), which was recognized in connection with *The Tale of Genji*. Significantly, it is a kana diary by a man, Ki no Tsurayuki's *Tosa Diary*, rather than the other diaries by women, that first reached canonical status. As Tomi Suzuki shows in her essay, it was not until the 1920s that Heian women's *kana nikki* (kana diaries) were recognized as literature worthy of study and fitted into a modern genealogy of "self-reflective literature" (*jishō bungaku*), as part of a larger "I-novel" discourse. It was only with the emergence of "women's literature" (*joryū bungaku*) in the modern period and the critical debate surrounding its emergence that the Heian women's tradition as we conceive it now was retroactively constructed.

CANON AND NATION BUILDING

Postcolonial critics have argued that the dominant canon, particularly as a result of official or state nationalism, can function as a tool of exploitation or political control by creating a larger sense of cultural homogeneity, a center of authority or standard that unites disparate individuals and groups while often denying the identity of a particular gender, class, or subgroup. In Meiji Japan, *kokumin*, generally translated in the following essays as "nation" and sometimes as "people of the nation," was a constitutionally defined notion of the nation that lay between the nation-state (*kokka*) and the various people that had been made new citizens of that state.[18] This notion was used to integrate the people culturally, politically, and socially into the new Meiji state, to construct what Benedict Anderson has called an "imagined community," a sense of a unified nation for disparate groups or localities that did not necessarily share common historical, religious, or ethnic roots.[19] As Kōnoshi Takamitsu argues in his essay, the *Nihon shoki* and the *Kojiki* were both created out of the need of the early Nara state to authenticate the Yamato (imperial) clan's worldview and its hegemony over other clans; and in the modern period, these same texts were reinterpreted as a means of establishing the Japanese people as a distinct race and as citizens of the modern nation-state. In a similar vein, Shinada Yoshikazu shows in his paper that in the mid-Meiji period the *Man'yōshū* was canonized as a "national poetry anthology" (*kokumin kashū*), an anthology of poems written by everyone from the emperor to the lowest commoner. In this view, the *Man'yōshū*, which was actually edited and composed by Nara aristocrats, reflected the unity of the new nation, in which the emperor and the people were perceived as belonging to the same body.

On the other side of the coin, canon formation has also been a means of resisting cultural hegemony, of establishing separate ethnic, national, and gender identities. Many of the new fields in North America, such as "Canadian Studies," "African-American Studies," "Native American Studies," and "Women's Studies," are deliberately engaged in building new literary canons (for example, in the form of new anthologies) as a means of strengthening their own ethnic, national, or gender identities amid a larger Eurocentric, androcentric discourse that has traditionally marginalized these groups or communities. Similarly, the kokugaku movement, which came to the fore in the eighteenth century and which established the foundation of the modern kokubungaku canon, was not only an attempt to free Japan from its position as a cultural colony of China, but also a movement by one group of scholars, mainly *chōnin* or urban commoners, to establish their own identity vis-à-vis not only Dōjō poets, who belonged to an aristocratic, court-centered wagaku tradition, but also kangaku scholars, who dominated the intellectual world and *bakufu* (military government) ideology at the time. In the nineteenth and twentieth centuries, the formation of nationalistic "traditions," particularly those based on vernacular literature, has also been crucial in decolonization, in movements of national liberation—in India, Korea, and elsewhere—which had to forge new national identities separate from that imposed by the colonizers. Canon formation, in short, has served as a vehicle both for control and for liberation.

As Eric Hobsbawm and scholars of nationalism have shown, seemingly nonpolitical spheres such as aesthetics, literature, and ethics have been critical—if not even more powerful than political institutions—in the process of constructing nation-states, whose members had to be unified through the development of a common *cultural* identity.[20] One consequence was that cultural phenomena that had been specific to a particular region or social community often with the passage of time became identified with the nation. Kabuki, for example, which had been viewed as a vulgar, popular entertainment for urban commoners, eventually became a respectable form of national theater. In the Meiji period, works of art from various historical periods were declared to be "national treasures" (*kokuhō*) and arranged in museums as the embodiment of "Japanese culture." *Ukiyoe,* which had been regarded as disposable decorations, were suddenly treasured as works of art representative of Japanese culture as a whole. As Karatani Kōjin has argued, critics such as Okakura Tenshin (1862–1913) saw Japanese art, particularly traditional art uninfluenced by the West, as a sign of superiority of both Japan and the "East," but the canon of Japanese visual art, which came to represent Japan abroad at the turn of the century, was in fact largely determined, as in the case of ukiyoe, by its desirability as a commodity in the West, by the tastes and demands of *Japonisme.*[21] In other words, the identity of the cultural tradition, which was intended to distinguish Japan from other nations and give it a sense of historical and social unity, was constructed in significant part in response to Western models or markets. European literary and dramatic models had a similar impact on the formation of the Japanese literary "tradition."

At the ideological heart of the national literature movement was linguistic nationalism, the belief that the nation was founded on a common language, the "national language" based primarily on spoken Japanese.[22] In Europe, the phenomenon of national literature emerged as early as the Renaissance, with the use of Romance languages, but it did not come to the fore until the rise of nationalism in the eighteenth and nineteenth centuries. In England, for example, the study of literature generally meant the study of the Greek and Latin classics, and English literature was not accepted into the curriculum at Oxford and Cambridge until World War I, an event that aroused nationalistic sentiments vis-à-vis other, rival, European nations. Prior to this point, English literature was regarded as a poor man's classics, studied by those without the means or ability to study Greek and Latin, much as the study of Japanese texts, of waka and monogatari, was the curriculum for women who did not have the opportunity to study kangaku. In the Meiji period, Ueda Kazutoshi (1867–1937), the leading advocate of kokugo and one of the pioneers of modern *kokugogaku* (national language study), argued in 1894 that "loyalty to the sovereign and love of the nation" (*chūkun aikoku*) and a common language were the two forces that united Japan as a nation, that the "national essence" (*kokutai*) was embodied in the

Japanese language.[23] This notion of a national language, which was strengthened by the importation of Western phonocentric notions and the *genbun-itchi* (union of spoken and written languages) movement, was contrasted with kanbun, a written language associated with China, a country that was in decline and that would succumb to Japan in the Sino-Japanese War. The result was a dramatic pedagogical shift away from the Confucian classics and the devaluation of Japanese writing in kanbun, which had been the language of religion, government, and scholarship.

The construction of a national literature and of a national language was critical to the formation of a strong nation-state, particularly in the face of powerful Western nations, which represented a model for modernization but not one for establishing a national identity. Even as they modernized, new nations had to distinguish themselves from other nations by carefully delineating their own national characteristics, which were perceived to be *unique* and to have existed over time, especially prior to foreign influence. One result, which was different from the kind of nationalism found in European nations, was the emergence in Japan of two forms of nationalism, Japanese nationalism and a broader Asian or East Asian nationalism. This may be one reason why kanbun, while diminished by the rise of Japanese nationalism, was not completely abandoned as part of national literature or national culture. As Kurozumi Makoto reveals in his essay, both the Chinese writing system and the field of Chinese studies continued to have a profound impact on Japanese culture, particularly as a means of ethical and moral education, which was critical to modern nation-building. In contrast to the kokugaku scholars, who looked back to the ancient period to find a pure form of Japanese literature, Meiji scholars, following the evolutionary, Enlightenment model of history, stressed progress across time, giving value to medieval and Tokugawa texts, which had never been part of the canon, and favoring the medieval mixed Chinese-Japanese (*wakan konkō*) style, which they saw as having more strength than the feminine style of Heian kana literature. One consequence was that both the aristocratic, emperor-centered literature of the earlier periods and the popular literature of the medieval and Tokugawa periods were treated together as part of a single national literature.

ELITE AND POPULAR CULTURES

Another central issue in canon formation has been its function as an exclusionary and controlling force, as a means of protecting or enhancing elite culture against the encroachments of popular or mass culture. The knowledge of or access to the canon, particularly to the language embodied in the canon, has often been used as a means of maintaining social distinctions and hierarchies. For example, elite aristocratic culture, represented by the Dōjō waka poets such as Nijō Yoshimoto (1320–1388), the founder of orthodox renga, drew stimulus from popular culture, from commoner (*jige*) renga poets, whether it be for new talent or inspiration. At the same time, the nobility drew sharp boundaries around the classical canon—*Tales of Ise*, *Kokinshū*, *The Tale of Genji*, etc.—in order to control, enhance, and transmit its value as cultural capital, the ultimate example being the *Kokindenju*, the secret transmissions of the *Kokinshū*.

One of the key distinctions between canonized texts and noncanonical texts is that canonized texts are the object of extensive commentary and exegesis or are used widely in school textbooks, whereas noncanonical texts or genres, no matter how popular, are not. The same applies to the modern distinction, which came to the fore in the late Taishō period (1912–1926), between "pure literature" (*junbungaku*), a notion nurtured by elite literary circles (*bundan*) and "popular literature" (*taishū bungaku*). A careful distinction must be made here between *popularity*, which implies accessibility and wider audiences, and *authority*, which implies privilege and pedigree. Equally important is the distinction between economic capital, the commercial value that may result from popularity and wider audiences, and cultural capital, which often grows precisely because its distribution is limited. Chikamatsu Monzaemon may have been popular in the Genroku period (1688–1703) and his plays may have made money for him and his sponsors, but they were not a sign of cultural privilege or authority until they were canonized in the modern period.

Canons are generally comprehended today as the instruments of entrenched interests, reproducing the values or ideology of dominant groups. However, as Barbara Herrnstein Smith has pointed out,

> the needs, interests, and purposes of culturally and otherwise dominant members of the community do not exclusively or totally determine which works survive. The antiquity and longevity of domestic proverbs, popular tales, children's verbal games, and the entire phenomenon of what we call "folklore". . . may be more or less independent of institutions controlled by those with political power.[24]

Two very different kinds of canon formation occurred in the late medieval period. The first was the one-to-one transmission of texts and knowledge by aristocratic poetry families linked to the imperial court, which culminated in the secret transmission of the *Kokinshū*. At the same time, we witness the popularization of Heian court culture and literary figures through various media, through such performance arts as nō drama, renga, haikai, and otogi-zōshi. Transmitted by traveling minstrels, artists, and performers, the stories and figures of Heian classical literature as well as the classical association of seasons and famous places, spread, often in abbreviated or reduced form, to various social classes and to the provinces. In contrast to the closed nature of the *Kokindenju*, the popularization of classical figures and associations was an open process, creating endless variations, many of which were apocryphal. Legendary personae such as Kakinomoto no Hitomaro, Ono no Komachi, Ariwara no Narihira, Izumi Shikibu, Sei Shōnagon, Saigyō, and others owe their popularity not only to canonized texts preserved by court nobility but also to noncanonical genres, such as setsuwa, otogi-zōshi, and *heikyoku* (recitations of *The Tale of the Heike* to the accompaniment of the lute), including visual or aural media, which are often sympathetic toward those deprived of power or rejected by society. As we can see here, popular culture, often driven by Buddhist proselytizers who used noncanonical genres and media to preach to illiterate audiences, had a profound impact on canon formation—a process that was diametrically opposed to the institutional attempt to enhance and preserve canonical value, as exemplified in the secret transmissions of the *Kokinshū*.

A salient characteristic of European cultural nationalism, particularly in Germany during the period of nineteenth-century Romanticism, was ethnic nationalism (the sense of a nation bound by blood and kinship ties) based on the idea of the folk. A similar phenomenon occurred belatedly in Japan in the late Meiji and early Taishō periods with the emergence of the notion of *minzoku* (folk), based on the belief that the spirit of the people could be found in commoner culture, often prior to writing. In contrast to the earlier mid-Meiji national literature movement, which saw the emperor and the people as one body, this national literature movement, centered on literary journals such as *Teikoku bungaku* (Imperial Literature, 1895–1917) and influenced by such nineteenth-century German Romantics and folklorists as Heinrich Heine (1797–1856) and the Brothers Grimm (Jacob, 1785–1863, Wilhelm, 1786–1859), saw the literature of the nation rising up from below. There was an increasing surge of interest in folk literature, folk songs, legends, and myths, all of which were thought to embody the essence of the Japanese people from ancient times. Through much of the Heian period, the *Man'yōshū* was known for two court poets, Hitomaro and Akahito, but in the late Meiji and early Taishō periods, the *Man'yōshū* was recanonized, as Shinada Yoshikazu reveals in his paper, with attention turned, for the first time, to the *Azuma-uta* (Songs of the East) and *Sakimori-no-uta* (Songs of the Border Guards), which were regarded as *min'yō* (folk songs), the songs of anonymous commoners.

The *minzokugaku* (folklore studies) movement, which emerged at the end of the Meiji period, came to the fore in the 1930s, and experienced a revival in the 1960s and 1970s, expanded this movement further. Minzokugaku, founded by Yanagita Kunio (1875–1962) and sometimes referred to as the new nativist learning (*shinkokugaku*), initially attempted to valorize the non-canonical, what was outside the established academic and state institutions of kokubungaku, seeking culture in "literature before literature," in oral transmission, and among marginalized groups (such as mountain people, women, and children), which Yanagita believed were the bedrock of the Japanese tradition. One effect of the growth of minzokugaku, which was incorporated into kokubungaku by Origuchi Shinobu (1887–1953) and others, was the assimilation of a vast body of noncanonical genres, particularly set-suwa, otogi-zōshi, and other forms of folk literature, into the literary canon, a trend accelerated in the postwar period by a new emphasis on popular literature.

The result of modern canonization was not simply, as in some forms of cultural nationalism, the imposition of a common high culture on a variegated complex of local folk cultures, but rather a mixture of aristocratic (emperor-centered) literature—which had been at the heart of medieval wagaku and Edo kokugaku—*and* popular literature, particularly that of the medieval and Edo periods. In short, while a significant part of the modern literary canon was formed through political nationalism centered on the notion of kokumin and the central, higher authority of the emperor, under which the nation was unified, another aspect of the canon was driven, at least in significant part, by popular nationalism, which centered on the notion of minzoku and which shared much with the eighteenth- and nineteenth-century Romantic, Herder-esque, notion of the folk, of the common people, who were thought to embody the primordial spirit of the nation.[25] From as early as the turn of the century these two strands of nationalism, while often politically opposed, intertwined and reinforced each other. For example, with the establishment of an emperor-based nation-state, the myths and legends of the *Kojiki*, which hitherto had been known only to a small group of intellectual elites, were incorporated into textbooks as part of Japanese history, rewritten to stress the "Age of the Gods" (*kami no yo*) and Amaterasu, the sun goddess, as the progenitor of an unbroken imperial line. After World War II, however, when emperor-centered nationalism was discredited, the *Kojiki* was stripped of its sacred status as part of imperial history. Instead of forming the "historical" foundation of the modern emperor-system state, it became the origin of a more broadly construed "folk literature," the grounds for which had been laid earlier by minzokugaku scholars who had connected the gods, myths, and legends of the *Kojiki* to a "living," oral, locally based tradition in the provinces and villages of Japan.

STRUCTURE OF THE BOOK

Canon formation is an unending process. A text achieves canonical status only to be revalued, transformed, or eliminated. Each of the essays in this book consequently moves across time not only to examine the different ways in which texts have been received but also to examine why each text has been interpreted or transformed in particular ways. This procedure, which requires diachronic movement and which shifts the focus toward historicizing interpretation, allows us to observe the shifting horizon of expectations and to explore the different discourses or sociopolitical configurations that have constructed the canon.

The essays in the first part, entitled "Nation Building and National Literature," focus on the modern construction of national literature (kokubungaku) or "Japanese literature" (*Nihon bungaku*) as part of the larger process of constructing Japan as a nation-state (*kokumin-kokka*), particularly as it relates to major texts from the ancient period. In "*Man'yōshū*: The Invention of a National Poetry Anthology," Shinada Yoshikazu shows that the *Man'yōshū*, which had been virtually unknown to the general public, was canonized in the Meiji period as a "national poetry anthology" that contained work by poets from all social strata, "from emperors down to commoners." Although there had been significant historical precedent for it, this approach differed significantly from earlier notions in that it was driven by a need to find a national epic or national poetry equal to that found in Europe and one that favorably reflected the national character. The *Man'yōshū*, valued by modern critics for its vigor, naturalness, and "direct" expression of "frank" emotion, was more suited in this regard than the *Kokinshū*, which was now condemned for its technical rhetoric. Shinada argues that there were two basic, interlinked movements. The first, which occurred in the mid- to late Meiji period (1868–1912) under the influence of global nationalism, was the notion that the *Man'yōshū* embodied the unitary character of the nation (*kokuminsei*), a view espoused by the bureaucratic elite and closely associated with the needs of the imperial system and modern nation-building. The second view, which appeared from the late Meiji through the early Taishō period and which inverted the top-down emphasis of the first view, was the notion of the *Man'yōshū* as the embodiment of the culture of the "folk" (minzoku) and of the "populace" (*minshū*), an idea supported by the followers of the *Teikoku bungaku* (Imperial literature) journal and by their "discovery" of so-called *min'yō*, or folk songs—a notion derived from the German concept of the *Volkslied* (folk song)—which they found in the Azuma-uta and Sakimori-no-uta sections of the *Man'yōshū*. The first view of the *Man'yōshū* was seriously attenuated after World War II, with the reduction of the emperor to a symbol, but the second, populist, folk view continues to sustain the view prevailing to this day of the *Man'yōshū* as a national song anthology.

In his essay, "Constructing Imperial Mythology: *Kojiki* and *Nihon shoki*," Kōnoshi Takamitsu reveals the different ways in which the *Nihon shoki* and the *Kojiki*, two of the most important Japanese classics in the twentieth-century canon, were repeatedly reconstructed in the attempt to legitimize different imperial and world systems. The two works were originally created by the early Nara *ritsuryō* state to authenticate the Yamato (imperial) clan's hegemony over other clans. Modern scholarship has generally regarded the *Kojiki*, the *Nihon shoki*, and records of ritual practices as manifestations of a single, preexisting mythology, but as Kōnoshi shows, these texts in fact represented heterogeneous mythological systems and authenticated the ritsuryō imperial system in different ways. Subsequent commentaries (such as the official lectures on the *Nihon shoki*) and textual reconstructions bridged the gaps among these various texts, constructing a unified imperial mythology as well as new mythologies. When the ritsuryō state system collapsed in the medieval period, the discourse on the *Nihon shoki*—including a body of subsidiary texts referred to as the "medieval *Nihongi*"—shifted direction and served to legitimize a new syncretic order that fused Buddhism, Chinese philosophy, and early mythology (Shinto) in a worldview that embraced India and China. In the Edo period, by contrast, Motoori Norinaga, a leading kokugaku scholar, attempted to strip away these medieval Buddhist and Chinese readings and recover *furukoto*, an ancient Japanese language that he believed preexisted foreign influence, had been shared by all the people of Japan, not just the ritsuryō aristocracy, and was to be found in the *Kojiki*, which was now more highly valued than the more Sinified *Nihon shoki*. In the modern period, when national language became a key to constructing the nation, Norinaga's stress on the ancient language opened the way for the *Kojiki* to become a central text for folklore scholars such as Origuchi Shinobu. At the same time, the *Kojiki* became the canonical text for the government doctrine of national essence (kokutai), which used imperial mythology (particularly the notion of an unbroken imperial line leading back to the gods) and divine sanction to legitimize a modern imperial system and to establish the Japanese people as a distinct race. In short, the discourse generated by the *Nihon shoki* and the *Kojiki*—which included numerous substitutional and subsidiary texts—served key functions that were frequently both religious and highly political: the legitimization of the early imperial state, the propagation of a syncretic medieval worldview, the recovery of the primordial Japanese language for nativists, the foundation for folklore studies, and the mythological and ideological justification for the modern emperor system, particularly as it related to the notion of kokutai—all issues related to national identity and origins.

The essays in the second part, "Gender, Genre, and Cultural Identity," draw deep connections between the subject of canon formation and national identity and the issues of gender and genre. In "Gender and Genre: Modern Literary Histories and Women's Diary Literature," Tomi Suzuki shows how the modern canonization of Heian women's diaries illuminates the larger issue of the modern construction of Japanese literature. In the first half of her essay, Suzuki examines the position of Heian kana literature in modern Japanese literary histories, which were first written in the 1890s and which, as a result of the phonocentric notion of "national language" (kokugo) and a new emphasis on direct expression, designated Heian kana literature, long associated with femininity, as the basis of "national literature." In this newly constructed body of "national literature," from which all the texts written in classical Chinese were eliminated, Heian waka, especially that of the *Kokinshū*, were devalued because they were not considered to be direct, unmediated expressions of emotion. Instead, the literary histories valued Heian vernacular prose texts, most of all *The Tale of Genji*, which was recanonized in an evolutionist framework as the great predecessor to the "realistic novel" (considered the most "advanced" literary form). It was in this context that Heian *kana nikki* (kana diaries) were first valorized (from the 1890s to the 1910s) as direct expressions of emotion and as a critical step toward *The Tale of Genji* as a realistic novel. It was not, however, until the emergence of the notion of *nikki bungaku* (diary literature) in the early 1920s—when the *watakushi shōsetsu* (I-novel) became the center of critical discourse as a result of the widespread establishment of the notion of *bungaku* (literature) as a privileged means of expressing and developing a "genuine self" (*shin no jiko*)—that women's kana nikki finally achieved canonical status. Heian women's poetic memoirs were labeled more specifically as *joryū nikki bungaku* (women's diary literature) in the mid-1920s—when the journalistic notion of *joryū bungaku* (women's literature) began to circulate widely in response to a sudden expansion in female readership—and promoted as a genuine prototype of modern women's literature. As Suzuki shows in her analysis of literary historical narratives through the 1980s, "women's diary literature" subsequently became a critical element in defining the Japanese literary tradition as "lyrical" and "self-exploratory."

In "Modern Construction of *Tales of Ise*: Gender and Courtliness," Joshua Mostow analyzes the changing interpretations of *Tales of Ise*, an anonymous mid-Heian narrative with a long history of medieval and Edo commentary, and relates Meiji, Taishō, early Shōwa, and postwar readings to issues of the modern nation-state, the emperor system, gender, and socioeconomic change. Mostow shows that in the Meiji period, *Tales of Ise*, while regarded as a resource for educating the new kind of woman required by modernity, was generally viewed, like the Heian period itself, negatively, as effeminate and degenerate, and lacking the true Japanese spirit, which was positively gendered as masculine. At the same time, the first Meiji edition of *Tales of Ise* presents Narihira, the protagonist, as a patriot in the service of the emperor (resisting the Fujiwara usurpers)—a political interpretation in keeping with the ideals of the Meiji Imperial Restoration. By contrast, in the Taishō period (1912–1926), which witnessed the emergence of "free love" (*jiyū renai*) and the "modern girl" (*moga*) and "modern boy" (*mobo*), *Tales of Ise* was positively reassessed, most prominently in Yoshikawa Hideo's *Shinchū Ise monogatari*, not only for its affirmation of "love," but also for the aestheticization or sublimation of that "love" through poetry, the mixture resulting in "elegance" (*fūryū*). In the early Shōwa (1930s-1940s) period, *Ise* was generally regarded as a repository of ancient and "pure" Japanese values. In the early 1940s, it became identified for the first time with "courtliness" (*miyabi*), or courtly elegance, which was associated with romantic love and women as well as with the imperial court and the emperor (to which Narihira was seen as being loyal). In the postwar period, *Ise* continued to be defined by gender and by miyabi, which became the defining characteristic of the work as well as of a national aesthetic closely associated with the emperor as national symbol. Although one scholar attacked the earlier feminization of *Ise* and saw miyabi as a male attribute, Katagiri Yōichi and other modern scholars in the

1970s and 1980s stressed the central role of women and love, presenting a highly feminine version of miyabi. Mostow argues that this stress on the feminine reflects the larger postwar categorization of Japan's "traditional" past as feminine, probably influenced by a post-defeat search for a more pacific Japanese past, by female-oriented cultural consumerism, and by a prominent tendency shared with other late industrializing countries for male elites to embrace the modern and to consign the custodianship of the "traditional" to women.

In "Zuihitsu and Gender: *Tsurezuregusa* and *The Pillow Book*," Linda Chance examines the Edo reception of *Tsurezuregusa* (Essays in Idleness, early 14th c.), which did not become the object of extensive commentary until the beginning of the seventeenth century, when it was brought before a new audience of commoners and townspeople by scholar-teachers who prized it, among other things, as a model of style and language, as a repository in kana of the high tradition, and as a guide to everyday life—values and functions that stand in striking contrast to the highly aesthetic readings that it has been given in the modern period. As Chance shows, gender and genre were critical factors in this canonization process: as a kana text by a male author—as opposed to a female text such as *The Tale of Genji*—*Tsurezuregusa* found considerable favor with male teacher-commentators such as the Neo-Confucian scholar Hayashi Razan (1583–1657). Equally important, *Tsurezuregusa*, with its grounding in continental philosophy, was canonized as a form of scripture, with emphasis on one or more of the three teachings—Buddhism, Confucianism, and Taoism. From the end of the seventeenth century, *Tsurezuregusa* was seen in a less didactic light, but it continued to have significant pedagogical functions, being dubbed the "Analects of our country," and serving, for example, as "lessons for women." By the eighteenth century, it had become the most influential work of literature in terms of style, both as a literary model and as the object of numerous parodies and variations. Today, *Tsurezuregusa* is known and classified as a *zuihitsu* (miscellany, that which "follows the brush")—a genre category central to almost all modern accounts of this text and one that encouraged more diverse and less didactic readings—but, as Chance points out, it did not become associated with this category until kokugaku scholars gave it this label in the late eighteenth century. And it was not until the post-Meiji period that *Tsurezuregusa*, along with *The Pillow Book*, became an example par excellence of this genre. Chance makes a revealing comparison: as was the case with *Tsurezuregusa*, *The Pillow Book* had been relatively neglected in the medieval period and suddenly became the object of commentary and parody in the seventeenth century. But due to differences of gender and sociophilo-sophical background, *The Pillow Book* was appreciated on a smaller scale, treated as a text of far less didactic importance, and selectively aimed at young female readers. As the connection to the notion of *zuihitsu* emerged in the late Tokugawa period, *The Pillow Book* also tended to be reduced to a generic precursor to *Tsurezuregusa*.

The essays in the third part, "History to Literature, Performance to Text," continue to pursue the issue of the construction of national literature, re-vealing the profound modal and generic transformations that occurred in the process. As we learn in David Bialock's "Nation and Epic: *The Tale of the Heike* as Modern Classic," *The Tale of the Heike*, although flourishing as an orally recited historical narrative, was not the object of extensive commen-tary or exegesis in the premodern period and was not recognized as *bungaku* until the 1880s, when modern disciplinary fields—such as history, literature, and philosophy—were reconstructed under European influence. Rather, *The Heike* had been regarded as a form of history, serving in the Edo period as an important historical document for legitimizing warrior rule. In the course of the Meiji period two contemporaneous yet distinct views of *The Heike* as lit-erature began to emerge. One view stressed its lyrical, tragic, and Buddhist elements, which gradually assimilated *The Heike* and other warrior chroni-cles to values more sympathetic to court culture and imperial rule. By stress-ing sacrifice and resignation, proponents of this view were basically refitting *The Heike* and other warrior chronicles for citizens of the imperial state. Another view, contemporaneous with the first, celebrated *The Heike* as the expression of a national (*kokuminteki*) spirit, as the Japanese equivalent of the national folk epic, a generic category used in Europe in the eighteenth and nineteenth centuries to evoke national identity and origins. This view, based on the implicit belief that the national folk epic evolved out of prim-itive, egalitarian warrior societies, was clearly antipathetic to the imperial ideology of the prewar period, which favored sacrifice and resignation to militant action. As a result, the epic reading of *The Heike*, although argued for as early as the Meiji period, was of less consequence in the prewar period in shaping a canonical view of the work. It was only in the postwar period that its appeal to heroic action, fraught with anti-imperial implications be-fore the war, could be harnessed to stimulate feelings of national solidarity. In contrast to Nara and Heian literature, which had been associated with the aristocratic culture and aesthetic lyricism, *The Tale of the Heike*, along with the medieval period (*chūsei*) itself, became allied, in this populist view, with an antiaristocratic, anticourtly culture, that of the folk or the "people" (*min-*

shū)—a view that blossomed in and dominated the postwar era, when the work was also seen, under Marxist influence, as part of a class struggle.

In "Chikamatsu and Dramatic Literature in the Meiji Period," William Lee examines the canonization of Chikamatsu Monzaemon's (1653–1724) *jōruri* (puppet) plays in the Meiji period. Though Chikamatsu's plays were popular in the seventeenth and early eighteenth century in the sense of being repeatedly staged, jōruri and kabuki, the two forms in which Chikamatsu worked, were not considered either by the performers or the intellectual elite to be literary genres or forms of serious literature, and consequently never became the object of commentary in the fashion of waka and monogatari. Furthermore, Chikamatsu's kabuki plays were never restaged after his death, and in the late eighteenth century his jōruri plays were performed only in heavily revised form. By the nineteenth century, jōruri as a dramatic form had faded. Lee examines two key groups of modern scholar-critics, one at Waseda University (centered on Tsubouchi Shōyō, a Shakespeare scholar) and the other at the University of Tokyo, who were largely responsible for Chikamatsu's modern revival and who, for the first time, regarded theater or, rather, "drama" (the English word preferred by many Meiji critics) as *a kind of literature*. Chikamatsu's modern canonization, which occurred under the influence of Western notions of genre and literature, thus marked a paradigmatic shift in which literary qualities were sought out in drama and in which literature came to embrace drama, including nō. Equally important, Chikamatsu's *sewamono* (contemporary plays), which centered on commoner life and which were seen as more "advanced" and "realistic" than his history plays (which had been at the center of the traditional repertoire), were revived and canonized as part of a "national" drama movement that attempted to create a drama comparable to those found in the "civilized" nations of the West and that made Chikamatsu a national icon.

The last section of the book, entitled "Language, Authority, and the Curriculum," examines the roles of language, pedagogy, and social change in canon formation. In his essay "*Kangaku*: Writing and Institutional Authority," Kurozumi Makoto examines the role of Chinese studies, the foundation of the central canon of the premodern period, with a particular focus on the issue of writing and the relationship of kangaku to other major forms of discourse—a complex role that has been obscured and erased by the modern notions of national language and "Japanese literature." Kurozumi shows that although *wabun* (Japanese prose) and *kanbun* (Chinese prose) are now thought to be antithetical languages, reflecting contrasting discourses, the two were in fact closely intertwined, with many aspects of kangaku—such as its reading and writing conventions as well as its kanji—incorporated into wabun, a synthesis that eventually resulted in the wakan konkō style. Kurozumi shows that while kangaku, the main discipline for the study and propagation of Confucianism, had a profound impact on the Japanese writing system and was closely associated with the authority of the Nara and Heian ritsuryō state, becoming one of the most influential forms of discourse, kangaku scholars themselves had limited political power compared to Buddhist institutions, particularly since the ritsuryō state did not depend on a meritocratic Confucian examination system and since kangaku was not able to establish its own deities and religious rituals, as Buddhism (and later Shinto) was able to. In fact, until the Edo period, with the exception of the hereditary *hakase* (scholars of Chinese) houses, those who studied and taught Confucianism and kangaku were primarily Buddhist priests.

Though it is generally thought that kangaku and Confucianism prospered in the first half of the Edo period and then faded away in the eighteenth and nineteenth centuries with the rise of kokugaku and Western studies (*yōgaku*), Kurozumi shows that in fact kangaku and Confucianism were relatively insignificant in the early Edo period but became extremely influential in the second half of the Edo period and far into the Meiji period. Most of the scholars of the new disciplines of kokugaku and yōgaku were in fact simultaneously scholars of kangaku, which provided the basis for these new disciplines. These scholars, who tended to be syncretic in orientation, appropriated kana in order to make Chinese texts accessible to a larger public. It was only as a result of subsequent attacks (from the late eighteenth century)— such as Norinaga's attack on "Chinese spirit" (*karagokoro*)—by "purifying" kokugaku scholars that kangaku came to be seen as a separate, and ultimately a lesser, discipline. While kanbun texts were eventually decanonized in favor of kana literature, Kurozumi shows that kangaku and Confucianism played a major role in constructing the modern nation-state, providing, as the example of the Imperial Rescript on Education (*Kyōiku chokugo*, 1890) demonstrates, the ethical and political framework for the creation of a new nation (kokumin). In the 1930s and 1940s, kangaku, which had been an integral part of Japanese education and culture for more than a thousand years, was finally displaced by Sinology (*Shinagaku*), which treated China as an object of scientific study separate from Japan, which now regarded itself as the center of Asia.

The underlying premise of the last essay, my "Curriculum and Competing Canons," which brings together different threads from the previous essays, is that the modern notions of "national literature" and national language have obscured what had been for many centuries a plurality of competing and intersecting canons, specifically those of Japanese learning, Chinese learning, Buddhist learning, and later Western learning. This essay pays particular attention to the changing nature of the pedagogical institutions, particularly the competing "house" (*ie*) system that developed in the late Heian period, the medieval temple schools (*terakoya*), and the private academies and domain (*han*) schools in the Edo period. Of particular interest are the consistent premodern subordination of wagaku texts to the Chinese and Buddhist canons—until about the late fifteenth century, when a significant reversal began to occur—and the affiliation of different social classes or communities with specific canons. In the medieval period, for example, the warriors in power (who set up their own schools, such as the Ashikaga university), the aristocracy who possessed many of the texts, and the priests who taught in the temple schools each gravitated toward a particular canon, Chinese, Japanese, and Buddhist, respectively. Equally important, however, was the crossover—the deep interest, for example, that elite samurai had in Japanese texts or that priests had in Confucian texts—and the fact that general education in late medieval temple schools involved a mixture of all three, with each canon fulfilling different pedagogical, religious, and social needs.

This larger overview reveals that many texts—such as *Wakan rōeishū*—were canonized for their pedagogical effectiveness in teaching reading, writing, and calligraphy. In fact, one can trace a gradual historical shift from a largely "writerly" canon, in which texts (such as *Ise, Genji,* and *Kokinshū*) were selected and canonized as models for writing or poetic composition—an emphasis that remained through the Meiji period—to an entirely "readerly" canon of classical texts, which were selected for the sole purpose of reading and moral instruction, in the years after World War II. In the premodern period kangaku texts were the primary vehicles for ethical or political training, but in the Meiji, Taishō, and early Shōwa periods this role was taken on by kana texts, medieval historical texts, military chronicles (such as the *Taiheiki*), and essays by Edo kangaku and kokugaku scholars, which played an increasingly ideological role (stressing filial piety, loyalty to the sovereign, etc.) in the immediate prewar period. After the war, however, with a radical "demilitarizing" of the canon, a number of the most widely used military chronicles and Shinto-related texts—such as *Jinnō shōtōki* (Chronicle of Gods and Sovereigns, 1339), *Taiheiki* (Record of Great Peace, early 14th c.), *Soga monogatari* (Tale of the Soga Brothers, mid-14th c.)—were removed from the high school curriculum, and more populist genres such as setsuwa and kyōgen were added. One of the most striking aspects of the postwar high school kokugo curriculum, however, is the dominance of nineteenth-century, largely European, notions of literature and genre (particularly as imaginative text exploring the self) in shaping the Japanese classical canon, coupled with the near elimination of philosophical, political, and historical texts, which had been an integral part of the prewar kokugo curriculum (not to mention medieval and Edo kangaku canons). The overall result was a narrowing down and shifting of the focus of a highly diverse canon toward texts that may be described as highly "lyrical" and "aesthetic"—today the two adjectives most frequently used by Western scholars to describe "Japanese literature."

Nation Building and National Literature

CHAPTER ONE

Man'yōshū: The Invention
of a National Poetry Anthology

SHINADA YOSHIKAZU

TRANSLATED BY KEVIN COLLINS

THE PRESTIGE OF THE MAN'YŌSHŪ

Among the many works now designated as Japanese classics, the *Man'yōshū*
(Collection of Ten Thousand Leaves, late 8th c.) enjoys a particularly prestigious position: it is valued as a masterwork of Japanese culture and an embodiment of the classical spirit. However, for more than a thousand years,
beginning with its compilation by members of the aristocracy in the Nara
period, the *Man'yōshū* had little or no connection to the overwhelming majority of the people inhabiting the Japanese archipelago. Despite the activity
of Heian waka poets, medieval renga masters, and early modern nativist
scholars (*kokugakusha*) and commoner poets, the *Man'yōshū* remained
largely unknown, even by name, until the middle of the Meiji era (1868–
1912). Today, by contrast, most Japanese possess a general familiarity with the
Man'yōshū, and it is not unusual to find someone who can recite a few well-
known verses by heart. Students, who usually read a handful of selected

poems from the collection, are taught, as part of the Japanese language (*kokugo*) curriculum, that:

> The *Man'yōshū* is Japan's oldest extant poetic anthology, with twenty volumes containing approximately 4,500 verses. Although there are a number of theories concerning the compilers and compilation of the collection, the most influential explanation maintains that it assumed its present form mostly as the result of the work of Ōtomo no Yakamochi in the late Nara period. Its poetic forms include the tanka [short poem], the *chōka* [long poem], the *sedōka* [5/7/7/5/7/7 poem] and poems in the form of *bussokusekika* [Buddha's footprint poem]. These are categorized in terms of content into the *zōka* [miscellaneous poems], *sōmonka* [exchange poems], and *banka* [elegies]. *The poets represented range from emperors to commoners, and the works in the collection are characterized by a simple and moving style.* The poems are generally divided into four periods according to the time of composition with the first period lasting until the time of the Jinshin Rebellion (672), the second until the movement of the capital to Nara (710), the third until the early Tenpyō period (729), and the fourth lasting until Tenpyō-Hōji 3 (759).[1]

This description appears in a 1998 first-year high school kokugo textbook, one that boasts the largest market share from among twenty such texts. In addition to enumerating the content and the variety of poetic forms and pointing out that the *Man'yōshū* is the oldest extant anthology, this passage stresses that the *Man'yōshū* contains works by poets from all social strata, from emperors to commoners, and that the expression is simple but moving, characterized by a frank and vigorous tone—features that have been extolled repeatedly in school texts, reference books, literary histories, and literary dictionaries for more than a century since the latter half of the Meiji period. One result is that the *Man'yōshū*, which was actually the product of the ruling class in the ancient period, has come to be regarded as a great cultural inheritance of the Japanese people as a whole.

In recent times, the *Man'yōshū* has become an object of veneration, drawing readers in unprecedented numbers. In response to the increased availability of *Man'yōshū* editions and commentaries, there has been a steady rise in the number of enthusiastic devotees and specialists. And yet only a small minority—mostly scholars of literature, language, or history; students (including those at "culture centers") and teachers of Japanese literature; and practicing tanka poets—have actually read through the entire collection or carefully studied even a portion of it. Even among those holding college degrees in Japanese literature, readership is actually quite limited. Approaching the *Man'yōshū* in its original form requires knowledge of the vocabulary and grammar of the archaic language used in the Kinki region during the seventh and eighth centuries. The classical language that modern Japanese learn at school, however, is either the language of the Heian period (794–1185) or that used in texts from later periods. Because the archaic language is not taught widely or systematically, it is rare for excerpts from either the *Man'yōshū* or the *Kojiki* (Record of Ancient Matters, 712) to appear on university entrance exams.

Only after modern critics acclaimed the *Man'yōshū* as a literary monument did it come to attract readers, a process related to the formation of a national culture. From the end of the Edo period, Japan embarked on the task of constructing a nation-state that would enable it to participate and compete in a larger global system. The formation of and modernization of this state, which was carried out through the early Meiji period, proceeded very much by design, following the model of various Western countries, but it occurred before the notion of the "people" (*kokumin*, literally "people of the nation") had acquired sufficient maturity or identity. In effect, the Japanese state became a vessel into which was poured the nation, or the nation's people. It was within this context that the *Man'yōshū* became a "classic of the people" (*kokumin no koten*), part of a canon through which the nation achieved its sense of cultural identity. Of the various works constructed and invented for this purpose, the *Man'yōshū* is no doubt the most representative.[2]

THE DREAM OF A NATIONAL POETRY ANTHOLOGY

Masaoka Shiki (1867–1902), the founder of modern haiku, is also remembered in the history of *Man'yōshū* reception as one of its leading proponents and scholars. He is often credited with being the principal voice in the modern reevaluation of this ancient anthology—a perception that is, as we shall see, somewhat inaccurate. From around 1892, Shiki devoted much of his energy to the transformation of the earlier *hokku* into modern haiku. He subsequently redirected his attention to the tanka and began to revolutionize this poetic form, as he had the haiku.[3] In 1898, he published a series of essays in the newspaper *Nihon* under the title, "Uta-yomi ni ataru sho" (Letters to Tanka Poets). In these essays, Shiki not only criticized the poetic mannerisms of the Keien school of Kagawa Kageki (1768–1843), which had dominated the contemporary poetic scene; he also tried to unseat the *Kokinshū* (Collection of Old and New Japanese Poems, 905), the first imperial anthology, as the authoritative standard for poetic composition. Shiki condemned the *Kokinshū*, which had been regarded as the paragon of the waka tradition for more than a thousand years, as an assortment of worthless poems lacking tension and verisimilitude. This sensational manifesto attracted rising poets like Itō Sachio (1864–1913) and Nagatsuka Takashi (1879–1915), who joined the group of Shiki's haiku followers. Adopting the *Man'yōshū* as the fountainhead for their own literary activities, these poets formed the Negishi Tanka society that continued to strive against Yosano Tekkan's (1873–1935) rival Myōjō school and emerged, after Shiki's death, as the Araragi school. Led by Shimaki Akahiko (1876–1926) and Saitō Mokichi (1882–1953), this offshoot of the earlier society came to occupy the preeminent position in the literary circles of the late Taishō period. Academic studies of the *Man'yōshū* interacted with this movement and similarly flourished.

However, Shiki's esteem for the *Man'yōshū* was fundamentally a stratagem to denounce the conservative poets of his day. In fact, Shiki had not thoroughly read the *Man'yōshū* at the time that he wrote his "Letters to Tanka Poets," and the main point of his argument—that waka had suffered a decline since the age of the *Kokinshū*—was by no means original. As Tekkan argued, several poets before Shiki had criticized the stubborn conservatism of the Keien School and praised the *Man'yōshū*.[4] As early as 1896—two years before Shiki's discussion—Toyama Masakazu (1848–1900), the president of the College of Letters at Tokyo Imperial University and a member of the House of Peers, remarked upon the superiority of *Man'yōshū* expression and the naturalness of its diction as opposed to the artificial language of the *Kokinshū*.[5] Toyama, who was—along with Inoue Tetsujirō (1855–1944) and Yatabe Ryōkichi (1851–1899)—one of the founders of the *shintaishi* (New Style Poetry) movement, made these comments in an effort to rid New Style Poetry of what he believed to be pointless affectation. Two years after these men published *Shintaishishō* (A Selection of Poems in the New Style, 1882), Suematsu Kenchō (1855–1920), who later served as Minister of Communications and Home Minister, wrote an essay, "Discussion of Poetry and Music" (*Kagaku-ron*), in which he attributed the demise of poetry during and after the Heian period to its estrangement from music. Citing *Man'yōshū* poetry, which he assumed to have been sung orally, Suematsu called for the creation of a modern poetry through the restoration of musicality.[6] As these examples reveal, the "rediscovery" of the *Man'yōshū* and its inception as national poetry extend back to the early 1880s, well before Shiki's influential "Letters to Tanka Poets."

It is significant that the discourse on the *Man'yōshū* as a national poetry anthology (*kokumin kashū*) was indirectly embodied in statements made by men like Toyama, Suematsu, and Inoue, who were leaders in the Meiji state. In addition to writing the official commentary on the Imperial Rescript on Education,[7] Inoue was an active establishment ideologue and, along with his favorite protégé, Takayama Chogyū (1871–1902), was a leader of the "national literature movement" (*kokumin bungaku undō*) in the latter half of the Meiji period. The linguist Ueda Kazutoshi (1867–1937), who helped to establish a standardized Japanese language and was an avid composer of New Style Poetry, may be included here as well. As the conspicuous contributions of these statesmen and ideologues to this discourse indicate, the establishment of a modern national poetry was more a matter of the nation or state than a literary matter. Inspired by their reading of European literary histories, these leaders were convinced that literature was "the flower of a people" (*kokumin no hana*) and that a nation-state that did not possess a resplendent and unique literature of its own could not be counted among the civilized countries of the world.[8] In Japan at this time, however, it was difficult to find such literature. As crude as they may have been, the poetic compositions of Inoue and others were created to meet this urgent need. Toyama and Suematsu made similar efforts in an attempt to improve Japanese theater. In any event, the enthusiasm that drove these men was the same energy that transformed the *Man'yōshū* into a national poetry anthology.

The poetry of the people was expected, first and foremost, to contribute to the spiritual unification of the nation. Contemporary literary and popular magazines such as *Waseda bungaku*, *Teikoku bungaku*, *Kokumin no tomo*, and *Taiyō* reveal the extent to which Meiji intellectuals envied and aspired to be national poets like Goethe and Schiller in Germany or Shakespeare in England. While repeating the names of the literary giants of the West, Meiji intellectuals, with a singular ardor somewhere between the heroic and the ludicrous, implored their countrymen to produce a great national poet or asked why Japan had never produced great poetic drama like that of Shakespeare. They intensely desired a poet who could be loved by and belong to all, young and old, high and low.[9] This was more than a literary ambition: the creation of such a poet was considered an indispensable part of Japan's efforts to vie with the Western powers.

Evidence of this desire can be found in the work of Haga Yaichi (1867–1927), who has been called the father of "national literature studies" (*kokubungaku*). In 1901, while studying in Berlin as an instructor at Tokyo Imperial University, Haga wrote to a friend back in Tokyo: "One thing that has deeply impressed me since coming to Germany is the fact that all of the people *from the monarch and his ministers to the workers in the fields* are able to enjoy the same literature and the same music."[10] Haga applied to German literature the same language used in reference to the *Man'yōshū*. Unfortunately for Haga and others, however, the value that they sought in the *Man'yōshū* was not to be found in the Japan of their own day: the prestige accorded to the *Man'yōshū* may indeed have been a kind of phantom generated from the ambitions and anxieties of the intellectual elite and projected upon an ancient text. Six years before this letter, someone whom we gather to have belonged to the same school as Haga wrote an essay entitled "On Methods for Compiling a Literary History," in which he expressed admiration for Goethe's lyric poetry and wistfully lamented the fact that long ago in Japan, as well, everyone from emperors to common field hands shared in the poetic world.[11] It was this unknown author's assertion that a situation that had existed in antiquity could be realized in the future. The author's esteem for ancient poetry, it should be stressed, stemmed more from a contemporary sense of mission than from a direct appreciation of the poetry itself.

Convinced that a national poetry had to possess both form and content that were appropriate for the literature of a new age, Inoue and others rejected the thirty-one-syllable tanka form and instead advocated and practiced New Style Poetry. Toyama went even further in rejecting five-seven meter. To give the poetry more complex content, they advocated widening the range of poetic diction; and to make the poetry more accessible to society at large, they urged the elimination of elegant language and rhetoric in favor of more direct expression.

The debate also led to a reexamination of the poetry of the past, which in turn resulted in speculation about the possible revival of the chōka, or long poem, which had flourished during the age of the *Man'yōshū* but was rarely practiced in subsequent periods. In extreme cases, the chōka was regarded as a form of epic poetry. This kind of interest further solidified the critical opinion that *Man'yōshū* poetry—the chōka in particular—was "grand and vigorous" (*yūkon*) in tone. In the same fashion, the *Man'yōshū* was admired for its "direct" (*shinsotsu*) expression of "unaffected" (*soboku*) emotion. Modern writers consequently could not hide their bewilderment when confronted with *makura-kotoba* (epithets), *jo-kotoba* (prefaces), and other rhetorical techniques of *Man'yōshū* poetry. Waka since the time of the *Kokinshū* was thought to have lost its vitality and to have become excessively technical and frivolous as a result of having been the exclusive possession of aristocrats who had cut themselves off from the common people. The *Man'yōshū*, by contrast, was perceived by Meiji intellectuals and literati as the reflection of a golden age in which their forebears wept and laughed together in song. Believing that they shared a literary bloodline with these natural poets of old, they convinced themselves that a modern national poetry was about to emerge. In all likelihood, the perception of the *Man'yōshū* as a national poetry anthology was a form of psychological compensation for the absence of such a modern national poetry.

The revival of nō drama may be considered a phenomenon in the same general vein. Nō, which had survived the Edo period under the patronage of various military houses (where it was referred to as *shiki-nō*), had lost its support with the coming of the Meiji Restoration and was, for a time, on the brink of extinction. Around 1880, however, it was renamed *nōgaku* (nō opera) through a conservative movement centered upon the imperial family, its peers, and prominent financiers. Kume Kunitake (1839–1931), who was deeply involved in this movement and contributed several articles to the magazine *Nōgaku* (first issued in 1902), argued that the origins of nō dated back to the very foundation of Japanese culture. In order to promote the development of this traditional entertainment as a national art form, Kume often compared the nō to European opera.[12]

The case provided by *Heike monogatari* (The Tale of the Heike), which David Bialock has discussed, offers another interesting point of comparison. In the modern period, one of the main lines of argument regarding *The Heike* and other *gunki-monogatari* (military tales) is the claim that they can be read as national epics (*kokumin jojishi*). As indicated earlier, Japan's failure to produce a grand poetic masterpiece was the source of considerable collective dismay among those who had become familiar with European literary achievements. One effort to fill this perceived void was manifested in the late Meiji period in a succession of lengthy, experimental works based upon Japanese history and legends. These include Inoue Tetsujirō's *Hinuyama no uta* (The Song of Mount Hinu), which was serialized around 1896 in the magazines *Teikoku bungaku* and *Taiyō*. Inoue fancied himself to be Japan's answer to Homer. In a case more directly related to *The Heike*, Yosano Tekkan and two others collaborated on a work entitled *Joji-chōshi Genkurō Yoshitsune* (The Saga of Genkurō Yoshitsune), which appeared in the pages of *Myōjō*. These attempts to create literary works in conformity with a Western epic were accompanied by an analogous attempt to discover the same qualities among works in Japan's literary past that could serve as psychological surrogates. In this sense, the transformation of *The Heike* into an epic ran parallel to the transformation of the *Man'yōshū* into a national poetry anthology. But while the notion of the *Man'yōshū* as a national poetry anthology became firmly established in the public mind, the idea of *The Heike* as epic remained unstable, preventing it from gaining the same kind of acceptance and popularity.

The Homeric epics were literary monuments to the turmoil of a transitional period during which the Greek people passed from a primitive to a civilized race. Western theory maintained, moreover, that such monuments were universal among all civilized races. If this were true, it would stand to reason that Japan, as a cultured society, should also possess an epic poem. At the same time, however, if one reflected on Japan's particular "national essence" (*kokusui*), which the Japanese were convinced was superior to that of any other nation on earth, then one would have to concede that the kind of warfare described in *The Heike* was anomalous—something running counter to the essence of the Japanese people. If there was one idea that accurately represented the character of the Japanese people and left nothing to be desired, it was the image of a harmonious world comprising a unified culture extending "from emperor to commoners." This was precisely the image that was discovered in the *Man'yōshū*.[13]

PRELIMINARY STAGES IN THE CONSTRUCTION OF A NATIONAL POETRY ANTHOLOGY

The fact that a national poetry anthology was invented does not mean that it was conjured from thin air. As is well known, the reputation of the *Man'yōshū* as Japan's oldest poetic collection goes back to the middle of the tenth century, when the compilers of the *Gosenshū* (Later Collection of Poems, 951) first attempted to decipher its difficult orthography. Since that time many poets have studied the *Man'yōshū* and attempted to make it a part of their own practice; the text has also been the object of criticism and exegesis from a very early period. The commercial success of Edo-period printers, who relied upon woodblock printing techniques, helped pave the way for the achievements of *kokugaku*, the nativist learning movement, by making ancient texts more readily available. In the mid-Meiji period, many of the works of these earlier nativist scholars, including some works that had never been published in their own lifetimes, were reprinted in movable type and became widely available. The accumulated knowledge and thought of eighteenth-century kokugaku scholars, particularly the "return to the past" movement advocated by Kamo no Mabuchi (1697–1769) and others, provided the conceptual groundwork for the creation of a national poetry anthology.

The from-emperor-to-commoners concept also had premodern precedents. For instance, we find this idea in *Toshiyori zuinō* (1115), a poetic treatise by Minamoto no Toshiyori (1055–1129), who wrote during the Insei (Cloistered Emperor) period (ca. 1086–1222), and in the preface to *Rin'yō ruijinshū* (Collection of Dust on a Forest of Leaves, 1670), an anthology of waka by early Edo commoner poets edited by Shimokōbe Chōryū (1627–1686).[14] Both accepted the idea that waka, as Japan's traditional form of poetic expression, had been composed since antiquity by everyone—from buddhas, gods, and emperors to the lowliest woodcutters and fishermen. This stance goes back to the two prefaces to the *Kokinshū* and the well-known assertion that "all living things compose poetry," which in turn had originated in China in the *Book of Songs* and its Han commentaries and involved the assumption that rulers could gauge the state of their realm through the songs sung by the people. The *Kokinshū* may have incorporated this idea since the imperial poetry collection was conceived as a cultural apparatus to support imperial authority. The fact that later imperial waka collections all featured anonymous poems is most likely related to this political aim.[15] The same interpretation was applied to the *Man'yōshū* even though it was not an imperial anthology. Implicit in the inclusion of poems such as the *Azuma-uta* (Songs of the East) and the *Sakimori-no-uta* (Songs of the Border Guards) in the *Man'yōshū* was the suggestion that Japan, as a small empire no less dignified than China, subsumed and possessed its own "Eastern barbarians."

For Toshiyori, this concept was more than mere tradition: waka was a Japanese custom reaching back to the Age of the Gods, and he argued for its universality by enumerating the poetry of children, beggars, artisans, thieves, and others on the margins of ordinary society. He praised their poems together with those by Shinto deities, buddhas, and sage-kings of the past, and he hailed stories in which the deities themselves had been moved by the power of waka. For Toshiyori, who felt that waka was in decline, these miracles evinced the wondrous power once possessed by poetry and reflected an ideal state that needed to be revived. He could not help adding that, in his own times, people no longer heard of such miracles. Ironically, while Toshiyori spoke of the universality of waka, this very assertion was based on the unspoken premise that such poetry was part of aristocratic culture.

A somewhat different picture emerges with Chōryū, more than five hundred years later, when the shogunate was already established and the political power of the emperor and aristocracy had been lost. Presided over by Retired Emperor GoMizunoo (1596–1680), the imperial court at that time had become a literary salon under the sway of the Nijō waka poets, who sustained their influence by means of secret transmissions. *Rin'yō ruijinshū*, the anthology of poems edited by Chōryū, included compositions by persons of no rank or office and may be seen as a demonstration of popular poetry against the closed nature of the circle of court poetry. His compilation of poems by samurai, merchants, farmers, and priests alerted his readers to the abnormality of court-dominated poetics. Like Toshiyori before him, Chōryū also clung to an idealized image of the ancient past in which waka was composed by everyone, including the poorest individuals.

The writings of *kokugaku,* or nativist scholars, who flourished in the eighteenth century, also touch on the popular nature of poetry. In *Kokka hachiron* (Eight Issues on Japanese Poetry, 1742), Kada no Arimaro (1706–1751) explained that the *uta* (song) was, like the folk songs of the common people, originally an oral form, and he emphasized the fact that great poetic immortals of the *Man'yōshū* like Kakinomoto no Hitomaro and Yamabe no Akahito were men of inconsequential rank. Motoori Norinaga (1730–1801), the most noted of the kokugaku scholars, also accepted uta in its broadest sense as a property of the people. But while grouping waka with lower-class popular songs to assert their universality, he contended that waka was the orthodox form of the uta. Regarding the old songs as primarily the product of the middle and upper aristocracy, Norinaga understood uta in its original sense to be synonymous with the aristocratic poetic style.[16] In short, the various early claims that all people are given to song were not necessarily declarations of an inherent social homogeneity. Commoners and nobility belonged to different worlds, and as long as this separation existed, there was a need to view waka as a common possession, bridging these two spheres— a distinction that marks off earlier views of the *Man'yōshū* from the modern notion of a national anthology.

As is well known, Mabuchi did more than anyone in the premodern period to champion a "return to the *Man'yōshū*," but he never attributed the value of the anthology to the breadth of the poets represented. For Mabuchi, the greatness of the *Man'yōshū* was to be found instead in the "forthright emotions" (*naoki kokoro*) and "sincerity" (*makoto*) expressed in its poems. In Mabuchi's opinion, waka started to decline when the masculine qualities of the *Man'yōshū* style yielded to the feminine properties of poetry from the *Kokinshū* onward. Mabuchi attributed the causes for this change to the transfer of the capital from the masculine area around the Nara capital to the more feminine Yamashiro region, where the Heian capital was located. Mabuchi's admiration for the *Man'yōshū*—as a masculine anthology—must be seen in the context of his goal of correcting what he believed had become the contemporary denigration of waka as "a frivolous diversion for women."[17]

Earlier poets and scholars who strove for a "return to the *Man'yōshū*" each discovered a different value in the collection, resulting in a far greater diversity of views than those held by their Meiji successors. Meiji intellectuals extracted the usable features of this premodern discourse and incorporated them into their own framework. The notion of poetic composition by all people, which had previously been used to stress the universality of waka, was now transformed into a representation of the unity of the nation's people. In the case of Mabuchi, the notions of masculinity (*masuraoburi*), straightforward emotions (*naoki kokoro*), and sincerity (*makoto*) were reformulated into the requisite attributes of a national poetry: namely, vigor, naturalness, and directness.

Most important, the earlier nativist scholars were not vexed, as their Meiji counterparts were, by the issue of the colonization by Western powers *or by Japan's place within a global system.* Though some hailed waka's long tradition and others emphatically stressed the nobility of the Yamato spirit, the fundamental basis for their ethnocentric discourse was a sense of inferiority and rivalry vis-à-vis Chinese civilization. Meiji nationalism, by contrast, was the product of intercourse on a global scale. In the modern period, Japan's perception of China went from high respect and emulation to derision and aggression. At the same time, the Japanese have come to recognize their culture as distinct and quintessentially East Asian vis-à-vis the West. In all likelihood, Japanese in the modern period eagerly embraced the stock description of the *Man'yōshū* for the comfort and encouragement it gave them: the implicit message was that no matter how disparate in rank, status, or wealth, they were all fellow citizens, sharing basic qualifications as members of the same community. In effect, the expression "from emperors to commoners" bestowed citizenship upon the monarch, or, to borrow Benedict Anderson's term, it "naturalized" the ruler into the nation-state.[18]

THE CONCEPT OF MIN'YŌ OR FOLK SONG

The modern transformation of the *Man'yōshū* into a national poetry anthology (*kokumin kashū*) occurred in two broad phases. The first of these, which took place from the mid- to late Meiji period, was discussed in the section entitled "The Dream of a National Poetry Anthology." This section will treat the second phase, which lasted from the late Meiji to the early Taishō period.

The late Meiji period witnessed the remarkable tanka (modern waka) movement and the erasure of earlier pessimism over its future. One result was the emergence of the view of waka as the underlying thread of Japanese literature from antiquity. This "extended continuity" of tanka formed the groundwork for the crucial associations between tanka and both the imperial system and the character of the Japanese folk or ethnos (*minzoku*)—that is to say, a people believed to share a common indigenous culture. One should be careful to note, however, that the principal leaders of this tanka movement, the members of the Myōjō school, were broad-minded in their interests and sought poetic inspiration from both the East and the West. For them, Meiji poetry encompassed New Style Poetry, a Western-inspired poetic form, as well as tanka and haiku. The Myōjō poets prized the *Man'yōshū* as a Japanese classic, but they did not regard it as their only canonical text. This accommodating attitude distinguished the Myōjō poets from Masaoka Shiki's successors, who had yet to exert their influence.

The discourse on the *Man'yōshū* as a national poetry anthology was fortified during this period by young scholars working in close alignment with journalists. The theoretical and systematic pursuit of a national poetry by these elite intellectuals—the first generation to have received a modern education from the elementary school level—led to a dramatic reversal in the way that the *Man'yōshū* was conceived: the from-emperor-to-commoner hierarchy implied in the mid- to late Meiji descriptions of the *Man'yōshū* was inverted. Instead of viewing poetry as a cultural property (of deities, the imperial family, and nobility) that disseminated downward to the populace, these intellectuals saw a more sophisticated poetry that was culturally based in popular (*minshūteki*) folk (*minzokuteki*) songs and that was cultivated through contact with foreign civilizations. This shift in perception was brought about largely by the importation of the German concept of *Volkslied*, or folk song, which was eventually rendered into Japanese as *min'yō*. For the next eighty years, this perspective would become the key premise in the study of the *Man'yōshū*, pervading every current of that enterprise, including the most advanced research.

In November 1894, students, graduates, and instructors at the College of Letters at Tokyo Imperial University organized the Imperial Literary Society (*Teikoku bungakukai*) with the express intent of creating a "national literature" (*kokumin bungaku*) that would serve as a central pillar of the national spirit. In January of the following year, they began publication of a monthly magazine, *Teikoku bungaku* (Imperial Literature). The passionate opinions of the contributors to this magazine were infused with and pushed forward by the nationalistic tenor of the next decade—the ten years between Japan's successes in the Sino-Japanese War (1894–1895), which worked public opinion into an unprecedented frenzy, and the Russo-Japanese War (1904–1905). This movement, which centered on the magazine *Teikoku bungaku* and which I shall call the "late Meiji national literature movement" (*Meiji kōki kokumin bungaku undō*), carried out its aims according to a three-point basic agenda: first, an inquiry into and a nurturing of the unique character of the people (*kokuminsei*); second, contact with and assimilation of the cultural and spiritual achievements of the advanced nations; and, third, a synthesis of these two projects. The members of the Imperial Literary Society, following a program cut from the fabric of German literary history, dreamed of a glorious day in the near future when Japan, like Germany, would dramatically turn out a succession of great writers. The first item on the agenda, the discovery and promotion of the Japanese national character, was to be achieved through the glorification of the Japanese classics, the writing of literary, cultural, and philosophical histories, and the collection and analysis of proverbs (*kotowaza*) and folk tales. The second item was to be attained by introducing past and present European literature, arts, and ideas and using them to stimulate those working in creative fields. The process of synthesizing these two endeavors was conducted in the pages of the literary magazine, which seethed with theoretical discussions of New Style Poetry and problems related to Japanese language and orthography.

From the very first issue, the notion of the Volkslied stood at the conceptual center of the *Teikoku bungaku* movement. In the 1770s, the German thinker Johann Gottfried Herder (1744–1803) saw the Volkslied as an essential means of seeking the spirit of a nation in popular culture. His compilation of folk songs into collections for publication inspired Goethe to compose lyric poetry in the manner of the Volkslied, thereby extending its influence to later Romantic poets. These earlier developments in Germany, which fascinated the members of the Imperial Literary Society, became the focus of repeated debate. However, in their haste to apply German concepts to the literature of their own country, the early participants in this literary movement failed to ask themselves just what in the Japanese tradition corresponded to the "folk song," which, they assumed, represented the character of the nation's people in pure form and was therefore good. While heralding the advent of New Style Poetry and calling for the expansion of poetic diction and the improvement of poetic forms, the members of the Imperial Literary Society were adamant that their goals be met through lessons learned from "folk songs," or *zokuyō* (popular songs), as the term was initially translated. Unfortunately, their choice of the word *zokuyō* was burdened by earlier associations with bawdy and vulgar popular songs and led to an indiscriminate clustering of urban songs with songs belonging to rural communal traditions.

Much of the resulting confusion was brought under control by Ueda Bin (1874–1916), a scholar of English literature and one of the important modern importers of European culture. Through Ueda's writings, the word *min'yō* (folk song) came to replace the term zokuyō as a description for the type of composition the literary movement wished to establish as one of its models. The word *min'yō*, which had previously appeared at least once (in a book review by the writer Mori Ōgai [1862–1922]),[19] was not coined by Ueda, but his repeated use of the term led to its widespread adoption. Ueda's writings also clearly indicated that the concept of min'yō—as opposed to zokuyō—excluded the types of songs performed by geisha in the pleasure quarters. In an essay in a special issue of *Taiyō* published in June 1900 under the title "The Nineteenth Century," in which Ueda introduced European literature of the past century, Ueda indicated that in each region of Europe, min'yō had served as a vital stimulus to the rise of national poetry. Even more important was an interview with Ueda published in the pages of *Teikoku bungaku* four years later in which he sought the foundation of a national music and called for the immediate compilation and collection of min'yō for that purpose.[20] His remarks attracted great attention both inside and outside the Imperial Literary Society, and writers began to compose poems in the fashion of min'yō, some even endeavoring to compile collections on a national scale.[21]

In calling for the recognition and appreciation of min'yō as national music, Ueda was consciously rejecting claims to that privilege made by traditional forms such as *gagaku* (court music), koto music, nō music, and shamisen music. Although each of these forms had long been potential claimants to the title of "national music," Ueda argued that each was, in reality, an exclusive form that had attained a level of accomplishment within only one stratum of society. According to Ueda, art that neglected to draw upon the sensibilities of the "populace" or "people" (*minshū*) could not be expected to engender a sense of national unity. For Ueda, minshū did not simply mean the people of the middle or lower classes; it evoked the people who sustained the culture of the nation.[22] The word *min'yō* was formed through a combination of the characters *min* (民) and *yō* (謡), which corresponded to the words *Volk* (folk) and *Lied* (song). *Min* conveyed the sense of both "people" (minshū) and "folk/ethnos" (minzoku)—people believed to share a common indigenous culture—but more importantly, in Ueda's ru-minations it first and foremost denoted kokumin, the people of the nation. As with Herder, the concept of the Volk was intended to fill in the gap be-tween the ideal of a nation and its reality. Min'yō were one of the diverse "traditions" that were required to create the necessary spiritual bond among the members of the emerging nation-state.

The attention given to min'yō parallels the sudden growth in folklore studies that developed alongside the late Meiji national literature movement. Investigations into the national character of the Japanese people began to ap-proach the issue from the perspective of ethnicity (*minzokusei*), the charac-ter of the folk. An instance can be found as early as the anonymous 1895 paper "On Methods for Compiling a Literary History," which contains the following passage:

> The brilliance of the thought of the people (kokumin) is not always expressed initially in the form of written letters. When collected and given literary ex-pression by poets, oral traditions such as legends, paeans, proverbs, and folk songs (zokuyō) should also be categorized as part of the literature of the peo-ple of the nation. In terms of literary history, the value of such works is not the least bit inferior to that of the great literary masterpieces.[23]

A few years later, *Teikoku bungaku* began to publish a number of studies related to proverbs, myths, and legends. Among those who attempted to compile collections of proverbs, none dedicated as much energy to the task as Fujii Otoo (1868–1945), who completed *Zokugen-ron* (A Study of Folk Sayings) in 1906, after ten years of research, and released his voluminous *Gengo daijiten* (A Comprehensive Dictionary of Proverbs, 1910) four years later. At the same time, remarkable strides in the area of myth and legends were made by Takagi Toshio (1876–1922), who, in 1904, marked the start of modern mythology studies in Japan with the publication of *Hikaku shinwa-gaku* (Comparative Mythology), which included many articles that he had published in *Teikoku bungaku* beginning in 1899. In contrast to earlier treat-ments of the *Kojiki* and the *Nihon shoki* (Chronicles of Japan, 720), which viewed these narratives as actual histories or collective memories of antiquity, Takagi dealt with these stories as the myths of the Japanese folk.

Takagi's work was soon followed by similar studies by writers in a variety of fields. After publishing Takagi's article, "A Study of the Hagoromo Legend," in March 1900, *Teikoku bungaku* carried similar works by Ueda Bin in June of the same year and, in the following months, articles by the English literature scholar Okakura Yoshisaburō (1868–1936) and the linguist

Shinmura Izuru (1876–1967). The appearance of Takagi's work in 1904 came at the same time that Tsubouchi Shōyō (1859–1935), one of the leading literary figures of the day, urged the synthesis of Western opera and traditional Japanese theater and music in *Shingakugeki-ron* (A Study of New Musical Drama). Shōyō's own literary efforts to demonstrate his theories included works—*Shinkyoku Urashima* and *Shinkyoku Kaguyahime*—based upon legends such as those of Hagoromo and Urashima. It is no coincidence that these were produced in the same year that Takagi published his study of Japanese myths and legends. Writers from a number of different fields were drawn to Japanese myths and legends at this time, reflecting the degree to which the notion of the Volk had earned general recognition as the source of national identity. It was in this context that the concept of *min'yō* or folk song was eventually applied to the *Man'yōshū*, which had already assumed the role of national poetry anthology.

In September 1902, after completing a year and a half of study in Germany, Haga Yaichi initiated a course at Tokyo Imperial University's College of Letters entitled "The Study of Japanese Poetry." Because this course was virtually the first systematic and organized attempt at understanding the whole of Japanese poetry, it made a profound impression on his students.[24] One of Haga's key points was the German distinction between *Volkspoesie*, the folk song compositions of ordinary men and women, and *Kunstpoesie*, the more artistically conceived and crafted works by professional poets. Volkspoesie and Kunstpoesie, terms that had been introduced by Herder more than one hundred years earlier and adopted in numerous histories of German literature, were translated into Japanese as *kokumin-shi* (poetry of the nation's people) and *gijutsu-shi* (artistically crafted poetry).

One of the students deeply impressed by Haga's lectures was Shida Gishū (1876–1946), who treated the issue of the Volkslied in a series of articles published in *Teikoku bungaku* in 1906 under the title, "A General Introduction to Japanese Folk Song."[25] Shida's study, which was the first to deal seriously with min'yō, was also the first to claim that the *Man'yōshū* preserved the earliest examples of min'yō, or folk songs. To trace the development of the Japanese national character, Shida advocated the systematic compilation of earlier min'yō and found an important initial source in the Songs of the East (Azuma-uta, contained in the 14th volume of the *Man'yōshū*), which he labeled "folk songs of the eastern region" (*tōgoku chihō no min'yō*).

The *Man'yōshū* contains more than 230 so-called Azuma-uta, which are commonly regarded as having been composed by people living in the rural eastern districts. It also includes the Songs of the Border Guards (Sakimori-no-uta), which are thought to have been the work of soldiers from the same eastern provinces, mobilized to protect Japan's western border. In addition, there are songs (uta) attributed to people living in the remote areas to the north and south, compositions thought to be by laborers who participated in the construction of the Fujiwara palace, and poems labeled as songs of street performers. These works have come to be regarded as the product of the "common people" (*shomin*) and have provided one important basis for viewing the *Man'yōshū* as a poetry anthology of the nation-people. With few exceptions, however, all these poems feature a telltale combination of five and seven syllables as their basic metrical unit. In other words, they employ a poetic form identical to that used by aristocrats in their poetic compositions, whereas even the songs found in the *Kojiki* and the *Nihon shoki* do not adhere to this fixed form with such consistency. The *Man'yōshū* compositions exhibit too great a formal regularity to have been orally composed by illiterate commoners. However, the notion of a national poetry anthology, fueled by longing and nostalgia, has prevented readers from acknowledging these basic facts. Although causing some hesitation, Shida was likewise not impeded by the fact that all 230 Azuma-uta were in the regular tanka (5/7/5/7/7) form used by the aristocracy. Despite these problems, his particular interpretation of the Azuma-uta as "folk songs of the eastern region" was to enjoy wide acceptance among *Man'yōshū* scholars for more than half a century.

Shida's goal was to recover as many past min'yō—the older the better—as possible. Since this task lay at the very root of the national literature movement, a certain license was justified by the urgent need to push forward, and before long, min'yō were discovered elsewhere in the *Man'yōshū*: eleven more examples came to light in volume 16. Shortly thereafter, folk songs were discovered in Heian court poetry collections, and in medieval and Edo period collections as well. Emboldened by his methodology, which convinced him that all min'yō share basic characteristics with only slight variations, Shida was able to discover one after another. These min'yō were invented rather than discovered, and in this particular case the mother of invention was, indeed, necessity.

The fruits of Shida's labor were harvested by his teacher, Haga Yaichi. In his *Kokubungaku rekidaisen* (Selections from National Literature from Past to Present), published in 1908, Haga conjectured that many of the anonymous poems of the *Man'yōshū* were either "Nara- or pre-Nara period min'yō":

When I read the *Man'yōshū*, I am naturally enamored of the professional literary poets like Hitomaro, Akahito and Yakamochi, but I have an even stronger fondness for the poems by the nameless poets in volumes 9, 11, 12, etc. In their frank depiction of deep emotions between men and women, these poems are quite unlike the artistically crafted poems of later ages. I have the same feeling as when I read China's *Book of Songs*. In the Songs of the East in the 14th volume, we find the voice of the people singing deep romantic emotions. These works probably fell outside the scope of Chinese influence.[26]

In 1914, in lecture notes titled "Literature of the Nara Period," Haga identified poems in volumes 11 and 12 as "poetry of the folk" and praised them accordingly. In the course of a few years, the min'yō, or folk song category, had, without any supporting evidence, swelled exponentially from Shida's original cluster of poems in volumes 14 and 16 to a powerful surge.

Haga had not always viewed the *Man'yōshū* in this light. In 1890, when he published *Kokubungaku tokuhon* (*Japanese Literature Reader*), he and his fellow editor, Tachibana Senzaburō, grouped the Nara period, when the *Man'yōshū* was compiled, together with the Heian period and labeled them both the *chūko* (mid-ancient) period. By including the *Man'yōshū* in a historical period when literary activity centered on the court aristocracy, Haga had, in effect, revealed that he did not believe that the folk or popular features of the *Man'yōshū* were that strong. A few years later, in 1898, in "Ten Lectures in Japanese Literary History," he did describe the anthology as including works by people from "emperors and princes at the highest levels to priests and nuns who had abandoned the world," but he also pointed out that more than half of the poets in the *Man'yōshū* were "urbanites living in the capital or officials belonging to the court."[27] Here Haga, no doubt concerned with the aristocratic culture and refined elegance of the court, plotted the popularization of waka as a downward vector, originating with the aristocracy and then "spreading out and flourishing." It was not necessarily the case that the aristocracy had co-opted popular culture for itself. By 1908, however, in his *Selections from National Literature*, Haga's emphasis had shifted to the side of the populace, or commoners. As we can see here, the reconception of the *Man'yōshū* as a national poetry anthology based on the notion of the folk (minzoku) had occurred by the last few years of the Meiji period.

This transformation is further corroborated by the work of Sasaki Nobutsuna (1872–1963), a well-known tanka poet who made substantial contributions to the textual and philological exegesis of the *Man'yōshū*. Beginning in 1905, at about the same time that Shida was publishing his papers, Sasaki lectured on the history of waka at the College of Letters at Tokyo Imperial University; the content of those lectures was released three years later as *Kagaku ronsō* (Waka Studies, 1908). In one of the essays in that collection, Sasaki praised the nameless poets of the *Man'yōshū* and voiced his admiration for volumes 13 and 16 and for the Azuma-uta in volume 14, which he designated as *shomin-shi* (commoner poetry).[28] He also maintained that the anonymous poems in volumes 7, 10, 11, and 12 were unremarkable when compared with the works of the known poets, but by the publication, seven years later, of a more systematic work entitled *Wakashi no kenkyū* (Studies in Waka History, 1915), he was prepared to recognize volumes 11 through 16 as "a collection of min'yō" and to hail the distinctive style of naïve simplicity of the poems in volumes 11 and 12.

The commoners "discovered" in these *Man'yōshū* poems were not portrayed as impoverished masses feeding off the cultural scraps left by the imperial court. To the contrary, they gloriously embodied the poetic voice of the folk, of the Japanese as a single ethnic community. Any similarity between their songs and those of the aristocracy was now taken to confirm the notion that min'yō had extended its influence upward rather than the reverse. The relationship between the poetry of the aristocracy and that of the commoners bore witness to a shared tradition that was believed to have flowed continuously in the ancient age through all Japanese, high courtiers and commoners alike. The aristocracy was not a privileged class under the influence of a foreign culture; its achievement was now believed to have been grounded in the spirit and energy of the folk. Since it stood upon the culture of the people like no other work, the *Man'yōshū* could be regarded as the wellspring of the Japanese national spirit and a great product of its culture.

TWO VIEWS OF THE NATIONAL POETRY ANTHOLOGY

As described earlier, the notion of the *Man'yōshū* as a national poetry anthology received the imprimatur of the academic world, leading to a situation where the Araragi poet Shimaki Akahiko could, in 1919, make the following statement with confidence and wide approval.

The *Man'yōshū* resonates with the poetry of the folk (minzoku). In it, all the Japanese people bare their souls to one another in song and candidly communicate their shared human emotions. So it was for everyone, from the emperor above, to the lowest fisherwomen scooping brine from the sea, to even the meanest beggars. We find in one poem an emperor delivering a song of love to a young girl gathering herbs, and in another a lowly girl baring her heart to a gentleman of rank. First among the distinguishing features of the

Man'yōshū is the way that the members of all social strata directly faced the real issues of their day and revealed the intensity of their emotions in song.[29]

In this paper, originally a lecture, Shimaki Akahiko describes the "progress among the populace" (*minshūteki hattatsu*) of "songs of the folk" (*minzoku no kayō*), which, existing outside the isolated world of Heian and post-Heian waka, inherited and preserved the "spirit of the *Man'yōshū*." In the apparent unity between the character of the folk/ethnos (*minzokusei*) and the character of the people/populace (*minshūsei*), we can see the degree to which the image of a national poetry anthology had extended, reaching as far as the leading poet of the Araragi school.[30]

In conclusion, two complementary factors went into the construction of the image of the *Man'yōshū* as a national poetry anthology. The first was the notion of the character of the people of the nation (kokuminsei), which was intermeshed with the imperial system. The second involved the concepts of minzokusei (folk or ethnic character) and minshūsei (character of the populace or people). The former, with its direct relationship to the needs of the nation-state, was pushed to an extreme in Meiji textbooks that uniformly lauded the *Man'yōshū*'s reverence for the emperor. In the Shōwa era, the Yokusan (Imperial Assistance) political organization that aided the government during World War II used passages from the *Man'yōshū* as a means to boost Japanese fighting spirit during the war. The ability of this first factor to sustain the national image of the *Man'yōshū* was understandably attenuated after World War II. The replacement of the first factor by the second, however, has permitted the notion of the *Man'yōshū* as a major Japanese classic to persist in the half century since the end of the war. Because it had been articulated in primarily cultural—as opposed to political—terms, the prestige of the *Man'yōshu* has been able to survive in the postwar period and withstand the reduction of the emperor to merely symbolic status.[31]

CHAPTER TWO

Constructing Imperial Mythology:
Kojiki and *Nihon shoki*

KŌNOSHI TAKAMITSU

TRANSLATED BY IORI JOKO

The object of this essay is to examine the various systems and discourses that have transformed the *Kojiki* (Record of Ancient Matters, 712) and the *Nihon shoki* (Chronicles of Japan, 720) into the "Japanese classics." Today these two works are regarded as the origin of the "Japanese," as the means by which we can understand the lives and thought of the people of the ancient period. In other words, the *Kojiki* and the *Nihon shoki* have been defined as the cultural foundation of both the folk and the nation, and they have been treated in that fashion in school textbooks approved by the Ministry of Education. But this discourse was constructed by a modern nation-state (*kokumin kokka*) whose ideological underpinning was the emperor system (*tennōsei*).

Indeed, from the time that they were first written in the early eighth century until the present, the *Kojiki* and the *Nihon shoki* have always existed in the context of the emperor system; the two texts were constantly reconstructed and reinterpreted for the purpose of enforcing or maintaining the legitimacy of the emperor. To understand this process we need to examine three historical stages: the ancient *ritsuryō* state, the medieval period, and the modern nation-state.

Modern scholarship has regarded the *Kojiki* and the *Nihon shoki*, along with early ritual texts such as *norito* (ritual prayers), as manifestations of a single, preexisting mythology. I shall argue, however, that these texts in fact represent different mythological systems that variously authenticated the political hegemony of the Yamato clan (imperial house) and its state system, a centralized autocracy based on comprehensive legal codes (*ritsuryō*) and on the assumption that all rightful power derived from an emperor who was above the law, a system that prevailed from the late seventh century to the late tenth century. As we shall see, the early commentaries and subsidiary texts generated by the *Nihon shoki* and the *Kojiki* wove together these heterogeneous mythologies to create a unified, imperial mythology. When the ritsuryō state system became defunct, the discourse produced by or imposed on these two texts took on other political and religious functions: in the medieval period, for example, the *Nihon shoki* became a vehicle for the propagation of a syncretic worldview; in the Edo period, the *Kojiki* served as a key text for nativist learning (*kokugaku*) and was regarded by Motoori Norinaga (1730–1801) as a repository of *furukoto* (ancient language). In the modern period, the two texts, building on their earlier reincarnations, served as the mythological and ideological underpinnings for the modern emperor system, particularly as it related to the notion of *kokutai* (national essence).

ESTABLISHMENT OF THE RITSURYŌ STATE AND FORMATION OF DIVERSE IMPERIAL MYTHOLOGIES

The *Kojiki* and the *Nihon shoki* were originally composed as a result of the need of the early ritsuryō state to authenticate itself; the construction of the ritsuryō state required an affirmation of its own world order. Since the first century C.E., the rulers of Wa (the name given the Japanese archipelago and its inhabitants by the Chinese) had maintained communications with the Chinese imperial court in a tributary relationship where the rulers of Wa offered tribute to the Chinese emperors in return for appointments as kings of Wa. The Japanese rulers were incorporated in this fashion into the Chinese imperial world order. But from the seventh century—at the time of the Sui (581–619) and Tang (620–907) dynasties—the rulers of Japan declined to maintain this tributary relationship with China. Instead, they attempted to establish their own world order by creating a miniature imperial order modeled on that of China, complete with Korea as a tributary state.[1] The *Kojiki* and the *Nihon shoki* legitimized the new ritsuryō state and the new world of the emperor by providing an account of how the world came into being and how that world became the present imperial system, that is to say, by tracing the origins of the emperor to the Age of the Gods, a mythological realm.

Despite their shared purpose and character, however, the *Kojiki* and the *Nihon shoki* differed fundamentally from each other in their formulation of this imperial world order. This difference is most obvious in their treatment of the imperial descent (*tenson kōrin*), which reveals how the emperor came to rule the world. Both texts agree that it is Ninigi, as the Heavenly Grandson, who descends from heaven, but they differ significantly on who issues the order for his descent and how it occurs. To authenticate the rule of the emperor over the land, the *Kojiki* gives Amaterasu, the sun goddess, a definitive and important role (of handing Ninigi the imperial regalia, the Yasaka curved beads, mirror, and Kusanagi sword), while the *Nihon shoki* gives her no role at all. In fact, Amaterasu as ancestress of the imperial house does not even exist in the *Nihon shoki*.

One influential theory is that the *Nihon shoki* represents an earlier stage and the *Kojiki* a more developed stage of the same narrative,[2] but this is not a matter of development. Instead, each text establishes the legitimacy of imperial rule in its own way, which is related to the larger worldview that each presents. The *Kojiki* gives no account of the formation of heaven and earth, and the opening sentence describes the appearance of a deity in heaven, or Taka-ama-no-hara (Plain of High Heaven), when the worlds of heaven and earth have already taken shape and begun to function.[3] The earth, Ashihara-no-naka-tsu-kuni (Land Amidst the Reed Plains), is molded by the deities of Taka-ama-no-hara, specifically by Izanaki (Izanagi) and Izanami, who come down to earth and give birth to the land. The world does not emerge from the earth; instead, a world takes shape as a result of *musuhi*, the creative energy that comes from and is active in Taka-ama-no-hara.

In the *Kojiki* the earth is dependent upon heaven; it is a relationship that is confirmed by the story of the Heavenly Rock Cave.[4] Amaterasu's self-concealment in the Rock Cave causes disorder in both heaven and earth—which are plunged into total darkness and chaos—and order is restored to both worlds upon her emergence from the cave (an action that fills both heaven and earth with light). In other words, the order embodied in and upheld by Amaterasu, the heavenly deity from Taka-ama-no-hara, extends all the way to earth. As the ultimate arbiter of both worlds, Amaterasu delegates the rule of earth to Ninigi—a delegation that gives legitimacy to the rule of the land by the progeny of Ninigi. This legitimacy is confirmed through the ceremonial worship of the mirror, which functions as Amaterasu's spirit. As the guarantor of the legitimacy of the emperor, Amaterasu can indeed be called the "imperial ancestress."

The *Nihon shoki*, by contrast, begins with an account of the formation of heaven and earth, with everything, in the beginning, commingled as in a bird's egg. From this primal chaos, *yin* and *yang* separate to become heaven and earth.[5] And in the midst of heaven and earth appear three pure male deities working according to the yang principle. Next, the principles of yin and yang operate together to form four pairs of male and female deities. Izanaki and Izanami, the last of these paired deities, are the embodiment of the yin-yang principles in physical form. Their intercourse gives birth to the world and its myriad deities, including the sun deity, the moon deity, and Susanoo. (In the *Kojiki*, these three deities are born from Izanaki alone.) The worlds of heaven and earth, born of the separation of yin and yang, are simply members of a contrastive pair; the earth does not depend on heaven for its existence. In the *Kojiki*, Izanami dies from burns she suffers while giving birth to the fire deity. This cannot happen in the *Nihon shoki*, since Izanaki and Izanami, as the embodiment of yin and yang, are the driving force behind the process of creation. The world must be completed by the two deities together.

In the *Nihon shoki*, Amaterasu, as the sun deity, is restricted to being one of the subordinate members in the world order created by Izanaki and Izanami. Having created the sun, the moon, the land, and all things on heaven and earth, Izanaki and Izanami attempt to create a deity to rule over the earth, but do not succeed. The determination of a ruler of the earth is left in the hands of the various deities born of Izanaki and Izanami, who continue the process of world formation. The descent of Ninigi takes place within the context of this formative process in which Amaterasu does not take an active role. Moreover, Ninigi's status as a heavenly deity does not give him any special privilege. As Emperor Jinmu (the first emperor) says, "There are many sons of heavenly deities."[6] It is not until Emperor Jinmu (a descendant of Ninigi) gains control over earth that the legitimacy of imperial rule on earth is established.

In the *Nihon shoki*, the narrative of Izanaki and Izanami is placed within the overall perspective of a worldview influenced by yin-yang philosophy, where the two deities function as the source of the creative force that shapes the world and where Izanami does not die. In the *Kojiki*, by contrast, Izanaki and Izanami create the land under the direction of heaven (Taka-ama-no-hara), following orders from the heavenly deities. These and other differences reveal that several different accounts of the imperial world order were produced for the ritsuryō state, which, being a literate state, depended on written texts to authenticate itself. Some older narratives no doubt preceded and are contained in these two texts, but they take on completely different meaning within the *Kojiki* and the *Nihon shoki*. It is thus futile to use these two texts to postulate the original forms of these mythological systems. Instead, we must look at the two texts as surviving exemplars of multiple, heterogeneous mythologies that later developed or emerged together into what we now think of as "imperial mythology."

Ritual worship also played an important role in legitimizing the ritsuryō state. The emperor presided over festivals and offerings to various gods, thereby exerting control over the system of state worship. At the core of this system were the seasonal festivals designated in the *Jingiryō* (Regulations Regarding Affairs of the Deities) section of the *Yōrōryō* (regulations of the Yōrō Era, ca. 718–20), beginning with the *toshigoi* (praying for harvest) festival in mid-spring (Second Month in lunar calendar) and extending to the late-winter (Twelfth Month) festivals of *tsukinami* (literally "monthly festival," celebrated in the Sixth and Twelfth Months), *michiae* (offerings on the road), and *hishizume* (pacification of fire).[7] These festivals occurred according to cycles (for example, the *toshigoi* was a festival meant to ask that no harm befall the harvest and that the seasons progress in order), with additional festivals for the alleviation of various disasters. As a whole, the festivals served as prayers for a prosperous and peaceful year and to guarantee the orderly functioning of the cosmos; by presiding over these rituals, the emperor became the ruler of the world, with the festivals guaranteeing the legitimacy of the emperor.

Scholars have generally believed that the myths of the *Kojiki* and the *Nihon shoki* present a ritual mythology, a mythology that explains or accompanies the rituals of the ritsuryō state. Such a view has been encouraged by the resemblance between the *norito* (ritual prayers) found in the state rituals and the myths, especially those in the *Kojiki*. However, the *Kojiki* and ritsuryō state rituals are basically different and are constructed on fundamentally different organizing principles. The *Kojiki* recounts the establishment of the existing world order, beginning with the formation of the world, while the ritsuryō rituals attempt to guarantee the orderly progression of the seasons. Until now, all of these (*Kojiki*, *Nihon shoki*, and norito) were seen as part of a single, preexisting mythology, but a single, unified mythology was

created only *after* the writing of the *Kojiki* and the *Nihon shoki*, through a
process of revision and reconstruction and by reworking the diverse, heterogeneous myths represented in these texts and state rituals. The early history
of the canonization of the *Kojiki* and the *Nihon shoki* is in fact the history of
the construction of a unified imperial mythology.

UNIFICATION OF IMPERIAL MYTHOLOGY
WITHIN THE RITSURYŌ STATE

As the Japanese ritsuryō state was being formed, various mythological and
ritual systems evolved to support its claim to legitimacy. These various elements—as represented by the *Kojiki*, the *Nihon shoki*, and actual ritual practice—formed more or less independently, possessing characteristics that
could not be completely reconciled with each other. The unification of these
multiple, heterogeneous, and potentially divisive strands took place mostly
through textual interpretation, especially of the *Nihon shoki* (which was the
subject of a series of official lectures), and through the formation of new
texts that reworked the contents of earlier texts. These textual reconstructions in turn penetrated and absorbed the rituals. For example, the texts
influenced the norito, transforming them so that the rituals and the mythology came together to form a "single mythology" (as well as a ritual mythology)—a process that one can see in the norito in the *Engi shiki* (Regulations
of the Engi Era, edited 927) and in the *Sendai kuji hongi* (Chronicle of
Ancient Matters, composed in early Heian).

A notable example of the process by which ritual and mythology were
brought together is *Kogo shūi* (Collection of Old Narratives, 807). As is clear
from its preface, the immediate motivation for the writing of *Kogo shūi*,
which was presented to the emperor in 807 by Imbe Hironari, was the assertion of the Imbe family's rights and prerogatives under the ritsuryō world
order. The *Kogo shūi* achieved these ends by reconstructing the text of the
Nihon shoki (to explain the origins of certain court rituals, especially the imperial enthronement ceremony, in which the Imbe family had traditionally
held key roles) and by reinterpreting the imperial enthronement ritual in this
new context.[8] The *Kogo shūi* remolded the account of Ninigi's descent in such
a way as to give Futodama, an ancestral deity of the Imbe, a crucial role in the
descent, thereby justifying the Imbe's role in the enthronement ceremony.

At the time, Amaterasu and Takami-musuhi said, "Now, earth (*ashihara no
mizuho no kuni*) is a land where our descendants shall rule as kings. Let the

Imperial Grandson (Ninigi) go and rule it. Together with heaven and earth, the Imperial Throne shall prosper without end." Wherefore Amaterasu bestowed the divine treasures, the large mirror and the Kusanagi sword, upon the Imperial Grandson, to be forever the heavenly regalia. (These are the so-called sword and mirror of the sacred imperial regalia.) They were naturally accompanied by a spear and beads. Wherefore she issued an edict, saying, "My child, look on this precious mirror as you look on my person. Keep it in the same room, keep it in the same hall, make it your ritual mirror." Whereupon she ordered Ame-no-koyane, Futodama, and Ame-no-uzume to attend the Imperial Grandson.[9]

Ninigi is here described as descending to earth accompanied by the mirror and sword of the "heavenly regalia." Moreover, Futodama is described as one who "shall, leading all the attendant deities, fulfill all his duties, just as in heaven" (28, 128). *Kogo shūi* goes on to describe the enthronement of Emperor Jinmu mostly in terms of the activities of Futodama's grandson, Ame-no-tomi.

Ame-no-tomi, leading the Imbe, carried the mirror and sword of the heavenly regalia, and placed them within the main hall. In addition, he hung the beads, laid out the offerings, and recited the *Ōtono hokahi* (blessing the main hall) prayer—found in another volume—then the *Mikado hokahi* (blessing the palace gate) prayer—also found in another volume. (35–6; 133)

Kogo shūi then goes on to state that in the reign of Emperor Sujin (tenth emperor), a new mirror and sword—transmitted to this day as the mirror and sword of the sacred imperial regalia—were made, while the original mirror and sword were enshrined, first at Kasanui (Nara Prefecture) and later (in the reign of the eleventh emperor, Suinin) at Ise. The worship of the mirror at Ise, the transmission of the mirror and sword as sacred imperial regalia, and the enthronement ceremony are explained as part of the myth of heavenly descent. In other words, the account of the heavenly descent, which differs from that in both the *Kojiki* and the *Nihon shoki*, is reconstructed as the myth of the enthronement ceremony. *Kogo shūi* thus aids in unifying not only the two mythological texts but also the texts and the rituals, in the process creating a new mythology of the regalia.

The official lectures on the *Nihon shoki*, held under court auspices six times from 812 to the latter half of the tenth century, served as the setting for a similar process.[10] The primary purpose of these lectures, which coincides with the compilation of the official histories,[11] was to reaffirm the fundamental basis of the ritsuryō state, both historically and mythologically—a process that occurred through exegetical reinterpretation. The *shiki* (personal notes) compiled in relation to these official lectures reveal that these lectures ultimately created a text distinct from the original *Nihon shoki*. These notes, which are mostly lost, are quoted extensively in *Shaku-Nihongi*, a late Kamakura commentary, in which the Japanese readings for the *Nihon shoki* are frequently determined by analogy to the vocabulary used in the *Kojiki*. In doing so, the *Nihon shoki* and the *Kojiki*, which were originally two separate entities, end up being treated as a single mythology.

This synthesizing effect extends to larger issues. For instance, the following entry from *Shaku-Nihongi* purports to explain the "seven generation of deities."

> Kuni-no-tokotachi, Kuni-no-sazuchi and Toyokumunu are all male deities, who form three generations. Next are eight deities combined in male-female pairs. Counting a pair of male and female deities as a single generation, we have four generations. Altogether there are seven generations. This all corresponds to the account in the *Kojiki*.[12]

According to this explanation, the "seven generations of deities" in the *Nihon shoki* are the same as those in the *Kojiki*, though in fact there are major differences.[13] The *Nihon shoki* divides its deities into groups of three male deities plus four pairs of male-female deities (3 + 4 = 7) as stated above, but the *Kojiki* describes a group of two single deities followed by five pairs of brother-sister deities (2 + 5 = 7). The *Nihon shoki* lectures thus synthesize and unify the two mythologies at the expense of the original texts.

The resulting unified, single mythology also infiltrated ritual practices. The wording of norito recorded in *Engi shiki* appears to correspond to the mythological accounts contained in the *Kojiki*, revealing that, in all probability, the earlier *Kojiki* influenced the later norito. We can postulate a similar influence of *Kogo shūi* over the wording of *Ōtono hokahi no norito* (Prayer for the Blessing of the Main Hall), which contains a reference to "the mirror and sword of the heavenly regalia" being presented to the Imperial Grandson.[14] This synthesizing of textual myths with state rituals was part of the process by which the *Nihon shoki* was canonized as the base text for the legitimization of the emperor.

In summary, in the Nara and Heian periods, during the time of the ritsuryō state, the *Nihon shoki* held the privileged position as the text that legitimized the emperor system, although there were other lesser sources such as the *Kojiki* whose authority could not be ignored. The discrepancies among the various sources were worked out through the discourse created by the official *Nihon shoki* lectures, a discourse that constructed a unitary imperial mythology and that spawned a group of subsidiary texts of the *Nihon shoki*, which in turn infiltrated the norito that were recited at state rituals and festivals. The *shiki* (notes of the *Nihon shoki* lectures) and *Honchō shojaku mokuroku*[15] preserve the titles of these subsidiary texts: *Yamato hongi*, *Jōgūki*, *Nihon shinshō*, *Kana nihongi*, *Rekiroku*, all of which are no longer extant, *Sendai kuji hongi*, *Tensho*, *Shunjū reki*, and others.[16] The most notable among these is *Sendai kuji hongi*, which was composed almost entirely of material excerpted from the *Kojiki* and the *Nihon shoki* and which incorporated so much of these two texts that during the medieval period it was regarded as a base text from which both the *Kojiki* and the *Nihon shoki* derived.[17] Although the *Nihon shoki* continued to be considered the authoritative source of imperial legitimacy, in actuality these subsidiary texts functioned as the basis for understanding the existing world order, substituting for and even replacing the *Nihon shoki*.

THE KOJIKI AND THE NIHON SHOKI
WITHIN MEDIEVAL DISCOURSE

With the establishment of the Kamakura *bakufu* (shogunate) at the end of the twelfth century, the central political administration of the country shifted into the hands of the shogunate, away from the imperial court at Kyoto. As the imperial court's hold over the political order collapsed and the ritsuryō system ceased to function, the earlier imperial mythology that had legitimatized the ritsuryō state as a miniature version of the Chinese empire could no longer validate the new world order. But just as the imperial court, which had been the center of the ritsuryō system, continued to exist in an altered capacity, the imperial mythology continued to function in a transformed version.

This need for a renewed accounting of the imperial system was most keenly felt by the Kyoto aristocracy, whose world continued to revolve around the emperor. Indeed, medieval commentaries on the *Nihon shoki*—written by scholars such as Ichijō Kaneyoshi (1402–1481) and Yoshida Kanetomo (1435–1511)—were produced at the imperial court for the aristocracy. Though medieval *Nihon shoki* commentators held lectures on occasion for elite warriors (for example, Kanetomo's son Kiyohara Nobukata lectured at the household of the Asakura family in Echizen province), the samurai who attended such lectures were more interested in learning and adapting the aristocratic traditions than in altering or going beyond them.

Medieval discourse presented not an imperial world but a Buddhist universal world, in which the *Nihon shoki* as a scriptural "book of the *kami* or
gods" (*shinsho*) was matched and united with the doctrines of Confucianism
and Buddhism. A good example is *Nihon shoki sanso* (ca. 1455–1457), Ichijō
Kaneyoshi's commentary on the Age of the Gods volume of the *Nihon shoki*.
The following two segments of this commentary deal with the beginning of
the world.

> a. From Chapter 1, Section 1 of the *Nihon shoki*: "At the beginning of cre-
> ation, the land *floated and wandered*, like playful fish floating at the top of the
> water."
> "Float and wander" (*fubiao*) means to swing freely (*yaodang*). It signifies
> the activation of the yang principle. Even though fish do not sleep at night,
> the water continues to flow regardless of night or day. The two principles al-
> ternate without cessation. This is why the analogy of fish and water is used.
> This corresponds to the passage in the *Kusharon*, where it says that the accu-
> mulated water, battered by fierce wind, gradually formed the Metal Wheel.[18]
> b. From Chapter 1, Section 4 of the *Nihon shoki*: "The sea-water dripping
> [from the tip of the spear] solidified into an island."
> "The dripping sea-water solidified into an island" signifies the apex in the
> action of the yin principle. According to *Kusharon*, the rising powers of
> *karma* called forth a great cloud, rain fell on the Metal Wheel, and the drops
> were like cart-wheels. Further, a wind arose in reaction, and in turn formed
> the Earth Wheel.[19]

In this instance Kaneyoshi confirms that the beginning of the world as re-
counted in the *Nihon shoki* corresponds with yin-yang philosophy, and at
the same time he meshes this interpretation with the account of the beginning of the world found in *Kusharon* (Abhidharmakosabhasya), a Buddhist
text.[20] Kaneyoshi sees all three—the *Nihon shoki*, yin-yang philosophy, and
Buddhism—as different ways of saying the same thing. Each tells of a single
"universe that came into existence at the same instant,"[21] producing three
different manifestations of a single core truth. As Kaneyoshi says, "the three
teachings are not discordant."[22]

This worldview, while grounded in Buddhism, did not elevate India
(Tenjiku) to the origin or center of all significance. Instead, it reaffirmed the
existence of Japan within a communal universe, consisting of three spheres or
countries (India, China, and Japan), represented by Buddhism (sutras),
Chinese learning, and Shinto (books on the *kami*, or gods), respectively.
Kokinshū engoki, a 1492 commentary on the *Kokinshū* (Collection of Japanese
Poems Old and New, early ninth century) that reflects the medieval religious

belief in *honji-suijaku* (origin-manifestation), states, "The Buddhas consider India to be their country of origin (*honji*), and Japan is a land where they appear as expedient manifestations (*suijaku*); but from the perspective of the Japanese deities (*kami*), India is a land where they appear as manifestations, and Japan is their country of origin."[23] This sentiment in turn leads to Yoshida Kanetomo's statement in *Nihon shoki jindai kan shō* (Notes on the Age of the Gods volumes of *Nihon shoki*, ca. 1500) that "Our country is like the seed, India like the flower and fruit, China like the branches and leaves."[24]

The well-known opening line of Kitabatake Chikafusa's *Jinnō shōtōki* (Chronicle of Gods and Sovereigns, 1339), "Great Japan is the land of the gods,"[25] reflects the same notion that "Japan is the country of origin" and runs counter to the idea, widespread during the medieval period, that because Japan is the home of Dainichi Nyorai (literally Great Sun Buddha, who is in fact Amaterasu, the sun goddess), it is a "Great Japan." Instead, Chikafusa's position reflects the type of sentiment apparent in *Kokinshū engoki* and *Nihon shoki jindai kan shō* that Japan is part of a larger universal world order that extends to China and India and that bases Japan's identity within a framework of this shared universality with other countries. The uniqueness of Chikafusa's thinking lies in his attempt to legitimize the emperor with the claim that Japan has maintained a "purity of lineage" since the Age of the Gods and through the belief that this purity is symbolized and authenticated by the transmission of the three sacred imperial regalia.

In the medieval period, the *Nihon shoki* became engulfed and supplanted by a group of subsidiary texts that are conventionally designated as the "medieval *Nihongi*."[26] As we have seen, subsidiary texts of the *Nihon shoki* had already begun to supplant the parent text during the ritsuryō period, in the Nara and Heian periods, but the focus of these subsidiary texts had been on supplying a unified mythology to support the ritsuryō state and legitimize the emperor. From the latter half of the Heian period, a new set of subsidiary texts embraced a new, pan-Asiatic worldview, replacing the discourse of the now defunct ritsuryō state. Disseminated through short, anecdotal, *setsuwa*-type tales, as well as in more extended formats, such as found in the sixth volume of the *Jinkei shō* (Notes on Dust and Rubbish, 1482), this discourse produced the "medieval *Nihongi*," a diverse group of texts that drew upon syncretic discourse based on the three teachings—Shinto, Buddhism, and Confucianism. In this framework, statements in the *Nihon shoki* that drew on yin-yang philosophy were seen as expressions of universality, and an even wider universality was sought by conflating the *Nihon shoki* with Buddhist texts. Those aspects of the *Nihon shoki* that Motoori Norinaga, the nativist learning scholar of the *Kojiki*, was to reject as "Chinese" or foreign were in fact the very aspects that medieval commentators valued as positive reinforcements of the new worldview.

NORINAGA'S TRANSFORMATION OF THE MEDIEVAL PARADIGM

Motoori Norinaga—whose nativist stance was in many ways the direct opposite of the medieval stress on universality and syncretism—sought the foundations of his world order in what he saw as the exclusive purity of primeval Japan, most particularly in the "ancient words" (*furukoto*) that had been spoken by the Japanese. This position required the expunging of all elements of the Chinese language, including the obfuscating veil of written characters and literary conventions. In this context, the *Kojiki*, hitherto a secondary text, became the central text while the *Nihon shoki* was shifted to a more peripheral position. As Norinaga wrote in *Kojikiden* (his extensive commentary on the *Kojiki*, completed in 1798):

> When, in early times, there were no such things as books, and words were transmitted solely by word of mouth, these words definitely did not resemble those found in the *Nihon shoki*; instead, they must have been similar to the style of the *Kojiki*. The *Nihon shoki* attempts mostly to imitate Chinese writings, employing literary embellishments, but the *Kojiki* does not concern itself with Chinese writings, seeking only to preserve the ancient, Japanese language.[27]

The issue here is how to recover furukoto, an enterprise from which the *Nihon shoki* is not completely excluded: although the "literary embellishments" incorporated into the *Nihon shoki* have obliterated furukoto from its pages, the text still served the purpose of supplementing the understanding of furukoto in the *Kojiki*. In his detailed annotation of the *Kojiki*, Norinaga in fact employed all available sources of furukoto (such as the *Man'yōshū*) and supplemented them with materials found in the *Nihon shoki*. Since the *Kojiki* itself was written with Chinese graphs, it was also necessary to read through the distorting effects. Hence, *Kojikiden* is peppered with statements such as "so long as the word is the same, the meaning of the character is insignificant" (158) and "these characters are substituted for each other because of similar pronunciation, without regard to their meaning" (353). Significantly, Norinaga does not focus on the legitimacy of the imperial system, as found in Nara and Heian discourse, but on the *Japanese people* inside and outside that imperial world order, a people who were united by furukoto. For the first time, the issue of imperial legitimacy was tied to a larger social world that extended beyond the aristocracy and imperial court to include commoners, and that was based on the notion of a common language and ancestry.

Norinaga's *Kojikiden* reads the *Kojiki* as a narrative of the world that begins from before the creation of heaven and earth and that reveals the world as it was shaped under the guidance of *musuhi*, or creative energy. According to Norinaga, Takami-musuhi and Kamu-musuhi, "the wondrous spirits that create and shape all things," created "all the myriad things and all the various interactions among them, beginning with heaven and earth itself" (129). Under the guidance of musuhi, the primal substance, which "drifted like jellyfish," was fashioned into heaven and earth, becoming a world.[28]

Norinaga's analysis of the opening lines of the *Kojiki* reveals his overall approach to the text. Norinaga takes the first four graphs, *tien di chu fa* (heaven-earth begin-initiate) and reads them as *ame tsuchi no hajime* (beginning of heaven and earth) by analogy with Hitomaro's *ame tsuchi no hajime no toki* (time of the beginning of heaven and earth)[29] and other similar phrases that Norinaga identifies as furukoto. Norinaga's reading ignores the last character in the phrase, *fa* (to initiate), which he explains away by saying, "This also means *hajime* (beginning)."[30] He then explicates the primordial substance that "drifted like jellyfish" (*kuragenasu tadayoeru mono*) by conflating the account in the *Kojiki* with that in the *Nihon shoki*:

> At the time, what was to become heaven and what was to become earth were still undifferentiated and mixed together, just as it says in the *Nihon shoki* [chapter 1, section 1], the first alternate text: "When heaven and earth were still mixed together." (135)

Norinaga criticized medieval discourse for distorting the original texts, but his innovative scholarship, which attempted to excavate the world of furukoto, also produced a new mythology that differed from that found in the *Kojiki* and the *Nihon shoki*.

Norinaga sought out what people had possessed prior to writing, which is why he looked to the beginning of the Age of the Gods as the foundation for understanding "everything about this world" (294). In *Kojikiden*, after explicating the names of the various deities that came into existence during Izanaki's purification (*misogi*), following his return from Yomi, the underworld, Norinaga writes:

People try to understand the Age of the Gods based on human affairs . . . but I base my understanding of human affairs on the Age of the Gods. . . . Everything about the world, the way in which good things and bad things, great or small, alternate from generation to generation, from time to time . . . is in accordance with the way things were done at the beginning of the Age of the Gods. This way is realized in a range of events beginning with the sacred intercourse between Izanaki and Izanami, with the birth of the islands and the myriad gods, and ending with the delegation of the three domains among these Three Noble Gods. (294–95)

It is through the accounts of the Age of the Gods that one comes to understand the nature of human existence.[31] The whole history of human existence is affirmed and understood through reference to the "beginning" as found in furukoto, centered on the *Kojiki*, in a process that, inspired by the emperor, flows undisrupted into the present. Language becomes the basis for canonizing the *Kojiki*. This world that Norinaga envisions is neither that of the early ritsuryō imperial state, nor is it the "three worlds" of the medieval period. Instead, as signified by the term *sumera mikuni* (land of the emperor), it is a world identified by allegiance to the emperor *and* by opposition to outside lands, most specifically China. This reading of the *Kojiki*, with its emphasis on a common language and common ethnic identity, would prove suitable for the modern, ethnically oriented, nation-state. But it would be a mistake to see Norinaga's opinions as the basis for the canonization of the *Kojiki* in the modern period. Instead, it was the modern state's need for a national canon that caused it to discover Norinaga.

KOJIKI AND NIHON SHOKI IN THE MODERN NATION-STATE

In the last decade of the nineteenth century, Japanese intellectuals began to reflect on the role of language within the modern nation-state, an issue crystallized in Ueda Kazutoshi's famous lecture, "Kokugo to kokka to" (National Language and the Nation, 1894), which stated that the nation-state needs to be founded on a common language.

It is our duty . . . never to fail to prevent any misguided deterioration of the unity of language or of the race in the history of our empire. . . . The citizens of our great nation, comprehending this, should love their native tongue with their heart, strive to protect and improve it with their minds, and build upon this foundation as a bulwark of national education.[32]

Literary history as an academic discipline developed in response to this kind of demand for national identity. In *Kokubungakushi jikkō* (Ten Lectures on the History of Japanese Literature, 1899), Haga Yaichi, one of the founders of modern "national literature" (*kokubungaku*), notes:

> For several thousand years, generations of our people have spoken the Japanese language, and today, we hold in our hands a corpus of literature composed in this language. . . . The singular history of our people can be found within the history of our national literature.[33]

Literary history is clearly required here as historical proof of a nation-state based on a "national language" (*kokugo*). Literary history becomes historical proof that "for several thousand years, generations of our people have spoken the Japanese language," that the Japanese people have maintained a unique unity throughout history, which in turn makes possible the present and future unity of the modern nation. In this regard, literary history functioned as an instrument in constructing and guaranteeing the unity of the nation—which was the primary task and concern of the modern nation-state.

It was in this context that the *wabun* (vernacular)-centered corpus of Japanese "classics" was constructed and that the *Kojiki* assumed a privileged status over the *Nihon shoki* as a national classic and as the repository of the oldest and most ancient folk tradition, a notion that was a modern manifestation of the "single mythology" paradigm. The establishment of the position of the *Kojiki* in literary history was in fact not completed until the advent of modern myth studies (*shinwa kenkyū*). In the third decade of Meiji (around the turn of the century) scholars such as Takagi Toshio began searching for the original state of the culture of the folk or people through a cross-cultural study of myth, carrying on intensive discussions in the pages of the journal *Teikoku bungaku* (Imperial Literature), a phenomenon related to the rise of such theories as that of "folk songs" (*min'yō*), which played, as Shinada Yoshikazu argues in his essay, a major role in the modern canonization of the *Man'yōshū* as a "national poetry anthology." These various discourses, which sought to create a foundation for a national literature, were ultimately absorbed into literary history.

With regard to the *Kojiki*, it is necessary to differentiate the ethnographic, cultural-lineage approach, beginning with Takagi Toshio's *Nihon shinwa densetsu no kenkyū* (A Study of Japanese Myths and Legends, 1925), from the school of philological, textual research led by Tsuda Sōkichi, who opened the way for a critical examination of what preceded the *Kojiki* and the *Nihon shoki*. Tsuda, seeking to define Japanese mythology beyond the scope of these two texts, established the practice of treating them, particularly the *Kojiki*, as repositories of ancient folk transmissions and legends. As a result, modern scholarship, both in the form of comparative ethnographic studies and textual criticism, provided complementary and philological evidence of Norinaga's view of the *Kojiki* (and to a lesser extent the *Nihon shoki*) as a repository of furukoto, as the ancient transmissions of the Japanese people. In short, the *Kojiki* and the *Nihon shoki* (with the former regarded as superior in terms of preserving the original transmission in verbal form) were established as classics that allowed for direct access to the ancient age of the folk. Here "Japanese mythology" (*Nihon shinwa*) became myth as the cultural basis of the folk and the nation, resulting in a modern construction of the "single mythology" paradigm, as well as a creation of a mythology that could affirm Japan as a nation-state based on an emperor system (*tennōsei*).

The ideological transformation of myth to authenticate the modern emperor system was derived from a view of history that saw Japan as the emperor's country—a perspective that found its most radical articulation in *Kokutai no hongi* (Fundamentals of the National Essence), edited by the Ministry of Education in 1935, which opens with an affirmation of the authority of the emperor based on the divine decree given at the time of the heavenly descent:

> The Great Japanese Empire is forever ruled by the emperor of a single and unchanging imperial line by virtue of the divine decree of the Imperial Ancestress. This is our eternal, unchanging national essence.[34]

The first part of *Kokutai no hongi—Dai nihon kokutai* (National Essence of Great Japan)—outlines the mythological basis for the legitimacy of the kokutai, focusing on the divine decree that occurs within the myth of the heavenly descent and substantiating it with numerous excerpts from the *Kojiki* and the *Nihon shoki*. The second part—*Kokushi ni okeru kokutai no kengen* (Realization of the National Essence within Japanese History)—historically traces the ways in which every aspect of the life of the nation (people), its national character, its ethics, and its national culture, are part and parcel of the kokutai as it exists under the reign of the emperor. In other words, the history of kokutai originates in and is maintained by the authentication of the emperor by divine decree (*shinchoku*).

Watsuji Tetsurō (1889–1960), the critic-scholar who wrote *Sonnō shisō to sono dentō* (Traditional Reverence for the Emperor and Its Manifestations, 1943), presented a somewhat divergent view of the emperor system. Watsuji saw the *Kojiki* and the *Nihon shoki* as expressions of ethical self-awareness that centered both on the emperor who, as a ritualistic, central figure, provided a totalizing unity for the people (nation), and on reverence for that emperor. For Watsuji, the *Kojiki* and the *Nihon shoki* marked the beginning of a long, continuous history of Japan under the emperor. Unlike those who viewed Japanese history as the history of the emperor's country, however, Watsuji saw the emperor's centrality as relying on moral authority rather than on political power. These claims of the legitimacy of the emperor based on divine decree were dismissed with Japan's defeat in World War II, but Watsuji's view—of ethical reverence for the emperor as a unifying figure— continued in the postwar period to legitimize the emperor as a symbol of Japan and of the unity of its citizens.[35]

Post-1945 critiques of the emperor system by Marxist and other groups have effectively severed the direct tie between the issue of national identity and the emperor. But scholars continue to manipulate the *Kojiki* and the *Nihon shoki*, seeking out the myth of an original people and society, a myth thought to be buried under layers of politically motivated distortions. In other words, the "single mythology" paradigm, of an original myth prior to the *Kojiki* and the *Nihon shoki*, continues to exist. Furthermore, the canonization of the *Kojiki* and the *Nihon shoki* by the modern emperor system and nation-state has been complemented by textual, philological criticism; ethnographic cross-cultural methodology; Marxist class analysis; and Japanese folklore study (*minzokugaku*). The present state of scholarship on the two texts is such that a leading scholar of mythology such as Yoshida Atsuhiko can unabashedly state that the myths in the *Kojiki* and the *Nihon shoki* are mirrors that reflect "the thoughts and perspectives that we the Japanese people have had from the distant past to the present."[36] The fundamental modern framework for the *Kojiki* and the *Nihon shoki* as the cultural fountainhead of both the people and the nation, which is inseparable from the "single myth paradigm" that has canonized these two texts, thus continues to limit the perspective and approaches to these texts. Unless we are able to historize this situation and go beyond these approaches methodologically, we will ultimately continue to construct "Japanese mythologies."

Gender, Genre, and Cultural Identity

CHAPTER THREE

Gender and Genre: Modern Literary Histories and Women's Diary Literature

TOMI SUZUKI

Heian women's poetic diaries and memoirs such as *Kagerō nikki* (Gossamer Diary, late 10th c.), *Izumi Shikibu nikki* (Izumi Shikibu Diary, early 11th c.), *Murasaki Shikibu nikki* (Murasaki Shikibu Diary, early 11th c.), and *Sarashina nikki* (Sarashina Diary, 1058–64?) are customarily referred to as *nikki bungaku* (diary literature), and more specifically as *joryū nikki bungaku* (women's diary literature).[1] Although they have been transmitted for more than a thousand years, these texts did not receive serious scholarly and literary attention until the first decade of the twentieth century; and it was not until the consequent establishment in the 1920s of what I call the "I-novel" (*watakushi shōsetsu*) discourse,[2] with its confessional, self-exploratory emphasis, that these Heian women's diaries were placed at the core of the Japanese classics. Indeed, the notion of joryū nikki bungaku has significantly shaped modern views of the Japanese literary tradition as a whole. As a consequence, it is possible, through an analysis of the canonization of Heian women's diaries, to shed light on the genre configurations and gender assumptions informing the modern construction of the Japanese literary tradition as a whole.

The canonization of Heian women's *kana nikki* took place in the larger context of the modern nation-state building process, of which the modern institution of *kokubungaku* (national literature and its study) became an integral part. In the first half of this essay, I will examine the position of Heian kana literature in modern kokubungaku and in Japanese literary histories written from the 1890s onward. Heian kana literature, long associated with femininity, was designated the basis of "national literature" as a result of the phonocentric notion of "national language" (*kokugo*) that emerged in close relationship with the *genbun-itchi* (union of spoken and written languages) movement and that increasingly stressed direct and unmediated expression. In this newly constructed body of "national literature," from which all the texts written in *kanbun*, or classical Chinese, were eliminated, Heian waka, especially the *Kokinshū*—a canonical text for a thousand years—were devalued because they were not considered to be direct, unmediated expression (as the *Man'yōshū* was increasingly thought to be). By contrast, new attention was given to Heian vernacular prose texts. Valued most was *The Tale of Genji*, which had already been canonized, but which was recanonized as the great predecessor to the "realistic novel," regarded by nineteenth-century evolutionist literary histories as the most advanced literary form and a mark of an advanced nation. Kana nikki were initially (from the 1890s to the 1910s) valorized through these two axes, as direct expressions of emotion and as a critical step toward *The Tale of Genji*, the realistic novel.

Women's kana nikki were then elevated to canonical status through the notion of nikki bungaku that appeared in the mid-1920s, when the I-novel became the center of critical discourse. In the mid-1920s, during a sudden expansion of industrial mass society, there was an institutional emphasis on the notion of *bungaku* (literature) as a privileged means to express and develop a "genuine self" (*shin no jiko*), a stance that lay behind the emergence of the I-novel discourse. Scholars and critics argued that lyrical self-expression and self-exploration were a unique characteristic of a long Japanese literary tradition that could be traced back to Heian nikki bungaku. This movement contributed not only to the modern canonization of Heian women's poetic memoirs, but also to the recanonization of such "self-exploratory" *zuihitsu* (miscellany) as *Tsurezuregusa* (Essays in Idleness, early 14th c.), a text by a male writer that was thought to bring to a higher form what had been started by women.

Soon after Heian women's poetic memoirs had been elevated under the rubric of nikki bungaku, they began to be promoted more specifically as joryū nikki bungaku in the mid-1920s, when the journalistic notion of *joryū bungaku* (women's literature) started to circulate widely in response to a sudden expansion in female readership. At this point, joryū nikki bungaku, which was now valued even more than realistic fiction because of its perceived emphasis on the "sincere" expression of the self, was promoted as a genuine prototype of modern women's literature. In postwar literary histories, Heian women writers—thought to have preserved the national folk (*minzoku*) tradition against overwhelming foreign influence—were cast as figures of resistance as well as symbols of the potential latent in a defeated and impoverished nation. Women's diary literature was gradually differentiated from the I-novel with which it had been closely associated since the 1920s and that was attacked in the postwar period as the embodiment of Japan's failed modernity. In the process it was recast as the epitome of the national tradition, prefiguring "true modernity."

THE FIRST MODERN LITERARY HISTORIES AND FEMINIZED NATIONAL LITERATURE

Among the texts now categorized as nikki bungaku, Tsurayuki's *Tosa Diary* (935) and *Murasaki Shikibu Diary* appear to have been widely recognized at least from the time of Fujiwara Teika (1162–1241), the influential early canonizer of the Japanese poetic tradition. This recognition was primarily the result of the privileged status of their authors in the poetic tradition: Ki no Tsurayuki (d. 945) was the compiler of the first imperial waka anthology, *Kokinshū* (Collection of Old and New Japanese Poems, 905), and Murasaki Shikibu was the author of *The Tale of Genji*, which Teika and his father Shunzei regarded as an indispensable source book for poetry composition. *Izayoi nikki* (Diary of the Sixteenth Night, 1279), an early Kamakura period travelogue, was also valued due to the position of its author, Nun Abutsu (?–1222), in a prestigious poetry family—she was the wife of Teika's son Tameie. In fact, most of the authors of the other women's diary texts such as *Gossamer Diary*, *Izumi Shikibu Diary*, and *Sarashina Diary* were recognized primarily as waka poets whose fame derived from their position in the imperial waka anthologies.

During the Tokugawa period, a number of commentaries were written on *Tosa Diary* by a wide range of Confucian and *kokugaku* (nativist learning) scholars. On a more limited scale, *Murasaki Shikibu Diary* also received serious critical treatment, primarily in connection to *The Tale of Genji* but also as a historical account recording the ceremony surrounding an imperial birth. By contrast, *Gossamer Diary, Izumi Shikibu Diary*, and *Sarashina Diary* received little attention, though there were some textual studies, commentaries, and woodblock editions of these texts.[3]

The position of these texts remained largely unchanged into the late 1880s, when the institution of *kokubungaku* was created as part of the process of modern nation-state-building. In 1890, the first modern literary histories as well as the earliest modern anthologies of classical Japanese literature were published: Ueda Kazutoshi's (1867–1937) *Kokubungaku*, an anthology of late Tokugawa and early Meiji works with a short preface; Haga Yaichi (1867–1927) and Tachibana Senzaburō's (1867–1901) *Kokubungaku tokuhon* (Japanese Literature Reader, 1890), an anthology of Japanese literature from Hitomaro to Bakin with a concise historical survey from ancient times through the Meiji period; *Nihon bungaku zensho*, a twenty-four-volume collection of classical and medieval literature compiled by Ochiai Naobumi (1861–1903), Hagino Yoshiyuki (1860–1924), and Konakamura Yoshikata (1861–1923) and published from 1890 to 1892; and Mikami Sanji (1865–1939) and Takatsu Kuwasaburō's (1864–1921) two-volume *Nihon bungakushi*, the first full-length literary history with abundant excerpts from ancient to late Tokugawa texts. Although Ueda's *Kokubungaku* and Haga and Tachibana's *Kokubungaku tokuhon* were anthologies intended to be used as textbooks, their perspectives and concerns were similar to those of Mikami and Takatsu. All of them considered literature as "reflections of national life" (*ikkoku seikatsu no shaei*) and tried to present, through concrete literary examples, the "development of the mentality of the nation" in order that "the nation's people will deepen their love for the nation," that "the national spirit" (*kokumin no seishin*) will be elevated, and that the "social progress and development of the nation will be furthered."[4]

Even as they emphasized the "national spirit" and the "national life," these Meiji scholars of national literature criticized kokugaku definitions of Japanese literature (*wabungaku*) for being narrow and rejecting "foreign" elements of Chinese or Buddhist origin and for valuing only ancient texts and thus misrepresenting the fullness of Japanese national literature. They aimed instead for a comprehensive representation of the historical development of national literature, stressing both the continuity and the progress of the "national spirit"—"continuity" and "progress" being signs of a civilized and advanced nation. The perspective of these Meiji literary histories was clearly shaped by nineteenth-century European literary histories, particularly

Hippolyte Taine's (1828–1893) *History of English Literature* (1864; English translation, 1872), and by Spencerian evolutionism.

Taine had focused on what he called the "three primordial forces"—"race, milieu, and moment"—but he was primarily concerned with the persistence of certain habits of mind of a particular "race," by which he meant the respective national characteristics of the English, the French, and the Germans.[5] The English race, for example, was characterized by its "stoic energy and basic honesty, heroic severity . . . exact knowledge of precise detail, and a great practical sense" whereas the French race was portrayed as "light and sociable," with a "facile, abundant, curious mind."[6] In the same manner, Haga and Tachibana, along with Mikami and Takatsu, characterized Japanese literature and Japanese mentality as "elegant and graceful" (*yūbi*) in contrast to the "heroic and grand" (*gōitsu, yūsō*) character of Chinese literature or the "precise, detailed, and exhaustive" (*seichi*) nature of Western literature.[7] Significantly, this characterization of Japanese literature as "elegant and graceful" would persist in subsequent literary historiography and have a lasting impact on the general view of Japanese literature as feminine.

Although the basis for such characterization was not presented explicitly either by Haga and Tachibana or by Mikami and Takatsu, two primary factors can be pointed out. First of all, it was at this time that the notion of bungaku became interchangeable with literature in the modern Western sense of the word. While these Meiji scholars continued to use the earlier Confucian notion of bungaku to mean "learning" or "studies,"[8] they disassociated the content of that learning from Confucian studies and criticized the Confucian view of bungaku for disdaining fiction and belles lettres.[9] At the same time, Meiji literary historians emphasized that although leisurely activities such as writing fiction and composing elegant *wabun* (Japanese prose) or Japanese and Chinese poetry were part of bungaku, these activities represented only a small part of the larger enterprise of bungaku. Even as they confirmed the recent elevation of the *shōsetsu* (novel), they emphasized that this genre was only one part of *bibungaku* (elegant writing, belles lettres).[10]

For Meiji literary historians, *gakumon* (learning) consisted of two large areas: bungaku and *kagaku* (science). Bungaku in turn embraced a large body of writings that included not only bibungaku, but also *ribungaku* (rational or intellectual writing), which spanned such disciplines as history, philosophy, and political science.[11] This broad notion of bungaku followed the European notion of humanities, which had been one of the major European definitions of literature.

The notion of literature as equivalent to the humanities was institution-alized in 1877 in the process of establishing Western academic disciplines at the University of Tokyo. Bunka daigaku, the college of bungaku or the division of humanities, consisted of two departments: (1) the department of history, philosophy, and political science (*shigaku, tetsugaku, oyobi seijigaku*) and (2) the department of *wakan bungaku*, or Japanese and Chinese classics. The same division of humanities was redivided in 1881 into three departments: (1) philosophy (*tetsugaku*), (2) political science and economics (*seijigaku oyobi rizaigaku*), and (3) Chinese and Japanese classics (*wakan bungaku*). In 1885, the department of Chinese and Japanese classics was split into the Japanese literature program (*wabun gakka*) and the Chinese literature program (*kanbun gakka*); in 1889 the Japanese literature program was re-named *kokubun gakka* (national literature program).[12]

While Meiji literary historians emphasized the comprehensiveness of bungaku as humanities, they had to deal with these various disciplinary divisions, particularly the narrower definition of literature, that is, literature as bibungaku or what they sometimes referred to as *junbungaku* (pure literature). Indeed, the movement from the broader notion of literature as the humanities to literature as "pure literature," with particular stress on human emotions, was reflected in the institutional rearrangement of bungaku mentioned earlier, with kokubungaku becoming a subdivision of the humanities. This shift corresponds to the change in the Western notion of literature from the comprehensive notion of literature as humanities found in eighteenth-century Europe to the narrower notion of imaginative literature that pre-vailed in the nineteenth century.[13]

Mikami and Takatsu's literary history defines junbungaku as follows:

> Literature is what skillfully expresses human thought, feeling, and imagina-tion by means of certain styles. Its purpose is to be practical and to create pleasure; and it transmits basic knowledge to the majority of people.[14]

Thought (*shisō*), feeling (*kanjō*), and imagination (*sōzōryoku*), as well as prac-ticality (*jitsuyō*) and pleasure (*kairaku*), were emphasized as the essential components of junbungaku. This notion of "pure literature" reflects the influence of Victorian literary discourse as represented by Matthew Arnold and as seen in Tsubouchi Shōyō's *Shōsetsu shinzui* (The Essence of the Novel, 1885–86). On the efficacy of bungaku, Mikami and Takatsu note:

> True bungaku can make the spirit of the nation's people graceful, elevated, and pure (*yūbi, kōshō, junketsu*); and while it enables the reader to experience

the spiritual pleasure of grace, elegance, and purity, it can transmit ethical, religious, and artistic ideas and truths and teach important moral lessons and
essential facts in a natural manner.[15]

"Elegance and grace," the characteristics given to Japanese literature by the
first modern literary historians, here become essential attributes and effects
of bungaku in the specialized sense, the raison d'être of kokubungaku as a
modern institutional discipline.

The project of these Meiji literary historians was deeply conflicted, torn
between the notion of bungaku in the broader sense, as humanities or gakumon in general, and bungaku in the more specialized sense, as junbungaku
or bibungaku, toward which they obviously felt considerable unease.
Although Mikami and Takatsu defined thought, feeling, and imagination as
the essential components of junbungaku, it is apparent that out of the three
essential components, they placed primary value on thought (*shisō*) and its
associated faculties, theory (*riron*), principle (*gakuri*), rationalism (*gōri*), and
reason (*suiri*). When talking about imagination, they noted that "the imagination of uncivilized people was foolish illusion (*mōsō*), whereas the imagination of civilized people (*bunmeijin*) was rational, a means of approaching
an ideal through reason."[16]

Furthermore, these Meiji scholars had to identify Japanese national literature (*kokubungaku*) as that which had the universal features of bungaku, as
well as unique national characteristics. Mikami and Takatsu defined a nation's literature (*ikkoku no bungaku*) as follows:

> A national literature is the body of writing in which the people of a nation
> have expressed their particular thoughts, feelings, and imagination in their
> national language. Literature is universal for all nations, whereas national lit-
> erature is particular to a nation.[17]

According to this definition, *kanbun* (classical Chinese prose) was excluded
from the body of the nation's writings. This was a precarious operation since
the major part of historical, philosophical, religious, and political writings,
the "thought" and "reason" aspect of bungaku, had in fact been written in
kanbun, and thus had to be excluded from Japanese literature.

This leads us to the second factor that underlay the characterization of
Japanese literature as "elegant and graceful": the emphasis on Heian kana literature as the basis of national literature, an emphasis that resulted from the
genbun-itchi movement and its phonocentric notion of a national language
(kokugo). These Meiji kokubungaku scholars valued the Heian period

highly for the creation of wabun, Japanese writings in hiragana—the basis of the writing system for the national language—and for the development of Japanese literary genres such as the *monogatari* (tale), *sōshi* (booklet), *nikki* (diary), and *kikō* (travel diary), all of which they saw as reflecting the "internal life" (*rimen*) of the period (as opposed to the "external state of the period recorded in kanbun texts"). But they also expressed dissatisfaction with the "elegant and gentle, yet effeminate and spiritless" literature and mentality of the Heian period.[18] Haga and Tachibana attributed these characteristics to the nature of the Japanese national language (*kokugo no seishitsu*), to the fact that these works were written mostly by women and that the content was little more than love romances (*enwa*), and, above all, to the fact that the literature of the time centered on the upper class.[19]

Mikami and Takatsu, echoing Tokugawa-period kokugaku sentiment, stated that the laudable "simplicity" and the "brave, gallant spirit of Japanese men" in the ancient period became "effeminate and spiritless under the influence of Buddhism," and turned "pompous and gaudy as they imitated Chinese manners."[20] Haga and Tachibana, by contrast, highly valued Chinese and Buddhist influence, which they thought "imbued literature with lofty ideas," and preferred the "more vigorous and manly" (*gōken*) Japanese-Chinese mixed style (*wakan konkō bun*) that developed in the medieval and Tokugawa periods.[21] Mikami and Takatsu likewise praised the wakan konkō style, which they believed fused *yamato kotoba* (Japanese words) and *kango* (Chinese words) into a higher style and which they saw as the product of a masculinized, "brave and gallant" period.[22] All of them glorified the "remarkable progress" of national literature in the Tokugawa period, particularly the "vast expansion of literary genres" that "embraced both upper and lower classes."[23] Even though they had to exclude a vast body of kanbun writing, Mikami and Takatsu cited wakan konkō-style essays by Confucian scholars such as Arai Hakuseki (1657–1725) as exemplary of Japanese prose. They apparently favored these historical essays and treatises over Tokugawa drama and fiction, especially late Tokugawa-period *gesaku* (playful fiction), which (with the important exception of Bakin's work) they disparaged for its "obscenity."[24] In any event, the central concern of these literary histories was not so much to show the uniqueness of Japanese national literature as to emphasize its continuous "development and progress," implicitly calling for the further progress of national literature, the fate of which was linked to that of Japan as a modern nation-state among Western nations.

Among Heian texts, from which kanbun texts were excluded, the Meiji literary histories paid particular attention to Heian vernacular fiction. Valued most was *The Tale of Genji*, which was recanonized as the great predecessor to the "realistic novel" (*shajitsuryū shōsetsu*), even though these scholars were uneasy about its "effeminate style" (*kiryoku no usuki*), which, they noted, "was inevitable because it was written by a woman."[25] Valued next, even over waka, were nikki such as *Murasaki Shikibu Diary*, *Gossamer Diary*, *Izumi Shikibu Diary*, and *Sanuki no Suke nikki* (Sanuki no Suke Diary, 1108), and kikō (travel diaries), which included *Tosa Diary*, *Sarashina Diary*, and *Ionushi* (1045). While following the genre division of nikki and kikō found in the *Gunsho ruijū* (Classified Collection of Writings, edited by Hanawa Hokiichi, 1819), Mikami and Takatsu characterized these closely intertwined genres as being similar to monogatari, "as entertaining rather than practical," and stressed their "literary value" as opposed to the practicality of kanbun.[26] In the time-honored manner, they placed greatest value on *Tosa Diary* and *Murasaki Shikibu Diary*, but for a slightly different reason: they praised both works for their "light (*keikai, keimyō*), concise, unstrenuous" style, in contrast to Tsurayuki's "showy and artificial" (*fukanaru iyami*) kana preface to the *Kokinshū*.[27] The phonocentric focus of national language and national literature resulted in the decanonization of Heian waka, especially that of the *Kokinshū*, which they claimed lacked direct, unmediated expression.

Despite the strong ambivalence that these Meiji scholars showed toward their own characterization of national literature as "elegant and gentle, excelling in grace yet lacking in magnificence or heroic grandeur," and despite the subsequent representation (during the Sino-Japanese and Russo-Japanese Wars) of national character as masculine, as marked by "military spirit" (*shōbu ninkyō*) and "loyalty and brave courage" (*chūkō giyū*), this feminine characterization of Japanese literature would continue into the postwar period, primarily because of a need to identify the uniqueness and continuity of the national language and as a result of the shift in the notion of bungaku from the broader sense of humanities to the narrower sense of imaginative literature that stressed human emotions.

In 1899, Haga, who had just become a professor of Japanese literature at Tokyo Imperial University, published *Kokubungakushi jikkō* (Ten Lectures on the History of Japanese Literature), in which he elaborated on the literary history presented in his *Kokubungaku tokuhon*. Here Haga attempted to explain the general character of national literature in terms of the national language, placing even greater emphasis on its continuity. Haga attributed the "elegant and gentle nature" of the language to a "form (*gaikei*) full of vowels" and to the "mild geographical climate (*onwana kikō, fūdo*)." He explained that national literature was first developed by women because of the mild nature of the mother tongue.[28] Though *Kokubungakushi jikkō* appeared several years after the Sino-Japanese War (1894–95), which had irreversibly damaged the authority of the Chinese literary and cultural tradition, Haga emphasized that the national language had incorporated kanbun and kangaku into its foundation for its own further development and expansion. (This no doubt reflects the general attitude toward China after the victory in the Sino-Japanese War.) While, in typical Meiji fashion, he attacked the *Kokinshū* as shallow, Haga also praised Tsurayuki's *Tosa Diary* for "promoting the national language and literature (*kokubun*) at a time when the kana writing and literature (*kanabun*) remained chiefly women's writings (*onnabumi*)." Citing Kamo no Mabuchi's famous characterization of the "masculine *Man'yōshū* and the feminine *Kokinshū*," Haga stated that Tsurayuki was not just the feminine (*onna-rashii*) poet that Mabuchi made him out to be, but also the most able person of a weak epoch. Haga, in short, attempted to de-essentialize or disentangle the ambivalent connection between the kana-based national language/literature and the feminine.[29]

FUJIOKA, TSUDA, AND EARLY TWENTIETH CENTURY LITERARY HISTORIES: THE VALORIZATION OF HEIAN LITERATURE

These gendered characterizations were drastically reconfigured in Fujioka Sakutarō's (1870–1910) *Kokubungaku zenshi: Heianchō hen* (Complete History of Japanese Literature: The Heian Court), the first modern extensive study of Heian literature, published in 1905, the year of Japan's victory in the Russo-Japanese War. Fujioka challenged the contemporary exaltation of *bushidō* (way of the samurai) as the "unique essence of Japan's national spirit," writing in his preface: "Bushidō has certainly contributed greatly to our present achievement . . . but should we consider bushidō the primary characteristic of the people of a nation with three thousand years of rich history?" To measure all past literature, particularly Heian literature, in this fashion was, he argued, to judge it according to a Tokugawa ethical system.[30]

Following earlier modern scholars such as Haga, Fujioka designated the Tokugawa and Heian periods as the two prominent peaks of Japanese literature, comparing the former to Europe after the Renaissance and the latter to the classical period of Greece and Rome. The Tokugawa period "promoted militarism while the Heian period promoted literature; one encouraged frugality while the other was extravagant; one minimized the position of women while the other had women whose literary talent even surpassed that of men and who dealt with men in an unflinching manner. . . . The former [society] was masculine whereas the latter was feminine; the first prized obligations and principles (*giri*), the second valued feelings and sentiment (*jōshu*)."[31] In articulating a bipolar, gendered contrast, which was latent in Haga's ambivalence toward a national literature based on a kana-based feminine language, Fujioka attempted to defend and promote the central significance of the "feminine" Heian period for both national literature and national character.

Echoing Tsubouchi Shōyō's earlier condemnation in *Shōsetsu shinzui* (The Essence of the Novel, 1885–86) of Tokugawa didactic prose fiction and his stress on realistic depiction of human feelings and social conditions (*ninjō setai*) as the essence of the modern novel, and drawing on Motoori Norinaga's defense of human feelings against "unnatural" ethical constraints (in his *Genji monogatari tama no ogushi*, 1799), Fujioka skillfully articulated and reversed the latent hierarchical polarity between a "masculine, strong" Tokugawa literature and a "feminine, weak" Heian literature by characterizing Tokugawa literature as the "slave of ethical constraints" (a sign of backwardness) and Heian literature as product of the "age of passion and natural human feelings," that is to say, as the precursor of advanced literature. According to Fujioka, "the everyday life of Heian aristocrats, who valued love without regard to obligations and who esteemed beauty without preaching the good (*zen*)," exemplified what Takayama Chogyū (1871–1902) had recently called the "aesthetic life" (*biteki seikatsu*).[32] Fujioka's endorsement of Heian literature was underpinned by his belief in the value of "passion and taste" (*jōshu*), "love" (*ai*, which included respect for women as equal partners in love), "nature" (*shizen*), and "beauty" (*bi*)—key terms both in Fujioka's book and in the new literary discourse developed since the early 1890s by Kitamura Tōkoku (1868–1894) and the Bungaku-kai group, by Takayama Chogyū, and by various romantic movements in the early 1900s. Fujioka's view of literary value also reflected the completion of the shift from the broader notion of literature to the more specialized notion of bungaku as imaginative literature that stressed human emotion. (Differential terms such as bibungaku or junbungaku started to disappear at this time, with literature becoming simply bungaku.)

In discussing the literary values of Heian texts, Fujioka privileged the "realistic novel" as the most advanced literary form, tracing the development of Heian prose narratives from the *Taketori monogatari* (Tale of the Bamboo Cutter, 910), "the first novel," through the "fact-based" *Yamato monogatari*

(Tales of Yamato, 951) and *Gossamer Diary*, to the *Utsubo monogatari* (The Tale of the Hollow Tree, 984), which "attempted to depict court life concretely through fictional characters," to *The Tale of Genji*, which he considered the best novel ever written in Japan. Fujioka valued fictionality over factuality, but this fictionality had to contribute to the realistic depiction of the innermost human feelings and of contemporary social conditions, a quality that Tsubouchi Shōyō had advocated earlier and that Fujioka found in abundance in *The Tale of Genji*.

While privileging the realistic novel, Fujioka also focused on the *mode of expression*, giving particular value, regardless of genre, to the "unaffected and straightforward expression of innermost feelings," which he found in the monogatari (such as *Tales of Ise*) and in the poetry of Ariwara no Narihira, Izumi Shikibu, and Saigyō.[33] By contrast, Heian waka, represented by the rhetoric of the *Kokinshū*, was given the lowest position, lacking both realism and direct emotive expression.

Fujioka, who evaluated the nikki according to these two criteria, emphasized the "incomparable literary value" of kana nikki as an "expression of intense emotion" in contrast to kanbun nikki, which "recorded all the details of daily events."[34] Fujioka saw *Gossamer Diary* as "an autobiography close to a realistic novel," which epitomized the larger evolution from a factual record to a fictional, realistic novel. Indeed, women's nikki, particularly *Gossamer Diary* and *Izumi Shikibu Diary*, were valued by Fujioka for being "close to the monogatari in spite of their titles as nikki," for possessing "the thematic unity of the pure novel, leaving out irrelevant daily trifles, and organizing all descriptions according to a central theme."[35] Interestingly, the hitherto unquestioned high position of *Tosa Diary* became problematic. While recognizing Tsurayuki's "merit as the first man to promote kana national writing" (kokubun), Fujioka extended the Meiji attack on the *Kokinshū* to Tsurayuki's *Tosa Diary*, which he criticized for stylistic overelaboration, detached analytical intellect, and lack of passion.[36]

Fujioka's study of Heian literature, which was grounded in the new literary discourse of the 1900s, profoundly shaped later views of Heian literature as well as national literature. Tsuda Sōkichi's (1873–1961) influential literary and intellectual history, *Bungaku ni arawaretaru waga kokumin shisō no kenkyū* (A Study of the Thought of Our Nation's People as Reflected in Literature, 1916–21),[37] a monumental project on the dialectical development between class-based society and literary history, further amplified Fujioka's literary perspectives, particularly his emphasis on love (*koi*) and nature in the national tradition as well as on the emotive mode of expression. Tsuda praised the works of "female literati" (*joryū bunjin*) for "directly depicting particular scenes or feelings, whether as a sincere confession of their own emotional lives or as a product of a fictional imagination."[38] Like Fujioka, he severely attacked Tsurayuki for lacking in passion and being a "man of intellect," not only in his poetry, but also in *Tosa Diary*.[39]

Nevertheless, like his male predecessors, Tsuda remained quite uneasy about the prominent position of women's writing in national literature; and, like Haga, he attempted to de-essentialize the association between women and the national language. Tsuda argued that the refined kana writing by Heian women should be understood as a characteristic of the national language (kokubun) in opposition to kanbun, a rough language not suited for the mimetic depiction of reality, particularly of the human heart. "Reality, thoughts, and feelings of the people of the nation cannot be represented by foreign written languages."[40] Here Tsuda confidently projected into the historical past of the nation a belief in the immediacy of the national language, clearly internalizing the phonocentric ideology of genbun-itchi. At the same time, Tsuda was also ambivalent about what he called "feminized national literature" (*joseika sareta kokubungaku*). A noted populist, he ultimately criticized the "spiritless," "self-centered," "materialistic," "degenerate," "urbanized and feminized aristocrats" of the period."[41]

DIARY LITERATURE IN THE 1920S: DOI, IKEDA, AND A SELF-REFLECTIVE LYRICAL TRADITION

The earliest use of the term *nikki bungaku* was in the early 1920s, in a long essay titled "Nihon bungaku no tenkai" ("The Evolution of Japanese Literature," 1920), which was included in *Bungaku josetsu* (Introduction to Literature, 1922), by Doi Kōchi (1886–1979), a scholar of English literature and a Taishō liberal, who approached Japanese literature from a comparative perspective. This book had a profound impact on the younger generation of literary students, including young kokubungaku scholars such as Hisamatsu Sen'ichi (1894–1976) and Ikeda Kikan (1896–1956), who promoted the notion of nikki bungaku from the mid-1920s.[42]

In contrast to previous modern literary histories, which were conceived in terms of linear, progressive development, Doi's history of Japanese literature was conceived as a spiral evolution of genres, moving from epic to lyric to narrative fiction (romance, novel) to drama (as well as philosophical and religious literature and criticism), and then back again to epic, lyric, etc. Doi saw the history of Japanese literature as three spiral cycles: the first from the ancient period of myths through the nō plays of the Muromachi period, the second from the time of *The Tale of the Heike* through the end of the Tokugawa period, and the third from the early Meiji period through the contemporary, mid-Taishō period, at which point he anticipated a new, fourth cycle. Despite his thesis of generic evolution, in which drama and critical literature constituted the final stage of the cycle, the notion of "lyricism" or "sincere expression of the self" occupied a central position in Doi's conception of literature. All of Doi's literary genres were in fact defined in terms of the development and growth of the "self." Emphasizing the "internal continuity of the spiritual life of the Japanese people," Doi ultimately characterized the "special characteristic of Japanese literature and the Japanese people" as being "particularly lyrical (*toku ni jojōteki*)."[43]

It was in this context that Doi valued Heian women's diaries for their "self-reflection" and placed nikki bungaku "midway between the lyric (*jojōshi*) and narrative fiction (monogatari)." For Doi, this "self-reflective attitude, which expressed the heightened lyrical moments of one's life, naturally developed into an attitude that sought to represent life by giving fuller play to one's imagination."[44] Doi's praise of Heian women's nikki bungaku became even stronger in another essay in *Bungaku josetsu* called "Kokumin bungaku to sekaiteki bungaku" (Literature of the People of the Nation and World Literature, 1921), where he introduced Goethe's notion of national literature and transnational world literature. In contrast to national literature, which was considered "an expression of the humanity conditioned by a particular cultural environment, history, and language," world literature was conceived, according to Doi, as "an expression of humanity freed from the restrictions of a particular time or place"; world literature was "an expression of humanity in its purest and most profound essence."[45] Doi emphasized the importance of the growth not only of the individual self, but also of the collective self of the nation into a greater, more universal humanity, a national self that could grow further through interactions with other national literatures. In this context, Doi picked from Japanese literature the *Man'yōshū*, *The Tale of Genji*, Heian women's diaries, and zuihitsu such as *Makura no sōshi* (The Pillow Book, late 10th c.) and *Tsurezuregusa* as texts that he believed had universal interest and "would win people's respect and affection when translated into foreign languages." Doi urged contemporary Japanese readers to realize the "hitherto unrecognized high value" of these works, which were "direct expressions of individual personalities."[46] So important was this international mission that in 1920 Doi himself translated into English *Sarashina Diary*, *Murasaki Shikibu Diary*, and *Izumi Shikibu Diary*.[47]

In the mid- to late 1920s, under the strong influence of the genre evolution theory espoused by Doi Kōchi and Kaito Matsuzō (1878–1952), Ikeda Kikan, the first scholar to do an extensive study of Heian women's nikki, further elevated the status of nikki bungaku by developing the notion of *jishō bungaku* (literature of self-reflection), a term first used by Kaito Matsuzō in introducing the genre-evolution theory of Richard Green Moulton (1849–1924), an English classicist and literary critic.[48] In a 1926 article, "Historical Examination of the Literature of Self-Reflection," Ikeda basically followed Doi's spiral evolution from epic through narrative fiction to drama/philosophy/criticism and then back to epic, but shifted the focus by tracing the cycle from lyric (morning, childhood) to epic (daytime, adolescence) to drama (evening, adulthood) and then to philosophy (night, old age), which he represented as the "literature of self-reflection" and which "included *nikki*, *zuihitsu*, *kikō*, *shōsoko* (letters), and *shiron* (critical essays)."[49] Stating that all literature was the "reflection of the individual personality (*kosei*)," Ikeda specifically defined jishō bungaku as the "literature of confession and prayer in which the author's individual personality attempted to tell the innermost truth (*jiko mizukara no shinjitsu*) most directly in the form of the I"—a phrase that resonated with contemporary I-novel discourse (Ikeda used the German word "Ich"). While pointing to the similarity between jishō bungaku and the lyric, which were "unified, direct expressions of the individual personality," Ikeda characterized jishō bungaku as "the contemplation of and reflection on the past" in contrast to the lyric, which was "a rapturous absorption with the present." Ikeda repeatedly emphasized the "spontaneity," "sincerity," and "purity" of jishō bungaku as an "autobiography of a genuine soul."[50]

In that same article, Ikeda traced the development of jishō bungaku in Japanese literature, valorizing Heian women's kana diaries as the first achievement in the "spirit of the self-reflection." Compared to the women's diaries, Ikeda found *Tosa Diary*, "the most famous kana diary," disappointing because "its creative motive and self-reflection could not be regarded as genuine." Instead, it was *Tsurezuregusa* that received Ikeda's highest respect for "delving into the innermost self to reach the underlying trans-individual spirit" and for "recording a life that sought ceaseless self-development to reach an ever higher unity." *Tsurezuregusa* was now recanonized as a "self-exploratory" zuihitsu text by a male writer who brought to a higher form what had been started by women.[51]

Ikeda shared with Doi an unsettled awareness of a rapidly expanding industrial mass society as well as a strong belief in cultivation of the individual personality as the ultimate goal of life and literature. In contrast to Doi's optimistic, forward-looking idealism and universalism, however, Ikeda's historical outlook is characterized more by a strong sense of loss and nostalgia for a lost home (*kyōshū*), which was widely shared after the 1923 Great Kantō Earthquake and which lay behind his devotion to classical texts. At the end of his 1926 article, Ikeda wrote:

> Today, the literature of self-reflection is at its zenith. This self-reflective current has caused us to contemplate our·national tradition, providing new perspective on our national literature. . . . Yet, will new lyrics be born when and where the literature of self-reflection prospers? . . . What has broken through the cultural deadlock of our time? What worth does the frothy propagation of proletarian literature have? The commonplace popular novel (*tsūzoku shōsetsu*) and mass popular literature (*taishū bungei*), which are now in vogue, should never be recognized as the mainstream of Japanese literature. . . . Yes, today is truly the *fin de siècle*, in which various opposing forces are locked in powerful combat and the grotesque taste in movies is consuming our spirit, and in which fatigue, skepticism, cowardice, and frenzy are swirling amidst vulgar and spiritless dogmatism.[52]

Ikeda's statements are clearly reflective of the literary and journalistic environment of the mid- to late 1920s, which witnessed a vast expansion of journalism and of the reading public as well as a growing class consciousness under the influence of Marxism. The question of the efficacy and validity of literature was raised in a series of journalistic debates over the authentic novel (*honkaku shōsetsu*) versus the I-novel, the I-novel versus the commonplace popular novel (*tsūzoku shōsetsu*), popular art (*minshū geijutsu*) versus bourgeois literature, bourgeois literature versus proletarian literature, the popular novel versus the artistic novel (*geijutsuteki shōsetsu*) or pure novel (*junsui shōsetsu*). All of these exchanges were part of a larger debate over what constituted the validity and essence of literature in an expanding mass society.[53]

Ikeda placed jishō bungaku and nikki bungaku in particular, at the core of Japanese literature, in opposition to "commonplace popular literature" and proletarian literature. He emphasized the centrality of classical Japanese literature as the prototype of "genuine and mainstream" (*seidō*) literature—characterized by pure expression of the self—in an age of rapidly expanding industrial mass society. This view was widely shared and promoted by other leading kokubungaku scholars. For example, in a 1926 radio lecture series on Japanese literature, Fujimura Tsukuru, a professor of Japanese literature at

Tokyo Imperial University, addressed the public on the importance of "popularizing kokubungaku without vulgarizing it." Fujimura characterized national literature as "a self-portrait drawn by the people of the nation, a people's autobiography, a sincere confession of their inner life" that "reveals the true nature of national life and national spirit." Following Haga's earlier argument but now addressing a mass public instead of elite students, Fujimura emphasized the importance of "understanding the national character and spirit of one's own nation" in order to "strengthen the whole body of the nation," particularly at a time "when a harmful social ideology [Marxism] had become a serious concern." Referring to the sudden growth of kokubungaku publications and students in the recent years, Fujimura stressed the necessity of knowing oneself as well as one's own nation through the study of earlier Japanese literature at a time when Japan, "having joined the world's top five nations," was about to "tread its own unique path instead of simply imitating other powerful nations as it had before."[54]

WOMEN'S DIARY LITERATURE AND A
GENEALOGY OF WOMEN'S LITERATURE

Ikeda not only promoted the notion of nikki bungaku but more specifically that of joryū nikki bungaku. In the process, he created a typology of "women's inner life experience," emphasizing the "eternal image" (*eien no sugata*) or "eternal agony" (*eigō no nayami*) of womanhood (*josei*). In his *Kyūtei joryū nikki bungaku* (Imperial Court Women's Dairy Literature, 1927), the first full-length study of Heian women's kana nikki, Ikeda expressed a "mixture of uncertainty and intense joy in exploring the hitherto uncultivated virgin forest" of *Gossamer Diary*, which had barely been studied until this point. Ikeda emphasized that, despite its apparent textual difficulty, *Gossamer Diary* was an "acute, living human document immediately relevant to all women in all situations,"[55] and portrayed each work of Heian joryū nikki bungaku as a "sincere confession" of a different aspect of womanhood, revealing the inner development of women. According to Ikeda, if *Gossamer Diary* expressed the "painful cry of a woman growing from a virgin into a wife and then a mother," then *Izumi Shikibu Diary* revealed the "unbounded passion, coquetry, purity, and courtesan nature of women," and *Murasaki Shikibu Diary* unveiled "the self-reflective, self-cultivating, and critical aspects of womanhood," thereby "transforming [Izumi Shikibu's] yearning for the opposite sex into a greater love for humanity."[56]

A similar typology of women's "universal inner experience" is found in another early discussion of joryū nikki bungaku, that by Hisamatsu Sen'ichi, a professor of kokubungaku at Tokyo Imperial University. In the same 1926 radio broadcast series as Fujimura's, in a lecture entitled "Diary Literature and Women," he defined nikki bungaku as "a faithful record of life which is written without the intention of creating a literary work but which turns out to appeal to readers as literature."[57] Stating that Heian women's diary literature "revealed the inner life of all women," Hisamatsu described "the feminine life (*josei seikatsu*) of a wife" in *Gossamer Diary*; "the feminine life of a widow" in *Murasaki Shikibu Diary*; and "feminine life of a sensitive literary woman who goes from maidenhood to marriage and then widowhood" in *Sarashina Diary*. The last work "records the development of the author's state of mind (*shinkyō*), from actual life to a yearning for a literary life and then, finally, to a religious life." Though Hisamatsu, like Ikeda, briefly mentioned Izumi Shikibu's passion and "unrestrained love life," he focused on the "spiritual progress" and salvation attained through self-cultivation and self-reflection that he found in women's diary literature as a whole.[58]

Ikeda Kikan and Hisamatsu Sen'ichi's promotion of Heian joryū nikki bungaku as the core of self-reflective mainstream Japanese literature coincided with the emergence of the notion of joryū bungaku (women's literature) as a distinct journalistic category in the mid-1920s, when the number of women readers and writers vastly expanded.[59] A shift in gender roles—which appeared as more women joined the urban work force and which was epitomized, for example, in the phenomenon of "modern girls" (*moga*) and "modern boys" (*mobo*)—triggered a conservative call for a return to the "natural" distinctions between men and women.[60] Kokubungaku scholars, who sought to preserve and promote the "purity of mainstream Japanese literature" amid these social and cultural changes, especially in the face of the growth of mass popular literature and proletarian literature, promoted Heian women's diary literature as "pure literature," as the quintessence of self-reflective literature, and attempted to present it as the genuine prototype of modern *joryū bungaku* (women's literature), a term that was given, often disparagingly, to the popular literature written at this time by women for a wide public of women readers.

From the mid- to late 1920s, a number of emerging women writers such as Miyamoto Yuriko (1899–1951), Hirabayashi Taiko (1905–1972), and Hayashi Fumiko (1903–1951) began to write autobiographical, confessional novels at a time when it was widely believed that the sincere expression and cultivation of the "genuine self" was the basis of all art—when the notion of the I-novel emerged as the dominant literary discourse. The term *watakushi*

shōsetsu (or *shishōsetsu*), which emerged in the early to mid-1920s, initially referred to certain contemporary autobiographical sketches whose authors appeared to write directly about their personal lives. But the concept became ~~BROAD~~
broader and more nebulous, generating a prolonged cultural discourse that
extended to a wide and disparate community of writers, critics, social theo-
rists, journalists, and historians. That discourse not only characterized the
modern Japanese novel as a form that directly transcribed the author's lived
experience (in contrast to the centrality of fiction in the Western novel) but
also emphasized the continuity of the confessional, self-exploratory, autobiographical nature of the "indigenous" Japanese literary tradition, describing
classical literature with such highly Western, romantic terms and phrases as
"immediacy," "directness," "lyricism," "spiritual search for the self," and
"unity with nature." Many women writers, for whom liberation from patri-
archal oppression was a central concern in the search for the "self," turned,
as did male writers and intellectuals of the time, to socialist, anarchist, and
Marxist proletarian movements—a tendency that kokubungaku scholars
such as Fujimura, Hisamatsu, and Ikeda found threatening.[61] Although
modern scholars and writers usually see these women's autobiographical novels as the direct continuation of a long tradition of women's diary literature,
the notion of modern joryū bungaku (women's literature) and of classical
joryū nikki bungaku as distinctive genres was in fact developed at this time,
in the latter half of the 1920s.

While modern women writers were no doubt encouraged by this glorious
genealogy, the close association of the notion of joryū nikki bungaku with *REJECTION*
that of the I-novel also caused some of them, particularly in the postwar pe- *BY*
riod, to become extremely ambivalent toward this female literary tradition, *ASSOCIATION*
primarily because of their disdain for the I-novel. Enchi Fumiko (1905–
1986), for example, repeatedly expressed her ambivalence toward *Gossamer
Diary*, which she pejoratively regarded as "the origin of I-novel-type women's
literature," which, in her words, was "connected to the author by an umbil-
ical cord." On the other hand, she considered *The Tale of Genji* to be the
most outstanding work of Japanese literature because it created a world distinct from that of the author.[62]

POSTWAR CRITICISM: SAIGŌ, AKIYAMA, AND
FIGURES OF TRADITION AND MODERNITY

The terms nikki bungaku and joryū nikki bungaku became naturalized in
the 1930s and 1940s, and increasing attention was paid to the literary qual-

ity of diary literature, to the philological study of the texts, and to the relationship between diary literature and the other related genres.[63] Particularly influential in the postwar period, when the study of women's diary literature continued to flourish, was the work of the so-called sociohistorical (*rekishi shakai gakuha*) scholar, Saigō Nobutsuna (b. 1916). Influenced by Marxist criticism and by the folklore studies (*minzokugaku*) of Yanagita Kunio (1875–1962) and Origuchi Shinobu (1887–1953), Saigō argued in a 1949 article, "Flowering of Court Women's Literature," that the remarkable achievement of Heian women's literature was due to the fact that these writers were the daughters of scholars of Chinese studies, "a kind of superfluous intelligentsia," whose social status had declined to the middle or bottom of the aristocracy, and who consequently possessed a critical perspective on contemporary society. Saigō explained that from their doubly negative social condition—the decline of their fathers' social status and their socioeconomic decline—these women carried out a "remarkable spiritual and intellectual revolution," creating the "literature of the folk using the writing of the folk" (*minzoku no, minzoku no moji ni yoru bungaku*). In his opinion, these women were liberated from traditional familial and religious bonds and could thus confront reality with a critical consciousness while still tapping the "young vitality of a folk tradition unaffected by the civilization of the Continent."[64]

Saigō emphasized that this flowering of women's literature was not the natural outcome of a young folk tradition preserved by women but instead was made possible through the stimulus of classical Chinese civilization which was mediated by Japanese male scholars, the middle-class intelligentsia. In *Nihon kodai bungakushi* (History of Japanese Ancient Literature, 1951), Saigō explained that these doubly alienated women writers, who were free from Chinese intellectual orthodoxy, maintained the "emotion and soul of the Japanese" while, as daughters of Chinese scholars, they absorbed the Chinese literature that was normally prohibited to women.[65] Saigō's praise of Heian women's literature was similar to that of earlier kokubungaku scholars such as Haga Yaichi and Tsuda Sōkichi in that he recognized the bridging role of Japanese women in carrying the "young, national folk tradition" from the "golden ancient period" (*kodai no ōgon jidai*) to the more developed medieval period. Reflecting a larger discourse on modernity and native tradition, women and the feminine were here posited as the custodians of tradition, resisting the constraints imposed by reason and the rigorous demands of public life, both of which reflected foreign influence.[66] Saigō suggested in the final sentence of his 1949 article that Heian women writers represented an example in which "historical backwardness could paradoxically be transformed into productivity" when backed by a "young folk tradition."[67] For Saigō, in short, Heian women writers became the supreme figures of resistance as well as a national folk tradition; they came to symbolize politically and socially marginalized postwar Japanese (male) intelligentsia who aspired to resurrect themselves through their ties to the national folk tradition.

In the postwar critical clamor over the proper development of modernity, the I-novel was widely regarded as the epitome of an "underdeveloped, failed, Japanese modernity," which had led to the war and which needed to be redressed. In a 1951 study that reflected these sentiments, Ikeda Kikan discussed the *Gossamer Diary* in relation to the I-novel. On the one hand, he criticized the author of the *Gossamer Diary* for her self-centered, limited concerns and narrow perspective, characteristics that were "similar to the weaknesses of the I-novel." On the other hand, Ikeda praised the author's "bold confession," which "revealed the contradictions and corruptions of aristocratic life" and which represented a "revolt against the traditional norms." Ikeda, in short, attempted to save the *Gossamer Diary* in particular and joryū nikki bungaku in general from a degrading association with the I-novel by stressing the resistance of the daughters of the *zuryō* (provincial governors), echoing a point made by Saigō.[68]

In a short article in 1954 titled "How Can Nikki Be Literature?" Ikeda Kikan presented a new focus on the notion of literary autonomy. While echoing Tamai Kōsuke's 1945 definition of the nikki as a record of actual facts, Ikeda argued that the *nikki* was not a purely objective record but was filtered through the subjective ideals and passions of the writing subject (*shutai*), a term that reflected postwar intellectual discourse on the establishment of the modern subject (*kindaiteki jiga*), specifically the subject of action. Equally important, Ikeda stressed the "autonomous value of expression," stating that "the writer [of nikki bungaku] emerges in front of us as a person in a literary realm, leaving behind the writer's empirical self."[69] This new concern for autonomy had become, in the postwar period, an emblem of modernity—of the modern self, of modern literature, and, by extension, of the modern nation-state—and would be fully developed into a major paradigm in subsequent years by Akiyama Ken (b. 1924), who would become the leading scholar of Heian literature from the 1960s.

In a 1954 article Akiyama defended women's diary literature against the postwar attack on the I-novel tradition, which was accused of lacking in social scale and in textual autonomy (independence from the author). He argued that the individual experiences of the authors of joryū nikki bungaku were sublimated into autonomous texts that had wider, universal human relevance despite their apparently limited social scope and dimension. Taking into account their sociohistorical background (as explained by Saigō), Akiyama emphasized the spiritual growth of these women authors, who, while accepting their limited existence as a result of the institutional oppression of women (polygamy, physical confinement, etc.), "attempted to prove their true humanity in literature" by objectifying the "truth of their private experience" in a literature that both "criticized and resisted reality."[70]

Echoing Saigō, Akiyama emphasized the relationship between the remarkable literary achievement of these women and their alienated, powerless existence. Women could develop "genuine" literature—from waka to autobiographical nikki bungaku to monogatari—precisely because their literary activity did not have practical use-value (in terms of gaining prestige, public glory, social advancement) in the public or political sphere.[71] In a 1963 article, he argued that the social taboos and institutional restrictions that prevented women from having access to the public world and to official scholarship paradoxically allowed them to develop a subject (shutai) of "free action and free perception" that led to the creation of an autonomous literary world. In this scheme *Gossamer Diary* became the great predecessor to *The Tale of Genji*, in which was created "a second reality" into which the female author "transferred her entire soul and body."[72]

Writing in 1965, Akiyama further explored the notion of transference (to an autonomous literary microcosm), proposing that the nikki bungaku text be approached as "the actual site of action" in which one could read the significance of the author's act of transferring her or his life into writing:[73]

LIFE AS WORDS

> That which was pent up and swirling around inside the author could not be dealt with as it was. One could only overcome it by transferring it to a world ordered by words, that is, by writing a nikki. Needless to say, nikki bungaku was not a kind of self-confession, or an I-novel, let alone a factual record. Nikki bungaku was essentially fictional. While based on an actual life, a nikki bungaku text constructed a space where the author's own self was transferred as a result of the demands of life. The more autonomous this space was, the more effective the transference of the self. Heian nikki bungaku represented the achievement of this literary method.[74]

Akiyama, in short, attributed to nikki bungaku all the positive qualities of modernist literature—autonomy of the literary text governed by the principle of a fictional construction in which the author's empirical self was transformed into a more essential and universal presence—qualities that were regarded by many postwar critics to be the opposite of those of the I-novel.

Tosa Diary, which had sunk in value since the time of Fujioka in the late Meiji period, was revived by Akiyama, who emphasized the significance of fictionality in the work, a fictionality that paved the way for subsequent women's diary literature. Akiyama argued that Tsurayuki's pretense of being a woman writer was a revolutionary disguise (*gisō*), a supreme fiction, that liberated nikki bungaku from the nikki as record while still drawing on the nikki form. Akiyama interpreted the last sentence of *Tosa Diary* in which the narrator notes, "I suppose the best thing to do is to tear up these sheets at once," as a "burlesque declaration of its non-use-value . . . thus paradoxically declaring the literary autonomy of nikki bungaku" from practical concerns.[75] Akiyama also suggested that the death of the daughter in this work might in fact be a fictional dramatization through which Tsurayuki expressed the intense sense of despair and loss that he felt in his actual public life.

The emphasis on the autonomy and fictionality of nikki bungaku promoted a discussion of its relationship to *monogatari*, to narrative fiction. New critical attention was given to the dialectical development of nikki bungaku and monogatari literature. Akiyama argued in 1981 that literary diaries such as *Gossamer Diary* and *Sarashina Diary* emerged only in juxtaposition to preexisting monogatari (written primarily by male scholars). Through their own lives these women authors created a new world of monogatari that had more complex and deeper human dimensions than earlier texts in that genre.[76]

As each of the nikki bungaku texts came to be studied as independent classics, Akiyama became concerned that the generic significance of joryū nikki bungaku was becoming blurred, and in 1986 gave the following warning:

> What is joryū nikki bungaku? Although the nikki bungaku is widely used as a literary historical term, we have to confirm anew just what nikki bungaku is. Each of the works lumped together under the genre of nikki bungaku is so unique that I am worried that as critical study of each work progresses, our understanding of the essential nature of this genre as a whole will become blurred and neglected.[77]

Akiyama argued that the significance of nikki bungaku as a genre must be maintained. For him, the value of joryū nikki bungaku was that it represented the transference of the author's empirical self or life into an autonomous and fictional world of literature. The more autonomous the fictional world was the more effective and genuine was this transference. Accordingly, for Akiyama, *The Tale of Genji* becomes the text with the highest value. The uniqueness of joryū nikki bungaku then, in contrast to monogatari, lies in the fact that the theory of transference from the empirical self to the literary self seems visible and self-evident. Akiyama's desire to consciously maintain the awareness of joryū nikki bungaku as an important genre seems to derive not so much from the desire to value certain joryū nikki bungaku texts (which are, after all, for Akiyama, inferior to *The Tale of Genji*) but from the desire to maintain, by using the genre of joryū nikki bungaku as a pretext, this fundamental principle of literature (bungaku) as the ultimate means of making and experiencing this transference.

Akiyama Ken attempted to distinguish nikki bungaku from the I-novel—which was attacked in the postwar period as the epitome of Japan's failed modernity—by stressing the autonomy and fictionality of nikki bungaku texts, thereby suggesting that Japan had a rich literary tradition whose authors wrote, not of a failed self, but of a self that could be realized through the higher realm of literature. On the other hand, by continuing to rely on the notion of the "genuine self" achieved in literature and by stressing the continuity of such a national literary tradition—for which joryū nikki bungaku functioned ultimately as a symbol—Akiyama continued to develop the paradigm and discourse that first canonized Heian women's literary diaries in the 1920s in close relationship to the notion of the I-novel.

Japanese male scholars and intellectuals had been highly ambivalent about a feminized national literature ever since the construction of Japanese national literature in the late 1880s. They had sought to present literature as useful and essential to a newly established nation-state and a modern bourgeois industrial society, a society founded on scientific principles, rationalism, and a competitive spirit, all attributes strongly associated with masculinity. But in identifying national literature with a phonocentric notion of national language, they had to turn to kana-based writing, which had been strongly associated with femininity, and eschew texts written in kanbun or classical Chinese, which had long been the core of knowledge and associated with rationalism and masculinity.

In fact, in Europe from the late nineteenth century, literature had become increasingly associated with femininity as the notion of literature shifted from a broader notion of literature that encompassed both the rational and the emotional to one that was increasingly bound to the private and the emotional.[78] This shift toward the feminization of literature was reflected in modern Japanese literary histories, where the case was even more complicated by the association of the national language with what was perceived to be highly feminized Heian culture. The result was that it was impossible for male scholars to dissociate Japanese literature and national character from femininity even though they privileged rationalism and science as the fundamental attributes of modernity and modern civilization. As we have seen, they refigured and rationalized the feminine associations of Japanese national literature by stressing the importance of the lyrical, self-exploratory tradition as the quintessence of literature, and by claiming that that tradition was critical to the development of the modern self in terms of both the individual and the nation in the face of a rapidly expanding industrial mass society. In the process, joryū nikki bungaku, or women's diary literature, became a salient symbol of the national tradition as well as a prefiguration of modernity.

But the very insistence of Akiyama's recent claim for maintaining this genre distinction (of joryū nikki bungaku versus monogatari and other genres), the anxious desire to preserve joryū nikki bungaku as a central figure in this literary configuration, paradoxically betrays the increasing disintegration of such a notion of literature (as representing an autonomous higher realm associated with "true modernity" and embodying national identity). The evolutionist hierarchical genre distinctions (with the novel at the top) have also lost much of their earlier authority. At the same time, there has emerged, both in practice and in criticism, an increasing interest in autobiographical writings, particularly those of women, as a vital means of representing and constructing identities. Having been firmly canonized, those autobiographical texts by Heian women, referred to as women's diary literature, will no doubt continue to produce a gamut of readings.

CHAPTER FOUR

Modern Constructions of *Tales of Ise*: Gender and Courtliness

JOSHUA S. MOSTOW

Ise monogatari (*Tales of Ise*) has been a canonical text since at least the late tenth century and a subject of commentary and exegesis since at least the early thirteenth. In every historical period, scholars and poets have read, quoted, and written about *Ise*. When we speak of "canonization" with regard to texts such as *Ise*, then, we are not speaking of a discrete event, a transformation that occurs and is thereafter complete: a text does not become canonical once and for all. Rather, after its first canonization, later readers are confronted, even challenged, by its very status as a canonical text, and as readers and scholars they must make sense of that status. As we shall see below, until the recent challenges to the established canons mounted by multiculturalism, feminism, and postmodernism, the demand of a canonical text upon a reader had always been the demand of reaffirmation: it was up to the reader to understand why a text had been valued in the past; it was not for the text to have to prove itself.

Canonization, then, is an ongoing process, and the issue is not *that* a text is canonical at any moment in time so much as *why*: what reasons are given for a text's privileged status at any historical juncture? These reasons, of course, are what the text is said to mean, how it is construed, indeed, how it is reconstituted and (re)constructed. For the meaning of a text—even a canonical text—is never fixed, but constructed anew by each generation so as to be relevant to the needs of that generation. Accordingly, the literary-historical question surrounding a text such as *Ise* is not whether a particular interpretation is right or wrong, but rather why such an interpretation arose at the historical moment that it did. In what follows I shall examine the construction of the *Tales of Ise*—largely in the academic realm—since the emergence of Japan as a modern nation, asking what the context of the modern nation-state does to the scholarly reading of this aristocratic text and how readings of *Ise* have responded to Japan's changing fortunes since the nineteenth century. It will be my contention that gender has played a formative role in the modern reception of *Ise*, resulting in a gendering of the entire Heian period as feminine, and *Ise* as a text embodying, for both good and ill, a kind of femininity.

ISE BEFORE THE ESTABLISHMENT OF THE JAPANESE NATION-STATE

Before examining the reception of *Ise* in the early modern period, I would like to review very briefly the history of the text up to the Edo period (1600–1868).[1] The consensus among modern scholars is that *Tales of Ise* is the product of a complex formation process, developing perhaps from a collection of poems by Ariwara no Narihira (825–880). While the text is generally believed to have achieved its present form sometime in the mid-tenth century, the actual manuscript used for the standard version, the so-called Tempuku-bon, is one collated by Fujiwara Teika (1162–1241) in 1234—some three hundred years later. In whatever form, however, *Ise* seems to have already achieved a kind of canonical status by the late tenth or early eleventh century, since it appears in several places in *Genji monogatari* (The Tale of Genji). The best-known of these appearances is in the famous "picture contest" episode, where it is matched against a more contemporary work (no longer extant), *Jōsanmi monogatari* (The Tale of Jōsanmi). The Right side, which puts forward *Ise* as their entry, champions the more established classics, in contrast to the more up-to-date works promoted by the Left. In such a contest, *Ise* finds itself fighting the rearguard action of a classic; in fact, Imanishi Yūichirō suggests that *Ise* loses to the *Jōsanmi* in terms of "literary

charm," and its only defense is the fact that it transmits the legacy of the poetic immortal Narihira; in other words, *Ise* can hold its own only by recourse
to extraliterary values.[2] Regardless, through its appearances in *Genji* and
through copies of Heian period illustrated scroll versions, we can be assured
of *Ise*'s popularity among the aristocracy from the Heian into the Kamakura
period.

It is to the Kamakura period (1185–1333) that the oldest traces of extant
commentary on *Ise* are dated. These have been attributed to Teika's descendants, and they engage in what Susan Klein has called a kind of religious "al-
legoresis" that interprets Narihira as a bodhisattva and ascribes mystical
meaning to the *Ise* text. Klein has argued that these readings were generated
not in the old capital of Kyoto, but among the marginalized poetic coteries
(*kadan*) of the east, where political power had moved with the establishment
of the Kamakura shogunate.[3]

Such religious interpretations were rejected in the Muromachi period
(1392–1573) by commentators who for the first time identified *Ise* as a
fictional text and who turned their attention most particularly to its poetry.[4]
This "sober scholarship," as Richard Bowring calls it,[5] continued into the
Edo period, and it was these commentaries that formed the basis for both
popularizations and parodies of the work, verbal as well as visual. Finally, the
"new commentaries" (*shinshaku*) are founded on the philological principles
of the *kokugaku*, or nativist learning, movement. While some of these, such
as Kada no Azumamaro's (1669–1736) *Ise monogatari dōjimon* (*Tales of Ise*: A
Child's Questions, 1716–36) directly attack earlier commentaries such as
Hosokawa Yūsai's (1534–1610) *Ketsugishō* (The Commentary of Vacuous
Questions, 1596), historically they are best characterized by such works as
Kamo no Mabuchi's (1697–1769) *Ise monogatari ko'i* (The Ancient Meaning
of *Tales of Ise*, ca. 1753), which, as Bowring remarks, "would not be out of
place today."[6] The source of this feeling of contemporaneity is important to
examine. In Bowring's words:

> Mabuchi's commentary is striking for the almost total lack of overt reference
> to past theories or even past commentators. It is this that gives rise to the gen-
> tle tone . . . because Mabuchi is not seen pushing his ideas against anyone in
> particular; but seen from a different angle it becomes an act of defiance, self-
> assurance, and independence, as if those who had gone before no longer even
> deserved passing recognition. So it is that we begin to find developing the
> kind of commentary that we look for today: not straight philology but rather
> helpful translations of difficult passages into a modern idiom and a concern
> that the sections are seen to make sense to the ordinary reader.[7]

In this "modern" approach the commentator erases history and debate so that the text will, first and foremost, "make sense." Both commentary and text become univocal, and the polysemy of the text is eviscerated. At the same time, the commentary tacitly assumes the role of spokesman for the text, creating that model of sacred text, or genius author, and critic as high priest, that we are so familiar with from New Criticism. And like New Criticism, this style of commentary completely ignores all opinion that has come before. Finally, the seemingly unlikely similarities between Mabuchi and New Criticism come from the common condition of modernity: both are writing for a new, essentially bourgeois, "ordinary reader," rather than for an aristocratic or cultural elite.

Fundamental to this modernity was the explosion in printing. In the Edo period *Ise* circulated in a large number of printed versions, from scholarly editions of Yūsai's annotated text, to more popular versions in contemporary translation, such as *Ise monogatari hirakotoba* (*Tales of Ise* in Plain Words, 1679). Many of these editions were illustrated. In fact, one of the last datable Edo period editions of the work is *Ise monogatari zue* (*Tales of Ise* Illustrated), with pictures by Gyokuzan (Okada Shōyū, 1737–1812) and a preface by Ichioka Takehiko (1749–1827) dated 1823.[8] The proliferation of publishing had already created gender-specific markets in the Japanese book trade by the early eighteenth century,[9] and the *Zue* edition shows many design elements that suggest it might have been geared more toward a masculine than feminine audience. Other editions, on the other hand, were clearly designed as textbooks for girls. By the end of the Edo period, then, there were many *Tales of Ise*, responding to a variety of markets, defined by both gender and education. To some extent, this profusion would be disciplined into a more limited set of normative readings with the establishment of the nation-state.

ISE AND VIEWS OF THE HEIAN ERA IN THE MEIJI PERIOD (1868–1912)

As Fritz Vos has written, "In the Meiji and Taishō eras the classics were widely published as books printed with movable type, but hardly any serious studies on the subject of the *Ise monogatari* appeared."[10] The only important work from this period that Vos mentions is *Kōshō Ise monogatari shōkai* (A Detailed Explanation of *Tales of Ise*) by Kamata Masanori, which was not published until 1919. In contrast to the relative neglect of *Ise*, the first Meiji period study of *The Tale of Genji* appeared in 1876[11]; the *Genji* was also partially translated into English in 1882,[12] and approvingly cited in Tsubouchi Shōyō's 1885 *Shōsetsu shinzui* (The Essence of the Novel). Mention of *Ise*, however, is found chiefly in relation to women's education.

In a two-part essay devoted to *Ise* in *Jogaku zasshi* (The Journal of Women's Education), published in 1885–86, the anonymous author likens *Ise* to the Chinese *Shih Ching* (Book of Songs), an analogy that allows him to use the same exegetical tradition as was developed for the Chinese text, maintaining that although, like the Chinese text, most of the poems in *Ise* seem to deal with romantic relations, in fact, they are about ruling the nation and ordering the home, based on the five Confucian virtues. Arguing for the centrality of the husband-wife relationship in Confucianism, the essay then becomes a diatribe against licentiousness (*in*), which, the author insists, *Ise* records so as to admonish against. In particular, the essay champions the virtue of "harmonious relations between husband and wife" (*kan-sho*), and so ends up enlisting *Ise* in the new Meiji-period emphasis on the nuclear family that the Christian thinkers associated with *Jogaku zasshi* believed essential for the modernization of Japan.[13]

The following year *Ise* appears in *Jogaku zasshi* again, this time in an unsigned editorial entitled "Women and the Work of Writing: On the Work of Writing being Convenient for Women."[14] Contemplating a future where women are potentially the full equals of men and competing for the same jobs outside the home, the writer insists that such women will still be the exception. Accordingly, he recommends writing as an occupation appropriate to the limited time available to wives and mothers at home, and one by which they can advance civilization. It is in this context that, drawing on models from both Japan's past and from more recent European history, the author mentions "Murasaki Shikibu's *The Tale of Genji*, Ono no Otsū's *The Tale of Jōruri*, Sei Shōnagon's *The Pillow Book*, Akazome Uemon's [*sic*] *A Tale of Flowering Fortunes*, [and] Ise's *Tales of Ise*," reflecting the traditional belief that the *Tales of Ise* were written, or at least finally edited, by the famous poet Lady Ise (fl. early tenth century).[15]

The possibility of women competing with men, at least on the political front, was eliminated by the Law on Associations and Meetings (*Shūkai oyobi kessha hō*), enacted by the Cabinet in 1890. In the same year the first history of Japanese literature, *Nihon bungakushi* (History of Japanese literature), by Mikami Sanji (1865–1939) and Takatsu Kuwasaburō (1864–1921), appeared. Significantly, *Nihon bungakushi* puts the Heian period into heavy service as the Other of modern Japan: the Heian period is Sinified and, borrowing from Victorian ideology, it becomes emblematic of a kind of effeminate, aristocratic leisure that stands in sharp contrast to the new manly, bourgeois definition of work.[16] Indeed, Mikami and Takatsu criticize the Heian period as an imitation of T'ang culture and condemn the Fujiwara for usurping political authority from the imperial family[17]—these two facts are connected in their minds due to the belief, promoted by scholars of the nativist learning (kokugaku) movement, that one of the key distinctions between China and Japan was that while Chinese history had seen a number of different dynasties, Japan had only one. Mikami and Takatsu idealize the Nara period (646–794), or an even more primitive age, before the introduction of Chinese culture. The corruption of the true Japanese spirit, gendered as masculine (*Nihon danshi no yūsō naru kifū*), is directly attributed to T'ang culture, and especially to Buddhism and its attendant concept of *mujō*, the awareness of the ephemerality of life. This awareness is seen as leading to cowardice and the effeminacy of body and spirit.

The distinction between men and women is essential, according to Mikami and Takatsu, and they see the confusion between the two exacerbated in the Heian period. This kind of insupportable ambiguity is mirrored in another aspect of the Heian period: the aristocrats' inability to distinguish between Buddhist divinities and indigenous *kami*, or gods. The operative concept is clearly *bunri*, or "separation," as expressed in the policy of "the Separation of Shinto and Buddhism" (*shinbutsu bunri*) enforced by the early Meiji government.[18] In it, an indelible connection was made between the separation of Shinto and Buddhism and what was called the "restoration of imperial rule" (*ōsei fukko*). More precisely, this ideology was read back in time, and the *lack* of distinction between Shinto and Buddhism was identified as the *cause* for the decline of imperial rule. In other words, Mikami and Takatsu see syncretization of foreign Buddhist and "native Shinto" beliefs by Heian aristocrats as a necessary condition for the usurpation of political authority from the imperial household by the Fujiwara clan, just as the forcible separation of Buddhism and Shinto was a necessary condition for the Meiji "Restoration." This construction is linked to a separation between the masculine and the feminine, and the natural rightness of monogamy. The end result is that the Heian period becomes one of effeminate polygamists who are led astray by clever Buddhist priests and whose feminized moral or intellectual aptitude cannot distinguish between gods (kami) and buddhas. The Fujiwara clan's usurpation of imperial authority is also seen as a confusion between ruler and ruled.

However, due to the development of both prose and poetry during the Heian period, Mikami and Takatsu cannot deny the importance of this period for the evolution of "national literature" (*kokubungaku*).[19] The authors proceed to discuss the literature of the period in terms of six genres, significantly reversing the traditional hierarchy by putting "*monogatari*, in other words, the literature of the novel" first and *waka* and poetic prefaces last, with "diaries, travel accounts, and chap-books, that is, miscellanies" (*sōshi, sunawachi zuihitsu*), and "historical forms of writing" in between. Traditionally, poetry had been ranked as the supreme category, while fiction had been relegated to a status beneath serious consideration. For Mikami and Takatsu, however, monogatari functions as an indigenous tradition of social and emotional representation while serving at the same time as the inferior and effeminate aristocratic contrast to the newly emerging bourgeois novel. The authors devote only one paragraph to the actual content of *Ise*—rather than its generic identification—and they heartily condemn Narihira's profligate behavior. They also argue that the work is closer to a poetic preface than a novel; as we have seen, these two genres form the antipodes of their evaluative classification scheme. To sum up, then, *Ise*, through the behavior of its protagonist Narihira, shares generously in the faults of the Heian period, and its only redeeming features in the eyes of Mikami and Takatsu are its antiquity and literary style.

During the first half of the Meiji period, while people in general knew some of the stories from *Ise*, and especially those used in the nō repertoire, there seems to have been little detailed knowledge of the text itself. The first Meiji edition of *Tales of Ise* appeared in April 1890, in the first volume of the *Nihon bungaku zensho* (Complete Works of Japanese Literature), a twenty-four-volume series edited by Ochiai Naobumi (1861–1903), Konakamura Yoshikata (1861–1923), and Hagino Yoshiyuki (1860–1924). The text is preceded by a short introduction, which refers to the protagonist as "Lord Ariwara no Narihira" (*Ariwara no Narihira ason*), a level of respect not seen in *Nihon bungakushi*, and which stresses his position as a military officer.

> When we reach the age of Emperor Montoku [r. 850–858], it is Minister Fujiwara no Yoshifusa who holds power. The Mikado wanted to confer the position of heir-apparent on his first son, Prince Koretaka, but since he was afraid of this Minister, he did not accomplish his true intent, and in the end it was his second son, Prince Korehito, by the Somedono Empress [Meishi], who ascended. He ascended the throne as Emperor Seiwa, and the Fujiwara clan's power expanded from that point on. As for Prince Koretaka, he lost the heir-apparency, and as the number of his attendants dwindled, it was only this lord [Narihira] who, because of his deep commitment to the imperial household, came and went [as regularly as] ocean waves; he lamented the times, and was saddened by the world. He even secretly schemed that, if there

were a chance, he would put down this threat and restore imperial authority. But since one twig cannot hold back a stream, in the end he had to stain his honor, make sport of the world, and hide his traces. We can see this sentiment in his poem:

omofu koto	What I think
ihade zo tada ni	I should not say, and simply
yaminubeki	give it up
ware to hitoshiki	since there is indeed no one
hito shi nakereba	who feels the same as I.

This being the case, we cannot know whether his illicit affair with the Nijō Empress, while she was a commoner, was a scheme to obstruct her entrance into court; or whether or not the hardships he endured in the East were part of a plan to muster a group of sympathizers.

When we think about it this way, this romance (monogatari) is not simply superlative writing, it should also be recognized that it contains matters that can supplement history. Moreover, this lord was not simply a young noble who was a licentious playboy, but he should also be known as being a loyal subject of completely sincere patriotism.[20]

Here the editors are recycling the theory that had been put forth most recently in the late Edo period by such kokugaku (nativist) scholars as Ueda Akinari (1734–1809), Motoori Uchitō (1792–1855), and Kanō Morohira (1806–1857), that *Ise* records Narihira's political rancor. In the context of the new Meiji state, this makes Narihira a patriot, and it is suggested that his various morally reprehensible actions may actually have been resistance against the Fujiwara hegemons. In such a reading, the penultimate episode, Episode 124, of which the poem is quoted above, takes on special significance, suggesting political sentiments against the Fujiwara that Narihira was forced to keep to himself. Contrary to this emphasis on Episode 124, as we shall see, late twentieth-century scholars see the *first* episode as the key to *Ise*, especially in its use of the term *miyabi* (courtliness). It is, then, interesting to note that in this first Meiji edition the term *miyabi* is not mentioned in the introduction, nor does it even occasion any comment in the notes to the text.

As Tomi Suzuki explains in her essay in this volume, Japanese attitudes toward the Heian period changed substantially after the Russo-Japanese War of 1904–05, especially because of the work of Fujioka Sakutarō (1870–1910). In his *Kokubungaku zenshi: Heianchō hen* (Complete History of Japanese Literature: The Heian Court, 1905), Fujioka begins his extended discussion of *Ise* by briefly tracing its popularity, from among the high-class literary women (*jōryū shijo*) of Murasaki Shikibu's day, to the male literati (*kajin bunshi*) of the medieval age, demonstrating that *Ise*, together with *Kokinshū* and *Genji*, formed the foundation of medieval national literature.

The majority of Fujioka's energy goes into dating the text, on the basis of authorship and style. By placing *Ise* before the Engi era (901–23), Fujioka can make it, along with *The Tale of the Bamboo Cutter* (*Taketori monogatari*), an important bridge between the simplicity of Nara-period texts and the masterpieces of the Heian era, arguing that it is completely uninfluenced by foreign literature. *Tales of Ise* forms a middle term between the supernatural elements of the *Bamboo Cutter* and the beautifully constructed plot of *The Tale of Genji*. Fujioka's chapter on *Ise* concludes with the suggestion that the prose of the text shares the same faults as Narihira's poetry: a frankness and lack of polish that makes it seem "at times like the words of a child." Yet the fact that Narihira's name has been preserved for posterity makes him a giant of sorts. This reputation is due not only to his poetry, but chiefly to *Ise*, and it is this text that becomes a model for later national literature, with the character of Narihira as a precursor to that of Genji. However, Fujioka, echoing Mikami and Takatsu, who saw the Heian period as one of decadence and decline, clearly does not see Narihira's legacy as solely positive: "When one thinks on the influence [*Ise*] had in this way on later ages, from the middle of the Heian period on through to its end, must not Narihira too assume some responsibility for customs lapsing more and more into frivolous seduction, and poetry as well coming to be valued and used only for amorous verses?"[21] In other words, whether viewed positively or negatively, the dominant image of the Heian period during Meiji was one of licentiousness. Looseness in morals was, according to both Confucian and Victorian discourses, a result of effeminacy. In this way, although there were attempts to rehabilitate Narihira as a patriot, the Heian period as a whole, and any work produced in it, become permanently gendered feminine.

ISE IN THE TAISHŌ PERIOD (1912–1926)

The first major modern study of *Ise*, Kamata Masanori's *Kōshō Ise monogatari shōkai* (A Detailed Explanation of *Tales of Ise*; 1919), appeared in the Taishō period, a period that saw the emergence of the critical concepts of both the "I-novel" (*watakushi-shōsetsu*) and "women's literature" (*jōryū bungaku*).[22] Yet Kamata's edition is essentially a compendium of earlier commentaries—from *Gukenshō* (Commentary of My Humble Opinion, 1460) by Ichijō Kanera

(1402–1481) to *Shinshaku* (New Explanation, 1818) by Fujii Takanao (1765–1841)—much along the lines of the *Shūsuishō* (Gathered Sheaves Commentary, 1680) by Kitamura Kigin (1624–1705). In his foreword, Kamata largely follows Fujioka's lead, ranking *Ise* as a foundational text together with *Genji* and the *Kokinshū*, and insisting that *Genji* developed out of *Ise*.[23] The Taishō era ended with the appearance in 1926 of two other studies: *Ise monogatari kasshaku* (*Tales of Ise*—A Living Interpretation), by Kobayashi Eiko (1872–1952), and *Shinchū Ise monogatari* (Newly Annotated *Tales of Ise*), by Yoshikawa Hideo (1882–1944). In between, however, appeared what seems to have been the first translation of the *Tales* into modern Japanese since the seventeenth century, *Shin'yaku e-iri Ise monogatari* (*Tales of Ise*, Newly Translated and Illustrated), translated by Yoshii Isamu, with illustrations by Takehisa Yumeji, in Taishō 6 (1917). Yoshii followed this the next year with his rendition of *Genji*, *Genji monogatari jōwa* (Tale of Genji Love Stories). This was one in a series *Jōwa shinshū* (New Collection of Love Stories) published by Oranda shobō, which repackaged classical works (other authors included Chikamatsu and Saikaku) with Takehisa's popular imagery, aimed at the new consumers of "women's literature."

In Kobayashi Eiko's volume, what we might call a "popular scholarly edition" of the *Tales*, the Teika variant is supplied with *kanji*, annotated with marginal notes (*tōchū*), and each of the episodes, which are unnumbered and presented in continuous fashion,[24] is followed by yet another translation into modern Japanese. The text itself is preceded by an introductory essay that considers the issues of authorship, the work's title, and the section on Narihira's journey to the East (Azuma-kudari). With regard to authorship, Kobayashi, who quotes extensively from Tokugawa period commentaries, comes to the conclusion that Narihira wrote the entire tale and argues that Narihira's loyalty to the imperial house and antagonism toward the Fujiwara necessitated that his writing be oblique. Two fundamental political causes are given for Narihira's unhappiness with life in the capital: Emperor Montoku's inability to resist Fujiwara despotism and name Imperial Prince Koretaka as crown prince, and Narihira's affair with the Nijō Empress. In other words, Kobayashi uses the same political interpretation of Narihira's actions that we find in many Edo period commentaries. However, Kobayashi rejects the authenticity of Narihira's journey to the East, and insists that his poems are based solely on his imagination. The meaning of the *Tales of Ise* then becomes simply an expression of Narihira's yearning (*akogare*) to visit the beauty spots of eastern Japan, a record of his unfulfilled longing to escape life in the capital. Such a view of travel was certainly not shared by the Japanese

of Narihira's day, who saw any travel away from the capital as a kind of ban-
ishment. One wonders if Kobayashi's reading may have been influenced by
her own unfulfilled desire to visit the places abroad whose images, through
photographs and films, had become part of the popular urban culture of the
Taishō era.[25]

Finally, Yoshikawa Hideo's *Shinchū* is marked by a renewed emphasis on
poetry, the importance of *Tales of Ise* to poetry, and the importance of poetry
to Japan. At the same time, *Ise* is now firmly classified as an *uta-monogatari*
(poem-tale).[26] This is also one of the first works of the modern period to emphasize *fūryū* ("elegance" or "courtliness").

> We can probably see Izanagi's and Izanami's "O, what a charming man," "O,
> what a charming woman" as a kind of exchange of poems (*waka no zōtō*). The
> great part of love poems seen in the *Kojiki* and *Nihongi* are exchanged poems.
> We also see the exchange of poems outside of romance (*ren'ai*). Isn't it a grace-
> ful custom (*yūbina fūzoku*) for young men and women to hint at their feel-
> ings through poetry? This trend does not weaken even when we enter the
> *Man'yōshū* age. In the Heian court, although this kind of poetry exchange is
> limited to the aristocratic class, it flourishes, and its momentum extends as
> far as the early modern period. Although there is surely no time or place, past
> or present, east or west, where there is no one conveying his or her feelings
> by means of poetry, the extent of this custom is a mysterious phenomenon
> that cannot be seen outside of our country. If one has evil intentions in one's
> heart, one cannot expect to have beautiful poetry. That young men and
> women, in an age of free love (*jiyū ren'ai*), without formal ethical restraints,
> were saved from becoming the slaves of sensual desire must surely be due to
> the influence of poetry's great virtue. *Tales of Ise* is a poem-tale that was born
> against the background of such a society. The whole of *Tales of Ise* is a poem-
> tale, and the great portion of it is a love-story (*ren'ai monogatari*).[27] . . . To the
> men of this age the way of love (*koi no michi*) was elegant (*fūryū*). The way
> of poetry (*waka*), too, was, of course, elegant. Therefore, to delight in poetry
> on the path of love must have been consummate elegance. *Tales of Ise* has
> recorded this consummation of elegance, and to see in it examples of the fate
> of men and women in love being controlled by a single poem, is something
> at which one cannot marvel enough.[28]

Behind Yoshikawa's analysis is the assumption, which appears to have been
popular in the 1920s, that poetry was somehow the primary means of conversation in Japan's ancient age.[29] The widespread composition of poetry
even in the Edo period is now seen as a uniquely Japanese phenomenon.
Another common idea, which we find in both Japanese and English writers
of the 1920s, is that beautiful poems are the reflection of a beautiful heart.[30]

Yoshikawa's valorization of "love" (*ren'ai*), a term not coined until the Meiji period, above even filial piety or loyalty, reflects Taishō cultural attitudes and would have been unthinkable either in the Meiji period or later in the 1930s and 1940s. At the same time, he calls upon Japanese poetry to save the nation from Western decadence: it is only poetry that allowed Heian youth—who like their Taishō counterparts lived in a period of "free love"—to escape the slavery of gross sensuality. The suggestion here is that poetry can do the same for the emerging *moga* (modern girl) and *mobo* (modern boy) of the day, whose images were linked in the popular mind with the practice of "free love," or rather that it is precisely because the *moga* and *mobo* do not write poetry that they are no more than slaves to their sensual desires. By contrast, the combination of love and poetry is the key to elegance (*fūryū*). The Taishō period here positively assessed *Tales of Ise* not only for its affirmation of "love" but for the aesthetization and sublimation of "love" through poetry, a process that results in "elegance."

The history of the term *fūryū* is incredibly long and rich, dating back to at least the second century A.D. in China.[31] However, by the late Edo period it appears to have had two basic meanings. One was related to poetry, where the term suggested the kind of literary freedom and dedication exemplified by Chinese and Japanese poet-recluses, and wanderers such as the famous haiku poet, Matsuo Bashō (1644–1694). On the other hand, the term could refer to a kind of opulent, exaggerated splendor most closely associated with the world of popular entertainment such as kabuki and the Yoshiwara pleasure quarters, and it often appears in the titles of ukiyo-e woodblock prints. By the Meiji period, fūryū is used by Iwamoto Yoshiharu in *Jogaku zasshi* to represent a kind of socially irresponsible literary Bohemianism.[32] On the other end of the spectrum, Kōda Rohan (1867–1947) used the term in his enormously successful story "Fūryū Butsu" (translated variously as "The Buddha of Art," "The Buddha of Elegance," and "Love Bodhisattva"),[33] where it clearly represents an artistic, semireligious ideal associated with Bashō but also tinged with eroticism. It seems to be in this sense that the term is applied to *Tales of Ise* in the Taishō period. In general, however, concerns about "free love" in the Taishō period were directed primarily at the behavior of women—the image of the *moga* was far more a topic for concern than her male counterpart. Whereas the Meiji period frowned upon licentiousness in whatever form or period it occurred in, Taishō critics constructed a distinction between the "elegant" dissipation of Heian aristocrats and the degraded sexuality of the young women of the present, and thus were able to recuperate *Ise* as a model of decorum.

ISE FROM THE BEGINNING OF SHŌWA TO
THE END OF WORLD WAR II (1926–1945)

The two major *Ise* studies of the pre-defeat Shōwa era are *Ise monogatari ni tsukite no kenkyū* (Research on *Tales of Ise*, 1933–1936), by Ikeda Kikan (1896–1956), and *Hyōshaku Ise monogatari taisei* (Grand Compendium of *Tales of Ise* Annotations, 1939), by Arai Mujirō. Ikeda's is a massive textual study that includes a variorum edition; it establishes the relations between textual lineages and proposes a theory of the text's development. It is only at the very end of this long work that Ikeda broaches the topic of value, and here too it is solely to discuss "the literary status of *Tales of Ise*."[34] Ikeda demonstrates the overwhelming importance of *Ise* by recounting the pervasive influence it had on all subsequent Japanese literature and by reciting the large number of commentaries and studies it has spawned. Both justifications are distinctly modern. This approach is in contrast to the view presented, for instance, four hundred years earlier by Hosokawa Yūsai (1534–1610), in *Ketsugishō*. For Yūsai and all medieval commentators the value of *Ise* was a given, and citation of later allusive variations (*honkadori*) by Teika or other poets served an educational purpose, not a rhetorical one. Yūsai knew that his audience would appreciate knowing how *Ise* poems were used by later poets, but the citation of such later allusions to *Ise* was not meant to be seen as "proof" of *Ise*'s importance, which was taken for granted. With Ikeda, on the other hand, such intertextual citations are part of an argument that demonstrates the importance of *Ise*, an argument that also presupposes a national literary canon in a way that Yūsai does not. This is because, at the most fundamental level, Ikeda is arguing for the value of Japanese literature as a whole, with *Ise* as one of its exemplars. Implicit in Ikeda's argument is a comparison of *Ise*, as a premodern native text, with modern Western literature. Yūsai relates the *Ise* text or poems to other poems, primarily for the practicing poet who would want to join in the conversation and write his own poem. The importance of *Ise*'s intertexuality, then, is founded on poetic praxis, and its relations with other literature (besides the Chinese classics) is of little concern. For Yūsai, the fact that *Ise* served as an intertext for medieval nō plays, or for the Edo-period novelist Saikaku, would have counted for nothing: he was interested only in how great poets had alluded to *Ise* and in how one could discover prestigious Chinese subtexts in it. With Ikeda, however, the desideratum is to demonstrate the influence of *Ise* on the breadth and depth of what is now defined as the Japanese literary canon, and so we are given citations from monogatari (especially *Genji*), diaries, nō linked verse, and even Chikamatsu's puppet plays (while the relationship to Chinese literature is passed over in silence).

For Ikeda, the importance of *Ise* also rests on its position as the first of what is now seen to be a discrete genre, the uta-monogatari, and as such, on its position in the historical evolution of Japanese literature. *Ise* is also important because it has inspired so much study and research, making it part of a newly established "big four," alongside the *Man'yōshū*, *Kokinshū*, and *Genji*. It is not that *Ise* is the subject of many studies because it is important, but rather that because it has inspired so many studies we know *Ise* must be important. The fissure between the modern and what came before can be seen in this loss of the self-evident and inherent value of the classics.

Ikeda's "defense" of *Ise* remains strictly literary, and there is no point at which he attempts to extrapolate from the text to an understanding of the nature of Japan, its culture, or its people. By contrast, Arai Mujirō's *Grand Compendium*, published three years later, is a deeply conservative work.[35] First Arai asserts the importance of *Ise* by emphasizing its comparative antiquity, arguing that its oldest stratum predates both *The Tale of the Bamboo Cutter* (ca. 910) and *Tosa nikki* (Tosa Diary, 935) and that it is "pure Japanese thought, pure national literature. One cannot see the slightest foreign influence."[36] Second, he rehearses the esteem with which *Ise* has been regarded throughout Japanese history, including an explanation of why it was neglected during the Meiji period. Arai argues that due to its focus on relations between the sexes, which it described in frank language, *Ise* was seen as unsuitable for textbooks, and so fell into disfavor. However, monogatari, he argues, are mirrors of their ages, and if there is a vice, it is in the age, not in the telling; if one were to exclude works because they discuss sex, then *Genji* as well and the *Man'yōshū* and the *Kojiki* would all have to be eliminated. For Arai, *Ise* becomes a kind of ethnographic treasure trove, taking up concerns more plebeian than aristocratic, and is thus unparalleled in its breadth and recording of "language, manners, famous products, and ancient practices." Its value lies, in short, in its being a record of the ancient age.[37] Clearly such evaluation owes something to the emergence of the folklore studies of Yanagita Kunio (1875–1962) and Origuchi Shinobu (1887–1953) in the previous decades.

In sharp contrast to Arai's study, with its emphasis on the non-aristocratic elements of *Ise*, is the November 1943 special edition of *Bungaku* entitled "Miyabi no dentō" (The Tradition of Courtliness), which was one of the most important scholarly works identifying *Ise* with "courtliness" (*miyabi*) or courtly elegance and which elevated the concept of miyabi to the level of a "national aesthetic" category.[38] Miyabi was not, in fact, a term in premodern aesthetic discourse, and it appears only once in *Tales of Ise* and a handful of times (as an adjective, not a substantive) in the *Genji*. The key passage in which the word miyabi appears is the famous first episode.

Once a man who had lately come of age went hunting on his estate at Kasuga village, near the Nara capital. In the village there lived two beautiful young sisters. The man caught a glimpse of the sisters through a gap in their hedge. It was startling and incongruous indeed that such ladies should dwell at the ruined capital, and he wished to meet them. He tore a strip from the skirt of his hunting costume, dashed off a poem, and sent it in. The fabric of the robe was imprinted with a moss-fern design.

> Kasugano no   Like the random pattern of this robe,
> Wakamurasaki no   Dyed with the young purple
> Surigoromo   From Kasuga Plain—
> Shinobu no midare   Even thus is the wild disorder
> Kagiri shirarezu   Of my yearning heart.

No doubt it had occurred to him that this was an interesting opportunity for an adaptation of the poem that runs,

> Michinoku no   My thoughts have grown disordered
> Shinobu mojizuri   As random patterns dyed on cloth
> Tare yue ni   Reminiscent of Shinobu in Michinoku—
> Midaresomenishi   And who is to blame?
> Ware naranaku ni   Surely not I.

People were remarkably elegant in those days [*mukashi-bito ha kaku ichi-hayaki miyabi wo namu shikeru*].[39]

In 1940 the literary scholar Endō Yoshimoto (b. 1905) published an article establishing that in the *Man'yōshū*, the Chinese characters for fūryū were in fact read "miyabi."[40] By associating the relatively rare term miyabi with fūryū, Japanese scholars were able to provide miyabi with a distinguished philosophical pedigree.[41] In the lead article of the 1943 *Bungaku* special issue, Okazaki Yoshie (1892–1982), one of the best-known "Japanese cultural aestheticians," makes it clear that miyabi, as fūryū, originated in China, and that even in the age of the *Man'yōshū* it was still to a great extent foreign in nature. By the Heian period, however, and starting with *Ise*, miyabi had become thoroughly Japanese:

> When we get to the Heian period, we note that the usage of the term "miyabi" has become extremely Japanese. In the examples of its usage in monogatari, there seems to be not the slightest trace of China. The phrase *ichi-hayaki miyabi* (extreme courtliness) in *Tales of Ise* refers to the action of the man who peeps in on the "fresh and charming women," cuts off the hem

of his fern-patterned hunting robe, and sends off a poem about it, so that, if we were to take the meaning of miyabi narrowly, it is the performance of an act of literary elegance suited to the occasion, while if we take it broadly, it becomes something that we must interpret as amorousness (*kōshoku*) or aesthetic taste (*biteki shumi*). This meaning derives from the same tradition as the poem-exchange between Ishikawa no Iratsume and Ōtomo no Tanushi [in the *Man'yōshū*] or, from China, we can also hypothesize the indirect influence of the *Wen-hsüan*'s "Rhyme-prose of the lecherous man who loves sex" (*Teng t'u tzu hao se fu*). However, in *Tales of Ise* it is something specifically Japanese; in other words, we can think of it as a mutual act that becomes an expression of a kind of love (*ai*), one that had developed since the age of *Kojiki* and *Nihon shoki*. Based on this kind of example, we can think of "miyabi" as signifying a Japanese cultural mode founded on love and beauty.[42]

Okazaki seems here to be straining to find something specifically Japanese about the idea of miyabi, something that has not been borrowed from Chinese culture. He claims that such uniqueness can be found in *Tales of Ise*, and especially in the Heian period, though it starts developing from the Nara era (646–784). For Okazaki, miyabi involves romance, or romantic love, which is seen as something poetic and mutual (*sōmonteki*).[43] Okazaki's use of this term suggests several things: first, that there is something inherently poetic about miyabi; second, that it is somehow linked to the earliest Japanese writing (having a linguistic foundation); and third, that it requires the active participation of women.[44]

Women in fact become the primary vehicles of miyabi in the concluding article in this collection, "Heian jidai no joryū bungaku to 'miyabi,'" ("Women's Literature of the Heian Era and 'Miyabi'") by Ikeda Tsutomu (b. 1908). Ikeda relates miyabi to *kami-asobi*, or entertainment for the gods, starting with the dance to lure Amaterasu from the cave in the *Kojiki*, and including the entertainment put on by the ladies-in-waiting at court for the emperor, who was also understood to be divine. Ikeda pays particular attention to Ono no Komachi, who is said in the *Kokinshū* to practice poetry in the same style as Princess Sotoori (*Sotowori hime*). Sotoori was the sister of the consort of Emperor Ingyō (r. 412–53). Although Sotoori too found favor with the emperor, she feared her sister's jealousy and stayed away from the palace and instead waited for the emperor's infrequent visits to her own home. Ikeda identifies this kind of devotion as miyabi, here a synonym for *misao* (fidelity/chastity). However, miyabi also entails turning the subsequent pain (*wabi*) of waiting into beauty through poetry, literally, "romanticizing" (*rōman-ka*) it. Here Narihira is introduced, and his political frustrations rehearsed. His fidelity to the imperial house is the cause of this pain that, just like Princess Sotoori and the ladies of the imperial harem, he transmogrifies into beautiful poetry.[45]

The final essay to mention is by Hasuda Zemmei (1904–1945), titled simply "Miyabi." He also links miyabi to the emperor, but much more explicitly in the context of the wartime imperial cult.[46] Hasuda, who is best known for a book on Motoori Norinaga, committed suicide on the Malay Peninsula on August 18, 1945, after the call for surrender and after shooting to death his Korean-born commanding officer. In his essay, Hasuda rejects any historical specificity to miyabi, which partakes for him of the divine. He does not gender it, and in fact makes no specific reference to *Ise* itself. Nonetheless, in conjunction with the articles by Okazaki and Ikeda, this essay gives us a sense of the reception of *Ise* in the contexts of the wartime imperial cult and the heavily nationalistic Japan Romantic School (*Nihon rōman-ha*), with which Hasuda was associated.[47] *Tales of Ise* is characterized by miyabi, where miyabi means "courtliness," and "courtliness" refers specifically to the divine emperor. Perhaps surprisingly, we will see this association of *Ise* with the emperor rearticulated in the 1970s.

ISE IN THE POSTWAR PERIOD

Very little notable scholarship on *Ise* was produced in the years immediately following the war: the bibliography in the Nihon koten bungaku zenshū edition of *Ise* cites no important piece of research from 1943 to 1954. Publications resumed in 1954 with *Ise monogatari kochūshaku no kenkyū* (A study of old commentaries on *Tales of Ise*), by Ōtsu Yūichi (1902–1983), who was also responsible for the *Ise* section of the Kadokawa Nihon koten kanshō kōza series (A Course in the Appreciation of the Japanese Classics, 1958). In Ōtsu's reading, *Ise* is fundamentally the "Narihira monogatari" (Tale of Narihira), which falls into two parts: "the various stages of love" (*ren'ai no shujusō*) and "the story of the Captain of the Right Horseguards." The latter discusses Prince Koretaka and all the other named figures in the *Tales*, but the political aspects of their relationships are not broached at all; the work is read primarily as a biographical and romantic text. Accordingly, in the first episode, miyabi is equated to love, and the final line is paraphrased as: "Men of old were people who really did fall in love in a flash like this." Moreover, Ōtsu's reading creates a kind of sanitized and juvenilized *Ise*, reducing the amorous encounter of the first episode to a case of puppy love:

The important point in this story is that even though the hero has had his coming of age ceremony, he is still a youth. In the Heian court, in contrast to the present day, the coming of age ceremony was early, and took place usually between twelve and fifteen to sixteen years of age. . . . Accordingly, although an adult in dress, we must expect that in body and mind he was still very childish, and yet he sends a wonderful poem. It is literally his first love. One more thing is how beautiful it is and what pure feelings he has.[48]

Interestingly, it was Ikeda Kikan who took the lead after the war in constructing an almost exclusively feminine Heian era. In 1953 he published *Heianchō no seikatsu to bungaku* (Life and Literature of the Heian Court). Despite its inclusive title, Ikeda himself states that his study grew out of a series of lectures entitled *Nikki bungaku to kyūtei seikatsu* (Diary Literature and Court Life) that focused on "literature and women's lives" or, more specifically, "the general life of the rear court (*kōkyū*)," that is, the imperial harem. In other words, the term *kyūtei* (imperial court) in Ikeda's title refers only to the harem, and not to any of the "public" or formal spaces where men conducted the business of government; the masculine has been almost entirely leached out of the Heian period.[49]

The first attack against this highly feminized view of *Ise* came in 1972 with the publication of an article by Watanabe Minoru entitled, "Minamoto no Tōru to *Ise monogatari*."[50] Here he places the origins of *Tales of Ise* in an exclusively male salon of "fūryū poets" centered around the Ki, Ariwara, and Saga Genji clans. The implications of such a genesis are spelled out more fully in his 1976 Shinchō edition of *Ise*. By emphasizing miyabi in his reading of *Ise*, Watanabe actually manages to evict women from the *Tales* almost entirely. In his view, *Ise* is not about love, but about the "courtliness" of a man like Narihira. This positions women in a much-reduced role, and is in marked contrast to the view of "woman as equal partner in love" championed by early scholars such as Fujioka and Okazaki. Watanabe insists that characters make their entrance not for the sake of a love story, but to demonstrate the actions of an "elegant" man. The focus is on "elegant" deeds, not character or plot.

Like Ōtsu, Watanabe believes that "what must not be passed over in reading . . . is surely the point that this hero is an aristocratic youth who has just barely become one of the adults." However, he insists that the young man's "Field of Kasuga" poem is about neither love (*ren'ai*) nor marriage, rather it is a poem in praise of the opposite sex (*isei sanka*). If the author's interest were in love or marriage, Watanabe argues, then certainly the sisters' reply poem would have been included, but instead not one word is mentioned of it: "What happens *between* the man and the sisters is not the subject of the first episode; the subject of the first episode is what the man does *in reaction to* the women."[51]

Whereas readings of *Ise* in the immediate postwar period threatened to lose the work in the overgeneralized category of "court women's literature" (*ōchō joryū bungaku*), Watanabe, writing in the 1970s, positions *Ise* precisely against and in contrast to women's diaries. He contrasts the assessment of individuals found in *Murasaki Shikibu nikki* (Diary of Murasaki Shikibu), where observations made over a long period of time are condensed into a definitive assessment of the person's character, so that individual actions are rarely the issue, and *Ise*, where a person's actions, rather than his character as a whole, are the concern. Whereas women's diaries present cumulative assessments of the overall *character* of individuals, *Ise* is concerned with specific *actions*, which carry their own significance and about which very little explicit comment is made. Watanabe suggests that such differences are gender-based.

Watanabe's analysis also touches on issues of cultural identity, as in the first episode, which becomes an allegory for a newly independent Japanese "spirit" (*seishin*). It is his view that the Heian aristocracy, having experienced the major disruptions and expenditure of time and energy involved in moving the capital (to present-day Kyoto) in 794, must have certainly had an awareness of themselves as part of a new era. He points to the eventual suspension of embassies to China as another indication of this energy (*ikioi*):

> Heian aristocrats were feeling their way toward a new spirit, one appropriate to their new age. Miyabi is what was born out of that groping—an aesthetic of the Heian aristocracy that was neither Chinese nor Nara-esque. In fact, I believe that *Tales of Ise* is a document of the discovery and declaration of that aesthetic. Both youth and violence accompany this discovery and declaration. The negation of "rusticity" (*hinabi*), the violence of the attack on being "still green" (*nama-gokoro*)—there is no doubt that the text was born out of these. . . . *Tales of Ise* is truly, like the man of Episode One, a literature of "violent elegance" (*ichihayaki miyabi*).[52]

Watanabe, then, sees miyabi as distinctly Japanese. This is in contrast to scholars such as Okazaki, Konishi Jin'ichi (b. 1915), Akiyama Ken (b. 1924), and Katagiri Yōichi (b. 1931), who trace the development of the concept of miyabi from the term *fūryū* (*feng-liu*) of Six Dynasties China.

Katagiri Yōichi's interpretation of *Ise*, which appears in the widely read 1975 Kadokawa kanshō Nihon koten bungaku series, accepts most of Watanabe's points (e.g., the political significance of the first episode; the rejection of Fujiwara politics that miyabi represented), but rejects Watanabe's conclusion, keeping both love and women very much part of *Ise*. In his brief preface to the 1975 Kanshō, Katagiri writes:

> The root of the conception of Japanese literature is the expression of feelings (*jojō*), and the genre that makes this its chief concern is of course poetry (waka). Poem-tales (uta-monogatari), which fix on the kernel of that poetry and abide there, are all the more representative of Japanese (*Nihonteki*) literature, due to the fact that they tell about the love life of a hero who expresses his feelings as the composer of these poems. Especially *Tales of Ise*, always loved by the people, has become a standard of people's literature (*hitobito no bungaku*). There is no other work that has been read so much by later ages. In the medieval era, in the early modern era, it has always been a "best seller." I am repeating myself, but this popularity is because *Tales of Ise* is literature of such Japanese emotional expression, and because it is a love story.[53]

Katagiri is insistent that *Ise* is a *Japanese* text, a *national* text, "the people's" text. He stresses this national aspect far more strongly than, for instance, Ōtsu in the earlier Kōza volume. And in an analogous fashion Katagiri reintroduces women, *Japanese* women, displaying a uniquely *Japanese* beauty. He does this in the first episode with his focus on a phrase in the text that has received relatively little comment in modern commentaries—*ito namameitaru onna*:

> The adjective *namamekashi* is "youthful," "fresh-looking," "graceful," and "elegant." Moreover, it describes a beauty of character that has an everyday unity of mind and body. . . . *Namameitari*, too, I think, can be interpreted as something close to that, the same sort of thing. It is not the perfected, gorgeous, Chinese beauty represented by the term *uruwashi*—it is a word we use to describe a woman who possesses a gentleness (*yasashisa*) that tugs at the heart nostalgically—a high-class, elegant gentleness that one can never forget. . . . It is indeed this that I think indicates the feminine ideal in *Tales of Ise*.[54]

Katagiri makes the same claim for the woman in Episode Two as well, and elsewhere. We see here the renewed, postwar categorization of Japan's "traditional" past as feminine, influenced, I believe, by both a post-defeat search for a more pacific Japanese past, and by the economic boom of the 1970s that fed a largely female-oriented cultural consumerism. Katagiri is clearly attempting to present the feminine version of miyabi. In many countries, postsecondary education has increasingly become a commodity, and this is perhaps even more so the case in Japan, with its highly developed middlebrow or popular academic publishing market and commercial "culture centers." Katagiri is presenting the *Tales of Ise* as popular culture, as a "best seller." And of course most students studying classical Japanese literature at university are women. It would be unwise to ignore these facts when considering the trends in scholarly interpretation during the same period. In Katagiri's hands, then, a certain *jokun* (education for women) aspect seems to be discovered in *Ise*, and gender-specific forms of miyabi established for both men and women; that is to say, men behave freely, even impetuously, without regard for social constraints, while women's miyabi is a "gentleness" that inspires such behavior in men.

By 1979, Akiyama Ken could declare in the lead article to a special edition of *Kokubungaku* devoted to *Tales of Ise* that: "'Miyabi' is now considered the main theme of *Tales of Ise*."[55] In his own essay, "Ise monogatari: 'miyabi' no ron" ("*Tales of Ise*: A Discourse on 'Miyabi'"), Akiyama brings together the work of a number of scholars, including Watanabe and Katagiri, on miyabi and *Ise*, but his own major contribution came in 1984, with the publication of "'Miyabi' no kōzō" ("The Structure of 'Miyabi'").[56] Here, for the first time since World War II, miyabi is elevated to an aesthetic category on a par with *yūgen* (mystery and depth) and *iki* (chic). For Akiyama, the miyabi presented in *Ise* finds its finest representative in the character of Genji, and the concept of miyabi includes in it a "celebration of the emperor" (*tennō sankō*) and "interference from and transcendence over the political world" (*seiji sekai e no haihan to chōetsu*). In fact, Akiyama implies that the emperor's transcendence over political realities, as a sign, makes him the guarantor of the Japanese tradition—"as the personification and preservation of a stable cultural tradition, the conceptual existence of the emperor has reigned in a normative fashion" throughout Japanese history.[57] Akiyama insists that while an aristocrat like Genji was obviously part of the elite of his period, he had no actual political power, and in fact transcended his power base and the political world entirely through an aesthetic way of life. Akiyama firmly anchors that aesthetic way of life in the imperial family, making the emperor or an imperial prince such as Genji the guarantor of a stable cultural tradition. The imperial family, then, reigns through Art and does not rule through Power. And so we come to the point of what might be labeled "constitutional miyabi," or "miyabi as a symbol of the people." That is to say, just as the emperor is placed supposedly "above" politics and serves as a "symbol" of the nation, so too miyabi becomes a cultural prerogative of the imperial house and an aesthetic category that "symbolizes" the nation. Miyabi is simultaneously an imperial prerogative and a part of the *Volk* (folk); it is at the same time a characteristic of the Heian period and an essential element of the Japanese today. Thus, as the originary source for this concept of miyabi, *Tales of Ise* became part and parcel of the postwar emperor system.

CONCLUSIONS

At the start of the Meiji era, the status of *Ise* was ambiguous. Some saw it as part of the vernacular literary tradition that should form the base for educating the new kind of woman required by modernity. Others saw it as the biography of an imperial patriot. Its subject matter (particularly love and sexual relations), however, made it incompatible with the moral stance that also seemed required by foreign imperial powers, and the work was consequently devalued.

One of the most significant actions on the part of a modern state is to encourage the writing of a teleological narrative, a story of the birth of a literature that mirrors and reinforces the birth of a nation. In nineteenth-century discourse, this teleological worldview was called "progress," and the Japanese were quick to adopt it. In a kind of literary Darwinism, *Ise* became valued for its chronological priority and its subsequent influence on later literature. More importantly, the entire *telos* of the Heian period became *The Tale of Genji* (a point of view still widely prevalent today), and *Ise* was valued as the seed-text that led to the glorious flowering of *Genji*. *Ise* also became representative of a distinct genre, the uta-monogatari (poem-tale), itself seen as a necessary link in the literary evolution that led to *Genji*. Yet, at the same time, for such authors as Yoshikawa Hideo, *Ise*, with its "elegance" and poetry, began to be read against the emergence of popular culture in the Taishō period. Inversely, *Ise*, as the embodiment of miyabi, a national aesthetic, was increasingly taken as representative of something that distinguished Japan from other modern nation-states. In other words, the more Japan was seen to become like "the West," the more texts such as *Ise* were taken positively to represent a prelapsarian world of "original" cultural values. This trend blossomed in the 1930s and early 1940s, when *Ise* was seen as a repository of ancient and "pure" Japanese values and was employed by those who, like Arai, would "overcome the modern" (*kindai no chōkoku*)—that is, the Euro-American construction of modernity.[58]

Yet, by the 1940s, *Ise* was not being valued for its indigenous "purity"; rather, through the concept of miyabi (courtliness), it was firmly linked to a continental heritage (the Chinese notion of *fūryū*, or elegance). However, thinkers such as Okazaki did not seem to have seen this linkage as a sign of imitative weakness. In line with wartime propaganda about the "Greater East Asian Co-Prosperity Sphere," Japan was now seen as the inheritor and guarantor—the heir apparent—of the great East Asian tradition, while at the same time bringing these inherited values to their right and proper fruition.[59] As a source for miyabi, *Ise* was appropriated for the kind of essentializing philological exercises exemplified by Kuki Shūzō's *Iki no kōzō* (The Structure of Iki, 1930), and it was the aspect of "resignation" (*akirame*) that became increasingly emphasized as the war years continued.[60] This approach is apparent in the 1942 article by Ikeda Tsutomu: Narihira suffers for the sake of the emperor and, though incapable of positive action, he transforms his pain into the beauty of Japanese poetry.

In the 1930s, however, in the lull before the storm, there was a surge in purely textual criticism, and it was this seemingly apolitical approach that was most quickly resumed at war's end. The postwar period saw a number of fine studies of the textual evolution of *Ise* and a renewed interest in the premodern exegetical tradition.[61] Ironically, despite such studies, the 1970s saw a wide scholarly consensus on the central identity of *Ise* as miyabi (though debate continued as to just what the term meant). Another important postwar trend was a romantic reading of *Ise* that focused on love and women, a reading far from the political interpretations (i.e., *Ise* as a manifestation of Narihira's political rancor against the Fujiwara) that had been offered for hundreds of years and as recently as the 1920s. It was this romantic reading, supporting the presentation of the Heian era as "feminine," that would be taken up by English language translators such as Helen McCullough. One thing that can be said with certainty about readings of *Ise* in the postwar period is that women may be in (Ōtsu, Katagiri, Akiyama), women may be out (Watanabe), but women are an essential axis around which the text is interpreted, an axis that was an essential part of modernity. As we can observe in any number of late industrializing countries, under the feminizing gaze of orientalism/imperialism, local elite males embraced the modern and assigned custodianship of the "traditional" to women.[62] In Japan during the 1950s and early 1960s, this general trend took on special valency due to the effects of the Occupation and a renewed gender-based separation of industrial labor.[63] Watanabe's renewed politicization and masculinization of *Ise* can be seen as a reaction against this trend. Nonetheless, the trend toward a feminine-oriented purveyance of culture was irreversible, and the postwar period has seen the ever-increasing entrance of women into cultural consumption of the "traditional."

This essentially consumer-oriented trend became particularly noticeable in the 1970s,[64] a time that coincided with the efflorescence of *Nihonjinron* (or the debate on what it means to be "Japanese")[65] and a renewed emphasis on Japan's "courtly culture" (*ōchō bunka*) and past. This dovetailed, to some extent, with renewed attention to modern "women's literature" (*joryū bungaku*), which is often seen to have its roots in the "courtly women's literature" (*ōchō joryū bungaku*) of the Heian era. While Akiyama Ken was a major figure in studies of Heian court literature, he also brought *Ise* into the orbit of a "national aesthetics" that was implicated in the postwar emperor system (*tennō-sei*). It seems an open question to what extent the emperor will in the future be proffered by Japanese thinkers and academics as not only the "symbol of the Japanese people," but as the presumed source and guarantor of Japanese "traditions." At least in the 1980s, *Ise* played a significant role in the construction of this "emperor as culture" approach to the self-definition of the Japanese. Its role in the twenty-first century remains to be seen.

CHAPTER FIVE

Zuihitsu and Gender: *Tsurezuregusa* and *The Pillow Book*

LINDA H. CHANCE

CANON AS HISTORICAL CONSTRUCT

During the Tokugawa era (1600–1867), certain Japanese texts received attention as objects of study with a particular eye to the needs of novices. Not all of them were appropriate for neophytes, due to textual and linguistic difficulties, but they were regularized and provided with co-texts in the form of emendations and commendations. In this body of transmitted texts we may identify a core that ever larger groups saw as embodying the cultural heritage of Japan, and that thus constituted a quasi-canonical conglomerate, but not a stable one. Works in this group—*Ise monogatari, Genji monogatari, Tsurezuregusa*—share an aura of authority that seems unassailable. Yet texts elected to the status of "classic," whether for reasons literary, political, or philosophical, suffered their ups and downs, drawing their champions as well as their detractors over the course of time. If this was axiomatic in the medieval period when literati copied out manuscripts in painstaking longhand, it was even more the case in the Tokugawa, when new technologies of dissemination flourished and the audience for the written word expanded beyond court, clergy, and the military upper crust. The popularity of any one piece of writing, moreover, was assessed differently by members of diverse groups, each representing particular habits of thought.

From about 1600 on, and especially with regard to pedagogy, the canon was an area of contestation, with multiple views on texts vying for recognition. Each interpreter, or "handler," as I sometimes think of them, of a text such as *Tsurezuregusa* (Essays in Idleness, early 14th c.) may have aspired to consistency within what was usually a holistic treatment, using strategies for exegesis based on monumentalizing assumptions, but the resulting field itself was full of sometimes widely divergent renditions (even the most outlandish of which nonetheless confirmed the text's emerging claim to sustained attention). When we say that a work "found a place in the canon" during the early modern age, then, there lies behind that emplacement a series of castings and recastings of the text, ranging from the didactic to the aesthetic, and invariably including parodical treatments that lampoon the reverence of well-intentioned commentaries. Participation extended to a variety of social classes whose motives in laying claim to the text, the version of the past it would represent, and the hold on the future it could have were many.

Tsurezuregusa was extremely suited, by virtue of flexibility, to the construction process attending the establishment of a classic. On the one hand, it offered contradictions and conundrums, which permitted the commentator to step in and execute a tour de force that was itself satisfying to the audience. On the other hand, it provided a sampler of written modes: in seemingly straightforward language it ranged from short, easily digested passages of the Heian-style idiom that was tortuous for students in its mother lode, *The Tale of Genji*, to crisp pronouncements in the Sinified vernacular commonly used for admonitions or religious tracts. *Tsurezuregusa* covered all manner of topics, a useful quality for a primer in popular education, while presenting historical names, both native and continental, that any educator would be more likely to want to impart to his pupils than the monikers of fictional characters. It is little wonder that even to this day it is a flagship work in early literary (not to mention moral) training.

Just what motivated the composition of *Tsurezuregusa* in the early to mid-fourteenth century may never be known, but the theory that it was produced to educate a certain prince serves as a comment on its significance in education since the seventeenth century. Today, selected episodes by Kenkō (c. 1283–c. 1352) are a fixture in textbooks for Japanese middle school and beyond. *Tsurezuregusa* also ranks high on many syllabi crafted to introduce Asian writing and thought in Western classrooms.[1] Educators hold it up as an eminently sensible guide for living a disciplined life, fleshing the text out through examples relevant to contemporary living. Even in such popular culture forms as spy novels or comic book renditions, the ambiance of a textbook survives, as scholars link up with comic artists to put a new spin on historical details.[2]

Spurred on in part at least by the continual focus of the teaching elite on why the text is important to latter-day readers, members of the literary establishment have renewed Kenkō for modern times—he was taken as a forerunner of the critical enterprise by Kobayashi Hideo, and is still a model for followers of the contemplative mode, such as the prolific nun Setouchi Jakuchō. Essayists and historians alike identify readily with Kenkō the paragon of taste, the brilliant stylist, or the Wordsworthian recluse, as early Western supporters saw him. Both in and out of Japan a primary function of *Tsurezuregusa* in the canon has been to provide exemplary nuggets of Japanese aesthetic wisdom, or wisdom that is aesthetic.[3] Excerpters need not apologize for the packaging of handy fragments, since these are considered the essence of the work. It has been treated as the perfect piece of literature for demonstrating Japan's flashes of genius, and the ideal context for piecemeal study of elements that contributed to the national heritage, yet this has not hindered attempts to analyze the text in total. Thus the work's fragmentary nature has become a utility, now an excuse for partial explications, now a challenge to uncovering the wholeness of its artistry.

Whether at the hands of educators or imitators, the highbrow or the shamelessly popular, this modern treatment is invariably carried out in terms of the generic category *zuihitsu*, literally "following the brush," which is generally presented as a typical native mode of miscellaneous writing with a long history. Precursors include the tenth-century *Makura no sōshi* (The Pillow Book, late 10th c.) of Sei Shōnagon and, less often, the early thirteenth century *Hōjōki* (Account of My Hut) by Kamo no Chōmei (1155–1216). This literary history was not, however, constructed until the modern period—for two centuries after its composition *Tsurezuregusa* was barely read at all, let alone read as zuihitsu. My purpose here is to examine the process by which the current canonical view of *Tsurezuregusa*, with its primarily aesthetic and formal thrust, emerged from a markedly different early modern process of canonization. The first half of the essay will discuss the discovery of the text by pedagogues, then its spread to broad public notice through the works of other writers, and finally debates over content, which eventually ended in a compromise view of *Tsurezuregusa* as transcendent masterpiece that speaks to human existence in an artful way. In the second half, I will take up the emergence of attention to the author Kenkō, concluding with an assessment of the part that gender has played in the formation of this corner of the canon.

LECTURES, COMMENTARIES, AND NEW AUDIENCES

Before the seventeenth century, *Tsurezuregusa* (composed during the first half of the fourteenth century) had drawn the attention of various camps. It had served as a resource for poet-priests writing on versification or the theme of impermanence, for warriors and merchants seeking to mold the behavior of their followers, for storytellers building layers of allusion into their repertoire, and for those Buddhist monks who were willing to use a secular source to echo their teachings. Each of those prior receptions, however, focused on limited portions of what was, after all, a work of great variety, and thus do not constitute attempts to argue for its canonization. Annotations of the whole are not extant from this early period; if they existed, it is likely they were the product of such traditional elites as the warrior-poet Hosokawa Yūsai (1534–1610), who described *Tsurezuregusa* as "a friend in my old age," or the noble Nakano'in Michikatsu (1556–1610).[4] It was only around the Keichō era (1596–1615) that *Tsurezuregusa* came before a new and wider audience, most significantly via lectures by Michikatsu's disciple, the poet Matsunaga Teitoku (1571–1653). Teitoku's reluctant entry into this endeavor signaled a new era of pedagogy with lasting consequences for an inheritance of texts that up until then had only slowly been finding new audiences.[5] Secondary sources seem to delight in noting that Teitoku—son of a linked verse (*renga*) poet and from an important warrior family, but not a member of the nobility—was thirty-three years of age when he went against the established practice of private transmission, urged on by his friend, the ambitious Neo-Confucian Hayashi Razan (or Dōshun, 1583–1657), a stripling of twenty-one.[6] Listeners at Teitoku's lectures were mostly young townsmen from the Shimogyō (Lower Capital) area of Kyoto who had never before been party to the transmission of such texts, and who had requested his teaching.[7] Razan was himself lecturing on his new annotations to the Confucian *Analects*, which would be only a part of his influential scholarship. Teitoku later apologized for his youthful indiscretion, which had angered his teacher Michikatsu. *Taionki* (A Record of Favors Received, c. 1645) contains Teitoku's account of his sadness whenever he recalls Michikatsu's refusal to make a gross expression of his anger.[8] In the nearly half a century between his sharing of what had been private knowledge and these reflections on his teacher, Teitoku was witness to an increasing circulation of texts and a trend toward printed commentary that would soon become a flood.

Razan's apologies, as reflected in his commentary *Tsurezuregusa nozuchi* (*Tsurezuregusa* Field Hammer, written in 1621 but not printed until 1667) were of a different order. He expresses no compunction about having transmitted intellectual property that had belonged to the nobility, but he does express ambivalence about the subject of his labors, a vernacular work that appears as a mere chicken in the wake of his thorough dispatching of it, done as with a knife meant for carving up an ox.[9] In his struggle to make the text a vehicle for spreading Neo-Confucian teachings, Razan does not necessarily hide or excise the contradictions in the text, but he does mold and pad it, as he says, "bringing in words of the Confucian classics, using Japanese proverbs to explain things, writing in syllabary" (as opposed to characters).[10] According to Razan's preface to *Nozuchi*, the first virtue of *Tsurezuregusa* as vernacular classic is the sex of the author:

> A visitor of mine said: "Most things produced in the world that are called *monogatari* (tales) or *sōshi* (books in Japanese) come from the hands of women. For this reason their language is full of flattery and strained laughter; they show no principles of instruction or admonition. One sees only attractively made-up forms, and does not hear a bold, manly style. One is troubled by their busyness, lost in their complexity. They run to the vulgar, or degenerate into lies. All of them are this way. The only exceptions are Ki no Tsurayuki's preface to *Kokinwakashū* and his *Tosa Diary*. These are quite a different matter than the speech of women. Even though it is not long after Ki no Tsurayuki writes until we find another man writing, there is only one, this Kenkō." In my spare time I have happened to look at *Tsurezuregusa*. I have drawn upon my guest's words in composing this.[11]

Razan's implicit dilemma as a Neo-Confucian pedagogue was that works in the so-called "women's style" *kana* syllabary were the easiest vehicle by which Japanese could learn to read, but the unfortunate fact was that females had written most of the kana masterpieces. On the other hand, Razan could comfortably praise Kenkō, a male author, and Tsurayuki, the tenth century reviver of the waka poetic tradition via the *Kokinshū*, who only *posed* as a woman when he wrote the first known vernacular journal, *Tosa Diary*. Near the end of his text, Razan admits that *Tsurezuregusa* copies the style of *The*

Pillow Book and *The Tale of Genji*, but is quick to note that Kenkō studied Tendai Buddhism, seemed familiar with Taoism, despised the world, and understood life, death, and change. Razan betrays an awareness of the typical strengths of vernacular writing, as he goes on to say that "Kenkō felt the passage of time, depicted the seasons, spoke of male and female love, and expressed his own feelings."[12] But for Razan and the early Edo Neo-Confucianists in general, literature only had meaning when it was made useful in everyday life and brought in line with the study of real things.[13] Any such utility in women's writings was overshadowed by latent female faults. It was important to avoid displaying female writers before the young Neo-Confucians and physicians, townsmen, and samurai who formed the lecture-hungry public. *Taiheiki* (Record of the Great Peace, 1338) and Razan's new annotations to the *Analects*, both subjects of Teitoku's lectures during the same period, fulfilled this requirement. Teitoku also spoke on *Hyakunin isshu*, which included women among the "one hundred poets, one verse each," but was edited by the appropriately gendered male Fujiwara Teika (1162–1241).

What evidence we have of Teitoku's lectures, *Nagusamigusa* (Comforting Leaves), is a collection of students' notes that was not compiled until 1652, a half century after the oral presentation. Teitoku approved them and wrote an epilogue, but it is difficult to ascertain how closely they reflect his talks of almost fifty years before.[14] At the end of his comments, Teitoku likes to gush about the wonder of it all, recommend a particular section to youth, or specify its usefulness. Teitoku's view of *Tsurezuregusa* as a handbook of utilitarian lessons comes from *Nagusamigusa*'s origin in lectures, as does his habit of referring to recent people and activities in the course of explication, including the military leaders Oda Nobunaga (1534–1582), Toyotomi Hideyoshi (1536–1598), and the tea master Furuta Oribe (1543–1615).[15] Although the notes are otherwise of no special interest, Teitoku's encapsulations of the *taii*, the "greater meaning" or main point of each segment, are unique and lead Donald Keene to proclaim that *Nagusamigusa* "ranks among the best commentaries of the Tokugawa period, because it goes beyond explaining the meanings of isolated words in the traditional manner and reveals an excellent understanding of the intrinsic value of the work."[16]

The effect of Teitoku's gesture of bringing the text to a wider public is seen clearly in the high demand for material on *Tsurezuregusa* throughout the seventeenth century. It was probably the catalyst for publication of the first extant full-length commentary, *Tsurezuregusa Jumyō'in shō* (Jumyō'in's *Tsurezuregusa* Treatise, 1604), authored by the physician Hata Sōha (1550–

1607), also known by his Buddhist names Jumyō'in or Ritsuan Hōin.[17] The annotations of *Jumyō-in shō* were printed without the original text of *Tsurezuregusa*, indicating that the readership was probably upper-class individuals who had access to manuscript copies.[18] In about 1648 Aoki Sōko wrote what would become the single most widely distributed book of annotations, the *Tettsui* (Iron Hammer), a handbook for lectures that extracted the gist of *Jumyō'in shō* and Razan's *Nozuchi*.[19] Many copies exist with their owner's notes crammed into the margins, including a set by the priest-scholar Keichū (1640–1701).[20] *Tettsui*, and by extension the enduring rage for expert commentary, were parodied in *Yoshiwara shittsui* (*shittsui* means "lose" or "sink in people's estimation"), a 1674 guidebook to women of the pleasure quarters (*yūjo hyōbanki*), in this case those in Edo's Yoshiwara district.[21] Publishers and others in the business of promoting the pleasure quarters wanted this information to seem as important as any classic.

Perhaps it is a measure of the potency that *Tsurezuregusa* enjoyed among commoners that some of the elite attempted to reassert their authority over it. Teitoku is given credit for reestablishing a secret tradition around the text with the so-called Three Important Matters (*san ko no daiji*).[22] By mimicking the transmission of esoteric points about the *Kokinshū* poetry anthology found in the *Kokindenju* (secret transmission of the *Kokinshū*), Teitoku reclaimed *Tsurezuregusa* as a court-related icon whose full meaning was inaccessible without an informant. According to some interpreters, this remystification was motivated by Teitoku's insecurity as a non-noble and by the reaction to the horror felt by the nobility at what he had wrought through this potentially democratizing move of extending access to one and all.[23] The "important matters" concerned details of little consequence. The third, for example, was *shiro-ururi*, a nonsense epithet applied to a priest by the eccentric abbot Jōshin sōzu of the Shinjō-in, whose story appears in Section 60:

> Upon seeing a certain holy man, this abbot gave him the name "Shiro-ururi." "What's that mean?" someone asked, to which the abbot replied, "I've never heard of such a thing myself, but if it did exist, it would look like this holy man's face."[24]

The explication of this "important matter" basically says there is nothing worth discussing here.[25] Seven Oral Secrets (*nana ko no hiji*) also came into being at some point, as those who had lost control of *Tsurezuregusa* tried to reassert themselves by claiming possession of keys that unlocked the obscurities of the text.[26]

Whatever the arguments, there was clearly a consensus throughout the Tokugawa period that *Tsurezuregusa* was worth reading. For early seventeenth-century circles, it was not only instrumental in education for its linguistic qualities, it also conveyed an idealized version of the past from an elite and conservative viewpoint. Its utility was enhanced by the fact that it brought in representations from outside the court as well. Unlike other specimens of the high tradition, its purview extended to folk tales and the contributions of the warrior class, making *Tsurezuregusa* an ideal text for a pedagogical practice that aimed beyond the traditional audience for literature. Although their views of the proper audience for *Tsurezuregusa* differed, both the secret transmitters and the open lecturers held similar beliefs in the value of the text as a repository of tradition.

PARODIES, IMITATIONS, AND VARIATIONS

Full-scale imitations of *Tsurezuregusa*, some tending toward parody, others fostering didactic views, began as early as 1599 and became increasingly popular as the text was taught to the public.[27] Aspects of Kenkō's manner of writing—terse, desultory, and classicized—spread through these imitations. A good example is *Inu tsurezure* (Mongrel *Tsurezuregusa*), a homoerotic text (a significant mode in Tokugawa literature) by Konoe Nobuhiro (1599–1649) that exploits the dogmatic capabilities of some *Tsurezuregusa* diction to instruct youths in the niceties of sexual relationships.[28] In 1660 Asai Ryōi (1612?–1691) wrote *Kashōki hyōban* (Evaluation of the Laughable Record), a commentary that pointed out the frequent allusions to *Tsurezuregusa* in Nyoraishi's (1603?-1674) *Kashōki* (Laughable Record, 1642), a *kanazōshi* that criticized society and the economic state of the country. Such repetitions and recastings of didactic snippets from *Tsurezuregusa* helped to set the era's understanding of the text. The text, in turn, provided an intellectual pedigree for timely formulations that could be readily appreciated. After Asai's commentary appeared, Nyoraishi became well known and was admitted to *daimyō* and *hatamoto* (bannermen) houses, thus gaining a new class of patron.

It was typical in the Edo period for books whose titles ended in "*kusa*" or "*gusa*" to be in the manner of Kenkō, as in the following examples.[29] *Hisomegusa* (Chatterings), alternatively called *Ōmu shin Tsurezuregusa* (The Parrot's New *Tsurezuregusa*, 1645), is close in tone to *Tsurezuregusa* in its mixture of topics, which include nature, society, ethics, morality, custom, and

the arts. The anonymous *Kuyamigusa* (Seeds of Regret, 1647) consists of
116 passages, each of which ends with a summation of what was regrettable
in the anecdote, warning youth away from such conduct. *Nigiwaigusa*
(Essays in Activity or Prosperity, 1682), by Sano Shōeki (1607–1691), opens
with a long preface modeled on its forerunner and covers many subjects,
primarily the arts and especially ritual tea, as well as salient items in
Tsurezuregusa.[30]

The various *kanazōshi* that borrowed elements of style from *Tsurezuregusa*
frequently focused on a single issue. For example, *Muyūshū* (Collection of
Travels in Dreams, 1650), at one time attributed to Kamo no Chōmei, is
largely Buddhist in outlook, but unlike many other kanazōshi it is not
bound to the beliefs of a single sect; it is said to combine an awareness of impermanence with an affirmation of life.[31] Groups who drew on *Tsurezuregusa*
for prestige or to demonstrate how their creed meshed with the new classic
ranged across the spectrum of society, even to the practitioners of ritual tea,
who had their own *Chajin Tsurezuregusa* (*Tsurezuregusa* for Men of Tea,
printed 1836). This text preserves the rhetoric and flow of the fourteenth-
century language while wittily replacing topics in the original text with those
on utensils, rules, and past masters of tea. The anonymous transmutation
features such epithets as "Even if a person is magnificent in every way, if he
does not know tea, it is disappointing, like a famous tea bowl without a bottom."[32] Kenkō's disappointment, expressed in his third section via an analogy to a sake cup without a bottom, was reserved for men who did not understand love.[33]

The early modern reception of *Tsurezuregusa* included theatrical variations as well. A number of *yōkyoku* (nō libretti) remain, ranging from the
story of the radish soldiers (*tsuchi ōne*) to one that features "the cultured
recluse of Narabigaoka," where Kenkō is said to have had a hermitage and
buried his mother. The play *Shiro-ururi* was built around one of the indeci-
pherable words in *Tsurezuregusa* mentioned earlier and incorporates an explication.[34] Chikamatsu Monzaemon (1653–1724) gave his audiences *Kenkō
hōshi monomiguruma*, "Priest Kenkō's Sight-seeing Cart," at the Takemoto-
za theater in Osaka, by 1710. His Kenkō makes the proper Buddhist choices
in the end, but not before the text is used to illustrate an incredible series of
dramatic and romantic entanglements.[35]

During the eighteenth century, as both literary model and object of parody, *Tsurezuregusa* became the most influential work of literature in terms of
style.[36] It provided a handbook of written models, from the Heian classical
style of *Genji* to the Sinified vernacular of religious tracts. Writers such as

Ihara Saikaku (1642–1693) also found inspiration there, as his posthumously issued parody, *Zoku tsurezure* (Vulgar *Tsurezuregusa*), demonstrates. *Shin Yoshiwara tsunezunegusa* (New Yoshiwara Constancy) of 1689 is a double-level parody, with Isogai Sutewaka's text and "annotations" by Yonosuke (Saikaku's alias).[37] The eighteenth century was an age of parodies that exploited the image of Kenkō as man of the world and possessor of *sui*, the age's ultimate sense of taste, which guided the denizens of the gay quarters. These treatments manifest a dual attitude—embracing the familiar Kenkō on whom all had been weaned, but rejecting righteous associations by which Kenkō was constructed as an orthodox locus of truth. For example, in the farcical *Ressenden* (Biography of the Sages, published 1763), Kenkō runs a house of assignation that Confucius's envoy Shiro (Tzu-lu) visits while investigating the state of leisure opportunities in Japan.[38] Such titles as "*Tsurezuregusa* in the Village of Love" (*Irozato Tsurezuregusa*), "*Tsurezuregusa* in Modern Form" (*Tsurezure imayō sugata*, 1721), "Courtesan's *Tsurezuregusa*" (*Keisei Tsurezuregusa*, 1737), "*Tsurezuregusa* River of Chic" (*Tsurezure sui ga kawa*, 1783, by Enkō hōshi, "the Priest who loves love"), "Puppy *Tsurezuregusa*" (*Koinu Tsurezuregusa*, 1789–1800, by Santō Kyōden), and "Monster *Tsurezuregusa*" (*Kaibutsu Tsurezuregusa*, also by Santō Kyōden) give a sense of what this literature was like.[39] The list of authors who dipped into *Tsurezuregusa* for allusions is a who's who of premodern literati. Even the scholar of things Western and *gesaku* pioneer Hiraga Gennai (1728–1779) wrote a "New *Tsurezuregusa*" (*Shin Tsurezuregusa*).[40] While *Tsurezuregusa* was clearly a prose model and springboard for many writers, it bears remembering that the wildest parodies were (and to this day still are) likely to incorporate explanations and viewpoints that originated in pedagogical contexts. Even as the text was read by more and more people of divergent classes, most came to it through the presentations of commentaries and lectures, which they seemed to regard as natural extensions of Kenkō's words. Both commentarial and parodical practice were, therefore, reflective of the esteem in which the text was held.

TSUREZUREGUSA AS SCRIPTURE: STRUGGLES FOR A SINGLE MEANING

Perhaps because of its surface ease and appeal, commentaries past and present often seem to present *Tsurezuregusa* as the gateway to the Japanese classical universe, if not its center. Such glorification of *Tsurezuregusa*, regardless of whether it was justified, colored the serious discourse around the text, particularly in the Tokugawa period. Analysts and disseminators of every stripe share exegetical assumptions that usually govern the treatment of scripture and canon. John B. Henderson identifies these in his study of Confucian and various other commentary traditions, *Scripture, Canon, and Commentary: A Comparison of Confucian and Western Exegesis*. To borrow Henderson's descriptions, which aptly characterize much of the thrust of these commentaries, many authors write from the perspective that *Tsurezuregusa* was "comprehensive and all-encompassing, containing all significant knowledge or truth." By studying this one book, a youth could acquire the sum of human values. His teacher could use it as a locus for displaying other knowledge. The text was, as Henderson puts it and as diverse handlers clearly believed, thought "well-ordered and coherent, arranged according to some logical, cosmological, or pedagogical principles" (even though these differed in the eyes of each individual). Annotations proceeded from the assumption that it was "self-consistent," with any internal contradictions "only apparent." And it was held to be "moral" and "profound," with "nothing superfluous or insignificant" between its covers.[41] It was in this context that Japanese dubbed *Tsurezuregusa* the "*Analects* of our country," Confucius' rival.[42]

In point of fact, *Tsurezuregusa* has a rich, arguably inconsistent content, but as Henderson observes, commentarial strategies arise across all traditions to deal with such contrary manifestations in canonical works. A notable trend in readings was to explain the text's "essence" through a single system of thought, often Buddhism or Confucianism, with Taoism or native Shinto as a third possibility. Buddhist interpretations had a long and active history. *Tsurezuregusa sankō* (published 1678), which records the 1674 lectures of Ekū (1643–1691), a priest of Jōfukuji in Kii, draws heavily on a tradition (transmitted from the early sixteenth-century monk Sonkai) of reading *Tsurezuregusa* as a reflection of Tendai teachings.[43] Katō Bansai (1621–1674), in his *Tsurezuregusa shō* of 1661, through a highly original analysis, focuses on the teachings of the Tendai text *Mo-ho chih-kuan*, or *Maka shikan* (The Great Calming and Contemplation) of Chih-i (538–597). In his most sweeping assessment, Bansai, a priest with training in *haikai* from Hosokawa Yūsai and Matsunaga Teitoku, remarks that the purpose of *Tsurezuregusa* is "to make the way of Tendai *maka shikan* approachable."[44] Bansai, who compares the expression of Buddhist teachings in the text to the translation of Sanskrit sutras into Chinese, elevates the *tsurezure* of the title to the embodiment of "absolute *shikan*," the sign of Kenkō's realization of "concentration and insight" or "calming and contemplation."[45]

From Bansai's time on there was a tendency among commentators to define *tsurezure* not as "idleness" or "tedium," its meaning in Heian women's texts, but as a more positive detachment, a state into which Kenkō willfully entered in order to meditate on the world. Bansai does not deny the presence of other ideas in *Tsurezuregusa*, however. He credits the inclusion of all paths (including the Neo-Confucianism that Jumyō'in and Razan had heralded) as the reason the text came to be useful in his century.[46] Although Tendai Buddhism was evidently Kenkō's primary allegiance, many seventeenth-century seekers of textual rationality were chagrined by Bansai's *shikan* interpretation. Okanishi Ichū (1639–1711), an Osaka physician and Danrin school haikai theoretician who studied with Nishiyama Sōin (1605–1682), singles out Bansai for special notice in his *Tsurezuregusa jikige* (*Tsurezuregusa* Explained Directly, 1686) as the most ridiculously overstated among the promoters of the mystic approach to the text. In a tone of distress he writes:

> The title of this book is similar to those for the chapters of the *Analects* and *Mencius*. The first word of the text is taken as the title of the whole. There are many troublesome explanations besides this [correct] one. In particular, the proposal in Bansai's [*Tsurezuregusa shō*] treatise for the ten meanings of *tsurezure* in the title is ridiculous. You should not accept it for a minute.[47]

Even in arguing that the title has no particular meaning, however, Ichū invokes the Chinese classics for comparison.

An opposing branch of thought is represented by *Tsurezuregusa kuge* (*Tsurezuregusa* Phrases Explained, 1661), by Takashina Yōjun (active ca. 1660). Known as a Confucianist reading, it encapsulates the text by stating: "Generally it starts with [the style of] the two women Sei and Murasaki, but it is of a truer blue than they are; Tendai teachings are the root, Lao tzu and Chuang tzu the leaves and branches."[48] Like Bansai, Yōjun does not ignore the variety of the text, but his statement that Kenkō outdoes Sei Shōnagon and Murasaki Shikibu at their own game reflects the status of *Tsurezuregusa* among male Neo-Confucian readers, unchanged since Razan's day.

Tsurezuregusa mondanshō (*Tsurezuregusa* in Paragraphs), the 1667 compendium of the haikai poet and classical scholar Kitamura Kigin (1624–1705), culls the work of predecessors of all persuasions and also contains the first attempt at a theory concerning the date of the original.[49] The writings of seventeenth-century Japanese indicate that the most charged battle for *Tsurezuregusa* occurred over which of the three teachings—Buddhism, Confucianism, and Taoism in the main, but also Shinto for some—was paramount in its pages. Kigin, who accepts the presence of gods, Buddhas, the

Confucian path, and Taoism as a product of the Japanese outlook (*Nihon no fūgi*), asserts that "viewing it as only Confucian, only Buddhist, or only Taoist and speaking of it just in the terms one prefers is at odds with Kenkō's intention."[50] This caveat reflects the fact that many did treat it just that way. Nanbu Sōju (d. 1688), a Neo-Confucianist with the Toyama domain, assessed the debate over the core teaching this way in his *Tsurezuregusa genkai* (Colloquial Explanation of *Tsurezuregusa*, ca. 1669):

> When Buddhists read it, they put it all down to Buddhism; when Confucianists lecture on it, they take it as entirely meaning the Five Virtues; poets manage to call it the Way of Poetry by elaborating on the flowery diction. None of this is correct. Kenkō's purpose is to take whatever will be of benefit to people from any of the teachings, and to express his own meaning with them.[51]

While the emphasis here is still on *Tsurezuregusa* as a didactic work, Sōju, struggling against readings that were holistic but frequently tendentious, cuts away the differences in creeds to try applying the text directly to life. In the cursory preface to the aforementioned *Tsurezuregusa Jumyō'in shō*, Hata Sōha remarks that Kenkō's Way combined Confucianism, Buddhism, and Taoism.[52] This intuition was often cited by commentators who favored the unity of the three teachings, or *sankyō itchi*, as the raison d'être of the text. Sōju's *Tsurezuregusa genkai* continues: "Thus he grasps the three teachings as one, and in the last analysis breaks through the thought of human existence as eternal, sees the rule of changeless changing and composes this book."[53] As Shimizu Shunryū, a Neo-Confucianist and haikai poet (b. 1626), opines in his *Tsurezuregusa shinchū* (New Annotations, 1667), "When I consider closely the entirety of this book, Buddhist concentration and insight form the bones, Taoism the meat, *The Changes* and the *Spring and Autumn Annals* the skin."[54] The corporeal metaphor illustrates neatly seventeenth-century readers' attempts to grasp the totality of the work, and to make its disparate parts function together.[55] This imperative to unify did not fade until the eighteenth century, when the text was recognized as a zuihitsu, or miscellany that "follows the brush."

In the latter part of the seventeenth century, commentaries gradually evolved away from the single-minded concern to use the text for instruction of values. For example, in his *Tsurezuregusa taizen* (The Complete *Tsurezuregusa*, 1677), Takada Munekata (active ca. 1675) poses the question of whether Taoism is vital to the text since in Section 13 Kenkō chooses Lao-tzu and Chuang-tzu as representatives of the "unknown friends of the past" that he likes to get to know through books. Takada writes in reply that "we should see this as meaning only that he enjoys the flavor of their prose and the excellence of their views. It is not that his mind is drawn to Taoism and he wishes to teach it to others."[56] He rejects didacticism in his explications, instead referring to Kenkō's assertions and their contradictions as "the custom of such a book" (*kore sōshi no narai*).[57] Like Kigin before him, Takada rejects various "isms" in an attempt to get closer to the literary roots of the text and establish why it is enjoyable.

It is fairly simple to organize a retrospective of *Tsurezuregusa* interpretations so long as didactic views predominate, with each commentator bent on clarifying his relation to the opinion of others. From the late seventeenth century this story becomes less informative, or at least less representative, as the impulse for new commentaries was growing weak. It was a time for summing up, organizing, and reflecting on the overall message of what had come before. Asaga Sansei's (active late seventeenth century) *Tsurezuregusa shoshō taisei* (Great Compendium of Various Writings on *Tsurezuregusa*, 1688) was the first book to use subtitles for the sections and a table of contents (accoutrements that we expect as a matter of course in modern editions).[58] Kanju (active early eighteenth century), who wrote the longest of the extant biographies, *Kenkō shokoku monogatari* (Tale of Kenkō in the Provinces, 1706), also put together *Tsurezuregusa shūsetsu* (Collected Explications of *Tsurezuregusa*, 1701). In this compilation of the best from among twenty-one commentaries available up to that time, Kanju calls for an end to the purely didactic reception apparent in many of them, and advocates acceptance of whatever is there in the text (that is, of the individual's aesthetic responses to it).

> There is a tendency to see the meaning of each section as a lesson. Such theories are difficult to believe. Each should be seen as it is, the lessons as lessons, the random comments as random comments, the feelings of love as feelings of love.[59]

Readers everywhere seemed oppressed by the sage that Kenkō had been made out to be, and they called for an end to the sentential superstructure erected around the text. According to Ise Sadatake (1717–1784), the author would have been shocked at how seriously Tokugawa readers took him: "That *Tsurezuregusa* would be revered as a sage classic of wise commentary and treated as a book of admonitions for people is something Kenkō never would have imagined."[60]

A final plea for a nondidactic reading comes from Kagami Shikō (1665–1731), whose *Tsurezure no san* (In Praise of *Tsurezuregusa*, 1711) claims to convey the views of his teacher Bashō.[61] The notions that Kenkō was fond of Taoism and wrote in order to instruct his readership are firmly rejected, ridiculed even, in the dialogue that introduces the main points of the commentary. Instead, Shikō stressed Kenkō's literary interests, experimented with formal categorizations of *Tsurezuregusa* fragments, and included Kenkō in his two prose collections:[62] his *Honchō bunkan* (Mirror of Literature in our Country, 1718), presents the third segment of *Tsurezuregusa* as a representative Japanese prose-poem, entitled "Rhapsody on Sensuality" ("Kōshoku no fu"), after Chinese terminology, and *Wakan bunsō* (Japanese and Chinese Belles Lettres, 1727) inserts Section 137 under the title "Rhapsody on Moon and Flowers."[63]

Lest we conclude, however, that efforts to learn something besides literary style from the text had been thoroughly supplanted, we should note that the eighteenth century saw the publication of an edition that stressed "lessons for women," *Jokun Tsurezuregusa* (1702). *Tsurezuregusa* also became a requisite for a bride's trousseau.[64] Ishida Baigan (1685–1744), leader of Shingaku (School of the Mind), put *Tsurezuregusa* on his lecture list along with the Chinese classics, and his followers kept up the trend.[65] Kangaku (Chinese studies) scholar Hattori Nankaku (1683–1759) inserted a Chinese translation of Section 31, on the writing of a letter to a friend after snow, into his biographical miscellany *Daitō seigo* (Stories of East Asia, 1750).[66] What appears generally to be a development away from didactic uses after the seventeenth century reveals as well a perpetuation of the edifying function, congruent with the text's role as a primer for model sentences, historical episodes, moral teachings, and so on. Responses to *Tsurezuregusa* ran throughout the Tokugawa period in a glorious ebb and flow, and often a clash, of claims to teach the text, enshrine the text, or steal the text. Our modern inheritance is not without a sediment from this history, if only in the form of a suspicious attitude toward didactic approaches and a concern to properly appreciate the work's aesthetic essence.

ATTACKS ON TSUREZUREGUSA

It would seem that Kenkō was the darling of the age, adopted by everyone (however much opposed their purposes were), but there was an occasional voice of dissent. The first of these was *Tsurezuregusa modoki hyōban* (Parodic Evaluation of *Tsurezuregusa*, published 1672).[67] In its fictional narrative, a man from Chikuzen comes to Edo, the big city, and gets a letter from home telling him about Kenkō. Hearing that one Shōbara nyūdō, a lay priest, has a copy of *Nozuchi*, the man from Chikuzen goes to ask for instruction, archly parodying *Tsurezuregusa* as a near-religious icon. The priest warns the man that this book will not be good for him, but they make arrangements for lessons. What follows is a relentless attack on Kenkō, with illustrative vignettes drawn from the priest Shōbara's wide travels in China, India, and Thailand. The attack begins by lambasting one of *Tsurezuregusa*'s "seven articles of self-praise," an episode in which Kenkō goes to a Buddhist lecture at Senbon and is approached by a heavily perfumed woman. Kenkō leaves the hall, and later finds out that there had been a plot to tempt him, which he praises himself for having avoided. Shōbara nyūdō chalks this up to Kenkō's self-conceit and love of display, arguing that people would never have arranged this test of his willpower had he not had a reputation for violating his priestly vows with the opposite sex. A real practitioner of the Way would not have reacted to this ploy at all, the priest adds. Then he tells a story to illustrate his point.

> Recently at Arima in Chikuzen at a lecture with the high and the low in attendance there was a man who became pale and seemed about to die. When people asked him how he felt, he replied in a small voice that his illness was acting up. They told him to leave if that was the case, but he countered "If I go it will disturb many people." So he bore it and left after the lecture was over; he went home, and died. Since he had been on the verge of death, it was difficult for him, but he did not leave. Why did Kenkō have to interfere with the lecture because a woman drew close to him?[68]

In succeeding passages Shōbara uses Kenkō against himself as well, taking *Tsurezuregusa*'s comments on evanescence at the Kamo horse races and the devotion to the Way shown by Priest Tōren, as signs that Kenkō should have known better than to behave as he claims to have at Senbon.[69] As we shall see, it is not far from *Tsurezuregusa modoki hyōban*'s sacrilegious roast to the images of Kenkō the dilettante recluse that flood the next century.[70]

THE FIGURE OF THE AUTHOR

Biographies of Kenkō were comparatively late to blossom, probably because what was known of his life did not suit the aims of educators. The most trusted sources, such as *Taiheiki*, contained outrageous evidence of a compromised existence. (Indeed, the modern scholar Shimamoto Shōichi proposes that an affirmative attitude toward sex was one of the aspects of *Tsurezuregusa* that ordinary people found endearing.)[71] *Taiheiki* was, like most Japanese historical tales, accepted as accurate history. In one episode, Kenkō writes a love letter on behalf of Kō no Moronao to the wife of En'ya Hōgan (Takasada, d. 1338).[72] Not only is Kenkō's image besmirched by this service for a violent warrior—the two did historically have dealings, even if the letter incident is fictional—the epistle does not achieve its intended ends with the lady. Kenkō's biographers, especially when writing to introduce *Tsurezuregusa*, were forced to explain, excuse, or as they often did, cover up this double failing. Fukakusa Gensei (1623–1668)'s *Fusō in'itsuden* (Biographies of Japanese Recluses, 1664), for example, has a sketch of Kenkō that sets the tone for portrayals based on his poetry collection, which emphasize the elegance of his life.[73]

The period of serious depictions was soon to end, however. Kurata Shōeki's *Kenkō denki* (Biography of Kenkō, 1685) was the last biography to be based on substantiated information. At some point as early as 1673, apocryphal portions of Tōin Kinkata's (1291–1360) diary *Entairyaku* (named after an abbreviation of one of Kinkata's titles) circulated. Since the authentic *Entairyaku* was the personal record of a noble who had associated with Kenkō during their lifetimes, it was seen as a solid biographical source, and spurious portions were especially potent in shaping the Kenkō legend. Here we see Kenkō shooting some pesky birds, which turn into foxes; hopelessly in love with one Chūgū no Koben, daughter of the governor of Iga; lecturing to the nobility on the imperial poetry collection *Shinkokinshū*; performing the Amidist *nenbutsu* chant with his contemporary Ton'a and giving gruel to the poor; and dying of illness (having refused medicine) in Iga after a visit from the noble Nijō Yoshimoto.[74] All of this contributed to the humanity of Kenkō, implying that he had firsthand knowledge of martial arts, love, and priestly compassion, as well as good standing vis-à-vis the nobility. Such details allowed interesting narratives to be created and encouraged unified biographical readings of *Tsurezuregusa*.

In Kenkō's case, several pluses outweighed his peccadilloes. He was a master of the court tradition, a professional not only in waka, but also in ritual and ceremony (*yūsoku kojitsu*). Helpfully, his perspective was that of an heir, not a founder. In addition to presenting things in a less recondite version than say, the Buddhistic treatises of a Fujiwara no Shunzei, Kenkō was himself a model for the kind of activity Tokugawa educators wished to inculcate, namely the study of the past. In other ways Kenkō, known in the Edo period as Kenkō hōshi [priest], was anomalous, but conveniently so. The motive for his holy orders was in question, for he maintained his ties with society while being a "priest." The advantage came in that as a *hōshi* he was a figure of spiritual authority, but not a purely religious icon with built-in sectarian barriers. The political affiliations of Yoshida no Kenkō, as some Edo materials call him, were sufficiently unattested that biographers could invent a genealogy. And invent it they did. The Yoshida moniker, derived from his family background (the Urabe had hereditary posts at the Yoshida shrine) but not, as was often averred, from any record of his residence, associated him with Yoshida hill, a site in northeast Kyoto that could be construed as a connection with the Yoshida Shintō sect, or simply taken as a sign of reclusion in the capital.[75] Tales of Kenkō the spy for the restoration government of Emperor Go Daigo could be used to put a loyalist spin on his work for the Northern Court line during the Nanbokuchō (Southern and Northern Court) period (1336–92).[76]

GENDER AND GENRE

The genre category *zuihitsu* is central to almost all present accounts of *Tsurezuregusa*. The thesis that Kenkō wrote whatever popped into his head has come to have extraordinary utility for moderns who are uncomfortable with the contradictions or lack of organization in the text. Until the late Tokugawa, however, the term zuihitsu was reserved primarily for Sinified compendia with scant literary flavor such as *Enpekiken* zuihitsu, the miscellany of Kurokawa Dōyū (a.k.a. Enpekiken, 1620s–1691), edited by Nanba Sōken in 1756. *Tsurezuregusa* had been linked to the category in the seventeenth century, but only by a brief comparison to continental works.[77] Although Japanese writers, the commentator Okanishi Ichū with his *Ichiji zuihitsu* (Zuihitsu of a Moment, 1683) among them, had begun to indulge a fancy for vernacular works they termed zuihitsu, these were still seen as following the Chinese style of encyclopedic compilations. Hence the lineage of miscellany that begins with *The Pillow Book* and pairs it with *Tsurezuregusa* is an anachronistic construction of the type often and necessarily propagated by literary histories. The remainder of this essay will focus on the actual—and undeniably significant—relationship between these works in the Tokugawa period and earlier.

One of the few who took exception to the Tokugawa promotion of *Tsurezuregusa* was the *kokugaku* (nativist learning) scholar Motoori Norinaga (1730–1801), who disliked its Sinified air of masculinity and Buddhist pessimism. Yet it was his fellow nativists who catalyzed the transformation of this text into the chief exemplar of the desultory zuihitsu form. As defined by Ishiwara Masaakira (d. 1821) in his *Nennen zuihitsu* (Year by Year Zuihitsu, 1801–1805), "a zuihitsu is something in which you write down things you have seen and heard, said or thought, the useless and the serious alike as they come to you."[78] Ishiwara claimed this freedom of the brush for both Kenkō and Norinaga, his own mentor. Ban Kōkei (1733–1806) drew *The Pillow Book* into the zuihitsu genre in his discussion of native modes, *Kuni tsu fumi yoyo no ato* (The Traces of Our National Literature, 1774), but the elevation of *The Pillow Book* seemed to invite more attention to *Tsurezuregusa*, even among those kokugaku scholars with sympathy for the supposed feminine content of ancient and Heian texts.[79] Once the two texts were given the same generic label, they were frequently discussed together, and such discussions tended to lapse into lip service for Sei Shōnagon, with more extensive acclamatory citation for Kenkō. *The Pillow Book* languished without adequate reassessment, perhaps paradoxically suspect because of its link to the work of Kenkō, a lay priest interested in philosophies that originated in the rival civilization of China.

It is only in orthodox post-Meiji literary history that both *The Pillow Book* and *Tsurezuregusa* are members par excellence of the zuihitsu class, but we cannot afford to forget that the canonization of *Tsurezuregusa* proceeded in the context of *The Pillow Book*. On balance, the Tokugawa record finds the two works in frequent company and read closely by many of the same people—just not under the zuihitsu umbrella. Their close link in the modern canon is justifiable, if for different historical reasons than are usually proffered. Prior to the sixteenth century, *The Pillow Book* and *Tsurezuregusa* were of comparably modest importance. *The Pillow Book* circulated during its author's lifetime, a proud statement of the sensibilities alive in the culturally brilliant court of Teishi, consort of Emperor Ichijō, but it was largely overshadowed for later readers by Murasaki Shikibu's monumental *The Tale of Genji*. *The Pillow Book* was a source for writers on poetics and court ceremonial, and Sei Shōnagon's name turns up now and then in collections of anecdotes. Some argue that Kenkō himself rescued it from obscurity as a literary model.[80] If it was kept from the top rank of influence by its relatively slight role as a source on poetry, such was also true of *Tsurezuregusa*. The latter work was seemingly not destined to join the high canon, having been written by a single individual who was on the political and cultural sidelines, and who even when he was at court held the lowest of ranks. The text was copied and passed down through a lineage of poet-priests. Shōtetsu (1381–

1459), his waka student Shinkei (1406–1475), Shinkei's disciple Kensai (1452–1510), and Shōtetsu's acquaintance Tō no Tsuneyori (1401–1494) all praise Kenkō's observation that flowers are not to be viewed only at their peak, nor the moon only when unclouded.[81]

Certain statements in *Chikubashō* (Hobby Horse Passages), an autobiographical work attributed to Shiba Yoshimasa (1350–1410), resemble Kenkō's comments on youth, old age, and talent, but in fact it praises *The Pillow Book* by name (along with *The Tale of Genji*) as a guide to life, commenting, "They are works that more than anything teach human behavior and the life of the heart; in addition they allow one to observe people with sensibility."[82] It is this kind of use of texts that medieval intellectuals found most interesting.

In the sixteenth century, a subtle yet noteworthy difference in reception greets the two texts. Although the number of manuscript copies made is roughly equal to that for *Tsurezuregusa*, *The Pillow Book* loses ground in the area of substantive commentaries. To account for this gap, we must keep in mind that old texts were being used to inculcate literary grammar and vocabulary as well as familiarity with ancient practices. We can speculate, based on the content of *The Pillow Book*, as to why it was not as favored for teaching: its Chinese references and information on Japanese history are much more limited than those of *Tsurezuregusa*. For at least one Tokugawa scholar, however, there was a further reason to prefer Kenkō. As Mary Ellmann reminds us, "The word feminine alone, like a grimace, expresses a displeasure which is not less certain for its being undefined."[83] In his commentary on the passage where Kenkō voices his debt to *The Tale of Genji* and *The Pillow Book*, admitting that everything has been said before in those texts, Hayashi Razan notes that "Kenkō himself says that this section resembles *The Pillow Book* and *The Tale of Genji*, but his power of the brush is not inferior to that of Murasaki Shikibu and Sei Shōnagon." It is no coincidence that he feels compelled in his praise of Kenkō's next section to quote the opening line of the *Hōjōki* of Kamo no Chōmei, the work of another medieval male recluse now sometimes linked generically to *Tsurezuregusa*.[84] Chōmei almost functions as a chaser for the unpalatable necessity of mentioning the two women.

It was Kenkō himself who brought Sei Shōnagon and Murasaki Shikibu into the fray by referring to their works, and Shōtetsu who saw to it that their presence was justified on scholarly grounds through his judgment that Kenkō inherited the zuihitsu form from Sei Shōnagon.[85] Generations of annotators repeated Shōtetsu's remarks with such regularity that to broach *Tsurezuregusa* was to enter the realm of women's writings almost automatically. Razan's overt rejection of distaff writing was more the exception than the rule. Yet once Razan's opinions were on the record (and the quality of his efforts meant that all who came after him relied on his work), many felt a need to respond to his charges, however delicately. Kitamura Kigin (1624–1705) defends the women in the most important treatise on *The Pillow Book*, *Shunshoshō* (The Spring Dawn Selections, 1674). His method in treating both Kenkō and Sei Shōnagon is to train his eye firmly on literary allusions and diction.[86]

Notwithstanding Kigin's work on *The Pillow Book*, *Tsurezuregusa* attracted the lion's share of commentarial attention in the seventeenth century, putting it on a par with the long-celebrated tales of both *Genji* and *Ise*. In just twenty years from the midpoint of the seventeenth century on, thirteen commentaries hit the booksellers, and by 1753, Yamaoka Toshiaki (d. 1780) could refer to "dust piles" of *Tsurezuregusa* selections.[87] One might suspect that the *Hōjōki* was the next most influential work of prose considered nonfiction, and indeed the modern designation of *Hōjōki* commentaries as "*kinsei gochū*," indicating the existence of five main works over the early modern period, seems to outweigh the common modern reference to the "*kinsei sanchū* (three early modern commentaries)" that deal with *The Pillow Book*. Such retrospective groupings are clearly misleading, however, since the actual proportion of commentaries is closer to three for *Hōjōki* to five for *The Pillow Book*. The fact of the matter is that the *Hōjōki* was not connected to the zuihitsu genre in the Tokugawa period, and is frequently left out of that genre today. The link between *Tsurezuregusa* and the *Hōjōki* that led some analysts to connect them was rather the place of both of their authors in the recluse tradition. A wedge was thereby driven between *The Pillow Book* and *Tsurezuregusa* due to the differing situations of court and grass hut. Sei Shōnagon provided a window into the Heian court, a historical possession to be cherished, but not imitated. Kenkō, on the other hand, offered a template of reclusive life, which, if one had to choose, was the preferred model for Tokugawa youth (not to mention a rage among literati from the seventeenth century on). Many Confucians writhed uncomfortably in the presence of his calls for Buddhist detachment, and yet it could be argued that this particular bonze maintained an ongoing, healthy concern with the world. The recluse's path might also be interpreted as a metaphor for the medieval way to study, a valuable outlook rather than a way of behavior. Books of notable priests from the past such as *Fusō in'itsuden* bring together Kenkō and Kamo no Chōmei, not in terms of their literary commonalities, but for their similar pursuit of solitude, purity of motive, and learning.

The relative attractions of these three works for Tokugawa readers become clearer when one considers who analyzed which combinations. With the prominent exception of Katō Bansai, chief commentators chose either to write on *The Pillow Book* and *Tsurezuregusa* or the *Hōjōki* and *Tsurezuregusa*. No one chose just the *Hōjōki* and *The Pillow Book* as objects of comment. It is possible to generalize that the first pair appealed to those with more literary careers—haikai poets in particular found Sei and Kenkō inspirational—while the second won over men of Confucian persuasion, who could argue about the comparative prominence of the three teachings in both texts.[88] Historically, however, there was no reason why *The Pillow Book* should not have had an equal or better claim to be a classic favored by all, since it had been promoted among nonreclusive men in the same breath as *The Tale of Genji* (the "two jewels of Heian literature"),[89] whereas *Tsurezuregusa* had been mostly bandied about by Buddhist monks, coming only later into the purview of unretiring types.[90]

One eccentric individual did choose to treat all three works. Most accept *Sei Shōnagon Makura no sōshi shō* (c. 1670), the first early modern commentary, as the work of the Buddhist Katō Bansai, who also wrote on the *Hōjōki* and, as discussed above, *Tsurezuregusa*. It will be recalled that by linking *tsurezure* (as detachment) to *shikan* (calming and contemplating), Bansai emphasized the Buddhist nature of *Tsurezuregusa*. He has been accused of having a rather old-fashioned approach for this, while his choice to stress Sei's classifying sections has also been labeled a medieval attitude. These are equally signs of his early modern mindset, however, for he allies Kenkō with the grass hut tradition and Sei with the court and its material practices. Of the three major commentators, only Bansai treated *The Pillow Book* in a didactic manner, noting that "the central point of it is not only to enjoy the leaves and flowers of words, and to make clear old customs, but it must be seen as teaching the real meanings of things." He does his utmost to trace the flow of each section logically and point out the teachings. Nevertheless, Kigin's annotations on *The Pillow Book*, most of which are content to stop at the level of tracing vocabulary and grammar, became the standard. Later commentaries branched out, but only so far as to identify the clothing and vegetation in the text. With the exception of Bansai, then, the trend in commentaries was to intellectualize *Tsurezuregusa* and treat *The Pillow Book* only in terms of its surface.

The Pillow Book did not fare well as an object of instruction, but its popularity is reflected in the degree to which it was parodied. Just as there was a *Mongrel Tsurezuregusa*, there was a *Mongrel Pillow Book* (*Inu makura*, 1606) that updates and imitates the style of the original. A brief quotation will serve to demonstrate the irreverence and pure fun with which writers treated *The Pillow Book*. The following list is an example of one of the striking component styles of Sei Shōnagon's text:

The Pillow Book:

Frightening things:
The bark of an oak tree.
A place where there has been a fire.
The prickly water-lily, the water-chestnut, and the chestnut-bur.
A man with lots of thick hair who washes and dries it.[91]

Mongrel Pillow Book:

Things that stand one's hair on end:
Talking about ghosts.
In winter putting on armor without underclothes.
A river of unknown deeps and shallows.
Malaria.
The prospect of an evening's conversation with one's boy favorite.
The house where a faith healer is praying.[92]

The modern scholar Inoue Minoru has argued that *The Pillow Book* became less valued for itself as the Tokugawa era went on, and more likely to be simply parodied.[93] This production of *inu* or "dog" parodies was perhaps one arena in which all three texts were seen in common: in addition to *Inu makura* and *Inu no sōshi* (1632) (to name only two parodies of *The Pillow Book*), *Inu Tsurezure* (1653), and *Inu Hōjōki* (1682) each play on the stylistic distinctiveness of the originals, mongrelizing the text for maximum wit.

A factor in the differing reception accorded Sei Shōnagon was that she was to be read by young females. Nothing better attests to the utility for women readers of both *Tsurezuregusa* and *The Pillow Book* than their standing as necessary items in a bride's trousseau, reported in *Shūsai kango* of 1753. This utility mandated partial reading, however. Sei Shōnagon offered the spectacle of a lively-minded woman matching wits with her contemporaries, both male and female. She obviously relished her victories over men and behaved in other ways that did not conform to the officially sanctioned ideal of femininity, which called for submission to strictly defined social roles of service and inferiority vis-à-vis men. In the *joshi ōraimono* (handbooks for girls), biography was replaced by hagiography.[94] Commentaries might respond to the troublesome stories of Kenkō's love letters or Sei's downfall, but inspirational biographies focused on the positive, trotting out episodes without censure. In handbooks for girls, Sei's impromptu poem on Mt. Hsiang—one of many moments over which she exults—becomes a model of "quick thinking and ready learning" (*tōi sokumyō*), illustrated by a poster-girl standing before a rolled-up blind. Biographies also highlight her father Kiyohara no Motosuke (d. 990), and occasionally Teishi, but ignore the medieval tales in which Sei received her comeuppance for challenging her male acquaintances.[95]

In contrast to *Tsurezuregusa*, which made its mark everywhere in the Tokugawa period, *The Pillow Book* was appreciated on a more limited scale. One reason was that *Tsurezuregusa* itself was seen as an acceptable alternative, a stand-in when one was needed, for the earlier work. Sei Shōnagon's opus frequently faded into the background as inspiration for the work in which Kenkō achieved the fullest and best realization of her fluid style, without her vices. Gender was not the only ground for *Tsurezuregusa*'s leading role, but at least within the educational context that so influences the propagation of canonical works, it was a factor in the construction of preferential readings.

MODERN READINGS

These preferences lost some of their force in the late nineteenth- and early twentieth-century Japanese literary histories—projects that by their nature inclined toward close attention to textual forerunners. Literary historians followed Shōtetsu in pointing to the link between *Tsurezuregusa* and *The Pillow Book*, even when they counted Chōmei's *Hōjōki* (Account of My Hut) as the third pillar of the formation of *zuihitsu bungaku* (miscellany literature). The status of Kenkō, Sei Shōnagon, and Kamo no Chōmei as important poets helped prepare their thrones in a lineage of Japanese literature defined primarily as lyrical. Regarded as personal essays, their three works appeared in survey after survey, although seldom did all get equal treatment. In his *Kokubungakushi jikkō* (Ten Lectures on the History of Japanese Literature, 1899), Haga Yaichi (1867–1927) spotlighted *Tsurezuregusa* and Kitabatake Chikafusa's *Jinnō shōtōki* (Chronicle of Gods and Sovereigns) as texts of their era that successfully blended male writing and female writing, preserving the integrity of the national literature. Haga's admiration for Sei Shōnagon as a learned woman with less of the weakness possessed by the other Heian women writers comes through when he emphasizes that her brush was critical (*hihyōteki*) and her prose strong. The "disorderly" (*zappaku na*) Priest Kenkō, on the other hand, pales somewhat in comparison to Kamo no Chōmei, who is credited with having done a better job of refusing worldly fame and withdrawing into seclusion.[96] Still, it was not uncommon for critics (who were of course overwhelmingly male) to behave as Ishiwara Masaakira had in his *Nennen zuihitsu*, using any mention of *The Pillow Book* not to initiate a dilation on her text, but to springboard into a comment on *Tsurezuregusa*. Doi Kōchi performs this substitution in his remarks on Heian tale literature, which praise both of these texts for their focus on moments, but which then use *Tsurezuregusa* as the typical work for an exposition of the virtues of zuihitsu literature. Later he explicitly judges diaries and essays capable of standing up to the court of world opinion, and of being worthy of translation into foreign languages because of their direct expression of individual personality (*kosei*).[97]

One salient theme among modern critics was this presumed commensurability with Western literary standards. Much as kokugaku scholars had eventually come to extol these native texts as local and equally remarkable versions of Chinese *suibi* (zuihitsu), literary historians sought out Western exemplars to serve as near equivalents. W. G. Aston's parallel of *Tsurezuregusa* and Selden's *Table Talk* implied that Japan, too, had its miscellany. It is interesting to note that in this arena, the female-authored text was not at an automatic disadvantage. Aston marvels at the effeminacy of Japanese literature in the Heian period, stating categorically "It has no serious, masculine qualities." Yet he is not unkind to Sei Shōnagon, extracting at some length "the best and most quotable in Japanese literature" from her "Pillow Sketches." "If we compare it with anything that Europe had to show at this period, it must be admitted that it is indeed a remarkable work."[98] Such generosity no doubt encouraged Japanese to rate the piece highly themselves.

What is perhaps not surprising in this series of resemblances between premodern evaluations of the native zuihitsu and emerging discussions of the genre and its representatives in the Meiji era and later is how *Tsurezuregusa* remains available to a variety of interpreters and purposes. For one, it continues as a primer in classical literature. A teacher's guide for a Japanese language textbook of 1902 is typical in choosing two didactically convenient episodes—a priest of the Ninnaji temple and the priest who practiced linked poetry (*renga*)—for reading practice.[99] For some, *Tsurezuregusa* becomes the irreducibly native, unique form; others perceive it as Japan's greatest inspiration for a modern literature that now participates in a global field. Kenkō is eulogized in the pages of the first *Bungakukai* journal of 1893 as a Japanese Romantic by Hirata Tokuboku (1873–1943), who waxes enthusiastic over his "bosom friend" in a passage laced with references to pale light and falling flowers.[100]

In contrast to such an assumption of long-standing intimacy with the text, we have the claims of Utsumi Kōzō to be the first to provide a truly modern annotation of *Tsurezuregusa*. In *Tsurezuregusa hyōshaku* (Commentary on *Tsurezuregusa*, 1911) Utsumi (1872–1935) asserts that the true meaning of the text had not been comprehended before him. His commentary embodied the influential doctrine of taste—Utsumi set the premise that human faculties divide into the logical (the domain of *risei*, or intellect) and the emotional, identified with taste (*shumi*). *Tsurezuregusa* is an explication of taste, and Kenkō the master of that realm.[101] This view of the text as unified and serene—not far from the conceptions of the Romantics—enters Western reception of the text through Sanki Ichikawa's preface to William N. Porter's English translation, *The Miscellany of a Japanese Priest* (1914). Close study will reward us, writes our guide, as it "indirectly conduces to the peace of the world at large." Ichikawa stresses the difference from the West: "There is a thread—a golden thread one might say—running through the whole of the *Tsurezuregusa*, which, as Utsumi aptly points out, may well be ascribed to the author's endeavour to inculcate good taste in everything, a taste which is peculiarly Japanese."[102]

As the Meiji era ends and the Taishō period begins, many feel that this special area of Japanese aesthetic competence must be held apart and rescued from neglect by Japanese literati, who have turned too much toward the green traditions of America, as Yosano Akiko (1878–1942) laments in her call for research on the classics.[103] Yosano, the only woman to translate *Tsurezuregusa* into modern Japanese prior to the postwar boom in student trots, writes of the past conjured up by Sei Shōnagon as a place to amuse herself. It is enough for Yosano to imagine sitting with Sei as she admires the empress Teishi.[104] In the same year as Yosano Akiko's translation appeared, Sano Yasutarō published his *Tsurezuregusa kōgi* (Lectures on *Tsurezuregusa*, 1932) in which he accuses current scholarship of repeating old errors.[105] For Utsumi, Yosano, and Sano, each in their own way, zuihitsu are a refuge from the complexities of modern life, not much tainted by any past life of politics and strife. Presentation of *Tsurezuregusa* to the West remains similar in Kurata Ryūkichi's 1931 abridged translation for the Wisdom of the East Series. L. Adams Beck compares Kenkō to his French essayist counterpart in the introduction:

Of the two he [Kenkō] is infinitely the more serene and detached, and has a sensitiveness of spirit much surpassing that of Montaigne, though he falls far below him in sustained and constructive ability. His observations are those of a man who has weighed worldly opinion and smiles at its pretensions compared with the beauty and abiding interest of the simple things of life—the mystic loveliness of nature, the wisdom of living creatures, the One Spirit dwelling in both which, moving also in man, awakens his deepest intuitions and unites him with them.[106]

The persistence of the generic term zuihitsu in the Taishō period may link to such attitudes about the classics and Japanese "ownership" of their unique literary heritage. A boom in the writing of zuihitsu encompassed many different authors and pieces ranging from lyric to comic to journalistic in tone. Beginning in late 1923, the journal *Zuihitsu* collected the works of Tokuda Shūsei, Akutagawa Ryūnosuke, Satō Haruo, and others. *Zuihitsu*, from personal fiction (I-novel or *shishōsetsu*) to literary criticism to the trenchant observations of the physicist Terada Torahiko (1878–1935), received wide acclaim. *Tsurezuregusa* and *The Pillow Book* became the quiet ancestors of this literary ferment, helping to tie newly emergent styles to the Japanese past.[107]

Tsurezuregusa's place in the education system meant that Japanese encountered it early in their lives as readers, leading, then as now, to some contempt for the overfamiliar entity. Attempts to counteract this effect tended to stress the familiarity, the personal, and the aesthetic, in a combination of contemporaneity and nostalgia. Satō Haruo (1892–1964), in the introduction to his modern Japanese translation of 1937, complains that *Hōjōki* and *Tsurezuregusa* have both been valued less than they deserve since Meiji educators made them mandatory reading for exams. His appreciation for Kenkō centers on psychological depth in the service of liberty, an attitude that he can hardly believe was a product of a time six hundred years in the past. In an afterward on the tradition of Japanese literature, Satō believes it necessary to express the nature of the people (*kokuminsei*) and thinks that Japanese literature succeeds in this best by leading with the emotional core that is *mono no aware*. He thus explains the transformation of the Naturalist literary movement in Japan into forms such as *shinkyō shōsetsu* (mental-state fiction) that closely resemble diary and zuihitsu literature.[108]

Today, when the aesthetic approach to texts that emerged in the late Tokugawa and that was reinforced through the Westernization of literary history predominates, *Tsurezuregusa* and *The Pillow Book* are revered. Most interpreters see the miscellany style of both as intrinsic to the texts and as determinative of the content (the freedom of the form creating the range and tone of the material). It may seem a virtue that Confucian and Buddhist partisans are no longer inclined to argue over the essential message of *Tsurezuregusa* or *The Pillow Book*, but it is worth remembering that to side-

step the intellectual allegiance of any passage on grounds that either is "a literary work of universal significance" is itself a narrow strategy with its own
history. Misogynists may be gone, but the reduction of *The Pillow Book* simply to the status of a precursor of *Tsurezuregusa* can still divert us from other
lines of evaluation. A look at the process of canon formation serves to re-
mind us that it may well be the contestability of a text that makes it canonical. That text which is available for the widest scope of rewriting, whether
due to its ambiguity or breadth, and that author who is most congenial to
the times, or easiest to refashion, seem to be the best candidates for the chain
of flash freezings that is canonization. Needless to say, the end result of such
a course cannot and should not be the last word on any text.

History to Literature, Performance to Text

CHAPTER SIX

Nation and Epic: *The Tale of the Heike* as Modern Classic

DAVID T. BIALOCK

The Tale of the Heike (*Heike monogatari*, ca. 14th c.) has often been described as the greatest Japanese narrative work after *The Tale of the Genji*. The suggestion of qualified praise reveals more than an objective assessment of *The Heike*'s literary qualities.[1] The seeming belatedness of *The Heike*, its distance in time from the perceived origins of what came to be defined as court culture, has been a critical factor in shaping perceptions of the work's place in the modern canon of Japanese classics. As Komine Kazuaki has recently put it, most modern discussion of *The Heike* has been organized around a concept of court literature that established an implicit trajectory of cultural flowering in *The Tale of Genji*, associated with the aristocracy (*kizoku*), followed by a decline connected to the rise of warriors (*bushi*). As a result, much scholarly analysis of *The Heike* merely completes or supplements a certain view of *The Genji*, reinforcing literary criteria associated with court culture.[2]

This court-centered view of *The Heike* took shape slowly over the course of the Meiji era and the years leading up to World War II, a period that saw the consolidation of the imperial ideology and of the canonical centrality of the court literature as its ultimate cultural expression. The characteristic emphasis on the lyrical, tragic, and pathetic elements in *The Heike*, and, above all, on the complex perception of loss summed up in the term *mujōkan* (view of impermanence), linked *The Heike* to a world of compensatory beauty. This view of *The Heike* achieved its most complete expression in the writings of the new romanticist (*Nihon rōmanha*) literary critic Yasuda Yojūrō (1910–1981), who once characterized *The Heike* as "this tale of sad humanity."[3] Although seldom mentioned in standard handbooks on the scholarly reception of *The Heike*, the numerous essays that Yasuda composed on *The Heike* in the 1930s were distilled from perceptions on the suffering and tragic fate of heroes found in the writings of such classical scholars as Fujioka Sakutarō (1870–1910) and Igarashi Chikara (1874–1947). This view of *The Heike* and warrior literature in general, together with the entire mythology of *hōgan biiki* (partiality for the Hōgan, or Yoshitsune, and by implication for the Heike), later found its way into English through Ivan Morris's widely read *The Nobility of Failure*, an examination into the Japanese worship of failed war heroes.

This sweetened view of *The Heike* was related to factors in Meiji political culture. The Meiji scholars who first undertook a literary appreciation of *The Heike* and other warrior chronicles were confronted with a much different set of assumptions: *The Tale of the Heike* as literature did not exist. Instead, *The Heike* and related works like *Genpei jōsuiki* (Record of the Rise and Fall of the Genji and the Heike, ca. late 14th c.) and *Taiheiki* (Record of the Great Peace, ca. late 14th c.) were parts of a historical discourse that had helped to legitimate warrior rule through much of the late medieval and Edo periods. The ideological liabilities of these works made them problematic within the context of the Meiji imperial restoration. A scholar like Haga Yaichi (1867–1927), who was instrumental in shaping the modern discourse on *The Heike* and other military chronicles, was often openly critical of the anti-imperial bias that he discovered in these texts. The seemingly neutral literary-aesthetic reading of *The Heike* grew out of and was reinforced by this more explicit ideological condemnation of warrior literature.

The court-centered view of *The Heike* did not go unchallenged, however. As the interweaving strands of an aesthetic and more explicitly ideological, court-centered discourse were woven into the appreciation of *The Heike* in the prewar period, complexity was added by a third and contemporaneous view of *The Heike* as national epic (*kokuminteki jojishi*). European literary history introduced to Japan in the early years of the twentieth century associated the epic with the folk, national origins, and even primitive democratic energies. *The Heike* as epic theory, in which both *The Heike* and the medieval period were identified with popular and national origins, managed to endow the work with a plenitude, power, and energy that it lacked in the court-centered view of the work. Kobayashi Hideo's short appreciation of *The Heike*, published in 1942, is perhaps the most famous articulation of this view. Writing on "Ujigawa senjin" (The First Man Across the Uji River), which describes the exploits of the warrior Sasaki Shirō Takatsuna, Kobayashi makes the following observation: "Rather than a psychological description, it is the movement of brawny muscle that we seem to feel in this description." "From the prose in this passage, we feel the sweat of men and horses and the light of the sun." In this celebration of action, Kobayashi is countering a critical view of *The Tale of the Heike* that understood its melancholy (*aichō*) opening, with its Buddhist message of impermanence (*mujō*), as the work's chief characteristic. *The Heike*'s author, Kobayashi goes on to argue in the same essay, was not a thinker (*shisōka*) intent on inculcating Buddhist doctrine, but just a person giving a voice to the times, "to the traditional spirit of an epic poet (*jojishijin*) that even the author did not fully understand."[4]

Kobayashi's view was not original. As early as 1901, Takayama Chogyū (1871–1902) had celebrated the Nietzschean amoralism of *The Heike* hero Taira no Kiyomori, and throughout much of the prewar period, *The Heike* was lauded by scholars like Takagi Ichinosuke (1888–1976) as an epic expression of primitive vigor much superior, in his view, to the enfeebled court literature. But it was not until the postwar period that the individualism and popular democratic appeal of the epic reading could be usefully exploited as both a critique of the emperor system and a rallying point for national solidarity. To speak of *The Heike*'s evolving canonical status is thus to recognize its embeddedness in a complex discourse about nationality, origins, and imperial ideology. It is this always shifting and problematic status of *The Tale of the Heike* in the literary canon from Meiji through the postwar period that will be the focus of this essay.

FROM HISTORY TO LITERATURE

Although the version of *The Tale of the Heike* that has come to be known as the Kakuichi variant (1371) is today the one most commonly selected for inclusion in school primers and for general publication, it has not always been the object of such exclusive esteem.[5] Throughout the medieval centuries and continuing right up to the Meiji period, it was merely one of numerous competing variants. Moreover, the kind of literary appreciation exemplified in Kobayashi's essay begins to appear only from about the mid-Meiji period on.[6] Prior to that time *The Tale of the Heike*, when discussed at all, was treated as a historical narrative.[7] Unlike *The Tale of Genji, Tales of Ise*, waka, and other works of the Heian period, *The Heike* had been the subject of a very limited tradition of literary commentary and exegesis. The few commentaries that did exist were focused on the factuality or truthfulness of the historical narrative, and hence on issues of legitimacy, or on explicating obscure words, many of these technical terms for warrior accoutrements and the like.[8]

In the 1890s and early years of the twentieth century, therefore, when Meiji scholars such as Haga Yaichi (1867–1927) and Fujioka Sakutarō (1870–1910) began to reappraise *The Heike* as literature, they were in effect conjuring literature out of a historical discourse. In 1890 Haga published the earliest attempt at a literary appreciation of warrior chronicles. The following year, *The Heike* was published in the *Bungaku zensho* series, and two years later, in 1893, *Genpei jōsuiki*, an important variant of the read lineage (*yomihon*), was published in the *Teikoku bunko* series of classics. For the first time, warrior chronicles were being made available to the general public in relatively inexpensive formats with the aim of marketing their literary qualities. This activity coincided with a crisis in historiography, and it is this event that provides Haga with the substance of his opening remarks in which he reflects on the need to reassess *Genpei jōsuiki* and *Taiheiki* (Record of Great Peace) for their "eternal and unchanging" (*eigō fuhen*) literary values, since they were no longer of use as historical documents. One of the first Japanese literary scholars to recognize the sundering of literature and history into two distinct domains of discourse, Haga writes: "In the ancient period, history (*rekishi*) had the same form as literature (*bungaku*); today, good history is not necessarily good literature. Works that might be faulted as history can have good points as literature. Thus, the critical standards for literature and history are in fact different."[9]

It was following the introduction of historical positivism at Tokyo Imperial University in the 1880s that a series of essays attacking the historical accuracy of *The Tale of the Heike, Genpei jōsuiki, Taiheiki*, and other military chronicles was published by Hoshino Hisashi and other historians.[10] This was part of a more general critique of the adequacy of traditional Japanese historiography as a basis for constructing a national history on a par with European achievements, but it was also intertwined with issues of power and imperial legitimacy that went all the way back to the medieval period and that had resurfaced with renewed vigor during the Tokugawa revival of Chinese-style historiography.

A recent essay by Sakakibara Chizuru sheds an interesting light on the importance of *The Tale of the Heike* in such debates as they simmered in the early decades of the nineteenth century. In 1817, a document was discovered at the residence of a warrior in the district of Nose that claimed that Emperor Antoku had not died at Dan-no-ura—as stated in the account given in *The Heike*—but had survived and even succeeded in making a clandestine visit to Nose. The document further stated that after his death in the following year Antoku was buried at the local shrine of Iwasaki Hachimangū, while a number of his retainers remained in the district, as did their descendants. As copies of the document were circulated under different titles, heated debates arose over its authenticity. In his analysis, Sakakibara shows how the activity of writing commentaries (*chūshaku*) and historical proofs (*kōshō*) by the various antiquarians who collected such documents—many of them also collected *Heike* manuscripts—could easily blur, under the pretext of establishing authenticity, into the production of ideologically motivated truth. He notes, for example, how some antiquarians criticized the Antoku document because the implication of a clandestine visit by Antoku to Nose opened up doubts as to the whereabouts of the imperial regalia and hence doubts concerning the legitimacy of the imperial line.[11] In a similar vein, other scholars found fault with *The Tale of the Heike* itself, attacking in particular the Sinophilic "Kane watashi" (Transmission of Gold) episode as an insult to the imperial house.[12] *The Heike*, a work which in modern times has been celebrated for its nostalgic evocation of the imperial past, was thus embedded in fractious historical and ideological disputes that went all the way back to the medieval period.

As the literature scholar Hyōdō Hiromi has shown, *The Tale of the Heike*, along with other military chronicles, had been instrumental in establishing a discourse that was used to legitimate warrior authority and changes of power from the medieval period right up through the Edo period.[13] As the inaugural work in this discourse, *The Tale of the Heike* set the pattern for two warrior houses, in this case the Heike and the Genji, succeeding one another as defenders of imperial power. Other variants of *The Heike*, including *Genpei jōsuiki* and the military chronicle *Taiheiki*, went even further in this strategy of reinforcing the prestige of warrior government vis-à-vis the imperial house. They did so by borrowing concepts from Sung political thought that (1) clarified the prerogatives of warrior authority in governing the realm and (2) provided legitimacy to the notion of dual imperial courts.[14] In *Taiheiki*, for example, warriors who fight on behalf of different emperors legitimate their cause by drawing on precedents from Chinese ethical thought and historical writings. As the medieval period progressed, a structure of alternating warrior rule by two different clans acquired the sanction of a quasi-official discourse. As a result, warrior chronicles going all the way back to *The Heike* became repositories of prior instances sanctioning warrior accessions to power. Oda Nobunaga (1534–1582), for example, traced his descent back to a Heike warrior who died at Dan-no-ura. And when Tokugawa Ieyasu (1542–1616) came to power, he signaled his break from Ashikaga rule, associated with the Northern Court, by linking his descent to the Nitta warrior clan, whose members had died fighting on behalf of the Southern Court.[15] Tokugawa Mitsukuni (1628–1700) extended this legitimation of *bakufu* (military) rule by ordering the compilation of *Dai Nihon shi* (Great History of Japan) with the aim of legitimating the Southern Court. One of the by-products of this project was the collation of all *Heike* variants, which resulted in *Sankō genpei jōsuiki* (The Corrected Version of the Record of the Rise and Fall of the Genji and the Heike), a further indication of the work's prestige as historical narrative.[16]

The Tokugawa revival of official historiography in the form of *Dai Nihon shi* rekindled the medieval debate on the question of imperial legitimacy. The establishment of the rival Northern and Southern Courts by Ashikaga Takauji (1305–1358) and Emperor GoDaigo (1288–1339) in 1336 had placed the legitimacy of the imperial line in doubt. In his historical tract *Jinnō shōtōki* (Chronicle of Gods and Sovereigns, 1339), Kitabatake Chikafusa (1293–1354) had come down in favor of the Southern Court. *Baishōron* (1349), an anonymous historical tract defending the interests of Ashikaga rule, supported the Northern Court. *Taiheiki* was more ambiguous. As Hyōdō has shown, *Taiheiki* incorporates two contradictory discourses. The first, outlined above, formalizes the principle of two legitimate imperial lineages, authorizing in turn the alternate rule of two military houses; the second provides a competing notion of imperial rule allied directly with the people (*tami*) and is centered on *Taiheiki*'s account of the alliance of Kusunoki Masashige (1294–1336) and other marginal figures associated with Emperor GoDaigo, which led to the short-lived Kemmu Restoration (1334–1336).[17] It was this portion of the narrative that would prove so useful in the elaboration of an imperial ideology from the Edo period on, to the degree that it appeared to authorize a transcendent emperor figure whose supreme political authority abolished the political middle ground occupied by the ruling warrior class. With the justification of warrior rule (with its layered hierarchy) eliminated, all ranks and classes could then be absorbed into the abstract notion of the people united under a single emperor figure.[18]

The Tokugawa bakufu's revival of official historiography and its recourse to historical precedents in the military chronicles for purposes of self-legitimation provoked a sharp defense of imperial authority that included an attack on the historical precedent of dual imperial courts. For the supporters of absolute imperial rule, the very notion of having to accord legitimacy to the Southern Court was anathema, since it suggested that the transcendent principle of one sole legitimate imperial line was in need of justification. The Confucianists Fujita Yūkoku (1774–1828) and his son Fujita Tōko (1808–1855), voicing opinions that would later be echoed by imperial loyalists throughout the Meiji and early Shōwa periods, filled their writings with harsh criticisms of *Dai Nihon shi* and lengthy vituperations on the evil of Ashikaga rule during the period of the Northern and Southern Courts (Nanbokuchō), while averring, in what would later become a commonplace in discussions by Shōwa ideologues, that Japan had never known the popular overthrow of an emperor.[19] After the Meiji Restoration and a period of some years during which the two-court theory had prevailed, the debate recrudesced in the 1906 textbook controversy over the accuracy of Nanbokuchō as a legitimate period designation. The matter was settled in 1911, when the name Yoshinochō, after the site of GoDaigo's Southern Court, was adopted as the official designation. The name Nambokuchō, meanwhile, was excised from all textbooks until the end of the Pacific War.[20]

It is within the context of such debates about warrior versus imperial legitimacy and the historical discourse of military chronicles that was its vehicle that the Meiji reappraisal of *The Tale of the Heike* and related works as literature must be placed. In redefining *Genpei jōsuiki* and *Taiheiki* as literature for a new readership, Haga insists on a careful discrimination between the two works, which, he notes, appeared within one hundred years of each other under similar political and social conditions. Writing about the emergence of *Genpei jōsuiki*, the earlier work, Haga points out that "it was a period when Kamakura dominance was already firmly established, and power throughout the land had fallen into the hands of warriors; the court had lost all of its authority." Although Haga reluctantly acknowledges the presence of a warrior spirit in *Genpei jōsuiki*, in his opening characterization of the work it is really its theme of "impermanence and vicissitude" (*mujō tenpen*) and what he calls its "piercingly sad and pathetic Buddhist elements" that he singles out for special attention.

With his commitment to an evolutionary view of Japanese literary development, which informed the approach of the newly trained literature scholars at Tokyo Imperial University, Haga was aware that *Taiheiki* ought to have marked an advance over the earlier *Genpei jōsuiki*. He discovered this advance not in the work's outward form, but in the transcendent realm of its inner content (*naibu seishin*); namely, a "spirit of imperial loyalism" (*kinnō no seishin*) that had been entirely suppressed by the warriors in *Genpei jōsuiki*. In discussing the chief literary quality of *Genpei jōsuiki*, therefore, Haga directs the reader away from its obvious warrior qualities, and defines it instead in terms of its pessimistic expression of a Buddhist philosophy of loss and impermanence. The warrior elements simply drop out of Haga's appreciation. In tallying the literary qualities of these two works, Haga ascribes to the inferior *Genpei jōsuiki* the expression of the Buddhist theme of impermanence announced in its Preface, the admonitory lesson of the Heike clan's fleeting glory, the theme of this world's sadness, and the work's immersion in what Haga somewhat condescendingly refers to as "girlish grief" (*joshi no hiai*). The author of the superior *Taiheiki*, on the other hand, evinces a spirit of imperial loyalism from beginning to end, declaims the heaven-sent punishment of the arrogant Hōjō warrior clan, and sheds manly tears of righteous indignation (*jōbu no kōgai namida*).[21]

LYRICIZING WAR

Haga's essay formulated several key elements that would shape one particular view of *The Heike*'s place in the emergent twentieth-century canon. Although still conceived in largely negative terms, these elements include the beginnings of a lyrical and religiously focused conception of warrior literature. Over the next several decades, as scholars sorted out and established texts for the numerous variants, attention gradually shifted from *Genpei jōsuiki* and coalesced around the Kakuichi text as the exemplary expression of a Buddhist worldview softened by a lyricism resonant of the courtly age.

For example, in an essay published in 1907 in *Teikoku bungaku*, the literature scholar Fujioka Sakutarō elaborates an aesthetic interpretation of *The Tale of the Heike* that takes up, in a more subtle fashion, Haga's attack on the martial elements in warrior chronicles. In his essay, Fujioka recognizes three periods of revolutionary change in Japanese history: the period of the Taika Reforms (645), the period of civil strife during the era of Juei (1182–85), and the Meiji Restoration. For Fujioka, both the Juei and Meiji eras are characterized by the clash between old and new values, although he is at pains to contrast what he characterizes as the relatively peaceful change of Meiji to the violent military upheavals of Juei. Fujioka's strategy here, as opposed to Haga's, is to acknowledge the martial ethos of Juei while taking care to remove Meiji from any possible taint by association. Hence, he characterizes Juei as heroic (*eiyūteki*), and Meiji as a time of peaceful transformation, when "high and low, noble and base work in close cooperation together." Moreover, just as Haga chose to dwell on *Genpei jōsuiki*'s pessimistic Buddhist sense of loss instead of the work's warrior qualities, Fujioka treats Juei as a time of personal loss symbolized by the sacrifice (*gisei*) of the Heike clan, and especially of the tragic (*higekiteki*) figure of Kiyomori. In Fujioka's literary interpretation, the violence of Juei is thus transformed from a historical event, whose political and moral implications still resonated in Haga's analysis, into a timeless aesthetic expression of tragic loss, and *The Heike* becomes a work of literature full of emotional resonance for those who are living during the painful transition of Meiji. Composed only two years after the end of the Russo-Japanese War (1904–5), Fujioka's tragic-lyrical meditation on *The Heike* appeared at a time of increasing militaristic expansionism and nationalistic fervor.[22] The paradox of canonizing the military chronicles as high literature by draining them of their military spirit can be partially explained by examining the problematic relationship between *chūgi*, a retainer's loyalty to his lord, and the imported notion of individualism (*kojin shugi*).

Starting in 1901, the critic Takayama Chogyū published a series of essays expounding a Nietzschean-inspired philosophy of individualism, which included an essay on *The Heike* hero Taira no Kiyomori entitled "Taira no Kiyomori ron" (An Explanation of Taira no Kiyomori). Takayama elaborated an ideal of extreme individualism and criticized state nationalism and the evolving emperor system, which he saw as fettering individual expression. The essay marked a break from Takayama's earlier embrace of Japanism (*Nihon shugi*); instead of subordinating the individual to the telos of the state, the superior individual now replaced the state as the locus of a transcendent spiritual power.[23] In an extract from the essay on Taira no Kiyomori subtitled "Hei shōkoku" (The Taira Chancellor), Takayama characterizes Kiyomori as a man never beset with a guilty conscience, and one "in whose eyes the world was no more than a personal possession. . . . Whether it was loyalty (*chū*), duty (*gi*), moral obligations (*taigi*), or the social duties of rank (*meibun*), he treated them all as if they were no more than names for a species of habit." Having noted that Kiyomori showed no reverence for the emperor, Takayama goes on to hail him as a prime example of individualism and egoism:

> In brief, he was a great man who transcended the ethics of his day. Expressed in the language of the twentieth century, he was an extreme individualist, an egoist. In the language of contemporary ethics, he was not an immoral man but an amoral man. He was not a good man, nor was he an evil man. Quite simply, he was an extraordinary individual, a man of robust temperament.

After summarizing Kiyomori's extraordinary life and defiant death, Takayama expostulates: "From ancient times, there have been numerous examples of heroic last moments that have moved people deeply, but I know of no example that equals Kiyomori's tragic death."[24]

Takayama's essay opened up new critical space in the evolving discourse on *The Tale of the Heike*. On the one hand, the tragic view of Kiyomori's death, which in Takayama's interpretation was the expression of an individualistic ethos at odds with all forms of state power, anticipates views that became more fully developed in the lyrical conception of *The Tale of the Heike*. But there is another side to Takayama's essay: an ethical breach that many writers on *The Heike* and other kinds of warrior literature would hasten to fill in and repair. Takayama opens up the possibility of accommodation between, on the one hand, elements of the Confucian-derived moral code such as *chūgi* (loyalty) and *taigi meibun* (correct relations between superiors and subjects), which informed the moral universe of the warrior chronicles, and, on the other hand, the ideal of unrestrained individualism imported from the West. For ideologues like Haga Yaichi, this could only be viewed in a perilous light, because warrior loyalty and the hierarchical structure of social obligations set forth in taigi meibun were historically grounded in notions of personal loyalty and networks of regional affiliation that were fundamentally at odds with, and even inimical to, the aims of Meiji state nationalism. In brief, loyalty, whether to oneself or to a group, when carried to an extreme could readily acquire an antiestablishment character. Full of strong and rebellious characters, the warrior chronicles lent themselves to populist and individualistic interpretations that could easily veer off into political stances at variance with the evolving emperor system (*tennōsei*).

In contradistinction to Takayama's bold and potentially subversive reading, one strand of the complex literary discourse taking shape around *The Tale of the Heike* involved domesticating the warrior chronicles into literature and the martial ethos into an ethic compatible with the imperial state ideology. The trend initiated by Fujioka's essay, the lyricization of warrior chronicles into high literature, was one response. A more forceful tack was taken in another essay by Haga Yaichi, "Chūkun aikoku" (Loyalty and Patriotism), also published in 1907, which took up and expanded on the ethical concerns of his earlier essay by explicitly redefining the warrior ethic of loyalty as loyalty to the emperor and the state. He begins with a general characterization of Japanese political culture by quoting Siebold, whose lecture he had attended while studying abroad in Germany: "Every Western country's revolution arose out of dissatisfaction with the king; as a result, the prestige of the royal house was diminished or entirely destroyed. In Japan, on the other hand, every revolution benefited the imperial majesty and increased its prosperity." And in his words, he sums up the matter: "For this reason, throughout the ages our nation (*waga kokumin*) has preserved a single national essence (*kokutai*) and has progressed with the progress of the times." For Haga, therefore, Japan had escaped the kinds of conflict between the sovereign (*kokuō*) and his subjects (*jinmin*) that have characterized not only Western nations but China as well, where "sovereigns arose from the midst of the people and either by force or by popular acclaim managed to seize the throne."[25] Haga supports this view by citing the Taika Reforms in ancient times and the Meiji Restoration in modern times.

Whereas Fujioka had disposed of the problematic medieval centuries by transforming them into an emotionally resonant aesthetic object, Haga dealt with them from a moral viewpoint.[26] He notes, for example, that the warriors Yoshitomo and Yoshinaka are placed under the category of "traitorous retainers" (*hanshin*) in *Dai Nihon shi*.[27] In his words they are not even rebels (*muhonnin*), but ruffians (*ranbōnin*) who lost respect for the throne and now stand as admonitory examples of retainers who have not observed their obligations to their sovereigns (taigi meibun). He then goes on to cite the examples of Taira no Masakado (who was officially declared a traitor by the Meiji government) and Takayama's hero Taira no Kiyomori, noting how the latter was censured in proper Confucian style by his own son Taira no Shigemori. Finally, Haga rounds off this section by redefining the warrior concept of loyalty, embodied in the master/retainer relationship (*shujū kankei*), as an expression of the subordination of the people (kokumin) to the imperial house (*kōshitsu*).[28]

By the first decade of the twentieth century, several competing views of *The Tale of the Heike* and warrior chronicles in general were beginning to emerge. Takayama's reading of warrior figures as heroic individuals, although it would later be taken up in modified form by proponents of the epic theory, would remain, throughout the prewar years, a decidedly minor view.

Haga's Buddhistic and Confucian readings, on the other hand, and Fujioka's treatment of *The Heike* as a lyrical work, with its emphasis on sacrifice (*gisei*), suffering, and tragic pathos, would grow into an orthodoxy that was reinforced by the prewar imperial ideology.[29]

By the Taishō period (1912–26), annotated texts of *The Tale of the Heike*, often including literary appreciations as well, were bringing the work to the general reader in more accessible, and in some cases more deluxe, formats.[30] One of the most important of these texts was the first Iwanami bunko pocket-sized edition, published in two volumes in 1929 by the literature scholar Yamada Yoshio (1873–1958), who had earlier completed a groundbreaking collation and study of all major *Heike* variants.[31] One of Yamada's avowed aims in publishing this edition was to make the Kakuichi text widely available to the general reader; it henceforth became established as the canonical text. Perhaps even more important was Yamada's preface to this edition, which distilled in lucid, scholarly prose a view of the Kakuichi *Heike* that would be echoed by almost every subsequent study through the postwar period.[32] He focuses, for example, on the Kakuichi *Heike*'s sympathetic and lyrical portrayal of the warriors and Taira heirs Tadanori, Tsunemasa, and Atsumori and devotes separate sections to the Kakuichi *Heike*'s sympathetic portrayal of the pathetic and defeated warriors Yoshitsune and Kiso no Yoshinaka, a portrayal that would become the standard, and in some respects the only acceptable, model of the valorous warrior.[33] Echoing Haga's ethical viewpoint, Yamada also lavishes several pages of his preface on Kiyomori's eldest son Shigemori as an exemplar of Confucian moral thought. All of the trends first articulated in the work of Haga and Fujioka are thus given a formal and lasting imprimatur.

Our initial paradox, the gradual enfolding of warrior ethos into aesthetic values, can now be accounted for. During the militarist prewar period, Japanese literature scholars and intellectuals did not readily embrace militaristic values. Instead, they preferred to highlight Japan's "native" propensity for a lyrical and aesthetic worldview. This antipathy to militaristic values grew, at least in part, out of attitudes shaped by the Meiji Restoration, which was celebrated as a rejection of the preceding centuries of warrior and feudalistic government and a return to imperial rule. It also explains the gradual occlusion of the warrior-dominated centuries spanning the Kamakura and Ashikaga shogunates (1192–1537) and the gender attributes applied to specific historical periods. As is evident in Haga Yaichi's characterization of *Taiheiki* as "manly" in his first literary appreciation of warrior chronicles, in the 1890s he and other literature scholars were still under the spell of the so-called masculine virtues of a Sinified style most fully realized, in their view, by Edo period literature. By the early years of Shōwa (1926–89), however, the Heian past was being fully gendered as feminine, traditional, and indigenous (as Tomi Suzuki and Joshua Mostow show in this volume). As a result, the early embrace of Edo and medieval culture and of Chinese elements was abandoned in the search for an indigenous tradition that also coincided with the extreme nationalism of the emperor system.[34] Having achieved a kind of cultural preeminence, the lyrical cadences of Heian prose, grounded in pathos (*mono no aware*) and exemplified in works like *Genji monogatari*, would wash in successive waves into appreciations of *The Tale of the Heike* as a work full of belated echoes of the fallen court culture. The finest expression of this view, and a distillation of *The Tale of the Heike* as a prewar canonical text, is found in the writing of the new romanticist Yasuda Yojūrō.

In the years leading up to the war, Yasuda published numerous essays on *The Tale of the Heike*, but it is his essay "Kiso kanja" (The Young Man of Kiso), published in 1937, that most fully presents the aesthetic view of the work that dominated in the prewar years and that constitutes a virtual poetics for reading the work.[35] Discussing *The Heike*'s famous opening passage on impermanence, for example, he characterizes it as "the supreme expression of Epicureanism. The descriptions in *The Tale of the Heike* are not, as we learn in our school lessons in moral conduct these days, a view of rise and fall as it pertains to the administrative policy of nation-states." Here Yasuda effectively removes the work from the domain of political and ethical concerns that so preoccupied Haga, Yamada, and other scholars and instead locates it squarely in a realm of aesthetic expression (*bigaku*) and emotional pathos, where it rivals the productions of court literature. Characterizing *The Heike* as a "solemn history," whose chief effect is "angst" (*fuan*), he writes: "It builds up this [mood] in its solemn battle scrolls, weaving it into a tragic song of grief, and in its rhythm that echoes in the soul, it gives rise to a succession of events; and because of that one abstract rhythm, it fashions all of these mighty events into a harmony."[36] The rhythm that Yasuda invokes here refers to the succession of defeated heroes, from the Heike warriors, including Atsumori and Tadanori, to the Genji warriors Kiso no Yoshinaka and Yoshitsune, all sacrificed to political expediency in the establishment of the Kamakura bakufu. Yasuda describes the death of warriors dying on the battlefield in rapturous terms:

> In this there is a kind of heroic karma (*yūdaina gō*). It is the karmic beauty of the warrior's fate described on the battlefield. Moreover, such karmic beauty, similar, for example, to the beauty of Izumi Shikibu's womanly charms, pos-

sesses an unchanging splendor. The feeling of wanting to kill and wanting to be killed, and the feeling of wanting to love and wanting to be loved, are all found in the same dwelling; one might characterize it as the expression of wild words and fancy language (*kyōgen kigo*), in which everything is a form of praise for the dharma vehicle."[37]

In this passage, Yasuda succeeds in conflating the beauty of dying on the battlefield with both the court aesthetic of erotic pursuit (*irogonomi*) and the Buddhist notion of expedient means (*hōben*). This dehistoricized reading of *The Heike* participates nonetheless in the ideological ferment of the prewar years. By characterizing the martial ethos of loyalty and sacrifice as the highest embodiment of Japan's traditional values, gendered here as feminine, he provides an existential ground for Japan's youth, who are faced with imminent war. War, as an expression of tragic fate, now becomes the sole means for "overcoming the modern"—that is to say, the quest for an essential Japanese culture uncontaminated by Euro-American constructions of the modern.[38] Thus Kiso no Yoshinaka's sacrifice to the exigencies of politics and history was never lost on the people (*minshū*), particularly the youth:

> The judgment of the people alone showed that Kiso's character was never evil. Rather, Kiso's misfortune was to fall victim to the deeply laid machinations of the court nobles and cloistered court faction of the day. In a word, he was no more than a sacrifice (*gisei*) to history. Hence, young people who understand Kiso all love him. They never think of the morning sun general (*asahi shōgun*) as an evil court enemy."[39]

Enveloped in an aroma of mono no aware (pathos), Haga's traitor has now become a role model for youth.

A POPULAR CLASSIC? THE HEIKE IN THE PREMODERN PERIOD

The view of *The Tale of the Heike* propounded by Haga, Fujioka, Yasuda, and other prewar writers has been an influential one, and it lingers on in the perceptions of readers even today. Despite *The Heike*'s variety in style and content, which includes large amounts of humorous and supernatural anecdotes as well as unvarnished celebrations of military prowess, chrestomathies or handbooks designed to introduce the work to high school students even today tend to favor passages that highlight Buddhist themes of impermanence, episodes focused on the tragic and lyrically portrayed defeat of warriors, and passages connecting *The Heike* to a Heian literary aesthetic.[40] The preponderance of postwar studies dealing with *The Heike's* placation motif (*chinkon*) as an explanatory key to the work, while ostensibly linked to popular folkloric approaches to the work, may also be attributed in part to the continuing ascendancy of Heian literature, with its fecund ideological matrix of passive suffering, loss, and a compensatory logic of aesthetic beauty. Yet if we are to understand the full magnitude of prewar views of the work, and the even more powerful epic reading of *The Heike* in the postwar period, we must also attend to its premodern reception, especially in its relation to medieval culture as a site of so-called popular energies.

As Haruo Shirane notes in his introduction to this volume, one must be careful to distinguish between popular canons and those official canons associated with the vested interests of particular centers of power and authority. Whereas the latter "reproduce the values of a dominant group," the popular canon, open and fluid, is more often "sympathetic toward those deprived of power." From its earliest beginnings, *The Tale of the Heike* has always straddled both of these worlds, particularly when one considers all its variants, including not only written texts but also those transmitted through an oral tradition. In this sense, it is best to view *The Heike* as a structure of interrelated texts and oral practices, with numerous points of contact with both established and evolving centers of power, and with marginal elements at the fringes of society. In its most authoritative forms, such as *Genpei jō-suiki*, it was considered to be a semiofficial history. At the same time, in any discussion of *The Heike* it is useful, indeed crucial, to consider its "popular" reception among local, regional, and urban audiences that were, if not always in opposition to, at least in an ambivalent position vis-à-vis emergent or established centers of power.

One of the chief sites for Heike recitation (*heikyoku*) during its formative period was the area in the capital around Yasaka Pagoda (*Yasaka tō*) and the Kiyomizu slope. Abutting upon one of the largest markets in medieval Kyoto, this region attracted a mixed crowd that included outcasts (*hinin, saka no mono*), prostitutes (*tachigimi*), female entertainers (*yūjo*), and merchants (*akindo*).[41] *Tōdōyōshū* (Collected Essentials of the Guild), an Edo period handbook transmitting guild legends and anecdotal advice on performance, sheds further light on the multiple social venues of *Heike* recitation as it was practiced by the guild of blind reciters: "before the Palace and Courtiers Hall, in the presence of Ministers and Generals, before nobles and Buddhist prelates, and in the countryside and rustic places."[42] *Kanmon gyoki*, a diary kept by GoSukō-in (1372–1456), the grandson of Emperor Sukō, records numerous instances of guild reciters performing privately for aristo-

cratic audiences. Ueki Yukinobu has suggested that such aristocratic patronage may account for the lyrical quality of many *Heike* variants. On the other
hand, we know that warrior houses were also important patrons of the guild.
As Hyōdō Hiromi has persuasively argued, the production of new clean
copies (*kiyogaki*) of the Kakuichi variant that took place under the patronage of the Ashikaga branch of the Seiwa Genji is a clear indication of the importance of *The Tale of the Heike* both as a ritually performed text and as a
history for the Genji warrior clan.[43] This certainly appears to have been the
case for the Ashikaga shōgun Yoshimasa (1436–90), who is reported to have
listened to the entire *Heike* over the course of twenty-nine sessions.[44]

In addition to the mansions of powerful aristocrats and warriors and the
liminal Kiyomizu slope and market area, other important venues were
prayer halls (*jidō*) and courtyards (*niwa*) of temples located in the capital, as
well as crossroads (*tsuji*). Kanjin Heike (subscription Heike), as the name
suggests, was performed before mixed crowds for the purpose of raising
money for temple repairs and other uses. Controlled to some extent by the
temples and often combined with Buddhist sermons (*sekkyō*), kanjin Heike
suggests the reappropriation of *Heike* recitation for the purpose of prosely-
tizing and disseminating Buddhist doctrine. It also indicates the existence of
competition between rival centers of authority for institutional control of a
broadly popular narrative tradition. In discussing the parallel form of *kanjin
nō* (subscription nō) that was performed along riverbanks (*kawara*), for example, Ogasawara Kyōko notes that the performances, which could attract
thousands of people from different social strata, including capital roughs
(*kyō warawa*), were convenient sites for the new warrior class to display its
power. Eventually, as Ogasawara notes, the bakufu would devise a system of
licensing in an attempt to control the boisterous crowds that gathered to lis-
ten to various kanjin performances, which, in addition to nō or sarugaku
and *Heike* recitation, also included "field music" (*dengaku*) and balladic
dances performed by women (*kusemai*).[45]

In the course of the medieval period, *The Tale of the Heike* flowed into
other genres, including various theatrical forms such as nō, martial balladic
dances (*kōwakamai*), puppet theater (*jōruri*), and kabuki, as well as oral-de-
rived narrative forms such as anonymous short tales (*otogi-zōshi*) and, in the
Edo period, the widely popular "books of the floating world" (*ukiyo-zōshi*).
All of this oral and written production must be counted an important part
of the popular reception of *The Tale of the Heike*.

The significant influence of *The Heike* on nō theatre is indicated by
Zeami's well-known advice, in his treatise *Sandō*, on composing plots for

warrior plays: "Should the source of the character central to the play be a famous Heike or Genji warrior, the play should be always composed in accord
with the accounts given in *The Tale of the Heike*."[46] This passage has given
rise to numerous interpretations. Matsuoka Shinpei has suggested that
Zeami was attracted to the Kakuichi *Heike*'s established aura of authority
and aristocratic refinement, as opposed, for example, to the rough-and-tum-
ble depictions of warriors in *Taiheiki*. His argument is that Zeami was attempting to appeal to his new warrior patrons by replacing the negative
image of warriors in the old-style *onigakari no shura nō* (demon-warrior nō),
which crudely depicted warriors suffering the torments of Buddhist hells,
with the new-style *shura nō* (warrior nō), whose characteristic mark was aristocratic refinement. In *Tadanori*, for example, Zeami fuses elements from
the *Heike* depiction of Tadanori with elegant allusions to *The Tale of Genji*,
showing Tadanori at the height of glory on the battlefield instead of suffering
in a Buddhist hell.[47] Since the demon-warrior type nō continued to be performed at temples at about the same time, we have further evidence of how
Heike discourse could be simultaneously pulled in contrary directions.[48]

Another genre that falls within the purview of *Heike* influence was
kōwakamai, or martial balladic dances. Out of the fifty or so extant kōwaka
texts, twenty are related to *Heike* themes. Having developed in a period of
Genji dominance in the course of the fifteenth century, *kōwaka* texts reveal
a shift in focus from Heike warriors, characteristic of *Heike* recitation, to
Genji warriors. Even more importantly, the sources for individual kōwaka
plots were derived not from a unique *Heike* variant, but from a combination
of several *Heike* variants and oral traditions not found in written texts, and
the plots selected tended to emphasize retainers rather than masters. As
Misawa Yūko has noted, the appearance of retainers in roles of prominence
strikes the characteristic medieval note of "low overthrows high" (*gekokujō*).[49]
Furthermore, the kōwaka texts were connected to such *Heike* read variants
as *Genpei jōsuiki* and the Enkyō and Nagato variants, which are full of battle narrative with a strong regional coloring that has entirely dropped out of
the more widely known Kakuichi variant and other variants of the recited
lineage.[50] Many of these read variants contain within them the nuclei of regional histories, and exhibit, on another level, the pull characteristic in *The
Heike* between the peripheries and centers of power and authority. Just as
Zeami's shura nō appears to have appropriated the aristocratic cachet of the
Kakuichi variant in order to enhance the prestige of the increasingly powerful Ashikaga warrior clan, kōwaka texts appear to have developed out of a
countervailing regional pull characteristic of other *Heike* variants.

With the emergence of jōruri and kabuki in the late medieval and Edo periods, the influence of *The Heike* continued unabated. This can be explained in part by the consolidation of warrior power in the bakufu and the concomitant prestige accorded by it to such *Heike* variants as *Genpei jōsuiki*. *The Heike*'s proliferating world is further attested to by the large and still unedited number of otogi-zōshi based on the work that have come down to us from the Muromachi period alone.[51] Representative examples of Edo period works are Ihara Saikaku's *Kōshoku seisuiki* (The Rise and Fall of Love) and a work by a different author entitled *Fūryū ima Heike* (Today's Modish Heike). The latter, which is presented as the oral retelling of a written narrative by a blind female reciter (*goze*), portrays Kiyomori as an Edo-style townsman (*chōnin*) fallen on hard times due to his luxurious ways. The influence of *The Tale of the Heike* during the Edo period was also evident in the emergence of large numbers of *fuhon* (musical scores) published for use by amateur reciters, an art practiced widely by literati (*bunjin*) and tea masters.[52]

The Tale of the Heike of the premodern period was thus a work that grew out of a complex interplay between rival centers of authority and the marginal sites at their fringes, continuously fragmenting and flowing into new genres and modalities. Most importantly, the premodern *Heike* was not identical to the Kakuichi variant that most people read today, but consisted of a variety of variously named texts and narrative traditions that appealed to different audiences and classes of readers. Its earliest impact on Meiji scholars and writers was as a work that had been refracted and reshaped by late Edo urban sensibilities, embodying two broad yet distinct traditions: a widely diffused popular tradition going back to the medieval period and a more carefully controlled textual form, slowly acquiring its own commentary and exegesis, that was read and managed by the aristocratic and warrior elites.[53] In the Meiji 1880s and 1890s, the popular tradition of *Heike* was as yet outside the purview of the rapidly consolidating discipline of modern classical scholarship. For Sekine Masanao and Tsubouchi Shōyō, for example, the popular tradition of *Heike* recitation (*heikyoku*) was a category of literature difficult to assimilate to the newly imported western genres of novel, drama, and epic poem. Instead, it was lightly dismissed by them as "street talk" (*kōdan gaisetsu*) and "unofficial history" (*yashi*), old-fashioned Chinese terms for designating unofficial forms of discourse, and of little use in the pressing task of building a national literature.[54] Scholars such as Haga Yaichi, on the other hand, sensitive to its elite status as historical narrative in forms such as *Genpei jōsuiki* and sensing as well the lingering menace of its tumultuous world, were quick to dislodge its semiofficial forms from their eminence as history, preparing the way for *The Tale of the Heike*'s subsequent rebirth as a useful work of national literature.

By the late Meiji and Taishō periods, as texts of *The Heike* were gradually established and made available to a wider readership, writers began to turn to the work itself for inspiration, giving rise to a new literary fashion for novels (*shōsetsu*) based on *The Tale of the Heike*.[55] In this way, a popularly based tradition of both oral and written provenance that had descended from the Edo and medieval periods gradually crossed with the first wave of romantic influences from the West. The result was a large number of *Heike*-inspired novels and plays. The former were an early harbinger of the popular novel (*taishū shōsetsu*), which would crest in Yoshikawa Eiji's postwar epic rendering of *The Heike* entitled *Shin Heike monogatari* (New Tale of the Heike). Many of these novels and plays teemed with the kind of strong-willed egoistic characters extolled in Takayama's essay on Taira Kiyomori discussed earlier.

Among the most widely read of these *Heike*-inspired works were *Takiguchi nyūdō* (The Lay-Priest Takiguchi, 1895) by Takayama, *Taira no Kiyomori* (1910) by Yamada Bimyō (1868–1910), and the play *Hotoke gozen* (Lady Hotoke, 1912) by Mushanokōji Saneatsu (1885–1976). Yamada's novel depicts a strong-willed Kiyomori, despised by the Fujiwara and suffering in poverty, whose endurance and self-esteem gradually win him a place in the world, while Mushanokōji's *Hotoke gozen* portrays Kiyomori and the dancer (*shirabyōshi*) Giō as two strong-willed lovers, with Giō eventually resolving to seek her personal fulfillment in the religious life. Other *Heike* characters commonly selected for novelistic and dramatic treatment were Shigehira, a subject of tragic fate, and Shunkan, who typified the expression of romantic despair.[56] Kikuchi Kan's novel *Shunkan* (1921) also shows the extent to which such modern adaptations of *The Heike* were helping to transform it into a useful vehicle of social propaganda. In Kikuchi's novel, the hard-working Shunkan ends up marrying an inhabitant of his island place of exile, Kikaiga-shima, and thereafter lives a life of domestic tranquility. Illustrating the new modern ideal of "achieving success by overcoming difficulties" (*jiriki kōsei*), the outsider/rebel has become a productive member of society.[57]

With their emphasis on a romantic philosophy of individualism, cast in a lyrical or tragic mode, these plays and novels contributed to a reconceptualization of *The Tale of the Heike* as an early manifestation of a literature of the self. At the same time, they lent themselves to the recasting of *The Heike* as a form of literature that could be incorporated into a progressive narrative

of Japan's national awakening. In the end it was its association with popular
Edo culture, with its urban coloring, together with its roots in the medieval
past that made *The Tale of the Heike* and the medieval period ideal material
for the proponents of the epic theory.

A NATIONAL EPIC

The dominant view of *The Tale of the Heike* in the prewar years was characterized by an increasing tendency among scholars to assimilate it to an earlier type of court literature, which was by then being identified as authentic
and pure. But there were other writers and scholars, equally vocal if less
dominant, who had been calling for a more consciously political reading of
the work that echoed nationalistic and democratic sentiments. Although he
never employed the term *epic*, the economist and historian Taguchi Ukichi
(1855–1905) had as early as 1882 privileged *The Tale of the Heike* and the historical period in which it emerged as the first real political expression of the
people. In his widely read *Nihon kaika shōshi* (A Short History of Japanese
Civilization), he stated: "In our country's history, the achievement of making a clear connection between politics and the conditions of the people
dates in fact from Hōgen [1156–58] and Heiji [1159–60]."[58] In the same passage Taguchi had strongly criticized the kind of court-centered history embodied in the *Rikkokushi* (Six National Histories) as of little use for ascer-
taining anything about the political conditions of the day (*tōji no seiji no
arisama*) or the conditions of the people (*jinmin no jōkyō*).[59] With their focus
restricted to activities centered on the court, such histories, in Taguchi's
words, were "lacking in what is essential for a nation." In privileging the warrior-dominated medieval centuries as the critical moment in Japan's national
awakening, Taguchi had in fact anticipated the view, which would become
dominant seventy years later in the postwar period, of *The Tale of the Heike*
as an epic. In the 1950s, Tani Hiroshi, one of the most vigorous proponents
of that view, would write: "Through *The Tale of the Heike*, the history of the
end of the twelfth century and its people thoroughly overwhelms us with its
revolutionary dynamic power and verisimilitude. Moreover, as if gushing
spontaneously out of this work, the truth (*shinjitsu*) of the people's history
(*minzokushi*) shines forth."[60]

The term *epic poem* (*jojishi*) became current from about the time the critic
and translator Ikuta Chōkō (1882–1936) published his essay "Kokuminteki
jojishi toshite no *Heike monogatari*" (*The Tale of the Heike* as a National

Epic) in 1906 in *Teikoku bungaku.* We must be careful, however, to distinguish the more systematic formulators of an epic *Heike,* such as Takagi Ichinosuke, from those who loosely characterized the work as an epic. Literature scholars such as Fujioka Sakutarō, Igarashi Chikara, and others liberally sprinkled their discussions of the work with terms such as *epic poem, lyric poem (jojōshi),* and *tragedy (higeki).*[61] Such literary terms, all derived from Aristotle's *Poetics,* were used by these scholars as a way to ascribe so-called universal traits to Japan's literary inheritance. As the imperial ideology strengthened its grip in the prewar years, the court-centered literature of the Heian and Taika Reform periods achieved canonical preeminence, with the so-called universal categories of the lyrical and the tragic regarded as timeless expressions of Japan's authentic spirit. It is within this context that the more radical use of the term *epic,* as the narrative of an aggressively popular (*minshūteki*) ethos, marks a subtle rupture with the outwardly more pacifistic claims of the imperial ideology.

In *"The Tale of the Heike* as a National Epic," Chōkō elaborates a scheme for Japanese historical periodization that juxtaposes negative periods of foreign cultural influence against periods of cultural purification. According to Chōkō, although the Heian and Edo periods were both great periods of purification, their literature was limited, in the Heian to the aristocratic class (*kizoku*), and in the Edo period to the commoner class (*heimin*). It was only during the Kamakura-Muromachi period that literature, mediated by warriors and priests who were neither strictly aristocratic nor commoner, achieved a truly national (*kokuminteki*) character. The supreme expression of this national literature, for Chōkō, was *The Tale of the Heike,* which he compared to other epics of world literature such as the Greek *Iliad* and *Odyssey,* the German *Nibelungenlied,* and the Indian *Mahabharata.*[62]

In 1910, four years after Chōkō's essay and three years after Fujioka's 1907 essay in *Teikoku bungaku,* two more essays were published on the epic characteristics of *The Tale of the Heike.* In April of that year, the scholar of religions Anesaki Masaharu (1873–1949) published an essay entitled "The Epic as the Confession of an Age," contrasting the epic's focus on "events" (*jiken*), as exemplified in *The Tale of the Heike,* with the lyrical and emotional content of poetry (*waka*). With the Homeric poems and the Indian *Mahabharata* as his examples, he notes that nearly every country had some great battle in its past that gave rise to an epic. The epics that emerged out of such periods of warfare, moreover, expressed as the works of no other age could, the true mind (*magokoro*) of a people.[63] For Anesaki, the period of the Genpei Wars narrated in *The Heike,* more than any other period in Japanese history, embodied just such an expression of a "nation's spirit" (*kokumin no seishin*), and this explains the work's enduring capacity to stir people's feelings.

In his 1910 essay, "*The Tale of the Heike* as an Epic," the novelist and critic Iwano Hōmei (1873–1920) invokes the examples of Dante's *Divine Comedy* and Milton's *Paradise Lost* in order to provide a Western parallel to *The Heike's* epic focus on religious and tragic themes. Hōmei singles out Tadanori's pursuit of poetic fame, the now famous episode of the warrior Nasu no Yoichi's archery exploit, and the drowning of the child emperor Antoku as examples of how the nation (*waga kokumin*) expresses its artistic (*bijutsuteki*) and religious spirit (*shintōteki seishin*) even in moments of extremity.[64]

In addition to their emphasis on universal qualities by comparing *The Heike* with other world epics, these essays are notable for their militant nationalism. In Chōkō's essay, the opposition between periods of foreign and indigenous cultural dominance, with the latter characterized as superior, anticipates the prewar critique of the modern, which would set Japan's own cultural past as a bulwark against an increasingly dominant, technology-driven West. In Anesaki's essay there is, for the first time, an open acknowledgment of war as a generator of great literature and a crucible for forging a national consciousness, while in Hōmei the singularity of the religious and aesthetic in Japanese culture serves as an important characteristic of Japan's national consciousness. In many respects, all three of these writers conceptualize Japanese literature in ways similar to Fujioka, especially in their preference for the religious and aesthetic, but what sets them radically apart is their militant nationalism, which derives some of its force from class antagonisms that first emerged in the strife of the warrior-dominated medieval centuries. This view is further illustrated in the work of the historian Tsuda Sōkichi (1873–1961), another proponent of *The Tale of the Heike* as epic.

As has already been noted, literature scholars such as Haga Yaichi and Fujioka Sakutarō did not readily accommodate conflict and class divisions in their narratives of Japanese literary history. This is especially evident in their tendency to downplay periods of violent change while privileging the fiction of peaceful change in the periods of the Taika and Meiji reforms. Tsuda's innovation in his multivolume study of Japanese literature entitled *Bungaku ni arawaretaru waga kokumin shisō no kenkyū* (A Study of the Thought of Our Nation's People as Reflected in Literature, 1916–21) was to locate the concept of the nation-people (kokumin) in the activity of a single agent: the Japanese language as it was embodied in a varied and historically contingent literature (bungaku).[65] In other words, Tsuda's national literature arose out of multiplicity and conflict, through an evolutionary and dynamic process of histor-ical change.

Tsuda characterizes *The Tale of the Heike* as both an epic poem (jojishi) and, in its emotional pathos, as a lyric poem (jojōshi). For Tsuda, the author stands outside the power struggles that form the substance of the narration, and this detachment from events gives him a freedom of judgment expres-sive of the broad viewpoint of the "people" (minshū). Moreover, Tsuda notes that the creation of "national heroes" (*kokuminteki eiyū*) such as Shigemori and Yoshitsune derives from the same popular spirit. In contrast to the liter-ature of the Heian period, where the main characters such as Genji and Ariwara Narihira were admired because of their social position, the heroes of *The Heike* and other military chronicles are respected as characters in their own right. Such military chronicles with their heroic figures, he concludes, "are important national poems, a national literature."[66]

The major prewar proponent of *The Heike* as epic theory, and the most vehement critic of all lyrical, Buddhist, and tragic readings of the work, was the literature scholar Takagi Ichinosuke, who was also one of the editors of the now standard Iwanami taikei edition that was published in 1959.[67] For Takagi, the chief elements of *The Heike*'s epic style were its simplicity, its virility, and its capacity when read out loud to affect the reader or listener al-most physically. These qualities, in contrast to the enervating effects of court literature, made it a pedagogically valuable work. As early as 1912, Takagi had written a doctoral thesis at Tokyo Imperial University entitled "The Tale of the Heike Viewed as an Epic" (*Jojishi toshite mitaru Heike monogatari*). Even in this early effort, however, Takagi's interest in the problem of a Japanese epic was being drawn further back in time to the chronicles of the ancient period (*kodai*).[68] Takagi's attraction to the ancient period was the result of several factors, including the prestige accorded the ancient period by nativist learning (*kokugaku*). But the most important factor was his study of Western theories of epic formation, particularly those of the German thinker Johann Gottfried Herder (1744–1803) and the Scottish medievalist W. P. Ker (1855–1923).[69]

Although Herder never succeeded in systematizing his ideas on the epic, by the time his writings reached Japan his name had become inseparably linked to the concept of "folk-poetry" (*min'yō*).[70] In his later work, Herder came under the influence of the philologist F. A. Wolf (1759–1824), who ar-gued that the Homeric poems were not the work of an individual poet, but the fragmentary remains of discrete, anonymous oral lays, whose total design was as much the product of late editing as any shaping influence of folk-memory.[71] The theory is evident in Ikuta Chōkō's essay, in which he lists five conditions that a work must meet in order to qualify as an epic. His first and second conditions, that the epic must have a "basis in myths and legends connected to the deeds of ancestors or heroes" and a structure that reflects "a synthesis and reworking by one or several people of short poems that have already passed through a long period of oral transmission among the people (kokumin)," embody the core of Herder's late intuitions on epic formation.[72] In brief, it was Herder's theory that epics arose out of a process of amalgamation whereby the popular songs (*Volkslied*) of a nation's immemorial past gradually coalesced into a much longer poem.

Herder's near mystical reverence for this primordial voice of the people was part of a much broader discourse of nationalism, whose first stirrings in Europe appeared in the eighteenth century. The theory and its link with nationalism is usefully summarized by Kwame Appiah: "Herder's notion of the Sprachgeist—literally, the 'spirit' of language—embodies the thought that language is not merely the medium through which speakers communicate but the sacred essence of a nationality. . . . From its inception, literary history, like the collection of folk culture, served the ends of nation-building."[73] In the course of the nineteenth century, with the Homeric poems serving as a model and inspiration, long forgotten works such as the Anglo-Saxon *Beowulf*, the French *Roland*, and the German *Nibelungenlied* were rediscovered one by one and then hailed as the primitive expression of the national spirit of their respective countries.[74] In some instances, this quest for origins even led scholars to collaborate in the creation of epics, a process exemplified in Elias Lönnrot's creation of the great Finnish poem, *Kalevala*. As this latter example suggests, the lack of an epic was tantamount to the lack of a national past.[75]

For Takagi, who was thoroughly familiar with such European theory on the folk-epic, the Japanese epic ought to have emerged in the ancient period, the privileged moment for the crystallization of a national consciousness. His first effort was to search in the ancient songs of the chronicles, the *Kojiki* (712) and *Nihon shoki* (720). He explored this problem in several essays published in the 1920s and 1930s.[76] In a 1933 essay, "Nihon bungaku ni okeru jojishi jidai" (The Epic Age in Japanese Literature), for example, Takagi boldly suggested that the speaker in one of the ancient songs was not the Emperor Jimmu, but a heroic individual (*eiyūtekina kojin*) representative of a collective heroic past.[77] Writing in a period of imperial fervor, Takagi was treading on dangerous ground. Later in this essay, he in fact retreated to the orthodox position that the *ware* ("I") or subject of this song was, after all, a "great figure like the Emperor Jimmu of tradition.[78] Takagi's intent is nonetheless clear: he wanted to restore the ancient songs of the imperial chronicles to what he felt was their rightful place in an epic tradition of a national heroic past.

With reluctance, Takagi concluded that the ancient chronicles yielded only fragmentary evidence of a heroic tradition that had been brought to nought by foreign, specifically Chinese, influences. As a consequence, he shifted his attention from the ancient period of the songs to the mid-Heian and medieval periods. There, in the soil of the provinces, far from the capital, he discovered that "simplicity and roughness" (*soboku soya na mono*), the hallmark of the epic spirit, first in the early military chronicles, and then, more fully, in *The Tale of the Heike* itself. Echoing Ker's distinction between the simplicity of the primitive epic and the over-refined complexity of the romance, but also drawing on the nativist attacks against Chinese influences, Takagi conceived the epic spirit as in a continuous battle to free itself from the enervating effects of Chinese words. Hence, the vital force of the epic spirit, even in such works as *Hōgen monogatari* (The Tale of Hōgen), *Heiji monogatari* (The Tale of Heiji), and *The Heike*, is diminished "because it was painted over by the extremely artificial expressions deriving from Chinese."[79] However, Takagi averred, when the epic spirit does break through, in the description of such warriors as Tametomo in *The Tale of Hōgen* or of the battle of Ichi no tani in *The Heike*, it has the irresistible power to move. It was as if the epic spirit had gushed forth whole from the legends and ancient songs of the chronicles, stripped of all secondary interests, no longer trammeled by artificial rhetoric (*gikōteki na shūshoku*) and carping criticism (*richiteki na hihan*).[80] For Takagi, this epic spirit, manifested in the individual words and rhythms of *The Heike*'s onomatopoeic prose, had a pedagogical value that far exceeded the kind of moral instruction Haga Yaichi and others saw as the chief value of warrior chronicles. He was full of praise for the exemplary value to young minds of strong warrior figures such as Tametomo, and he condemned the standard textbook emphasis on the Confucian-minded Shigemori.[81]

Like Yasuda Yojūrō, Takagi showed a strong anti-intellectual bias, but it was a bias that inclined toward militant action rather than the aesthetic stance and the values of sacrifice, tragic pathos, and beauty associated with the Buddhist and court ideals embraced by Yasuda. Takagi's brand of popular nationalism, and its vehicle of expression, the warrior chronicles reconceptualized as epic, was, in subtle ways, at variance with the dominant state-nationalism of the prewar period. Takagi was writing, moreover, in the 1930s, a time of renewed interest in the classics and in those very court values that he viewed as anathema to the epic spirit of *The Heike*.[82] All of these factors, combined with its suggestion of an anti-imperial bias, contributed to the relative neglect of Takagi's epic theory in the years preceding the war.[83]

THE POSTWAR EPIC RESURGENCE

In the years following World War II, interpretations of *The Tale of the Heike* reflected the shift from the static, essentialist presentation of history that had prevailed in the prewar period to a dynamic, dialectical-materialist reading of events, which placed conflict, change, and transformation at the forefront. Among the key architects of this theory were Marxist historians such as Ishimoda Shō (1912–1986) and Tani Hiroshi (1914–1984) and literature scholars versed in historical methodology such as Nagazumi Yasuaki (1908–1995).[84] Part of a larger group known collectively as the sociohistorical school of criticism (*rekishi shakai gakuha*), these scholars transformed the timeless literary qualities that had been privileged in prewar views of *The Heike* into expressions of class struggle.

The first blow struck in this reassessment of both *The Heike* and the medieval period was Ishimoda Shō's ground-breaking study *Chūseiteki sekai no keisei* (The Formation of Medieval Society). It was in such an intellectual climate, when efforts were being made to dismantle what became known as the emperor system (*tennōsei*), that the epic theory of *The Tale of the Heike* took on a new life, achieving a near orthodoxy among literature scholars in the 1950s and 1960s.[85] One of Ishimoda's principal aims was to reconceptualize the medieval period (*chūsei*) as a dialectical critique of the earlier ancient (*kodai*) period.[86] In brief, he viewed the late-Heian and early medieval periods during which *The Tale of the Heike* took shape as a stage for the enactment of a class struggle between an urban-based aristocracy and an agriculture-based warrior class rooted in peasant culture. The role of mediating this class struggle fell to the wandering figure of the *biwa hōshi*. Transmitters of an ancient oral tradition (*katari*) going back to the clans and people (*minzoku*) of the ancient period, they moved freely across social strata and produced over time a synthesis of clashing cultural traditions that came to be embodied in the new harmony of *The Tale of the Heike*.[87] The result of this historical process, according to Ishimoda, was the creation of a truly national literature. To take just one example, whereas prewar scholars had viewed the Buddhism in *The Heike* as the world-weary expression of aristocratic nostalgia, Ishimoda argued that Pure Land Buddhism transformed itself from the pessimistic expression of a negated urban aristocratic culture into an affirmative anti-aristocratic expression with broad general appeal.[88]

In the work of Nagazumi, the contradictory motifs of the heroic and the tragic, which had been emphasized by Takagi and the more orthodox literature scholars respectively, became the clash between competing viewpoints.[89] Hence, in their heroic dimensions, the three major figures of Kiyomori, Kiso no Yoshinaka, and Yoshitsune, together with a host of minor heroes, all represent the viewpoint of the people (minshū). The second great motif, the tragic presentation, gives us the viewpoint of the aristocratic class, for whom the defeated Heike came to evoke their own fallen and disempowered state. In a wider view, these same contradictory elements embodied, for Nagazumi, the dissonance of ancient cultural effects that had lingered into the medieval period. In true Marxian fashion, *The Tale of the Heike* thus became the clash between historical periods as well, and in this clash Nagazumi discovered its distinctive epic quality. In the same way, the so-called mixed Chinese-Japanese style (*wakan konkō bun*), which is often singled out as *The Heike*'s chief literary quality in school textbooks, became the linguistic equivalent of clashing cultural traditions resolved into a new characteristic style.[90]

CONCLUSION

In the work of Ishimoda, Nagazumi, and other postwar proponents of the epic theory, the medieval period in which *The Heike* emerged was transformed from a marginal, problematic moment in Japan's imperial past into the central, epochal moment of Japan's national awakening. In its capacity to both incorporate and then harmonize social conflict and change, and to find a place for a wide range of moods—from the tragic to the heroic, from the comic to the pathetic—the theory developed by these scholars helped to make *The Tale of the Heike* into a powerful metaphor for Japan's postwar economic transformation. It was during these very years, from 1950 to 1957, that Yoshikawa Eiji (1892–1962) serialized his immensely popular *Shin Heike monogatari* in the *Asahi shinbun*, a labor which the novelist and critic Masamune Hakuchō (1879–1962) compared to the creation of a national epic. Yoshikawa himself, sensitive to the new postwar political climate, contrasted what he called the closed world of *The Tale of Genji* with the openness and international spirit of *The Heike* typified in Taira no Kiyomori.[91]

The epic theory's dominance lasted well into the 1970s. In the fourth edition of the *Kōjien* dictionary, published in 1955 and revised several times since 1969, *The Tale of the Heike* is still defined as an epic poem (jojishi). However, in view of its complexity and the diversity of its different variants, *The Heike* resists easy classification. A multifarious work of various historical provenances, with diverse regional, class, and gender affiliations, had been made to speak in the monological voice of the nation. With scholars now less concerned with defining the work as an expression of nationality, an invigorating appreciation of complexity is being restored to our understanding of *The Tale of the Heike* and its numerous variants.

CHAPTER SEVEN

Chikamatsu and Dramatic Literature in the Meiji Period

WILLIAM LEE

In a recent article entitled "Why Study Canonization?" the Canadian comparatist Milan Dimic wrote that the study of canonization "will permit us to explain better how canons are created, for what purpose and with what results."[1] Examining a given case of canonization not only provides insight into the discursive and ideological context operative at the time of canonization, but it also helps us to understand how canonization has affected the subsequent critical reception of the literary work. I shall try to show that studying the process whereby Chikamatsu Monzaemon's works were given canonical status in the Meiji period allows us to see not only what role discussions of the theater in general and Chikamatsu's work in particular played in the discourse of that period—and thereby shed some light on the distinctive features of that discourse as well as its underlying ideological concerns—but also how this canonizing discourse privileged certain approaches to and perceptions of Chikamatsu's work that continue to shape interpretations of his plays even today.

CHIKAMATSU IN THE EDO PERIOD

Before we turn to the Meiji period (1868–1912), it will be useful to have some idea of the reputation of Chikamatsu and his work prior to that period, since this is the position against which all reformulations brought about by canonization must be measured. As the author of more than one hundred works for the jōruri puppet theater, as well as some thirty kabuki plays, Chikamatsu (1653–1724) was a major figure in the theater world of the Kamigata (Kyoto and Osaka) region. Within this imposing corpus, moreover, were many popular successes.[2] Yet despite this productivity and commercial success, recognition did not come easily to Chikamatsu, either in the actor-centered kabuki or the *gidayū* (chanter)-centered jōruri theater. Indeed, the critique of actors, *Yarō tachiyaku butai ōkagami* (Great Mirror of Male Stage Actors, 1687), speaks derisively of Chikamatsu's publicizing himself as a jōruri and kabuki "author" (*sakusha*).[3] Even after it had become more common to identify the playwright on theater programs (*banzuke*), Chikamatsu's position as a writer was not comparable to that of a modern author. This was because kabuki play production was a collaborative process, with both the troupe leader (*zamoto*) and financial backers (*kinshu, ginshu*) having a say in the choice and construction of the plot, and with the actors themselves involved in working out the action and dialogue. In jōruri as well, Chikamatsu often worked closely with the troupe leader, and the success of some of his most popular plays, including *Kokusenya kassen* (The Battles of Coxinga), can be attributed in part to Takeda Izumo I (d. 1747), whose efforts to ensure popular success for his theater led to an emphasis on special effects and spectacle.[4]

While recognition for Chikamatsu's playwriting ability during his lifetime was thus circumscribed by the production process and economic realities of the commercial theater, his name nonetheless did live on during the rest of the Edo period (1600–1867). Three years after his death, for example, the jōruri history *Ima mukashi ayatsuri nendaiki* (A Chronology of the Puppet Theater, 1727) declared Chikamatsu to be "the tutelary god of playwrights" (*sakusha no ujigami*), while the late eighteenth-century *Sekai kōmoku*, a manual for kabuki playwrights, gives the titles of many of Chikamatsu's plays for reference.[5] The high esteem in which Chikamatsu was held by subsequent generations in the theater world can also be seen in the number of playwrights who adopted his name, the most notable being the jōruri playwright Chikamatsu Hanji (1725–1783). In the popular world of amateur gidayū chanting, too, Chikamatsu's work enjoyed a lasting reputation, as is evident by the large number of his plays still being published in the form of *jōruri-bon* (jōruri texts) until late in the Edo period.[6]

In addition to amateur chanters and those involved in the theater world, Chikamatsu also enjoyed a reputation among some Edo period scholars and writers. It was the Confucian scholar Hozumi Ikan (1692–1769), for example, who recorded Chikamatsu's thoughts on playwriting and art in his *Naniwa miyage* (1738).[7] Among the literati, the *kyōka* (comic waka) poet and comic writer Ōta Nampo (1749–1823) discussed several of Chikamatsu's plays in *Zokuji kosui* (Inspiration for Common Ears, 1788), while the *gesaku* (fiction) author Ryūtei Tanehiko (1783–1842) left in his *Jōruribon mokuroku* (Jōruri Text Catalog, 1818) the most comprehensive listing of Chikamatsu's plays undertaken during the Edo period.[8] These examples, however, should not be taken as evidence that either Chikamatsu or his plays were held in high esteem by the intelligentsia in general. Most Confucian scholarship of the period, for example, was focused on the Chinese classics or later commentaries; Confucian literary theory itself did not even include drama as a genre. Similarly, scholars of the *kokugaku* (nativism learning) school were primarily employed in philological studies of the waka poetry or prose narratives (*monogatari*) of the Nara and Heian periods. Indeed, due to the elite prejudice against popular entertainment, most scholars as well as writers working in more traditional genres would not have considered jōruri or kabuki texts worthy of serious study. Hozumi Ikan, who was personally acquainted with Chikamatsu, thus represents somewhat of an exception among Confucian scholars. It should also be noted that both Nampo and Tanehiko, despite their samurai backgrounds, were popular writers; Tanehiko, in fact, even wrote for the jōruri theater at one point in his career. It would be unwise, therefore, to read into these scattered examples of familiarity with or praise for Chikamatsu's work anything like the widespread acceptance by the educated elite characteristic of the established literary canon.

As for the general public or average theatergoer, here too one cannot assume a general familiarity with Chikamatsu's work, though in this case for quite different reasons. Subsequent developments in the theater world, including the introduction of the three-man puppet, an increasing emphasis on spectacle, and a tendency toward collective authorship of plays, produced by the mid-eighteenth century a very different theater from the one for which Chikamatsu had written. The popularity of jōruri at this time also had an impact on kabuki, the producers of which quickly adapted current jōruri successes for their own theaters. As a result, none of Chikamatsu's kabuki plays were restaged after his death, and those of his jōruri plays that were performed were inevitably adapted, revised, or even totally rewritten to meet the demands of the new theater. Most people in the late Edo period thus would not have been familiar with Chikamatsu's original work, and it can probably be concluded that many would not even have known of him at all. This especially would have been the case in the city Edo, where in the late Edo period jōruri was seldom performed and there were fewer stagings of kabuki adaptions of Chikamatsu's plays than in the Kamigata region.[9]

MEIJI PUBLICATIONS AND THE THEATER REFORM SOCIETY

While Chikamatsu's work was known and admired by Edo-period theater professionals, amateur chanters, and some writers, this recognition did not extend to the intellectual community at large or to the general public. All of this changed during the Meiji period. By 1905 a number of modern editions of Chikamatsu's works had been published, countless articles on Chikamatsu written for both academic and more popular journals, and the first attempts undertaken to perform faithful reproductions of Chikamatsu's plays on the stage. Most of this activity, moreover, had taken place in Tokyo. It is thus not only in the discourse of the Meiji period, but especially that of Tokyo, the power center of the nation, that the canonization of Chikamatsu's work must be located. This geographical factor must not be overlooked, for surely an important step in Chikamatsu's canonization was to make of him a national rather than a mere regional icon.

This canonization process would not have been possible without greater accessibility to texts of Chikamatsu's plays. The first step, therefore, was the modern reproduction of Chikamatsu's originals, most of which by this time were to be found only in the libraries of rare book collectors. The pioneer in this area was Hayashi Tamiji (1857–1922), owner of the publishing house Musashiya sōshokaku. Beginning in 1881, Hayashi began publishing modern editions of Chikamatsu's plays, and during the next dozen years he went on to publish some fifty Chikamatsu texts, culminating in the publication in 1892 of two large collections, *Chikamatsu jidai jōruri* (Chikamatsu's historical jōruri plays) and *Chikamatsu sewa jōruri* (Chikamatsu's contemporary jōruri plays), which between them reproduced a total of eighteen plays.

According to the introductory remarks contained in one of the first editions, the aim behind the Musashiya's publication of Chikamatsu's plays was "to disseminate these masterworks to even the most remote places." The motive for this can be found in the suggestion that Chikamatsu's language could help "to nurture the seed of composition."[10] Hayashi and the Musashiya, in other words, were little concerned with the historical nature of Chikamatsu's texts. Nor were they interested in providing texts that could be used for a Chikamatsu revival in the theater: indeed, the musical annotations used for jōruri chanting were omitted and the texts were published in a form more suitable for reading. The intent, in short, was educational, and as the emphasis was on language, the project itself can be said to reflect the early Meiji interest in language and education.

Whatever their intended purpose, it was these Musashiya texts that were read by Meiji period scholars and critics and thus prepared the way for the Chikamatsu boom that took place during the 1890s. At this point, there were two currents of scholarship and criticism, both of which played a role in the canonization of Chikamatsu's works. The first began with the theater reform movement carried on by Tsubouchi Shōyō and his colleagues and students at Waseda University. The second was centered around the graduates of Tokyo University's short-lived Classics Training Course (*koten kōshū-ka*), along with their colleagues from the Department of Japanese Literature. As Michael Brownstein has pointed out, it was the members of this second group who laid the foundations for the study of national literature (*kokubungaku*) and who in 1890 published a number of works that "provided the prototypes for all later scholarly anthologies and literary histories, and defined as well the canon of classical Japanese literature for the modern era."[11]

While there can be no doubting the importance of the kokubungaku scholars in the establishment of the Japanese canon, in the case of Chikamatsu the discourse of theater reform was equally if not more instrumental. This is not only because Chikamatsu was a playwright and his works—albeit in later adaptions—were still occasionally performed in the theater. Nor is it simply due to the fact that intellectual interest in the theater actually preceded the activities of the kokubungaku scholars. It is, rather, because the discourse of the reform movement was the first to employ a radically new conception of the theater. Put simply, this was the conception of the theater or, better yet, "drama" (the English word preferred by many Meiji critics), as *a kind of literature*. Historically, both kabuki and jōruri had been first and foremost live theater, and it is precisely the emphasis on performance that accounts for the frequent rewriting and adaptation of popular plays and the lack of an independent tradition of dramatic literature. The treatment of Chikamatsu as a writer and the acceptance of his works into the literary canon thus reveals a basic shift in assumptions about both literature and theater, a shift that is of the same order as the epistemic shifts or "inversions" analyzed in Karatani Kōjin's *Origins of Modern Japanese Literature*.[12] That is to say, the discovery of dramatic literature involved both a fundamental reformulation and the repression of the historical nature of this reformulation, which enabled the conception of the theater as literature to operate as an unspoken assumption and which later allowed the Waseda and Tokyo University groups to debate with each other over the nature of Chikamatsu's plays. For although the two sides differed from each other in many respects, both implicitly subscribed to the assumption that Chikamatsu's texts represented a kind of literature.

The effort to reform the public theater, like other reform movements of the 1870s and 1880s, was basically a top-down social phenomenon; and as in other reform movements, motivation came from the conviction that in order to advance its image and position in the world Japan would have to show that it had become a modern, "civilized" nation on a par with the industrialized powers of the West. Those of the governing and educated elite who had been to Europe were well aware of the important cultural role played by the great theaters of the European capitals, and thus in calling for theater reform they were also calling for the creation of a "national" theater of their own. Japan at this time had several traditional theaters, including nō, kabuki, and jōruri. The leading contender for the position of national theater, however, was kabuki. As for the others, jōruri still enjoyed popularity among amateur chanters; there was also a boom during the Meiji period of so-called "women's chanting" (*onna gidayū*), especially in Tokyo. The fact that much of this activity took place on the amateur level or in small variety theaters (*yose*), however, was no doubt one reason why jōruri was not seen as a candidate for a national theater.[13] Nō, on the other hand, was given serious consideration by at least one high-ranking government official, Iwakura Tomomi (1825–1883). While abroad in the early 1870s as head of a government mission, Iwakura had attended opera performances, and this apparently gave him a new appreciation of the value of the nō theater. Accordingly, on his return he set about helping to revive nō, which was then on the brink of extinction. Through Iwakura's offices, nō performances were viewed by members of the imperial family in 1876, and former U.S. President Ulysses S. Grant was invited to view a performance of nō during his visit to Japan in 1879. With Iwakura's death in 1883, however, interest in nō by the ruling oligarchy dropped off.[14]

It was kabuki, then, that became the leading candidate to take on the role of a national theater. Although some official measures were taken as early as 1872, it was not until the mid-1880s that a concerted effort at kabuki reform was mounted. At the center of this movement was the Theater Reform Society (Engeki kairyōkai), founded in 1886. Among the society's regular and supporting members were Prime Minister Itō Hirobumi (1841–1909), Foreign Minister Inoue Kaoru (1835–1915), and Education Minister Mori Arinori (1847–89). The de facto chairman of the society was Itō's son-in-law, Suematsu Kenchō (1855–1920), who had just returned earlier the same year from a nine-year stay abroad, including two years spent at Cambridge.

According to its "prospectus," the three major aims of the society were

1. to put an end to the evil customs of the theater and to foster the development of a better theater;
2. to make the writing of plays an honored profession; and
3. to construct a theater building suitable for the performance of drama and other stage arts, including music.

Elaborating on these goals, the prospectus criticized kabuki plays for being "lewd" and "vulgar." A reformed theater, it argued, would be one that "the upper classes can view without embarrassment." Such a theater, however, would be dependent on better plays, and this in turn would require encouraging "scholars and men of letters" to become playwrights.[15] These aims were repeated and other recommendations were made by individual members of the society in pamphlets and speeches of that year. Suematsu, for example, called not only for the adherence to Western dramatic principles such as the three unities and the separation of comedy and tragedy, but also for the abolition of such typical features of kabuki performance as the *hanamichi* (runway), the *chobo* (chanting of the narrative to musical accompaniment) used in plays derived from the jōruri theater, and the *onnagata* (female impersonator).[16] Another member of the society, Toyama Masakazu (1848–1900), added to this list the *kurombo* (veiled stage assistant) and scenes dealing with prostitutes and the licensed prostitution quarters.[17]

Potentially, the aims of the Theater Reform Society had major implications for the kabuki world, and it is hard to imagine how anything resembling traditional kabuki could have survived had all the society's recommendations been implemented. The society was short-lived, however, and its direct impact minimal. Nevertheless, the reform movement did have some indirect and lasting consequences. The interest shown in kabuki by the elite, for example, helped to dispel the traditional prejudice against the kabuki world, and eventually the way was opened for writers from the outside to enter the field. Another by-product of the movement was the impetus it gave to the serious consideration of kabuki as a historical theatrical genre. Any attempt at reforming kabuki, after all, implicitly required first a recognition of what kabuki was. Of course, the reformers rejected much of what they saw, but there were some aspects of kabuki that they could accept, even in a climate of reform based on Western models.

It is in the discourse of reform itself that the first hints of a more positive evaluation of kabuki can be found. Toyama, for example, expressed a preference for the older plays in the repertoire, claiming that some of them approached Shakespeare's work in transcending the particular time and place in which they were produced.[18] Suematsu as well conceded that in the past Japan had some playwrights of worth. "A Shakespeare," he argued, "may not appear for generations, but even though Chikamatsu Monzaemon and Takeda Izumo cannot be counted in the same class, it does not seem as if anyone will appear soon to rival them."[19] No doubt this remark was meant to emphasize the unlikelihood of any of the existing playwrights contributing to Suematsu's vision of a reformed theater. The mention of Chikamatsu and Takeda does suggest, however, the possibility of co-opting part of the native tradition for the reform movement. Moreover, that this distinction should fall to writers, and in particular to writers for jōruri, who were considered to have exercised more control over their texts than their counterparts in the actor-centered kabuki, further suggests that if there were room in reformist discourse for a rehabilitation of the theater of the past, this would be conceived as a *literary* theater.

TSUBOUCHI SHŌYŌ AND THE CHIKAMATSU BOOM OF THE 1890S

The critic who more than any other was responsible for making the study of the theater a respected scholarly pursuit was Tsubouchi Shōyō (1859–1935). In the history of Japanese literature Shōyō is best known for his *Shōsetsu shinzui* (The Essence of the Novel, 1885–86), as well as for his association with Futabatei Shimei, author of *Ukigumo*, arguably Japan's first modern novel. In the context of his own career, however, the mediating role Shōyō played in the development of modern Japanese prose fiction ranks a distant second when compared to his nearly lifelong devotion to the theater. Soon after the publication of *The Essence of the Novel*, Shōyō turned his attention to the theater, and from then until his death in 1935 his activities ranged over virtually every aspect of the field. In addition to his critical work on the theater, Shōyō also produced a number of original plays of his own, as well as a complete translation of Shakespeare. To this must be added the activities of his Literary Arts Association (Bungei kyōkai, 1906–13), which was responsible for the staging of several plays by modern European playwrights.

As wide-ranging as Shōyō's activities in the field of drama and the theater were, it could be said that they were really only different aspects of one common project: the creation of a national theater. Shōyō's research into Japan's theatrical traditions and his study of foreign models, in other words, must be seen in the context of an ideological and discursive environment in which considerations of the native culture were always accompanied and shaped by an awareness of the West. This applies even to those of Shōyō's works purporting to deal specifically with historical Japanese theater. In such works the examination of the Japanese tradition is always haunted by the question of national identity and by the example of the West, and thus the option of reform is never entirely absent.

What Shōyō saw in the theater of the West and found lacking in traditional Japanese theater was a literary quality. He was therefore critical of the Theater Reform Society's emphasis on theater architecture and questions of morality, and in his own contribution to the reform debate unequivocally stated his position that reform of the theater depended above all on producing better scripts, and that this required the recognition of dramatic texts *as literature*:

> The reform of play scripts is the essential basis of any theater reform, and unless this is carried out, all other reform measures will be of no avail. . . . Since, fundamentally, the main purpose of the theater, as of the novel, is to portray the truth (the truth of human emotions, the truth of social conditions), to be so concerned with extraneous matters as to kill this truth is a dangerous priority.[20]

It was thus by equating drama with the novel that Shōyō brought the whole discussion of theater and theater reform into the realm of literature. While his definition of the aim of literature may sound like a recipe for a nineteenth-century European novel, no doubt Shōyō's reading of Shakespeare, whom he had already started translating by this time, also lay behind his ascribing literary value to dramatic texts. In any case, like other reformers, Shōyō was aware of the great prestige Shakespeare's plays enjoyed and the scholarly attention they received. That Japanese theater lacked such attention was evidence to him of its deficiencies.

It is not surprising that traditional kabuki plays should be seen as defective when viewed as literature, given the primacy of stage performance in historical kabuki and the consequent lack of an independent tradition of dramatic literature. Shōyō's critical assumption that theater *is* literature prevented him from accepting this, however, and led him on the one hand to a critique of traditional kabuki, and on the other to an effort at reforming the contemporary theater. In order that the picture he painted of the traditional theater be not entirely negative, lest it undermine the possibility of a new national theater built on the foundation of the past, a third alternative, one already suggested by Suematsu and Toyama, was to find in the tradition at least some limited or potential literary quality. This Shōyō found in the jōruri of Chikamatsu, particularly in Chikamatsu's *sewamono* (contemporary plays). In his "Preface to a commentary on *Macbeth*" (1891), for example, he likens Chikamatsu's sewamono to Shakespeare's works, and suggests that "Shakespeare is a larger version of Japan's own Chikamatsu Monzaemon."[21] This mention of Chikamatsu in a discussion of Shakespeare was surely no accident, for it was precisely by comparing Chikamatsu with Shakespeare that the Japanese theater was shown also to have a literary tradition. Yet if the two playwrights really were comparable, why was it that Shakespeare enjoyed universal praise while Chikamatsu was hardly appreciated in his own country? This discrepancy Shōyō could only attribute to the lack of a critical tradition in Japan, and he went on to speculate what sort of reputation Chikamatsu might have enjoyed had his work received the same wealth of critical commentary and interpretation that Shakespeare's had.[22] While Shōyō's argument here is tautological, his point being that Chikamatsu had not been acclaimed a great playwright because not enough critics had come forward to declare him as such, it does confirm what we now know to be true of any instance of canon formation, namely, that canons are not self-evident or ideologically neutral but are produced by just the sort of scholarly activity and discourse Shōyō pointed to in the case of Shakespeare and that he found lacking in Japan.

If Chikamatsu had been deprived of such critical attention in the past, he was now about to receive it. As mentioned earlier, the next year, 1892, the Musashiya came out with its two-volume collection of Chikamatsu's plays. This was followed in 1896 by the Min'yūsha's two Chikamatsu volumes, *Sōrinshi gikyoku* (Chikamatsu's Plays), and by the two volumes edited by Aeba Kōson (1855–1922) for Hakubunkan's *Teikoku bunko* series (1896–97).[23] In

CHIKAMATSU AND LITERATURE IN THE MEIJI PERIOD   189

the meantime, other critics had entered the field. In 1892, for example, the romanticist Kitamura Tōkoku (1868–1894) wrote about Chikamatsu for *Jogaku zasshi*, while Uchida Roan (1868–1929) included a lengthy section on Chikamatsu in his *Bungaku ippan* (Outline of Literature), and in 1895 Takayama Chogyū (1871–1902) had three Chikamatsu essays published in the journals *Teikoku bungaku* and *Taiyō*.[24] During all this time Shōyō and his students at Waseda University continued to study and write about Chikamatsu, and in 1896 they established the Chikamatsu Study Society (Chikamatsu Kenkyūkai). Over the next few years Shōyō, Shimamura Hōgetsu (1871–1918), Satō Meiyō (d. 1937), and others wrote a number of articles for the journal *Waseda bungaku*, which in 1900 were collected and republished as the book *Chikamatsu no kenkyū* (Studies of Chikamatsu).[25] The year 1896, truly a monumental one in the institutionalization of Chikamatsu studies, was also marked by the debate between the Waseda and Tokyo University schools.

One result of this activity was the beginning of a movement within Chikamatsu studies of ascribing a privileged position to his *sewamono* (contemporary plays), despite the fact that his *jidaimono* (history plays) actually take up a far greater place in the total Chikamatsu corpus.[26] As Shōyō argued in "The Japanese History Play" (1893–94), it was precisely due to their literary quality that the sewamono deserved this privilege:

> The *literature* of the Japanese theater world has never suffered from a deficiency of good writers, whether Chikamatsu Sōrinshi [Monzaemon] in the past or Furukawa [Kawatake] Mokuami more recently. There are not a few plays, *at least if one restricts one's vision to the domain of the sewamono*, which by virtue of superior texts written by men of superior skill almost approach the Elizabethan drama.[27]

Given Shōyō's likening of Chikamatsu to Shakespeare, it comes as no surprise that he here again brings in the Elizabethan drama as a point of comparison. In both cases, however, the emphasis on the sewamono reveals this to be an oddly selective comparison. Shakespeare, after all, did not write anything resembling the sewamono, and there are few examples of the closest Western equivalent (domestic tragedy) that date from the Elizabethan period. Were one seriously to go about comparing Chikamatsu's works or the jōruri and kabuki of the Edo period with Elizabethan drama, then surely a more obvious object of comparison would be the more common jidaimono. For Shōyō, however, the lack of literary quality made the jidaimono unworthy of such a comparison. In "The Japanese History Play," for example, the positive assessment of sewamono quoted above is immediately followed by a critique of jidaimono, which are described as "nonsensical" and "implausible."[28] This contrast suggests that for Shōyō the literary quality of sewamono lay in their realism, or to paraphrase his earlier statement on the "main purpose" of theater, in their truthful depiction of human emotions and society. The contrast also implies that, whereas the sewamono could be accepted into the canon as is, the jidaimono would first have to be reformed. This is indeed the main point of Shōyō's essay, and after reviewing a number of attempts at reforming the history play, he goes on to make his own recommendations, most of which are based on Western theory or practice.

This was not the first example of the privileging of the sewamono in discussions of Chikamatsu. A year earlier Roan had taken a similar position in his *Bungaku Ippan*:

> Among Chikamatsu's one hundred or so works, those dealing with historical topics, such as *Battles of Coxinga* and *Soga Kaikeizan*, still lack the quality of "drama." His sewamono, on the other hand, are much more advanced and are fine examples of Japanese "drama."[29]

What is of interest here is that Chikamatsu's jidaimono are said to "still lack" the essential quality of drama, while the sewamono are described as "much more advanced." In addition to privileging the sewamono on the basis of literary quality, as Shōyō had done, Roan also suggests that the superiority of the sewamono over the jidaimono is the result of the historical evolution of drama as a genre. As will be seen later, this conception of evolutionary progress in literature and drama was one shared by the kokubungaku scholars.

As for the direction of this progress, Roan is clear that it lies in the creation of "tragedy." Quoting from the now famous passage in *Naniwa miyage* about Chikamatsu's "pathos" being a matter of "restraint," Roan interprets this as the technique of incorporating into the plot a conflict or reversal that will ensure a tragic outcome.[30] He then attempts to demonstrate this by analyzing the play *Shinjū Ten no Amijima* (Love Suicide at Ten no Amijima). As the analysis makes clear, the reason for the selection of this play as a representative of Chikamatsu's "masterpieces" is its theme of *giri* (duty, obligation). It is giri, Roan attempts to show, that provides the necessary complications that lead to the tragic end of Jihei and Koharu, the play's protagonists. In this, Roan anticipates Shōyō's famous statement that the essence of Chikamatsu's drama lies in the "conflict between *giri* and *ninjō* (human emotion)."[31]

One other feature of Roan's discussion of Chikamatsu that deserves comment can be found in the following passage:

The majority of Chikamatsu's sewamono express the fate of human beings moved by "love." In this Chikamatsu's work cannot be said to express the "myriad minds" found in that of Shakespeare; nonetheless, the degree of insight into human nature is unparalleled in Japan.[32]

Here we see again the inevitable comparison with Shakespeare. What is of note, however, is the language. Like the terms "drama" and "tragedy," the word "love" (ren'ai) is given a gloss to ensure its English reading. To describe the relationship between Jihei and Koharu in Shinjū Ten no Amijima as one of "love," however, is to apply a modern concept in a context where it does not belong. As Karatani has pointed out, the modern notion of romantic love (ai, ren'ai) was first diffused into Japanese society by Meiji period churches, and it was only beginning with that period that such "love" can be said to have existed.[33] The case with the terms "drama" and "tragedy" is similar: far from being self-evident, universal concepts, these are Western notions that owe their currency in Japan to the Meiji period study of foreign literature. Why Chikamatsu was singled out by critics such as Shōyō and Roan, therefore, and why his works achieved canonical status in this period, can in part be explained by the fact that such Western concepts seemed to apply to his works better than any others in the Japanese tradition. It was precisely this attempt to see Chikamatsu's work in terms of such purportedly universal concepts that led the Tokyo University kokubungaku scholars into a debate with Shōyō and his colleagues at Waseda University in 1896.

THE TOKYO UNIVERSITY – WASEDA DEBATE

While the initial impetus for the debate came from the Tokyo University group's formal commencement in 1896 of Chikamatsu studies under Ueda Kazutoshi (1867–1937), interest in Chikamatsu among the university's kokubungaku scholars had actually begun several years earlier and was already evident in Nihon bungakushi (History of Japanese Literature, 1890) by Mikami Sanji (1865–1939) and Takatsu Kuwasaburō (1864–1921). As Brownstein argues, although the emerging discipline of kokubungaku was linked to the Edo-period tradition of kokugaku, it also drew on two important concepts prevalent in Western theories of literature at the time: the notion that a literature expresses the unchanging national character or sentiment of a people, and that literature progresses as society evolves, and thus a nation's literary history displays changes in its level of civilization. The first point was in accord with the views of earlier kokugaku scholars, who since the Edo period had focused on ancient Japanese texts, which were seen to embody the national spirit. Where the young kokubungaku scholars broke with their kokugaku counterparts was in extending the era of "classical" literature up to the late Edo period and including writings in the mixed Japanese-Chinese style (*wakan konkō bun*) as well as popular works in the vernacular.[34] This was a reflection of the other major assumption of the modern scholars, the notion of evolution or progress in literature, which suggested the need to carry on literary history up to the present and to include new genres and literary styles. In order to see this as progress, however, this Edo period literature had to be related to positive social evolution. This is one further reason why Chikamatsu's works were singled out for praise. Unlike earlier "classics," his plays were not only written for a popular audience, his sewamono were, along with the fiction of Saikaku, among the first literary or dramatic works to give substantial treatment to the lives of the common people. That Chikamatsu and Saikaku's careers overlapped was probably another factor. And although the haiku poet Matsuo Bashō cannot be labeled "popular" in the same sense as Chikamatsu and Saikaku, the fact that he was a contemporary allowed for the construction of an early "golden age" in Edo period literature, one that came to be known as the period of Genroku literature, after the name of the calendrical era (1688–1704).

This treatment of Chikamatsu's plays as literary works and their acceptance into the literary canon reveals yet another way in which the kokubungaku scholars differed from their kokugaku predecessors: if the study of the popular literature of the Edo period represented a major departure, so too did the inclusion of drama in the field of literature. This new development no doubt also had much to do with the study of Western works by the kokubungaku scholars. In the West, drama has always been considered a genre of literature, and as Earl Miner has pointed out, Western poetics is somewhat exceptional in the world in being founded on drama and in its emphasis on mimesis.[35] In order to demonstrate that Japan had a comparable literary history, therefore, the kokubungaku scholars had to show that Japanese literature too contained a dramatic tradition. Haga Yaichi (1867–1927) and Tachibana Senzaburō (1867–1901) thus included in their 1890 anthology, *Kokubungaku tokuhon* (Japanese Literature Reader), a nō and a kyōgen play, as well as a scene from Chikamatsu's *The Battles of Coxinga*.[36] Similarly, in their *Nihon bungakushi* published in the same year, Mikami and Takatsu discuss not only nō and kyōgen and provide samples of each, but also deal at even greater length with Edo-period theater, focusing especially on Chikamatsu, as well as providing excerpts from two plays, one of them, again, Chikamatsu's *The Battles of Coxinga*.[37]

Through their efforts to construct a literary history that would rival that of the West, kokubungaku scholars thus came to share with reformers and Shōyō the assumption that drama was a kind of literature. It is worth stressing, however, that they arrived at this position via a different route. Whereas the reformers and Shōyō, acutely aware of the prestige of drama in the West and the literary fame of playwrights such as Shakespeare, were convinced that theater *should have a literary quality*, kokubungaku scholars were led through a consideration of literary history to the conclusion that literature *included* theater. And since kokubungaku scholars were also concerned with discovering in Japan's own literary history a national essence, their task was not simply one of detecting a literary quality in Japanese theater but of reconstructing a dramatic tradition that, on its own terms, would rival or even surpass that of the West. Thus Mikami and Takatsu praised nō as "an example of the special kind of literature that arose in the Muromachi period," one that "shines with a brilliant light in the history of Japanese literature" (153). The authors were even more enthusiastic about the achievements of Japanese dramatists in the Edo period, especially Chikamatsu, whom they labeled "the Oriental Shakespeare [*tōyō no Shekisupiyaa*]" (430). Whereas Shōyō's statement that Chikamatsu was a Japanese version of Shakespeare implies some sort of similarity or equivalence between the two playwrights, the appellation "Oriental Shakespeare" suggests a similar stature but also an essential difference, one corresponding to the difference between East and West. This is not to say that the authors were seeking to embed Japanese drama in a cultural tradition that included the cultures of other Asian countries. Indeed, despite words of praise for Chikamatsu's familiarity with Chinese as well as Japanese literature (438), Asia here functions as yet another "Other" against which to construct a national tradition and identity. The scene from *The Battles of Coxinga* chosen to illustrate Chikamatsu's brilliance, for example, is none other than the one in which the Japanese character Watōnai, armed with a charm from the Ise Shrine that imbues him with the power of the "Land of the Gods," upstages the cowardly Chinese by defeating a ferocious tiger with his bare hands (447–53).

Rather than dwelling on the comparison between Chikamatsu and foreign models, then, it is largely in terms of the native tradition that Mikami and Takatsu discuss Chikamatsu's achievements. This is done by first discussing early Edo-period jōruri and then arguing that Chikamatsu "infused jōruri with an unusual power that brought the form to a true state of brilliance" (437). As for the source of this power, the authors make clear that it is to be located in Chikamatsu's command of language. The highest praise is given to his "literary style" (*bunshō*) and "choice of words" (*jiku*), which are said to allow the reader or audience to see clearly the minutest details and envision the characters as if they were before their very eyes (438–39). While this attention to detail and language is here claimed to be an important feature of Chikamatsu's work, it can also be said to characterize the approach of the kokubungaku scholars themselves. The lack of such attention to language and other details was in fact one of the charges that the kokubungaku scholars of Tokyo University leveled at Shōyō and the Waseda group during the 1896 debate.

The opening salvo in the debate came in the form of a brief anonymous article published in *Teikoku bungaku* in March 1896.[38] The article begins by complaining that "there are some in this world who are in such a rush that, after having read through only a part of Chikamatsu's works, they immediately begin searching for his view of life, jump from there to a discussion of the traits of the characters, quickly move on to a comparison with Shakespeare, and then attempt to expound a theory of drama" (205–6). While the author of the article does not deny the value of such research, he does argue that "things have their proper order," and thus before indulging in such bold theorizing one must first thoroughly study the "language and customs" of Chikamatsu's time. The article goes on to say that, as the first step in this necessary basic research, the Tokyo University group has started preparing an index of the words used in Chikamatsu's sewamono, adding that by expanding such an index to include words from other contemporary sources it could serve to illuminate not only Chikamatsu's work, but also the literature of the Genroku period as a whole (206).

In its response published the next month, again anonymously, the Waseda group, while politely commending the kokubungaku scholars for their research efforts, suggested that if their true aim was to investigate Genroku era language and customs, then instead of Chikamatsu they would be better off studying "realistic" fiction writers such as Saikaku (207). To this came a reply the following month from the Tokyo University side, arguing that to study Chikamatsu was not simply a means to acheive a better knowledge of Edo period language and customs. Speaking for himself, the author claimed that he studied Chikamatsu's works precisedly because it was those works he wanted to know better. He insisted, however, that in order to achieve this end, a thoughout knowledge of the language, people, and affairs of Chikamatsu's time was absolutely essential, and thus he added his approval to the passage in the Tokyo University group's opening attack, which criticized the Waseda side for its tendency to skip over details and jump to broad conclusions (208).

Although articles from both sides continued to be published for several months, the arguments soon began to repeat themselves. While the debate petered out with no clear victor, it does reveal much about the state of dramatic criticism in the Meiji period. On the one hand, there was Shōyō and the Waseda group who were willing to grant a certain autonomy to dramatic form and sought to find in the work truths that transcend linguistic or historical particulars. For the Tokyo University kokubungaku scholars, on the other hand, an understanding of a dramatic work could only be achieved through the exhaustive study of the details of language, sources, and historical background. While it is possible to see these as two theoretically opposed approaches to the study of drama, it is important also to historicize these approaches in terms of the underlying ideological issues and agendas. The Meiji period, after all, was one in which, through their encounter with the West, the Japanese became acutely aware of themselves as a people. It is thus possible to see in the two approaches two different strategies for using Japanese drama as a means of constructing national identity. For the reform movement and for Shōyō and like-minded critics, the strategy lay in discovering in the Japanese tradition dramatic forms and themes that were comparable to those found in the West. For the kokubungaku scholars, on the other hand, the project of creating a national identity involved the construction of a history of Japanese drama that could stand as the equal to that of the West but that at the same time would reveal the particularity of Japanese culture. In Chikamatsu's sewamono, critics such as Shōyō and Roan believed they had discovered clear evidence of a Japanese dramatist who excelled at the portrayal of human emotions and the construction of tragedy. At the same time, the kokubungaku scholars not only saw in jōruri proof of a vibrant indigenous dramatic tradition, but also found in Chikamatsu a playwright who, through his extensive knowledge of the literature of the past, his talent for creative innovation, and his magical command of language, demonstrated the particular genius of that tradition.

CONCLUSION: AFTER THE MEIJI PERIOD

Both of these critical trends continued into the post-Meiji period. In 1928 a theater museum was established at Waseda University to commemorate

Shōyō's seventieth birthday and the completion of his translation of Shakespeare's works, and became the base for a number of theater scholars, most notably Kawatake Shigetoshi (1889–1967), who carried on Shōyō's brand of theater research. The kokubungaku approach to theater history, meanwhile, continued to be practiced at Tokyo University during the same period under the leadership of Takano Tatsuyuki (1876–1947) and Shuzui Kenji (1899–1983). In the postwar period there have been some innovations in theater scholarship, but also much continuity. Arguably the most influential of postwar studies of Chikamatsu has been *Chikamatsu josetsu* (Prefactory Remarks to a Study of Chikamatsu, 1957), by Hirosue Tamotsu (1919–1993), which adopts a Marxist perspective in order to relate Chikamatsu's plays to their historical background.[39] Hirosue's approach is still largely literary, however, and indeed the greater part of this work is devoted to an attempt to trace the development of tragedy through Chikamatsu's successive sewamono. On the other hand, there have been some postwar Japanese theater historians who have questioned the use of literary analysis in elucidating and evaluating works created for the traditional theater, and there have been some important attempts to analyze Chikamatsu's work from the point of view of performance.[40] Too often, however, criticism of Western-derived literary analysis goes hand in hand with an essentializing cultural approach driven by the ideological attempt to overcome both Westernization and modernization by insisting on the unique national character of the traditional, that is, pre-modern, Japanese theater.[41]

Despite these innovations, Chikamatsu is still heralded today on many fronts as the Japanese genius of tragedy and a master in the portrayal of the lives and emotions of the common people. This is only possible, however, by concentrating on his sewamono and dismissing his kabuki plays and jōruri jidaimono as either vehicles for actors or more primitive examples of the genre of jōruri. This preference for his sewamono is also still very much evident in literary anthologies and selected editions of his works, the most telling example being the two Chikamatsu volumes in the Shōgakukan *Nihon koten bungaku zenshū* series (1972–75), which include all twenty-four of the sewamono and not a single jidaimono or kabuki play. The situation is not very different in English: Donald Keene's *Major Plays of Chikamatsu*, which remains the best introduction to Chikamatsu for Western readers, contains a total of ten sewamono and only one jidaimono. On the other hand, there are two new Japanese "complete" editions: the *Chikamatsu zenshū* published by Iwanami (1985–92), which includes not only all of Chikamatsu's *jōruri* works but his kabuki plays as well, and the *Shōhon Chikamatsu zenshū*

(1977–89), which produces in facsimile form the original editions of all extant jōruri plays known to be Chikamatsu's work as well as many others of uncertain authorship. These collections, however, are used principally by specialists who engage in the kokubungaku form of literary research.

In sum, then, the situation today is not very different from that of the 1890s, and in this sense the Meiji-period treatment of Chikamatsu can be said to have resulted not only in his canonization, but also in establishing views of and approaches to his work that are now taken for granted. I can only suggest that any advance in our understanding of Chikamatsu's works and their historical importance must come from a dialectical process in which, starting from a broad knowledge of Chikamatsu's corpus, a theoretical framework is constructed that can adequately comprehend the variety within that corpus. At the very least, such a framework must go beyond the simplistic reduction of Chikamatsu's drama to the conflict between giri and ninjō. Toward this end it must be able to relate the tragedy in Chikamatsu's sewamono to his more numerous jidaimono and kabuki plays, most of which take the form of tragicomedy, while at the same time relating both kinds of plays to their performance context and historical moment. In the meantime I shall be content if my analysis of the treatment of Chikamatsu in the Meiji period has helped to explain why his works were canonized at that time and why we read them today the way we do.

APPENDIX
Chronological List of Editions of Chikamatsu's Plays

Hayashi Tamiji, ed. *Chikamatsu chosaku zensho.* 2 vols. Maruzen, 1881–82.

———. *Chikamatsu jidai jōruri.* Musashiya sōshokaku, 1892.

———. *Chikamatsu sewa jōruri.* Musashiya sōshokaku, 1892.

Sōrinshi gikyoku. 2 vols. Minyūsha, 1896.

Aeba Kōson, ed. *Chikamatsu jidai jōruri.* Hakubunkan, 1896.

———. *Chikamatsu sewa jōruri.* Hakubunkan, 1897.

Mizutani Futō, ed. *Zoku Chikamatsu jōrurishū.* Hakubunkan, 1899.

———. *Chikamatsu kessaku zenshū.* Waseda daigaku shuppanbu. 1910. (39 jōruri and 3 kabuki plays.)

Tadami Keizō, ed. *Chikamatsu jōrurishū*. 3 vols. Yūmeidō, 1910–14. (42 plays.)

Takano Tatsuyuki and Kuroki Kanzō, eds. *Chikamatsu Monzaemon zenshū*. 10 vols. Shunyōdō, 1922–24. (127 jōruri and 17 kabuki plays.)

Kitani Hōgin, ed. *Dai Chikamatsu zenshū*. 16 vols. Dai Chikamatsu zenshū kankōkai, 1922–25. (104 jōruri plays.)

Fuji Otoo, ed. *Chikamatsu zenshū*. 12 vols. Osaka Asahi shimbunsha, 1925–28. (147 jōruri plays.)

Takano Tatsuyuki, ed. *Chikamatsu kabuki kyōgenshū*. 2 vols. Rokugōkan, 1927. (27 kabuki plays.)

Shigetomo Ki, Shuzui Kenji, and Ōtomo Tadakuni, eds. *Chikamatsu jōrurishū*. 2 vols. Nihon koten bungaku taikei. 49–50. Iwanami shoten, 1958–59. (6 jidaimono and 14 sewamono.)

Keene, Donald, trans. *Major Plays of Chikamatsu*. New York: Columbia University Press, 1961. (10 sewamono and 1 jidaimono.)

Mori Shū, Torigoe Bunzō, and Nagatomo Chiyoji, eds. *Chikamatsu Monzaemon shū*. 2 vols. Nihon koten bungaku zenshū. 43–44. Shōgakukan, 1972–75. (24 sewamono.)

Chikamatsu shoshi kenkyūkai, ed. *Shōhon Chikamatsu zenshū*. 36 vols. Benseisha, 1977–89. (145 jōruri plays.)

Chikamatsu zenshū kankōkai, ed. *Chikamatsu zenshū*. 17 vols. Iwanami shoten, 1985–92. (114 jōruri and 30 kabuki plays.)

Language, Authority, and the Curriculum

CHAPTER EIGHT

Kangaku: Writing and Institutional Authority

KUROZUMI MAKOTO

TRANSLATED BY DAVID LURIE

Today texts such as the *Kojiki*, *Man'yōshū*, *Genji monogatari*, and *Heike monogatari* are taught in school as "Japanese classics." They are extensively studied by scholars and critics and are widely acknowledged to embody the essence of Japanese culture. But, almost without exception, it was not until the late Edo and Meiji periods that these texts became part of the canon. This process began with the *kokugaku* (nativist learning) movement in the mid-Edo period and was spurred by the establishment of the modern academic field of "national literature" (*kokubungaku*), the expansion of the educational system, and the demands of the national literature movement.

Prior to that time, however, there was another major literary canon in Japan, written in kanbun, a system of writing that employs Chinese graphs (*kanji*). It is a genre that has fallen into disuse, although Japanese students are still taught kanbun grammar in high school. From the Nara period through the late Edo period, kanbun texts commanded authority and were the object of *kangaku* (Chinese studies), a broad and systematic discipline whose importance continued well into the modern period. Why then did kokubungaku rise and kangaku fall? This shift did not become apparent until the late Edo period and did not become irreversible until the Meiji period, but to understand the causes it is necessary to go back to the ancient and medieval periods and examine the complex history of the relationship between kanbun and *kana* (vernacular syllabary) and between kangaku and *wagaku* (Japanese studies). I shall then analyze the sociopolitical and religious functions of kangaku and the changing position of kangaku and kanbun vis-à-vis kana and other vernacular discourses in the medieval, Edo, and modern periods. In so doing, I intend to show that while kanbun and kana are often thought of as antithetical writing systems, with their respective disciplines and canons in competition with each other, they were in fact closely interrelated, as were kangaku and kana-based disciplines, with kangaku eventually helping to give birth to kokugaku in the late Edo period and continuing to have a significant impact on national language, culture, and political discourse in the Meiji period.

THE DOMINANCE OF CHINESE WORDS AND THE GENESIS OF THE 'KANA' SYLLABARY

Japan had no writing system prior to the arrival of kanji culture. According to written documents, this began in the time of Emperor Ōjin in the early fifth century, although there are even earlier traces of characters inscribed on metal and stone. At first writing was used by immigrants from Korea and China and their clans, primarily for the official business of domestic and foreign politics,[1] but in the sixth century, the learning and technology of kanji culture, starting with Confucianism and Buddhism, began to be imported and had an enormous impact on Japan's ancient state and culture. If it had not been for the stimulus of kanji culture, what was once a loose confederation of clans would probably not have moved toward the formation of a large unified state.

Influenced by the establishment of the Sui and Tang dynasties in China, in the seventh century Japan began constructing the so-called *ritsuryō* state, a centralized autocratic system of political and economic control in the service of the imperial ruler and based on a system of codified law. During the development of this early state, which reached its peak in the ninth century, kanji was the only system of writing, and texts in classical Chinese, or kanbun, written either by Chinese or Japanese, were the only means of studying Buddhism and Confucianism. The *Kaifūsō* (the eighth-century collection of *kanshi*, or poems written by Chinese by Japanese poets), may be considered a hallmark of ritsuryō state culture. Several imperial kanshi anthologies of the first half of the ninth century, as well as the *Kojiki*, *Nihon shoki*, and *Manyōshū*—all three now considered to be classics among Japanese classics— were written solely with kanji.

Even after the ninth century, kanji and kanbun were the central means of writing by men (court nobles and clergy). The *Rikkokushi* (Six Official Histories, beginning with the *Nihon shoki*), the ritsuryō rules of etiquette and their commentaries, various types of correspondence and public records, Buddhist and Confucian scriptures, educational writings, ritual texts, and even the diaries and memoranda of male nobles all continued to be written either in Japanese using only kanji or in kanbun. The principal arenas of kanji and kanbun, in other words, were public society, religion, learning, and technology, all of which were connected to the framework of the ritsuryō state. Though it has often been thought that the ritsuryō state lost its polit-ical and economic authority in the mid-Heian period, when warriors gained various political rights, it is clear that the framework of the ritsuryō state continued for a long time, lasting even until the Edo period.[2] Indeed, it was under the ritsuryō system that warriors were formally appointed to court po-sitions. It is even possible to claim that that framework took on new mean-ing, being revived and amplified, from late Edo into the Meiji period. Even the Edo *bakufu* (shogunate) was based on the cultural framework of that sys-tem. Until as late as the middle of World War II, official government docu-ments were written in kanji and *katakana* (a phonetic syllabary closely con-nected to kanji). Even today scholars of kangaku are called upon to decide the names of imperial reigns such as the Chinese compounds Shōwa and Heisei (as opposed to Japanese designations such as Miyabi 1 or Aware 3).

While kanji and kanbun were associated with the public sphere, with re-ligion and learning, they also had a literary and artistic dimension. Even after the mid-Heian period, members of the nobility and courtiers continued to write Chinese prose and poetry (*kanshibun*) and compiled kanshi antholo-gies, and during the medieval period literary production flourished in the Zen monasteries of the Five Mountains (Gozan). Throughout the Edo pe-riod and extending into the Meiji period, Chinese studies (kangaku) flourished, and the literary production of kanbun and kanshi was so prolific that it would be impossible to read all the texts that have survived from that time. It is important to note here that it was under the influence of and amid a vast expanse of discourse in Chinese that kana literature first appeared.

In their earliest form, kana were simply kanji that were used to capture the oral voice. In the *Kojiki*, utterances are written with kanji used for their sounds, as in "*ana ni ya shi e wotome wo*" ("Oh my! What a good girl!") *Kojiki*

1: 4), from the scene of sexual intercourse between the gods Izanami and Izanagi. Proper names, songs, and children's ditties were also recorded this way. Words and utterances that could not be semantically expressed with kanji or in kanbun were written as a series of sounds by means of kanji selected for their pronunciations (*on*). Much of the *Man'yōshū* was also recorded with this type of writing, which employs kanji as kana (referred to as *magana* or *man'yōgana*).[3] Apparently, the term *kana* was not originally thought of as indicating a category separate from kanji, as it is today. Because kanji were originally the only graphs, they were considered the true script, while the kana syllabary was thought of as a temporary script—a situation reflected in the terms *mana* and *kana* (literally, "true names" and "temporary names"). Magana were also used as graphs for notating (alongside the kanji of the base text) *kundoku*, the Japanese convention for reading kanbun, which seems often to have been read aloud.[4]

Beginning in the second half of the ninth century, *katakana* and *hiragana* were formed by simplifying the magana phonographs. The katakana set of signs, which came from the magana used to supply readings for a kanbun text, were created by taking part of a kanji and using it as an abbreviated written sign. Hiragana, on the other hand, came from the magana used to record individual utterances, names, and poems, and were created by cursivizing (*sōka*) the entire kanji graph. Magana continued to be used in more public or formal contexts, while hiragana appeared in everyday, informal situations, when writing flowed in an easy, relaxed manner. Hiragana were originally called *onnade* (woman's hand), which suggests that it was not used in public contexts. The two processes leading to the formation of katakana and hiragana had differing emphases and nuances. Kanji were associated with public, academic, and religious spheres of life and with solemn or sacred occasions, and katakana, which provided the reading for the sound of each graph, reflected respect for the kanji and classical Chinese prose (kanbun). By contrast, hiragana was not associated with this high valuation of kanji, but emerged out of a world that implied intimacy and was used to express the spontaneous aural flow of the native language.

This difference in character persisted long after the creation of hiragana and katakana. Even when it had become possible to write in Japanese in nonkanbun styles, a kanji-laden, katakana style was used for more serious writing, and a hiragana style with fewer kanji was used for smoother and more graceful writing. In the government school textbooks from the Meiji 20s (roughly 1890s) onward, in the lower grades of elementary school, when learning about writing was the objective and when students were made to practice reading out loud, words were written in katakana. In the higher grades, once students had become accustomed to reading and writing, the books employed hiragana writing, although katakana continued to be used for technical subjects.[5] Moreover, until the middle of World War II, government texts were written mainly in katakana and kanji, as were 70 to 80 percent of magazines and other printed materials. Although the authority of katakana has diminished today, it is used for foreign words and is favored by bureaucrats. The use of katakana for onomatopoeia, which began in the Edo period, also reflects an emphasis on sound.

Interestingly, for a long time the more fluid hiragana was written without the relative size of the graph being regulated: despite the fact that there was a one-to-one correspondence between graph and sound (vowel syllable), large and small graphs were directly linked together in cursive fashion (called *tsuzukeji*). Regulation of the size and placement of the graphs did not come about until the printing of Motoori Norinaga's *Kojikiden*, which began in 1790,[6] and it appears that the spatial separation of individual hiragana graphs did not occur until the shift from woodblock to movable type printing. Hiragana continued to be chosen as a script that, unlike katakana, could be written in continuous cursive form (*kuzushigaki*). The fluidity and intimacy of hiragana also resulted in a refined aesthetic. In contrast to early documents in katakana, which appear in academic and religious contexts, beautifully rendered cursive hiragana are found in writings that were frequently preserved as art objects.[7]

It should be noted that hiragana literature (*waka* collections from the *Kokinshū* on, women's diaries, and *monogatari*) began appearing in the mid-Heian period, in the tenth and eleventh centuries. While this development deserves attention, its importance has been exaggerated, creating the mistaken impression that the Japanese language of the Heian period was centered on hiragana-based documents and that this constituted the main stream of linguistic culture. As Tsukishima Hiroshi has noted, even though masterpieces of hiragana literature did appear, "They certainly were not representative of the whole: kanbun texts continued to be produced, and occupied the dominant position that they had in the previous age."[8]

KUN AND KUNDOKU: THE INTEGRATION OF CHINESE INTO THE JAPANESE LANGUAGE

The oral power of the native language that could not be expressed by kanji and kanbun influenced the formation of both katakana and hiragana. The kundoku reading conventions that produced katakana, which arose from a refusal to accept kanbun as Chinese writing, involved preserving the visual kanbun text while rearranging it into Japanese word order during the reading process.[9] The reader looks at the Chinese words while vocally transposing them into the flow of oral Japanese, a process that involves retaining the syntax of Japanese at any cost.

At the same time, the native language had a profound effect on the use of individual kanji. At first kanji were pronounced with "*on*" readings that derived from their original Chinese sounds, but most kanji used in Japanese were also given "*kun*" readings that signified native words. Those aspects of the native language that could not be expressed in kanji were initially recorded in magana (man'yōgana) and eventually katakana and hiragana. At the same time, the *kun* readings of graphs, which coexisted with the *on* readings and were often determined by referring to Chinese dictionaries,[10] were not just raw assertions of the oral world; rather, they were an attempt to maintain a high degree of contact with the world of kanji and kanbun while favoring the native oral language. This linguistic consciousness, which valued both Chinese and Japanese and promoted contact and fusion with Chinese from within Japanese,[11] involved not only the relationship of *kun* to *on*, but also that between kana and kanji.

During the Nara and early Heian periods, many Japanese intellectuals were bilingual in Chinese and Japanese, having studied on the continent or immigrated from China. However, the situation changed after the mid-ninth century, when exchange with the continent came to an end. The Tang system became unstable, and its cultural leadership began to deteriorate, with the result that the various peoples on the periphery became independent, creating their own individual writing systems.[12] From the end of the ninth century, the period from which the earliest documents with katakana glosses (*kunten*) for kundoku reading remain, a new generation grew up within the native language and no longer read kanbun directly.

The situation in Japan contrasts with that in Korea, which was geographically closer to and had stronger ties with China. Whereas the Japanese, with their greater sense of autonomy from China, devised the kun and kundoku systems as well as their own various kanbun styles, and incorporated kanji into the native language, the Koreans embraced Chinese more fully and did not introduce similar practices into the Korean language.[13] For this reason Japanese has an extremely "high rate of kanji use," as Nakata Norio puts it.[14] Rather than rejecting Chinese, the Japanese achieved a delicate balance between the imported language of Chinese and the native language, and even as the Chinese language per se became more distant, the kanbun lineage continued to develop in Japan.

CHINESE STUDIES AND THE PLURALIZATION
OF AUTHORITY

A major change in the position of Japanese vis-à-vis kangaku occurred at the beginning of the Heian period, in the latter half of the ninth century, due partially to the deterioration of the ritsuryō system. At that time the oral language gained authority with the emergence of hiragana writing—a shift symbolized most dramatically by the appearance of the *Kokinshū* (Collection of Japanese Poems Old and New, 905), the first imperial waka anthology and the first official document to be written in the hiragana script and style. Although hiragana had been called "woman's hand" (onnade) and had been associated with the private (in contrast to the public and male association of kanji and kanbun), in the *Kokinshū* this "feminine" writing took on a certain public character and authority.

The ascendancy of aristocratic cultural values exemplified in the *Kokinshū* also altered the world of kangaku. In Tang China, civil service examinations were systematized in 640, and the government-sponsored *Gokyō seigi* (*Wu-ching cheng-i*, The Correct Significance of the Classics) commentary was selected as an official text, which emphasized the five Confucian classics and considered literature and history to be of lesser importance.[15] The situation in Japan was the opposite. The university (*daigakuryō*), academies, and examinations, which were established under the ritsuryō system in the eighth century, were not considered to be elements of a large recruiting system.[16] The position of university professor (*hakase*) had been considered low ranking, and as those positions became hereditary, learning was pursued as "house studies" (*kagaku*) of hakase families. There was no consolidated set of annotations to the classics, like *Wu-ching cheng-i*; rather, Japanese scholars had a strong preference for historical or literary texts such as the *Wen-hsüan* (Anthology of Literature). The position of the Confucian classics (the Myōgyōdō curriculum), which had been at the center of scholarship, declined, while that of literature and history (the Monjōdō curriculum) steadily rose. These tendencies became even more pronounced after the Heian period.

That ability in kangaku alone was not a determinant of position and power is illustrated by the fate of Sugawara no Michizane (845–903), an eminent kangaku scholar, poet, and political figure. Having risen from professor of literature (Monjō hakase) to minister of the right, Michizane fell victim to a plot by Fujiwara no Tokihira (871–909), lost his position in court, was exiled, and died in disgrace. Eventually, to placate his angry spirit, he was deified as Tenjin, the god of learning, literature, and Confucian cultivation—much as in China, Confucius, the god of learning, was worshipped in the *shih-tien* (*sekiten*) festival. Tenjin was revered by hakase scholars, and in the late Edo period, Tenjin was worshipped in *terakoya* schools. As Michizane's transformation suggests, even though knowledge of kangaku was important, it was not the primary qualification for advancement in the political world. Despite its linguistic and cultural importance, kangaku was external to political legitimacy itself and to the essentials of governance. It is revealing that the scholars (*hakase*) depicted in Heian monogatari are depicted comically, as remaining in obscurity despite their pride and intellectual authority.

Religious conditions in Japan also contributed to the decline of the study of the Confucian classics. The failure of Confucianism to play a significant role in official promotions or enjoy state sponsorship can be traced, at least in part, to its inability to establish its own religious ceremonies. After the Han dynasty (206 B.C.E.–220 C.E.), the study of the Confucian classics was supported in China by important rites and ceremonies such as the worship of Heaven and funeral rituals, and through "hidden wisdom" such as magic, divination, and fortune-telling. In Japan, however, such collective and state rites were monopolized by the worship of *kami* (gods) and by Buddhism. The only successful Confucian ritual in Japan, it seems, was the *sekiten* (*shih-t'ien*) festival, which celebrated Confucius and his disciples. In the sixth century, in the pre-ritsuryō period, when a foundation for rites was established, Buddhism and Taoism, but not Confucianism, flourished in China and Korea—a fact that deeply influenced the form of Japanese religious ritual. While some Confucian ideals were embraced, for example, in the *Nihon shoki*, the scale of the bureaucracy required by the Japanese state was smaller than in China, and because of the clan system, it was not particularly necessary to install an examination or educational system as the basis of the state society. Japan's political leaders probably hoped to establish the preexisting kami rites at the core of the state.[17] "Heaven" (*ten*), which was at the center of Chinese Confucian rites, was replaced in Japan by the "god of heaven" (*ama tsu kami*), and the legitimacy of the state was grounded in the lineage deriving from the "seed" (*tane*) of that god, thereby linking virtue to an external source. Various rites of Taoism and Confucianism were absorbed into the system of kami worship, but priority was given to Buddhism, which had magical powers and involved fewer political complications. The Nara period (eighth century) witnessed the gradual syncretism of Buddhism and kami worship, and after the ninth century this extended throughout the country. Heian rites and ceremonies took place in a world in which the gods were closely linked to Esoteric and Pure Land Buddhism. The deification of Sugawara no Michizane and the observance of the *kangakue*, a Tendai Buddhist festival that promoted learning, were the natural outcome of this process. With his deification as Tenjin, a kami, Michizane put down roots in the soil of Japan; in a similar fashion kangaku lived on in Buddhist form.

Instead of becoming an independent social or religious institution, kangaku became a literary and technical (a means of documentation) field in a syncretic environment of Buddhism and kami worship. Significantly, *hakase* scholars were specialists in Confucianism, but their influence did not come close to that of the Buddhist priests. Those who studied Confucianism were in fact primarily Buddhist priests and Shintoists. In the medieval period, Shintoists, along with members of the nobility, produced commentaries, did research, and gave lectures on the *Nihon shoki*, a kanbun text. Kangaku was also linked with divination and fortune-telling, and was regarded as a kind of hidden wisdom behind politics and ritual, as it had been in China. As the portrayal of Taira no Shigemori (Kiyomori's son) in *The Tale of the Heike* reveals, and as depicted in other monogatari and setsuwa (folk literature)— especially in the works of mixed kana and kanji—the idealized image of government and conduct was imbued with the Confucian virtues of benevolence, righteousness, courtesy, and wisdom, as well as loyalty and filial piety, virtues that were important in court culture. Another measure of the political and moral authority of kangaku was the fact that the warriors of the Kamakura bakufu also wrote their history, the *Azuma kagami* (Mirror of the East), in kanbun (albeit in a heavily Japanized style).

Indeed, until wagaku (Japanese studies) or kokugaku (nativist learning) became established fields of study in the Edo period, one could say that there was no learning (gakumon) outside of kangaku. Kangaku provided both the framework and the medium for every aspect of religious, governmental, and literary endeavor. At the same time, it gave birth to the system of writing kana and *kanabun* (kana prose) that included elements that undermined and opposed kangaku. Thus, while Japanese kangaku did not maintain Confucianism at its absolute center, it did not mean that the authority of kana and kanabun displaced that of kanji and kanbun. Instead, there arose a general trend toward linguistic and cultural syncretism, a "Japanese/ Chinese (*wakan*) fusion."

The tradition of elegant kana prose and poetry epitomized by the *Kokinshū* (905) was no more than one piece of a larger whole. The period in which the imperial waka anthology appeared was one in which, on the whole, Chinese and Japanese elements coexisted harmoniously.[18] The image of the Heian period as effeminate and devoid of kangaku culture is thus highly misleading. Many of the nobles plotted revolts, energetically carried out business at their provincial private *shōen* estates, or even, in some cases, relocated to the countryside and became warriors. The perception that the Heian nobility were fully represented in the *Kokinshū* and *The Tale of Genji* or that they were like the effeminate figures depicted in the *Tale of Genji Picture Scrolls* (*Genji monogatari emaki*) emerged later, as a contrast to the fierce image of the warriors who had seized power. This perception began to circulate during the Muromachi period, after the study of Heian waka and monogatari had become the object of highly retrospective classical study.[19] When we look at the entirety of Heian culture, however, we find Chinese and Japanese harmoniously syncretized, each an important element in Japan's linguistic culture.

THE EXPANSION OF EARLY MODERN CHINESE STUDIES AND ITS MIXED NATURE

Throughout the tumultuous medieval period, specialists in kangaku—with the exception of a few Shinto shrine families, hereditary hakase scholar families, and educated court nobles—were almost all Buddhist priests who wrote Chinese poetry and prose and studied Confucian texts as "outer classics" (*geten*). The "inner classics" (*naiten*) were Buddhist texts, usually sutras. Until the early modern period, Buddhist priests who wrote Chinese poetry and prose were in fact the largest and most skilled group of intellectuals who dealt with kanji and kanbun. In the provinces these priests functioned as teachers; they served as administrative and diplomatic secretaries for the warriors who held power and as intellectual and magic consultants, performing divinations and rituals during battles and on other occasions. When peace arrived and the age of the Edo bakufu (1600–1867), or military government, began, the priests expected their role as educators to expand, but this was not the case. Rather, greater stress was placed on the Confucian values relating to social and public conduct and political rule. Thus, the Confucianists (called *jusha* in the Edo period) gradually gained a degree of influence with kangaku or Confucian study (*jugaku*) as their discipline, claiming that Buddhism was a superstition with no role to play in the world. Even so, in the first part of the early modern period, that influence was relatively insignificant. In the 1640s, Matsunaga Sekigo (1592–1697) wrote in the *Irinshō* that "at present, Buddhism prospers in this country"[20]; in the 1680s Kumazawa Banzan (1619–91) stated that of Confucianists "there are not more than two or three in ten thousand," and that "when compared to the

Buddhists, the scarcity of Confucianists is as a single drop in a vast ocean" (*Shugi gaisho*, I and IX).

In *Studies in the Intellectual History of Tokugawa Japan* (1951), Maruyama Masao presented a highly influential narrative of early modern Confucianism: although Neo-Confucianism (the Chu Hsi school) was established as the official ideology of the shogunate, it was soon overthrown by Japanese-style Confucianism and by kokugaku (nativist learning), a process through which Japan achieved modernity.[21] According to this schema, during the first half of the Edo period Confucianism was the central system; when it disappeared during the latter half it allowed for the emergence of the modern state. But the fact is that Confucianism was insignificant at the beginning of the early modern period, prospered increasingly in the latter half of the period (the eighteenth and nineteenth centuries), and continued to grow in the modern period. The Maruyama model, which views Confucianism and the old regime in terms of their backwardness and eventual collapse, puts forth a perspective that may be called a modernist version of kokugaku. This view of Confucianism, which was created from an amalgam of modernism as a form of "leaving Asia" (*datsu-A ron*) and of Japanese ethnocentrism (*Nihon chūshinshugi*) gained currency in the modern period, especially during the "imperial restoration" and "civilization and enlightenment" periods of early Meiji (1870–80) and during the postwar period of "modernization" (1945–90). But the reality is that kangaku and Confucianism steadily gained influence in the latter half of the Edo period and continued to be significant in the modern period.[22]

It would thus be a mistake to believe that early modern kangaku and Confucianism formed a monopolistic system. During the Edo period, scholars continued to write high-quality kanbun, although a more Japanized "pseudo-kanbun" and *sōrōbun* (epistolary style writing) came into increasing use. The advent of printing brought about a homogenization of various linguistic norms while expanding the audience for writing. Literary texts in popular demand and instructional texts were inevitably written in kana, a mixture of kana and kanji, or kanbun with kunten glosses.[23] Rather than rejecting the medium of kana, kangaku scholars and Confucianists used it to propagate their works, much as Buddhist priests had done in the medieval period. *Kanashō* (kana commentaries) that explained key kanbun passages, proverbs, and episodes in kana were composed; many important Chinese and Korean kanbun texts were published in Japanese editions (*wakoku*) that furnished kunten; *genkai* (commentaries in everyday Japanese) also appeared.

As the term *genkai* suggests, people who worked with kanbun viewed the relationship between Chinese and Japanese in terms of a difference between formal and colloquial languages. Rather than avoiding the colloquial language, they used it extensively to explain the more formal language of kanbun. Revealingly, Ogyū Sorai (1666–1728), perhaps the most noted early eighteenth century advocate of original kanbun study, thought that explications of Chinese texts should be made in everyday colloquial Japanese rather than elegant classical Japanese. In the linguistic context of Japan, where Chinese and Japanese had already been mixed together, the prevalence of Chinese and kanbun was not necessarily antithetical to the use of various forms of wabun (Japanese) styles or languages. As suggested earlier, this kind of mutually supportive writing system differed significantly from that found in Korea, where Chinese and the native language (*hangul*) were often mutually exclusive.[24]

In terms of the content of religion and thought, early modern Confucianists were not particularly opposed to other religious traditions. They occasionally attacked Buddhism, and to a certain extent they were able to replace Buddhist priests in their role as middle and upper class intellectuals, but they were ultimately unable to eradicate the deep-rooted rituals and social influence of Buddhism. Interestingly, just as they did not reject kana and kana writing, the early modern Confucianists did not entirely reject the Shinto tradition. Most Confucianists in fact practiced Shinto (*kami* worship) and propounded Confucian-Shinto syncretism. Moreover, many of them were nationalistic to the extent that, despite their esteem for the Chinese classics, they saw no historical or political value in China itself. Yamaga Sokō (1622–85), for example, thought that the Japanese should refer to their own country as "the central kingdom" (Chūgoku), and Yamazaki Ansai (1618–85) argued that the teaching of Confucius implied that if Confucius were to attack Japan, the Japanese should fight against him.[25]

In China and Korea, the Confucianists who advocated Neo-Confucianism were conspicuously idealistic and looked down on folk beliefs and older forms of thought and religion. In Japan as well, Confucianism, especially Edo period Neo-Confucianism, tended to be idealistic and highly ethical but not in such a way that required a rejection of kana or Shinto. At the same time, Japanese Confucianism was unable to create Confucian state rites and continued to absorb Shinto and Buddhist elements. Moreover, Japan never had a Confucian meritocracy (employing a state examination system), and most early modern Confucianists were lower-class samurai and townspeople (*chōnin*) who were not from the government bureaucracy. Rather than pursuing an idealistic or elitist fantasy that had no chance of fruition, Japanese

Confucianists sought out an appropriate, respectable place within the indigenous cultural tradition, choosing a strategy of populism that employed established cultural elements or traditions to gain access to a wide audience.

Edo period scholars of kangaku studied not only the Confucian classics, but also pursued military science, natural science, general history, Japanese history, and other disciplines. From the end of the seventeenth century, as the level of Confucian studies rose, excellent commentaries on the classics—such as those by Yamazaki Ansai, Itō Jinsai (1627–1705), and Ogyū Sorai—appeared, and in the eighteenth century textual criticism and philological study emerged in large volume. In addition to the Confucian classics, Edo period kangaku scholars studied various subjects such as the philosophy of the Hundred Schools (*shoshi hyakka*), history, and natural history, as well as Chinese poetry, literary prose, and vernacular fiction. Needless to say, many also composed waka and wabun letters.[26] If Japanese Confucian scholars had this tendency, which did not appear in the more elitist, classics-centered Confucianism of China and Korea, it goes without saying that the general educational curriculum did not restrict itself to the Confucian classics, but combined study of the Confucian classics with various other Japanese subjects.

This open and syncretic attitude fostered disciplines that later came to be distinct from kangaku, most importantly, kokugaku and Western studies (*yōgaku*). Today there is a tendency to think of kokugaku and Western studies as specialized disciplines of independent origin and character, but most of the scholars who were involved with these emerging disciplines were in fact kangaku scholars. Non-kanji/kanbun texts were initially supplementary subjects within kangaku. However, when, in the latter half of the eighteenth-century *wagaku* (Japanese learning), kokugaku, and *rangaku* (Dutch studies) became independent domains, kangaku was set apart as distinct from them. Kokugaku scholars such as Motoori Norinaga claimed territory for kokugaku by criticizing Confucianism, just as Confucianists had earlier sought to promote their specialization by criticizing Buddhism. However, these claims were made by a purifying vanguard to which the majority of scholars, not to mention ordinary people, had no connection. In fact, the attack on and rejection of an absolutized *karagokoro* (Chinese spirit) as advocated by Norinaga was not generally embraced, and even a number of kokugaku scholars such as Ōkuni Takamasa (1792–1871) or Hirata Atsutane (1776–1843) tolerated kangaku. While, in the larger historical perspective, the mainstream did not reject kangaku, Norinaga's claims had the effect of establishing a hierarchical difference between Chinese and Japanese, privileging kokugaku and Shinto and reducing kangaku to a supplementary status. The criticism of kangaku thus did not result in its rejection so much as the creation of kokugaku and Shinto as specialized disciplines and the establishment of a Shintoistic tradition at the center of the world of thought and culture.

THE CHARACTER AND ROLE OF KANGAKU IN THE EDO PERIOD

As the level of kangaku rose during the middle of the Edo period, Chinese and Korean texts were imported in great numbers, and the composition of Chinese poetry and prose was encouraged. At the same time, an attempt was made to adapt the techniques and approaches of these imported texts to Japanese literature. Not all scholars approved of the mixed, half-Japanized approach to kangaku, however. For example, Ogyū Sorai insisted on the authority of the original Chinese texts and the original Chinese pronunciations; he even studied conversation, which Edo period kangaku scholars, whose main activity was deciphering written texts, did not normally consider relevant. In *Gakusoku* (School regulations, 1717), Sorai rejected *kundoku* as "roundabout reading," claiming that it ultimately led only to understanding the text from within the tradition of Japanese, and advocated "direct reading" so that "we ourselves meet with Confucius morning and evening, and the sages appear before us." But even Sorai, who disliked Japanese kanbun, or creolized Chinese, renounced comprehension through sound, stating that he wanted "none other than to read Chinese graphs with the eyes" and feeling that he was not capable of being truly fluent and living in Chinese.[27]

The relationship of early modern Japanese kangaku scholars to the Chinese language in most cases centered around texts that were remote objects. The analytical focus on texts as linguistic objects resulted in the development of a sophisticated interpretive methodology and complex research into grammar, vocabulary, and usage.[28] At the same time, this distancing of the Chinese language led to an appreciation for the native tradition, a kind of linguistic nationalism. Japanese scholars who did not have any particular agenda applied the tools and discipline of kangaku to their own language. Intellectuals began to emerge who chose to pursue wisdom and morality, not through kangaku but through the more congenial language of Japanese. This shift provided the linguistic and cultural foundation for the birth of kokugaku (nativist learning) and was the reason that paradoxically many Japanese kangaku scholars came to hold, consciously or unconsciously, an imperial, ethnocentric worldview.[29]

As kangaku flourished in the mid- to late Edo period, many deeply learned philologists, essayists, educators, and intellectuals emerged all over Japan. Izawa Ranken (1777–1829), Yasui Sokken (1799–1876), and Shibue Chūsai (1805–58)—whom Mori Ōgai (1862–1922) wrote about in his biographies at the beginning of the Taisho (1912–26) period—were drawn from this generation of kangaku scholars. Behind this proliferation of kangaku was a phenomenon often referred to as the "explosion of education" (*kyōiku no bakuhatsu*)—with the establishment of the many local schools of urban commoners (*terakoya*), private academies (*shijuku*), and domain schools (*hankō*) from the latter half of the eighteenth century—as well as the increased growth in publishing.[30] Kangaku functioned as a common educational base amid this increased production and circulation of knowledge, connecting people from various classes and areas.

In the final years of the Tokugawa shogunate, or bakumatsu period (1853–68), kangaku in fact provided the foundation for a political and ethical consciousness necessary for the formation of a nation (*kokumin*) and a nation-state (*kokka*) and that went beyond the establishment of Confucian ethics. The writing of kangaku scholars such as Rai San'yō (1780–1832), who was famous for his kanshi (Chinese poetry) and for *Nihon gaishi* (Private History of Japan, 1829), written in kanbun, had a special rhetorical attraction that inspired people to have high ambitions.[31] Most of the "patriots" (*shishi*), the young men who volunteered themselves for political action during the bakumatsu period, were students of kangaku. Because Japanese literature, particularly waka and monogatari, tended toward amorous lyricism and private sentiment, it was to kangaku and kanbun literature that one turned for ethical and political enlightenment. Early modern kangaku also filtered the philosophical content of the Chinese classics in ways that reflected Japanese culture. For example, the Confucian notion of steadfast loyalty to one's superiors was accepted, while the concept of a corresponding right of the lower classes to resist was not, and the close interpersonal values of loyalty and sincerity were valued over the Confucian virtue of benevolence (*jin*) or the requirement that the ruler provide for the common good. These transformed elements of Confucianism would be repeatedly invoked and reproduced in the modern period.

THE FATE OF CHINESE STUDIES IN THE MODERN PERIOD

The beginning of the Meiji period was marked, above all, by the wholesale importation of Western knowledge and literature. Western studies (*yōgaku*) had a profound impact on educators and the intelligentsia. While various types of conflict developed between nativist Shinto thought and Western ideas, resulting in the need to renew kokugaku for modern purposes, nativist Shinto thought became central to the authentication of the state. Kangaku, by contrast, was relegated to an ambiguous position between Western studies and kokugaku, with its continued importance open to question.

In the Daigakkō (the forerunner of Tokyo University and the Ministry of Education), which had been established in 1869, scholars of kokugaku, then called *kōgaku* (imperial studies), plotted to abolish the *sekiten* festival honoring Confucius and expand their own position, thereby provoking a severe conflict with kangaku scholars, who were placed on the defensive—a situation similar to the contemporaneous anti-Buddhist movement to separate shrines from temples in which Shintoists and kokugaku scholars attempted to expand their domain by suppressing Buddhism.[32]

The more extreme actions of these Shintoists and kokugaku scholars were checked by the extensive Westernization that occurred from around 1872, and when the national university and school systems were established by the education laws of 1886, kokugaku was divided into *kokubungaku* (national literature or national literature study), *kokugogaku* (national language study), and *kokushigaku* (national history study), thereby dividing the power that kokugaku had possessed during the bakumatsu period.[33] Kokushigaku, the new discipline of Japanese history, can in fact be seen as either a kangaku-tinged version of kokugaku or as a kokugaku-tinged version of kangaku. Many of the early Meiji kokushigaku scholars were people such as Shigeno Yasutsugu (1827–1910) or Kume Kunitake (1839–1931) who had originally been kangaku scholars.

In the early Meiji period, kangaku was seen as representative of the old regime and was therefore consigned to the periphery, becoming subject to attack, not only by kōgaku or kokugaku-Shinto scholars, but also by those who supported Europeanized modernization. Many proponents of enlightenment, starting with Fukuzawa Yukichi (1834–1901), attacked Confucianism and argued for limiting or abolishing the use of kanji.[34] These anti-kanji polemics appeared again after Japan's victory in the Sino-Japanese War (1894–95). Nevertheless, the Meiji period was an age of Confucianism and kangaku—in fact, it may be the age in which Confucianism and kangaku penetrated Japanese society most deeply. Not only did the Edo tradition of kangaku culture persist, *kango* (Chinese-based vocabulary) became essential to the unification and integration of the nation and state. In the effort to eliminate dialects and regional linguistic differences and to those who wished to profess knowledge, exert authority, and proclaim public-spiritedness, kango was a necessity.[35] Government offices and universities constructed and used new Chinese words or compounds, as did numerous magazines and newspapers.

Chinese also became a medium for the importation of Western knowledge and thought—even, occasionally, of Western philosophy. There were even scholars of kangaku and Western studies, like Nakamura Masanao (1832–1891) who actively attempted to fuse the two: "In the future those who wish to enter into the inner chamber of Western studies should prepare by cultivating strength in kangaku."[36] Many areas of Western studies in the Meiji period were in fact based on kangaku. However, as with kokugaku, which was nurtured by kangaku but later became a separate field that abandoned its mother discipline, the growth of Western studies in the Meiji period eventually led to the rejection of kangaku. To the Westernized intellectuals of "Taishō (liberal) culturalism" (*Taishō kyōyōshugi*), the older discipline was a thing of the remote past.

But during the Meiji 20s (1887–96), a period marked by reaction to Westernization and by the formation of nationalist thought, the need for a Confucian East Asian ethics became evident. Although based on the Shinto tradition linked to the emperor, the Imperial Rescript on Education (1890) expounded Confucian ethics—what might be described as a modern state version of the Shinto-Confucian syncretism developed in the Edo period. In order to foster the development of a unified "people" (*kokumin*), both kangaku and Confucianism became necessary for intellectual, moral, political, and practical purposes. It is even possible to say that Japanese Confucianism, which never had an examination system, finally managed in the Meiji period to link up with Shinto rites and construct a Confucian state system.

Nevertheless, the kangaku and Confucianism emphasized by the modern state were not the same disciplines that had earlier stressed Chinese literature (*kanbungaku*) or "Eastern tradition." In contrast to kokugogaku (national language study) and kokubungaku (national literature study), which were placed at the center of Japanese culture in response to the requirements of nation-building, kangaku and Confucian study were marginalized and their content diluted. In the social hierarchy of scholarship and knowledge, kanbun as a topic of instruction was given low priority, taught in the middle school curriculum along with "ethics" (*shūshin*) and "physical education" and then rarely revisited in subsequent curricula. The suppression of kangaku increased after the Sino-Japanese War (1894–95), as political confusion grew in China. Asian ideals seemed outmoded and superfluous for Japan, and kangaku was disdained by scholars of Western studies as well as by kokubungaku scholars.

Subsequently, however, toward the end of Meiji, the fortunes of kangaku rose once again. Schools and academic societies devoted to various kinds of kanbun literature sprouted up, accompanied by numerous scholarly publications.[37] Proclaiming the movement as a "kangaku renaissance," Taoka Reiun (1870–1912) in 1896 claimed that kangaku would perform "the great task of the Japanese people: to answer the call to become pioneers in fusing Eastern and Western thought." The "kangaku renaissance" was connected to an inflated sense of mission that emerged in the wake of the Sino-Japanese and Russo-Japanese (1904–5) Wars and was based on the notion that as Asia or the East (*tōyō*) became more politically confused, it was up to Japan to take a position of leadership and represent Eastern thought and learning. The scholar Endō Ryūkichi also thought that kangaku and Eastern philosophy were necessary "spiritual training" (*seishin shūyō*) for the general population.[38]

This situation was actually connected to a more scholarly movement that led to the establishment in Japan of modern Sinology (*Shinagaku*). In 1895 the journal *Teikoku bungaku* published an unsigned article entitled "Genkon no kangaku" (Kangaku Today), in which the author begins by lamenting the fallen state of today's kangaku scholars and noting that "the people of our country have the responsibility both to develop China (*Shina*) politically in the future and to promote China's learning from the past." The article concludes with the statement that "the movement among young and able kangaku scholars and philosophers toward scientific research in Sinology should be a thing of great joy for our academic community."[39] This prediction came true with the establishment of lectures in Sinology at Kyoto University in 1906 and with the work of scholars such as Naitō Konan (1866–1934) and Kanō Naoki (1868–1947). This new discipline was articulated as a "science" (*kagaku*), the formation of which had been influenced by Western studies of East Asia (*tōyōgaku*). The term *Shinagaku* was in fact an attempt to transcend the long cultural history associated with kangaku by creating a new discipline that treated its subject (China) scientifically.[40]

The statement by Naitō Konan in his preface to *Shinaron* (Discussion of China, 1914) that this book "thinks for the Chinese in place of the Chinese" (*Shinajin ni kawatte Shinajin no tame ni kangaeru*) has been criticized by the modern critic Koyasu Nobukuni as "imperialistic discourse" with a "transcendent point of view."[41] Naitō's supercilious attitude toward Asia may have been due to the new authority of "science" and "learning," to Japanese ethnocentrism, and to a new Sinocentrism (*Chūkashugi*)—as opposed to

Eurocentrism—in which Japan stood in for Chinese civilization (*Chūka bunmei*). Throughout the early Showa period (1925–45), as kangaku and Eastern philosophy were emptied of content and became increasingly ideological, the new Sinology reacted against this trend, and its adherents showed a noticeable sense of superiority toward the old kangaku scholars. As kangaku was increasingly manipulated for ideological purposes and Sinology became a new academic discipline, those aspects of kangaku derived from China—the literary and artistic aura, the ethical and political ideals, and the East Asian cosmological view—gradually faded from sight. From the end of Meiji through the Taishō period, intellectuals such as Natsume Sōseki and Mori Ōgai attempted to bring back those lost qualities, but with the coming of the Shōwa period, only the most imaginative people could recall the beautiful image of culture and learning that had once been evoked by kangaku.

CHAPTER NINE

Curriculum and Competing Canons

HARUO SHIRANE

In *What Is a Classic?* T. S. Eliot describes a single, monolithic canon, a stable of texts and writers from which we add and subtract. But the fact of the matter is that such a single canon has never existed; instead, there have only been competing canons, which differ in their nature, status, and function.[1] This essay examines the nature of these competing canons in Japan—particularly the Chinese studies (*kangaku*) canon, the Buddhist canon, and the Japanese studies (*wagaku*) canon, which eventually intertwined with the nativist studies (*kokugaku*) canon—in order to recontextualize and reveal the relative position of what is now referred to as "Japanese literature" or *kokubungaku* (national literature). The Japanese literary canon as it is presented in modern literary histories, both in English and in Japanese, grew out of modern notions of literature, particularly as imaginative or creative writing, and was closely related to modern notions of national language and identity. Prior to the nineteenth century in Europe, literature meant the whole body of valued writing in society: philosophy, history, essays, and letters as well as poetry. What made a text "literary" was not whether it was fictional—the eighteenth century was uncertain about whether the novel was literature at all—but whether it conformed to certain standards of "polite letters."[2] Similarly, in Japan, from as early as the Nara period and extending through the Edo period, literature as highly valued writing encompassed a wide body of historical, philosophical, religious, political, and poetic texts, with no particular emphasis on the fictional. Due to both Chinese and Buddhist influences, fiction, in fact, was generally considered a negative characteristic, which resulted in the need for complicated defenses of literature. The modern notion of Japanese literature as kana-based imaginative writing thus represents only one stream of what was considered to be serious writing in Japan.

In the first half of this essay I explore the complex and historically fluctuating position of the wagaku canon within school curricula and the nature of its premodern subordination to the Chinese and Buddhist canons. I then examine the manner in which the present Japanese literary canon was constructed through modern middle school and high school textbooks. Throughout, I am concerned not with interpretations of the text so much as with the sociopolitical or pedagogical function of the text. As we shall see, the present canon of Japanese literature was determined as much by the needs of elementary and secondary education—in which the primary function of the canon was to teach reading and writing or to provide fundamental guidelines for moral and social behavior—as it was by more advanced institutions such as the university or by scholars and critics who have made the text an object of exegesis and competing interpretations. Furthermore, by presenting an overview of more than a thousand years of canon formation, we will be able to see how diversified the various curricula actually were, how they interacted, and how dramatically they changed, not only across time, but also from one community or class to another, before being shaped and replaced in the nineteenth century by what Benedict Anderson has called an "imagined community," a modern sense of a unified nation, language, and literature for what was in fact a highly variegated cultural landscape.[3]

When useful, I have made a distinction between what I call a "readerly" canon, a set of authoritative texts that initially were to be *read* for purposes of moral, religious, social, or political education, and a "writerly" canon, a set of authoritative texts whose initial function was, throughout most of the premodern period, to teach prose or poetry composition, a key social and literary practice.[4] In writing about the European canon, John Guillory has noted, "It has long been known by historians of literature that the process we call canon-formation first appeared in ancient schools in connection with the social function of disseminating knowledge of how to read and write.

The selection of texts was a means to that end, not an end in itself."[5] This is particularly true of the wagaku canon, which was first constructed by court *waka* (classical Japanese poetry) poets in the medieval period primarily for the practice of poetry. Even the canonization of *Genji monogatari* (*The Tale of Genji*, early 11th c.) and *Ise monogatari* (*Tales of Ise*, late 10th c.) was initially for the purposes of constructing models or sources for poetry. By contrast, kangaku was centered on a "readerly" canon, though some of its texts also served as models for the composition of Chinese poetry or elegant prose. Gradually, the wagaku canon came to serve other purposes, including those of Buddhism and Shintō; and in the eighteenth century it was used by kokugaku, which, openly competing with kangaku and Buddhist studies, sought to establish a "readerly" canon in Japanese, employing wagaku texts for moral, religious, political, and social purposes, much as the Confucian classics had been used.

THE NARA AND HEIAN PERIODS: CURRICULA AND HOUSE TRADITIONS

In the Nara and Heian periods, the term *gakumon* (learning) generally meant kangaku, the study of writings in Chinese, which focused on three main areas: Confucian classics, Chinese histories, and Chinese belles lettres (particularly Chinese poetry). Initially, the University (*daigakuryō*), the *ritsuryō* state institution for training government officials founded in the latter half of the seventh century, had two curricula: Confucian studies (Myōgyōdō), with about four hundred students, and mathematics (Sandō), with about thirty students. According to a rule established in 701, the two required texts for the Confucian curriculum were the *Analects* (*Lun-yü, Rongo*) and *The Classic of Filial Piety* (*Hsiao-ching, Kōkyō*) plus a choice of other texts.[6] In 730, the university expanded to include a law curriculum (Myōhōdō), which studied the *ritsuryō* legal codes, and a curriculum of letters (Monjōdō or Kidendō), which was of much lower status and focused on *The Anthology of Literature* (*Wen-hsüan, Monzen*), and the lexical work *Erh-ya* (*Jiga*). Later, the three Chinese histories (*sanshi*)—Ssu-ma Ch'ien's *Historical Records* (*Shih-chi, Shiki*), *The History of the Former Han Dynasty* (*Han-shu, Kanjo*), and *The History of the Later Han* (*Hou-han-shu, Gokanjo*)—were added to the Monjōdō syllabus. In the course of the eighth and ninth centuries, the Monjōdō dramatically increased in size, reflecting the growth in the importance and popularity of Chinese history and literature. By the ninth century, however, when the university had attained its peak, powerful clans (particularly the northern branch of the Fujiwara) began to monopolize the bureaucratic posts, which became hereditary, giving the upper nobility little incentive to send their sons to the university. One consequence was that education for almost all the upper aristocracy was carried out at home with tutors.

Elementary education for the nobility began with textbooks such as the *Mōgyū* (*Meng-ch'iu*), a T'ang elementary textbook with 596 four-character lines describing famous figures in Chinese history: *Senjimon* (*Ch'ien-tzu-wen*, One Thousand Characters), a Six Dynasties collection of 250 four-character phrases that was used for calligraphic practice; *Hyakunijūei* (Hundred Twenty Poems), a collection of 120 five-character line poems on various aspects of the cosmos by the Chinese T'ang poet Rikyō (Li-chiao, 645–714)[7]; and *Wakan rōeishū* (*Japanese and Chinese Poems to Sing*, edited by Fujiwara Kintō, 1012), which matched 588 famous phrases from Chinese poetry with 216 Japanese waka and which was also used for calligraphic practice. For more practical matters, the aristocracy began using *ōraimono* (epistolary textbooks), such as *Meigō ōrai* (Akihira's Letters, by Fujiwara Akihira, late 11th c.), which contained model letters on topics ranging from borrowing and lending money, promotions, and Buddhist matters, to composing poetry.[8] The nobility then went on to study the more advanced texts found in the Myōgyōdō (Confucian) and Monjōdō (Chinese literature) curricula—especially Ssu-ma Ch'ien's *Historical Records* and the *Wen-hsüan*—as well as other Chinese texts outside the Confucian curriculum such as *Lao-tzu, Chuang-tzu,* and *Collected Works of Po Chü-i* (*Pai-shih wen-chi, Hakushi monjū*).[9]

For Heian aristocratic women, who were not allowed into the university and who were also educated at home, three central cultural accomplishments were calligraphy (*tenarai*), poetry composition (*utayomi*), and music (*koto-hiki*), which meant playing the *wagon, sō no koto,* or *biwa* (lute). The practice of waka composition and calligraphy was begun at the same time, usually by copying out some famous poems from the preface to the *Kokinshū* (*Collection of Old and New Japanese Poems*, 905). A passage in the *Makura no sōshi* (The Pillow Book, Section 23) suggests that for aristocratic women learning meant the study of Japanese poetry (waka), particularly the *Kokinshū*, which was often memorized in its entirety. The most highly educated women such as Murasaki Shikibu and Sei Shōnagon—who were probably tutored by their fathers, who were scholars of Chinese—also read texts from the Chinese canon, especially *Collected Works of Po Chü-i* and *Wen-hsüan*.

With the gradual breakdown of the state university system from the mid-

Heian period onward, higher education and scholarship became privatized into "family learning" (*kagaku*), the profession and privilege of a particular family or clan, which inherited the knowledge and texts of a particular field. Even within the state university system, only certain families were able to enter a particular field and achieve the rank of professor (*hakase*) in that area. The Monjōdō curriculum, for example, was limited to families such as the Sugawara, the Ōe, and certain branches of the Fujiwara, while the Myōgyōdō curriculum was limited to the Nakahara and the Kiyohara families.[10] Often two or more families would alternate at a particular position in the university, leading to fierce competition among families, who developed their own closely guarded interpretations and scholarship.

MEDIEVAL CURRICULA: PRIESTHOOD, SAMURAI, AND NOBILITY

Scholarship in the medieval period was carried out primarily by two main groups: priests, who belonged to different Buddhist schools, and aristocrats, who were members of different families (*ie*). Each major Buddhist school—for example, the Tendai in Ōmi province, the Six Schools in Nara, Shingon at Tōji and Mount Kōya—developed its own complicated form of scholarship. The same was true of the aristocratic scholar families that emerged in the Heian and Kamakura periods—from the Monjōdō and Myōgyōdō families to the Japanese poetry families. Each possessed certain texts and a body of knowledge and scholarship that was passed on from one generation to the next. Learning generally meant following a "way" (*michi*), which implied both an abstract "way" (such as the "way of the Buddha") and a hereditary profession (*kashoku*) carried out by a specific family. To study the way of poetry (*uta no michi*), which was established sometime in the late twelfth century and which became the heart of wagaku (Japanese studies), meant to study with one of the established, hereditary poetry families (*uta no ie*), such as the Rokujō or Mikohidari, which treated both the texts and the knowledge of the texts as family possessions. This kind of monopolization and privatization of learning, which eventually led to an emphasis on secret texts (*hihon*) and secret transmissions (*hiden*), also emerged in most of the other fields in the medieval period, from martial arts (*bugei*) to performing arts (*geinō*). These canons were determined not by their popularity or by the consensus of a wide audience of readers, but rather by the authority or monopoly that a particular family was able to establish over a specific profession.

One consequence of this process was that the shape of the waka canon was a direct reflection of power struggles among hereditary poetry families. In the late twelfth century, the Rokujō family, one of the leading poetry families, embraced a broad and eclectic poetic (waka) canon that included poems from the *Man'yōshū* (Collection of Ten Thousand Leaves, late 8th c.). By contrast, the Mikohidari family, led by Fujiwara Shunzei and his son Fujiwara Teika, which eventually prevailed over the Rokujō family, favored restricting all poetic diction and models to the *Sandaishū*, the first three imperial poetry anthologies, beginning with the *Kokinshū*. Shunzei and Teika regarded the mid-Heian texts, *Sandaishū*, *Tales of Ise*, *The Tale of Genji*, and to a lesser extent, *Wakan rōeishū* and *Collected Works of Po Chü-i*, as the foundation (*moto*) for the practice of waka, which they believed had badly deteriorated in the two centuries following the *Kokinshū*. This ideal was realized in the poetry of the *Shinkokinshū* (*New Collection of Old and New Japanese Poems*), an imperial anthology edited by Teika and others in 1205 and the culminating achievement of the Mikohidari family. One consequence was that the *Sandaishū*, *Tales of Ise*, and *The Tale of Genji* became the central canon for the study of waka for the next eight hundred years, at least for the poetry circle organized around the imperial court, commonly referred to as Tōshō or Dōjō (court) poets. The Mikohidari family saw the hundred-year span from Emperor Daigo's reign (r. 897–930), when the *Kokinshū* was edited, to that of Emperor Ichijō (r. 986–1011), when *The Tale of Genji* was written, as a cultural golden age, an image that remained unchanged until the nineteenth century. The influence of this historical model, centered on *The Tale of Genji*, was so great that in subsequent periods correct Japanese grammar and kana system (*rekishiteki kanazukai* or *kyūkanazukai*) became identified with that of this particular period even as the grammar and kana system deviated from this ideal.

By the late Heian period, the notion of scholarship or professional education, which had centered on kangaku, had expanded to include fields that were more native in origin such as waka, calligraphy (*shūji*), and music (*kangen*), each of which developed similar private traditions and family styles (*ieyō*). As the fortunes of the aristocrats plummeted, they turned to their Heian court heritage—both possession of the actual manuscripts and knowledge of the texts—as a means of sustaining their identity and authority. The emergence of wagaku, which centered on the study of waka, and the canonization of Heian kana texts were not simply a matter of waka poetics but involved nothing less than the survival of a particular class that was in danger of rapidly disappearing.

Despite the rise of wagaku, which was monopolized by court-affiliated aristocratic families, the central canon for the nobility still remained Chinese or Buddhist. As the introduction to Priest Chōken's *Genji ippon kyō* (Genji One Volume Sutra, 1176) reveals, the genre hierarchy as it existed in the late Heian and early medieval periods was, roughly speaking, from top to bottom: (1) Buddhist scriptures; (2) Confucian texts; (3) histories (*shisho*), specifically Chinese histories such as *Historical Records*; (4) Chinese poetry and elegant prose (*bun*) such as *Wen hsüan*; (5) Japanese poetry (waka); and (6) vernacular tales (*monogatari*) and other kana texts including *nikki* (diaries). The genre hierarchy follows the Chinese model, with Confucian texts, histories, and poetry held in highest regard, while fiction is relegated to the bottom. The most highly regarded curriculum, at least from the Buddhist priest's point of view, was the Buddhist one, followed by the Confucian canon. Next came the two highest Chinese literary genres, history and poetry. At the bottom were the two native genres in kana, waka and *monogatari*, with poetry accorded a much higher status than prose fiction. Even for Kamakura scholars such as Kitabatake Chikafusa (1293–1354), a pioneer of Shinto and nativist thought, Japanese texts did not take precedence over Chinese and Buddhist texts.

However, by the late fifteenth century, in the Higashiyama period, the situation had reversed and Japanese texts clearly stood above Chinese texts in the aristocratic curriculum, along with a switch of emphasis in the Buddhist canon from esoteric texts to Pure Land texts.[11] This curriculum focused overwhelmingly on Heian court texts, particularly *The Tale of Genji, Tales of Ise, Sagoromo monogatari* (Tale of Sagoromo, 1058–80), *Wakan rōeishū*, and on the imperial waka collections.[12] The nobility also read early kanbun histories of Japan such as *Kogo shūi* (Collections of Old Narratives, 807)[13] and the "age of the gods" volume of the *Nihon shoki* (Chronicles of Japan, 720)—which was treated by Muromachi scholars such as Ichijō Kanera (1402–1481) and Yoshida Kanetomo (1435–1511) as a religious text—and kana histories such as the *Ōkagami* (Great Mirror, 1025), a history of the Fujiwara clan. The attention of the medieval nobility, whose public functions were gradually confined by the warrior government to matters of court ceremony, also focused on kanbun diaries and court records—such as *Shokugenshō* (On Official Duties and Their History, 1340), a record of Japanese administrative practices by Kitabatake Chikafusa—that preserved knowledge of Heian court positions and rituals.

The aristocracy continued to consider kangaku an integral part of their culture and education even in the Muromachi period. Largely as a result of the long Myōgyōdō tradition, the nobility focused overwhelmingly on Confucian texts. The most popular texts were the *Classic of Filial Piety*, which was highly valued in Japan as an easy-to-read first book on moral training for children, and the *Analects*, followed by *Great Learning* (Ta-hsüeh, Daigaku) and *Middle Way* (Chung-yung, Chūyō), both used as introductory textbooks and reflecting the new trend toward Sung Neo-Confucianism (which emphasized the Four Books, or *Shisho*).[14] The Gozan (Five Mountains) Zen priests, who actively imported Neo-Confucian scholarship and became a powerful intellectual and cultural force in the Muromachi period, inspired a new field of Confucian studies and eventually became, along with the Kiyohara family, the leading scholars of kangaku. The Gozan Zen priests studied both the Buddhist canon—the main texts of the Tendai, Kegon, and various Jōdo (Pure Land) schools—as well as a wide range of Chinese texts, including *Lao-tzu, Chuang-tzu, Hsün-tzu*, Chinese histories, and Chinese literature, especially *Santaishi* (*San-t'i-shih*, Three Styles of T'ang Poetry), and *Kobun shinpō* (*Ku-wen chen-pao*, True Treasury of the Ancient Style). Significantly, with the exception of Shōtetsu (1381–1459), a waka poet and a follower of Fujiwara Teika, these Zen priests had relatively little interest in *Genji, Kokinshū*, or other kana literature.

In the medieval period, warrior leaders constructed private classrooms and libraries in their homes called "learning places" (*gakumonjo*), where they invited eminent Confucian or wagaku scholars to give lessons on the *Analects, The Tale of Genji, Tales of Ise*, and other texts. These samurai elite, desiring to be associated with high culture, also supported institutions of higher education, the most notable being the Kanazawa bunko—a library attached to a temple school in Kanazawa (present-day Yokohama) and supported by the military leader Hōjō Sanetoki (1224–1276) in the late Kamakura period. Another important school was the Ashikaga gakkō, a university established by the Ashikaga military government and staffed by Buddhist priests, which flourished in the Warring States period (1477–1573). The curriculum for the Ashikaga gakkō initially included both Buddhist and Chinese texts, but from the fifteenth century, following guidelines set down by Uesugi Norizane (1410–1466), the Ashikaga governor of the Kantō region who revitalized the school in 1432, the official curriculum, which was designed to be accessible to beginners and which was strictly Chinese, consisted of the following stages: (1) commentaries on elementary writing texts such as *Senjimon* and *Mōgyū*[15]; (2) Confucian classics, beginning with the Four Books, especially *Great Learning* and *Middle Way*, followed by the more difficult Five Classics; (3) works of various philosophers, *Lieh-tzu, Chuang-*

tzu, and *Lao-tzu*, and, finally; (4) Chinese literature, that is to say, *Historical Records* and *Wen-hsüan*. According to a count of book titles at the Ashikaga gakkō, which reveals more accurately the reading interests of the students, 76 percent were Chinese texts, with the most widely used being the Four Books and Five Classics, followed by Chinese histories and literature, with a strong emphasis on books on divination (*ekigaku*), a discipline prized by samurai in battle and a central part of the curriculum. The school also taught military science, using Chinese military texts such as *Rikutō* (*Liu-t'ao*) and *Sanryaku* (*San-lüeh*), medicine, and astronomy—all practical fields for the samurai. Another 16 percent of the book titles were Buddhist texts, and 7 percent were in Japanese, including *Wamyō ruijushō* (the first Chinese-Japanese dictionary), *Wakan rōeishū*, *Azuma kagami* (the first warrior house history, written in late Kamakura period), *Goseibai shikimoku chū* (Commentary on *Goseibai shikimoku*, 1232, a book of warrior codes), and Chikafusa's *Shokugenshō* (On Official Posts and Their History, 1340)—all of which fell outside the regular curriculum.[16] The school, which drew its students, including many samurai youths, from all over Japan, sent its graduates to various parts of the country to become teachers, thereby providing education for the entire nation.[17]

While the curriculum of the Ashikaga gakkō suggests that the elite samurai were interested overwhelmingly in the Chinese and Confucian canon, the fact is that the provincial daimyō in the Warring States period (1477–1573) eagerly pursued and patronized Japanese studies, particularly the Heian courtly tradition, and practiced a wide range of performing arts, especially waka and *renga* (linked verse), which depended on a knowledge of the Japanese classics. The provincial lords such as the Asakura in Echizen, the Hatakeyama at Noto, the Ōuchi in Suō, the Takeda in Wakasa, and the Imagawa in Suruga, and their chief vassals collected and studied texts such as *The Tale of Genji*, *Tales of Ise*, and the *Kokinshū*, which lay at the heart of the aristocratic canon, as well as other kana-based texts such as *The Tale of Sagoromo* and *Eiga monogatari* (Tale of Flowering Fortunes, 1092).[18] The most widely used waka texts were Fujiwara Teika's *Eiga no taigai* (Essentials of Composing Poetry, 1241), Ton'a's *Gumon kenchū* (Answers to Silly Questions, 1363), and Teika's *Hyakunin isshu* (One Hundred Poets, One Poem Each, 1235)—a reflection of the stature that Fujiwara Teika (1162–1241) and Priest Ton'a (1289–1372) of the Nijō school had gained by this time. These texts were read primarily as part of the practice of poetry, but for these provincial warlords, the Heian classical texts, particularly *The Tale of Genji*, which they commissioned paintings of, also represented something that they desperately wanted: an association with court culture and with the emperor. The provincial daimyō also collected Buddhist texts—especially *Hekiganroku* (Blue Cliff Notes) and *Rinzairoku*, two Rinzai Zen texts, and *Hokekyō* (Lotus Sutra)—as well as a range of Chinese texts, from the standard Confucian texts to Chinese histories and Chinese poetry by Po Chü-i and Huang T'ing-chien.[19]

In contrast to the elite warriors, who were tutored at their homes by *kuge* (court nobility) scholars, renga masters, or Buddhist priests, or who helped sponsor centers of learning such as the Ashikaga gakkō, the average samurai's primary education was learning the martial arts at home and reading and writing at a local temple school.[20] *Mijikagami* (Mirror of My Life, 1617), an autobiography by Tamaki Yoshiyasu, a samurai retainer of Mōri Motonari, a daimyō of Aki province (modern Hiroshima), records his schooling in detail, from the age of thirteen, in 1564.[21] The curriculum for the first year ranged from reading Buddhist sutras in the morning, specifically the *Heart Sutra* (*Hannya shingyō*) and *Lotus Sutra*, to studying *Teikin ōrai* (Household Lesson Letters, late 14th c.), an epistolary handbook for learning *iroha* syllabary, kana, and kanji, to reading a legal code text (*shikijō* or *shikimoku*) and mastering two moral training books: *Dōjikyō* (Lessons for Children), a collection of 320 five-character aphorisms for everyday life, and *Jitsugokyō* (True Word Teachings), a collection of 96 five-character phrases asserting the value of wisdom over money—both of which were widely used in ethical training in the medieval and Edo periods.[22] The second year focused on reading actual Confucian texts (Four Books and Five Classics) plus *rōei* (poems to be sung)—probably *Wakan rōeishū*—and two Chinese military classics, *Rikutō* and *Sanryaku*. The third year concentrated on Japanese texts: "*Kokinshū*, *Man'yōshū*, *Tales of Ise*, part of *The Tale of Genji*, *First Eight Imperial Poetry Anthologies* (*Hachidaishū*), listening to lectures on other poetic texts, practicing the way of waka, visiting the traces of Hitomaro and Akahito, and learning the style of Teika and Ietaka."[23] Calligraphy, which progressed from *sō* (running style) and *gyō* (semicursive style) to *shin* (square style) over the three years, was an integral part of the curriculum.

Sekyōshō (Mirror of Society Collection), a late medieval moral training text, shows the schedule at one temple school: 6–9 A.M. (reading sutras), 10 A.M.–noon (calligraphy), 1–3 P.M. (reading texts), 4–6 P.M. (various games and performing arts), 7–9 P.M. (poem-tale, musical instruments), 9–11 P.M. (free time). The various performing arts (such as nō singing), games (*sumō*, *kemari*, archery, *shōgi*, etc.), and light reading (such as poem-tales) were done after 3 P.M., as a form of recreation, after the main curriculum (sutras, writing, and reading) was finished.[24] As the schedule suggests, the temple schools, which became widespread from the fifteenth century, offered a diverse mixture of Buddhist, Chinese, and Japanese texts, as well as the opportunity to engage in a range of native performing arts, all of which reflected the cultural interests of the provincial warrior lords. As Yonehara Masayoshi points out, the samurai interest in both Chinese-style education and the practice of waka and *renga* was reflected in their extensive portraiture of Tenjin (Sugawara Michizane, who had visited China), Hitomaro, and Sōgi—the god of learning, the saint of waka, and the godfather of renga, respectively.[25] Tamaki Yoshiyasu's temple education may have been an ideal one for a samurai during the Warring States period, when young warriors could only study between periods of service in the field. According to one account, during a twenty-one-month siege (1563–65) of a castle of the Amago in Izumo Province, Kikkawa Motoharu (1530–86), the son of Mōri Motonari, the daimyō from Aki Province, copied forty volumes of the *Taiheiki* (Record of the Great Peace, late 14th c.), a Muromachi kana history that became an educational handbook for samurai in the late medieval and Edo periods.[26]

In the early medieval period, a significant gap existed among the warriors in power, the aristocracy in possession of many of the texts, and the priests who were scholars and teachers. Furthermore, each of the three dominant groups—the aristocracy, the samurai elite, and the priesthood—gravitated toward a specific canon, Japanese studies, Chinese and Confucian texts, and Buddhist texts, respectively, associations that were to have an enormous impact on the configuration of the Japanese canon as we know it today. More important, however, a significant overlap existed among the three. The Muromachi Zen priests, for example, were scholars of both Buddhist and Chinese texts, particularly Chinese history and poetry; the nobility in turn specialized not only in Japanese texts but in Confucian texts as well; and the samurai, while officially committed to a Confucian curriculum and the study of military histories, were deeply involved in waka and renga. In a surprisingly systematic manner, the temple schools provided fundamental instruction in all these cultural areas. Education consisted of a mixture of a "writerly" canon, texts for learning how to compose poetry, and a "readerly" canon, mainly Confucian and Buddhist, intended to develop moral and religious consciousness as well as social and political skills.

EDO PERIOD CURRICULA: FROM TERAKOYA TO HAN SCHOOLS

Education in the Edo period was dominated by a number of different types of schools, which were often defined by social class: (1) *terakoya* (literally, "temple schools"), for the elementary education of commoners; (2) the various organizations for the performing arts (such as *haikai, renga*, tea, incense, *nō*, etc.), which were usually open to all classes; (3) *shigaku* (private academies), for more advanced students of different social backgrounds in a variety of fields; (4) the Shōheikō, the official school established by the Tokugawa bakufu, for bakufu retainers and other samurai; and (5) *han* (fief) schools, created by the various daimyō for the education of their own samurai.

Terakoya, which focused on the utilitarian skills of "reading, writing, and the abacus,"[27] were private elementary schools run for profit by former samurai, *chōnin* (urban commoners), or those in other professions—such as Buddhist priests, Shinto priests, doctors, or town mayors (*risei*)—who managed the school on the side.[28] In contrast to medieval temple schools run by Buddhist priests in the provinces, the terakoya first emerged in the large cities, particularly in the early years of the eighteenth century, and spread to smaller cities in the next several decades before extending to the provincial villages in the 1830s and 1840s.[29] The curriculum typically began with calligraphy practice with *hiragana* (usually using the *iroha* syllabary poem), *katakana*, and numbers (*sūji*), and moved on to copying place names in vocabulary-building *ōraimono* (epistolary textbooks) such as *Kunizukushi* (All Provinces) before proceeding to *Senjimon*, the Chinese calligraphy handbook. Reading practice, which was often indistinguishable from calligraphy practice, normally focused on moral lessons from *Jitsugokyō* (True Word Teachings), on the Four Books, on medieval ōraimono such as *Teikin ōrai* (Household Lesson Letters, 1350) and *Imagawajō* (Letters from Imagawa Ryōshun, 1326–1414), or on new Edo period ōraimono, tailored specifically for the social class or occupation of the students, such as *Shōbai ōrai* (Merchant Letters), the one most widely used by urban commoners,[30] or *Nōgyō ōrai* (Farmer's Letters). *Shōbai ōrai* taught proper etiquette in dealing with customers, emphasized the dangers of greed, and cautioned against using money for drink, pleasure, clothes, and other material luxuries. A popular geography ōraimono was *Tōkaidō ōrai* (Eastern Highway Letters), which described the fifty-three stations on the Eastern Highway in 7/5-syllable rhythm.[31] On rarer occasions and at a more advanced level, students read literary texts such as *Selected T'ang Poems* (*Tōshisen*), Teika's *Hyakunin isshu*, part of *The Tale of Genji*, the kana preface to the *Kokinshū*, or *Wakan rōeishū*, which was used for calligraphy practice.[32] The choice of texts varied considerably, depending on the social class, the locale, and the profession and interests of the instructor: former samurai often offered instruction in Chinese studies (e.g., a warrior history such as Rai San'yō's *Nihon gaishi*),

Shinto priests taught wagaku, Buddhist priests explicated sutras, doctors gave insight into medicine, and town mayors explained some aspect of law (*hatto*).

The terakoya was usually divided by gender, often with separate rooms or facilities for boys and girls, and the young women were assigned to a much more meager, female-oriented curriculum that focused on Confucian-based, ethical texts such as *Onna Imagawa* (Women's Imagawa, 1687), which also served as a calligraphic handbook, and *Onna daigaku* (Great Learning for Women, early 18th c.), along with some Japanese texts such as *Hyakunin isshu* or *The Tale of Genji*.[33] Sometimes the wife of the *terakoya* teacher or a female teacher would teach supplementary subjects such as sewing, etiquette, tea ceremony, and flower arrangement, which were considered a part of a young woman's training. The daughters of commoners attended terakoya in relatively limited numbers (by one count, a little over one-tenth of the entire terakoya enrollment),[34] while daughters of wealthy families or elite samurai continued to receive their education at home. *The Tale of Genji* was in fact read from the medieval period as a *jokun*, an educational guide for young women.[35] A significant portion of Japanese courtly literature thus entered the popular sphere and imagination through women's education.

The latter half of the seventeenth century through the middle of the eighteenth century witnessed a spectacular growth in the wealth of the upper chōnin, who used their leisure time and surplus capital to pursue performing arts (*geinō*)—such as nō singing (*utai*), tea ceremony (*chanoyu*), flower arrangement, various musical instruments (such as the *taiko*, or large drum), and haikai. A revealing passage in *Shōbai ōrai* (Merchant Letters) notes that "if one's family has the extra wealth and leisure, one should take occasional lessons in waka, renga, haikai, flower arrangement, football (*kemari*), tea, nō song, dance (*mai*), drum (*tsuzumi*), large drum, flute (*fue*), lute (*biwa*), koto, etc."[36] These performing arts were developed and taught by specific schools (*mon*), which identified with a single founder (*iemoto*), and only those belonging to and certified by those schools could teach the established curricula. While certain schools, such as the Hayashi family Confucian studies school, the Satomura family renga school, or the Nijō waka school, were closely affiliated with the shogunate or the imperial court, most of the schools, such as those of haikai, tea, flower, utai, etc., were open to commoners, who flocked to them in large numbers. Matsuo Bashō (1644–1694), as the iemoto of one of these schools, was eventually transformed into a god, due to the ingenuity and industriousness of his disciples, who created branch schools all around the country. Haikai masters such as Matsunaga

Teitoku (1571–1653), the founder of Teimon haikai school, were concerned primarily with what I have called the "writerly" canon, texts necessary for the practice of a particular art, but they also contributed to formation of the "readerly" canon. These haikai poets, who were generally urban commoners, explored *The Pillow Book* and *Tsurezuregusa*, neither of which had received substantial notice by aristocratic waka poets and had consequently not become the object of secret transmissions and aristocratic family traditions. It was due in large measure to the attention of these Edo period haikai poets and scholars that *The Pillow Book* and *Tsurezuregusa* became two major texts in the Japanese canon. *Tsurezuregusa* in fact became the most widely published Japanese classic in the Edo period, achieving the status of the "*Analects* of Japan."

During this period the different fields of learning, each with its respective curriculum and canon, gave rise to private academies (*shijuku*) for more advanced students, the equivalent of modern middle school through college. These private academies generally took students regardless of social background (as long as they paid), including women, and often offered a different ideological perspective than that espoused at the han or bakufu schools. Of the roughly 1,500 different private academies thought to have existed in the Edo period, the greatest number were Confucian academies, followed by nativist (kokugaku) academies, and then Western learning (*yōgaku*) schools. Itō Jinsai's (1627–1705) Kogidō (Horikawa School, established in Kyoto in 1662), one of the most notable Chinese studies academies, is said to have had 3,000 students—samurai, nobility, and chōnin—from all over the country. By the end of the Edo period, there were 107 Western learning academies in Edo alone, not to mention those in Nagasaki and Osaka.

In the Edo period, the caretakers of wagaku, the aristocratic court (*Dōjō*) poets, were gradually displaced by kokugaku scholars, primarily of commoner background, who took a more rational, linguistic approach to ancient texts and rejected the medieval notion of secret transmissions based on house lineage. At the Suzunoya at Matsuzaka (Ise Province), one of the most famous kokugaku academies, Motoori Norinaga (1730–1801) lectured over a period of years on the *Man'yōshū* (which earlier kokugaku scholars had transformed into a major kokugaku text), the *Kokinshū*, *Tales of Ise*, *The Tale of Genji*, and *Kojiki* (*Record of Ancient Matters*, 712), a hitherto relatively minor history that Norinaga incorporated into the center of the Japanese canon and that would consequently overshadow the *Nihon shoki*. Norinaga also taught on a more sporadic basis texts such as the *Shinkokinshū*, *Tosa Diary*, *The Pillow Book*, *Hyakunin isshu*, *Tale of Flowering Fortunes*, *Tale of Sagoromo*, and *Shokugenshō*. Significantly, the kokugaku canon, which was based mainly on texts from the Heian and Nara periods, did not include medieval and Edo kana-based texts, not even *Tsurezuregusa*, which no doubt revealed too much Buddhist (foreign) influence for kokugaku scholars. In contrast to the medieval wagaku canon, which was primarily a "writerly" canon created by medieval poets for the purposes of composing poetry, kokugaku scholars, while concerned about the canon as a key to composing waka, constructed a largely "readerly" canon in which many of the same texts were reconfigured to provide moral, religious, social, and political alternatives to the texts in the Confucian and Buddhist canons. Significantly, the earlier canonizers of wa-gaku texts—such as Shunzei, Teika, Sōgi—were major poets of waka or renga while kokugaku scholars such as Motoori Norinaga (1730–1801) tended to be scholars rather than poets.

The kokugaku schools can be seen, at least in part, as an attempt by one group, mainly urban commoners, to compete with the aristocratic court (Dōjō) poets, the Buddhist clergy, and the Confucian kangaku scholars, who had dominated the spheres of learning in the medieval period. However, as the modern scholar Odaka Michiko has pointed out, many of the earlier forms of learning and teaching, especially the secret transmissions of the Dōjō court poets, continued to thrive in the Edo period.[37] The secret transmission of the *Kokinshū* passed from Hosokawa Yūsai (1534–1610) to Prince Toshihito (Hachijō no miya) to Emperor GoMizunoo (1596–1680), who formed the center of a group of court waka poets. The tradition of the *Kokin denju*—which centered on a "writerly" canon very different from the one constructed by kokugaku scholars—continued to be practiced at the Gosho, the imperial palace, until as late as 1840. By associating itself with the emperor and the imperial court, the Dōjō school was able to maintain its authority—regarded as the highest in the poetic world—until the end of the Edo period.

The han (fief) curriculum, which varied greatly from school to school and which viewed education from the point of view of the ruling class of warriors, initially focused almost exclusively on kangaku, particularly Confucian studies, concentrating on the Four Books and Five Classics, as well as Chinese histories.[38] In the late eighteenth century, as the need for more practical skills became evident, a limited number of han schools added calligraphy, wagaku, arithmetic, and astronomy to the curriculum. By the 1820s and 1830s, han schools, particularly those in contact with the Dutch or threatened by Western military powers (such as those in northern and western Kyūshū), also included Western learning (*yōgaku*), a new field that encompassed practical areas such as science, medicine, military affairs, shipbuilding, and western languages (Dutch and English). By the time of the Meiji Restoration, 68 of the 592 han schools taught yōgaku, and 92 wagaku, which in some schools appeared in the form of kōgaku (imperial study), the study of Japan as country of the emperor.[39] Generally speaking, the han schools did not include Japanese histories in the curriculum, but the crisis at the end of the Edo period brought about some change. The *wakan* (Japanese-Chinese) curriculum at the Matsumoto (Nagano) han school, for example, included Japanese histories in kanbun such as *Honchō tsugan* (*Mirror of Japan*, compiled by Hayashi Razan and others), *Kokushi ryaku* (*Digest of National History*, 1826), *Kōchō shiryaku* (*Digest History of the Imperial Court*, 1823), and Rai San'yō's *Nihon gaishi* (*Private History of Japan*, 1829).[40] The curriculum of Gakushūkan, a han school founded in 1713 by the Kishū (Kii) han, had initially been restricted to kangaku, but by the late 1860s it had shifted to a three-pronged curriculum of kokugaku, *rangaku* (Dutch learning), and military study; and then, after the change to the prefecture system in 1871 (Meiji 4), it added *yōgaku*, in the form of English, French, and German, while continuing to teach a limited amount of kokugaku in the form of such texts as the *Kojiki*, *Shokugenshō*, *Nihon shoki*, *Ryō no gige* (834), *Man'yōshū*, and *Kokinshū*.[41] In short, there was never a single dominant canon, but rather different types of canons, which overlapped. Kanbun histories of Japan, which began in imitation of Chinese historiography, gradually entered into the field of kokugaku, and kokugaku moved into the han curriculum—a movement reflected in the early Meiji educational curriculum.

THE MODERN PERIOD: FROM WRITING MODELS TO NATIONALISM

The Gakusei (Educational system) edict of 1872 created an elementary school (*shōgaku*), middle school (*chūgaku*), and university (*daigaku*) system on a national basis, but it would be many years before the system was actually constructed.[42] The 1886 Middle School Edict (*Chūgakkōrei*) divided the middle school, which was intended to provide higher education for boys, into two levels: a five-year, prefectural *jinjō chūgakkō* (normal middle school), and a two-year, state *kōtō chūgakkō* (higher middle school).[43] In 1886 the Meiji government also established the Teikoku daigaku (Imperial university) system, eventually creating nine universities for advanced learning and research, each with five fields, in law, medicine, engineering, humanities (*bun*), and science (*ri*).[44] In 1899 the Kōtō jogakkō rei (Higher Women's School Edict) officially established a higher women's school system to provide secondary education (usually four years) for women and to be the equivalent of the men's chūgakkō.

In Meiji Japan, school children did not read actual pre-Meiji texts, either in classical Japanese (*bungo*) or kanbun, until the normal middle school (jinjō chūgakkō). In the postwar period, classical Japanese and kanbun became even more remote and were not taught until the high school (kōtō gakkō) level. The modern canonization of classical Japanese literature as it occurred through public educational institutions, where these texts had the widest impact, is thus best viewed by looking at prewar middle school (the equivalent of high school and the first two years of college in the postwar period) and postwar high school textbooks. While these textbooks, which were frequently edited by the leading professors at the imperial universities, do not necessarily reflect the latest popular tastes or the most recent scholarship, they directly reveal the manner in which the canon was shaped by institutional power and authority.

In the years immediately following the 1872 announcement of the gakusei system, the middle school language curriculum remained similar to that found in Edo period han schools. The curriculum was divided into three areas—*kokugogaku* (national language study), *shūji* (calligraphy), and *kogengaku* (classical language study)—which were often taught by kangaku teachers from the former han schools, who mixed traditional kangaku texts—such as *Wen-chang kuei-fan* (*Bunshō kihan*, Prose Models) and *Tso-chuan*—with late Edo kokugaku texts in kanbun such as Rai Sanyō's *Nihon gaishi*. In 1880, kokugogaku and kogengaku were replaced by the *wakanbun* Japanese and Chinese language curriculum, which implied, in an age when kanbun still reigned supreme and was taught for the practical purpose of learning to write, that kana-based texts had a significant place alongside Chinese texts. Such Japanese texts as the *Genpei jōsuiki* (*Record of the Rise and Fall of the Genji and the Heike*, late 14th c.), *Tale of the Heike*, *Tsurezuregusa*, *Tosa Diary*, and *gabun* (neoclassical) texts by Edo scholars and poets were added to the curriculum at this time to teach the writing of Japanese as well.[45]

The 1886 Middle School Edict placed the middle school curriculum under the direct administration of the Ministry of Education, stipulating that only those textbooks certified (*kentei*) by the Ministry of Education could be used, and renamed the language curriculum "Kokugo naishi kanbun" (Japanese language and Chinese writing), a title that would remain unchanged for most of the prewar period. In 1890, the Imperial Rescript on

Education (*Kyōiku chokugo*) was promulgated, establishing a national ethic of fidelity to the emperor (*chūkun*) and love for the nation (*aikoku*) based on Confucian ethics. In the following year, the first modern literary histories as well as the earliest modern anthologies of classical Japanese literature—such as Haga Yaichi (1867–1927) and Tachibana Senzaburō's (1867–1901) *Kokubungaku tokuhon* (A Japanese Literature Reader, 1890)—were published, establishing a new literary paradigm based on European genre models (of drama, novel, epic, etc.). The result of the new national educational policy and the new literary histories and anthologies was the establishment of a middle school curriculum that was highly Confucian in orientation, deeply influenced by new literary paradigms, and guided by the new notion of a national language (*kokugo*) based on kana.

Haga Yaichi and Tachibana Senzaburō's *Kokubungaku tokuhon*, a groundbreaking anthology, presented a short history of Japanese literature followed by representative kana-based texts from each of the major historical periods, including poetry (*Man'yōshū*, *Kokinshū*, *Shinkokinshū*, haiku), drama (nō, kyōgen, jōruri), prose fiction (*The Tale of Genji*, *Tale of the Heike*, *Jinnō shōtōki*, *Taiheiki*, etc.), and a number of Edo essays by scholars and poets (e.g., Motoori Norinaga, Arai Hakuseki, Muro Kyūsō). In contrast to the earlier curriculum, which stressed kanbun texts, the government-certified middle school textbooks from the 1890s onward, no doubt inspired by the new national literature model and history presented by Haga, Tachibana, and other scholars, anthologized many of the national language texts now considered to be part of the canon of Japanese classical literature. *Chūtō kokugo tokuhon* (Middle School National Language Reader, edited by Nakamura Akika, 1893), for example, included *Man'yōshū*, *Tales of Ise*, *Tale of the Bamboo Cutter*, *Tosa Diary*, *Kokinshū*, *The Pillow Book*, *The Tale of Genji*, *Sarashina Diary*, *Ōkagami*, *Tale of Flowering Fortunes*, *Konjaku monogatari* (Tales of Times Now Past, 1120), *Hōjōki*, *Heiji monogatari* (Tales of Heiji, 1219), *Hōgen monogatari* (Tales of Hōgen, 1219), *Uji shūi monogatari* (Collection of Tales from Uji, 1189), *Jikkinshō* (1252), *Izayoi nikki* (Diary of the 16th Night, 1279), *Tsurezuregusa*, *Jinnō shōtōki* (Chronicle of Gods and Sovereigns, 1339), *Tale of the Heike*, *Masukagami* (Greater Mirror, 1376), and *Taiheiki*. While the Edo period kokugaku canon was restricted almost entirely to ancient and Heian texts, these textbooks included texts from every major period, particularly medieval military narratives (*gunkimono*) such as *The Tale of the Heike* and *Taiheiki*, medieval collections of folk literature such as *Konjaku monogtari* and *Uji shūi monogatari*, and medieval essays such as *Hōjōki* and *Tsurezuregusa*, none of which had been part of the Edo period kokugaku canon (probably due to the fact that, like most medieval popular texts, they showed heavy Buddhist influence). In contrast to the medieval wagaku canon, which had centered on poetry and poetry-related texts, this curriculum was heavily weighted toward histories in kana, including Heian histories. In *Nihon bungakushi* (History of Japanese Literature, 1890), the first full-length literary history, Mikami Sanji (1865–1939) and Takatsu Kuwasaburō (1864–1921) note that Heian histories such as the *Great Mirror* and *Tales of Flowering Fortune* are good examples of national literature not only because they are written in *kana*, but also because they resemble in style and presentation the "novel" (*shōsetsu*), now considered the most advanced of literary genres.[46]

Kokugo textbooks from the 1890s selected texts for the practical purpose of serving as models for writing the national language (kokugo). In the preface to *Chūtō kokubun tokuhon* (Middle School Japanese Reader, Meiji shoin, 1896), one of the most widely used textbooks of this period, Ochiai Naobumi (1861–1903),[47] the editor, writes: "In the first year, the student should imitate the style of the Meiji period, in the second year the student should imitate the style of the Tokugawa period, and in the third year the student should imitate texts of the classical (*chūko*) period. In all cases, texts have been selected that are rhythmical and elegant and that are sufficient to serve as models for student composition."[48] Following this policy, the first two volumes drew together fifty pieces by contemporary Meiji authors (many of whom wrote in literary Japanese, or *bungo*); the third through sixth volumes gathered roughly fifty pieces from neoclassical essays from the Edo period; and the seventh through the tenth volumes brought together fifteen medieval and Heian texts.[49] The volumes, in short, were arranged in order of difficulty, beginning with Meiji writings, proceeding to Edo writings, and then ending with medieval and Heian texts at the most advanced stage. The Meiji textbook editors viewed medieval and Edo period writing, particularly the *wakan konkō* (mixed Japanese-Chinese) style, which combined Chinese graphs with classical Japanese grammar, as the suitable model for contemporary writing. The Meiji canonization of *Genpei jōsuiki*, which Haga Yaichi praises for fusing the "sadness of *wabun* with the strength of kanbun," in fact had much to do with its being regarded as an exemplar of the *wakan konkō* style.[50]

One of the most striking aspects of middle school textbooks in the 1890s is in fact the extremely heavy use of Edo period essays in the neoclassical style (*gikobun*), a style that combined classical grammar with Chinese graphs. These *gikobun* essays were written by both kangaku and kokugaku scholars and poets and other *bunjin* or poet-painter men of letters. According to one count, Meiji textbooks include as many as 170 different neoclassical Edo texts, of which 51 are drawn on two or more times.[51] The most widely used of these essays include *Unpyō zasshi* (Various Records of Clouds and Grass, 1834, attributed to Yanagisawa Kien), Kan Chazan's (1748–1827) *Fude no susabi* (Wanderings of a Brush), Ban Kōkei's (1733–1806) *Kinsei kijinden* (Biographies of Eccentric People of the Edo Period, 1790), Arai Hakuseki's *Oritakushiba no ki* (Record of Brushwood For Burning, 1716) and *Tokushi yoron* (Discussions of History, 1712), Matsudaira Sadanobu's *Kagetsu sōshi* (Stories of Flowers and Moon, 1818), Tachibana Nankei's (1753–1805) *Saiyūki* and *Tōyuki* (Travels West, Travels East), Yuasa Jōzan's (1708–1781) *Jōzan kidan* (Stories by Jōzan, 1739), Muro Kyūsō's (1658–1734) *Sundai zatsuwa* (Casual Talk at Surugadai, 1750), Motoori Norinaga's *Tamakatsuma* (Jeweled Basket, 1795–1812), and Miura Baien's (1723–1789) various writings (*Baien sōsho*). In *Kokubungaku tokuhon*, which also draws heavily on essays by Edo intellectuals, Haga praises kangaku scholars such as Arai Hakuseki (1657–1725) for developing a mixed Japanese-Chinese (wakan konkō) style that could communicate Confucian thought to "the average person, that was even easy for women to understand," and prefers this writing to the pure (almost entirely kana) neoclassical style of kokugaku scholars, which had a limited vocabulary.[52] One consequence of this kind of view was that these Japanese essays—such as *Oritakushiba no ki* and *Tokushi yoron* by Arai Hakuseki—became among the most widely used texts in Meiji middle school textbooks. These essays by Confucian scholars, along with other mixed style writing by kokugaku scholars, not only functioned as models for literary prose composition, but also provided moral, heavily Confucian education as well as essential knowledge about various fields (in the Meiji enlightenment mode)—three key functions of the 1890s kokugo curriculum.

A stylistic experiment was initially made in the early Meiji period to create a new Japanese literary style based on classical waka texts, but a more practical style of literary prose (*bungobun*) using classical grammar was soon developed by contemporary writers such as Mori Ōgai (1862–1922) and Kōda Rohan (1867–1947). This Meiji literary prose style, which was a form of neoclassical *gabun*, or elegant prose, was in turn gradually supplanted by *genbun itchi* (unification of the spoken and written languages) style.[53] The first results of the genbun itchi movement were seen in texts such as Futabatei Shimei's *Ukigumo* (Floating Clouds, 1887–89) and Yamada Bimyō's *Musashino* (1887), but it was not until 1908–10 that it began entering into textbooks in significant form, and it did not become dominant until the late Taishō period (1912–26).[54] As the literary style was gradually displaced by the genbun itchi style and classical Japanese lost its practical function as a writing model, classical texts took on other functions, which were increasingly ethical and ideological.

Medieval and Edo period moral training textbooks such as *Jitsugokyō* and *Dōjikyō* had stressed filial piety (*kō*) and loyalty (*chū*) as the means by which the child paid back an obligation (*on*) to his or her parents. This idea was linked via the *Classic of Filial Piety* (*Kōkyō*), a popular Edo period Confucian textbook, to the idea that the same filial piety and loyalty should apply to the subject's relationship to the ruler. The 1890 Imperial Rescript on Education, which combined these traditional Confucian virtues with a family-based notion of the nation, emphasized fidelity to the sovereign and love for the nation, thus mandating all schools to carry out the Meiji government's objective of transforming the people into *shinmin* (subjects of the emperor). Ueda Kazutoshi (1867–1937), the modern pioneer of kokugo (national language) study, argued in 1894 that "loyalty to the sovereign and love of the nation" (*chūkun aikoku*) and a common language were the two forces that united Japan as a nation, that the "national essence" (*kokutai*) was embodied in the Japanese language.[55] The underlying premise here was that kokugo was, according to one 1911 regulation, "the dwelling place of the nation's spirit" (*kokugo wa kokumin seishin no yadoru tokoro*),[56] and that the Japanese classics were a key means of understanding the "national essence." One consequence of this policy was that Meiji textbooks gravitated toward medieval and Edo period kana-based warrior literature (such as the *Taiheiki*), which had emphasized such virtues as self-sacrifice and loyalty. The *Taiheiki* story of Kusunoki Masashige (d. 1336), who came to the aid of Emperor GoDaigo when the emperor was betrayed by Hōjō Takatoki, was frequently used as an example of *chūkun*.[57] Another *Taiheiki* example was the description of Kusunoki Masatsura's mother, who suppresses her own emotions and gives up her child for the sovereign. The ideal mother, in other words, was one who sacrificed herself not only for her family, but also for the nation.[58]

By the 1930s kanbun also took on an increasingly ideological function. From the beginning of the Meiji period, kokugo had been established and identified in opposition to kanbun, which was of foreign derivation. The extended conflict in the early Meiji period between the kokugaku scholars (from the Kōgakusho) and the kangaku scholars (from the former Shōheikō and han schools) with regard to the proper balance between kokugaku and Chinese texts in the kokugo curriculum resulted in the kokugaku scholars eventually subordinating kangaku to kokugaku. Despite various subsequent attempts to degrade or eliminate kanbun, however, it remained an integral part of the kokugo curriculum, primarily because Chinese graphs were seen as integral to kokugo and because kangaku, particularly the study of the Confucian classics, was regarded as essential to moral education, a key function of the kokugo curriculum.[59] As literary or classical Japanese (*kobun*) gradually became separated from contemporary Japanese prose (*gendaibun*), which became the central language of the kokugo curriculum, both kobun and kanbun came together under the rubric of the "classics" (*koten*), where they remain together today in the postwar curriculum. In the prewar period they began to share similar ideological and ethical functions. As the teacher's guide to the 1943 government middle school textbook notes,

> Through Japanese prose as the classics (koten), one should make the students master the tradition and expressions of the imperial country and cultivate the life of the nation (*kokumin*) as well as the creative culture of the imperial country. Through kanbun as the classics, one should make the students master the culture, thought, and expressions of the imperial country and of East Asia (Tōa), and one should contribute to the cultivation of the national spirit.[60]

The government textbook on kanbun published in 1943, for example, draws on Rai Sanyō's *Nihon gaishi*, a kanbun warrior history that had been used in the han schools, to demonstrate such notions as national spirit (*kokutai*), loyalty (*chūsei*), and military valor (*yūbu*). Thus, kanbun of both Japanese and Chinese origin served as an important means of cultivating the nationalistic spirit, including a sense of the Greater East Asia Co-Prosperity Sphere.

THE POSTWAR CURRICULUM: DEMILITARIZING THE CANON

Shortly after the end of the Pacific War, when Japan came under the control of the Allied Occupation forces, the Ministry of Education declared that the object of postwar education was the establishment of a peaceful country and ordered the elimination of all textbook passages dealing with military life and nationalist ideology. Even passages such as "Kurikara tōge" (Yoshinaka at Kurikara Pass) and "Yumi nagashi" (Yoshitsune's Lost Bow), which describe the actions of brave soldiers in *The Tale of the Heike*, were excised.[61]

Orders were also given to eliminate moral training (*shūshin*) from the curriculum and to prohibit public discussion of concepts such as "national essence" (*kokutai no hongi*), "the way of the imperial subject" (*shinmin no michi*), and national Shinto. The result was the disappearance of over half of the wartime curriculum, including almost all *gunki monogatari* (military chronicles), Shinto-related histories, and numerous Edo period *gabun* essays on valorous soldiers and great men.[62]

Though kangaku was eliminated from the national language canon in the Meiji period, medieval military chronicles and kana essays by Edo kangaku scholars provided an important means of "nationalizing" Confucian ethics in Meiji textbooks. By contrast, postwar textbooks, in reaction to the prewar militaristic and ultranationalist use of kana texts, constructed a largely "peaceful" and "democratic" Japanese canon, which was populist in orientation and which significantly diminished the role of the warrior culture that had been incorporated into the canon by Meiji textbooks.[63] Those writers who had no association with military or imperial history—such as Bashō and Kenkō—maintained their high status from prior to the war, while the curriculum as a whole shifted toward commoner culture, particularly toward popular literature, with a noticeable growth of interest in humor and such genres as *setsuwa* (folk stories), *kyōgen* (comic drama), fiction, haikai, and jōruri. Waka and *kayō* (folk songs) that dealt with nature and simple human emotions (rather than the emperor) were also added to the canon.

Jinnō shōtōki (Chronicle of Gods and Sovereigns), which Kitabatake Chikafusa originally wrote to legitimize Emperor GoDaigo's imperial restoration and which was a major text in Meiji and prewar textbooks, was decanonized after the war. Prewar kokugo textbooks, which began in the 1930s to introduce the notion of Japan as the "land of the gods" (*kami no kuni*) and present the emperor as a divine being, focused on passages such as "Three types of imperial regalia" (*sanshu no jingi*), "Duty of the imperial subject" (*shinmin no tsutome*), "Way of the vassal" (*jinshin no michi*), and "Great Japan is a land of gods" (*Ōyamato wa kami no kuni nari*), passages that authenticated the imperial system by stressing an unbroken imperial lineage since the age of the gods. Today, due to its earlier association with *tennō* (emperor) ideology, *Jinnō shōtōki* does not even appear in most collections of classical Japanese literature despite its importance for understanding medieval syncretic thought.[64]

An even more dramatic fate awaited the *Taiheiki*, which was perhaps the single most important text in the entire prewar period, comparable in stature to *Tsurezuregusa* and *The Tale of the Heike*. In the Edo period, the

Mito school, which directly contributed to the ideology behind the Meiji Restoration, linked Kusunoki Masashige to the legitimization of GoDaigo's Southern Court; and, as Hyōdo Hiromi points out, imperial restorationists such as Yoshida Shōin from Chōshū looked to Masashige as a model for revolt against the Tokugawa military government.[65] Many of the *Taiheiki* selections in prewar textbooks focus on figures such as Kusunoki Masashige, or Kusunoki's son Masatsura, who exemplify the virtue of loyalty either in terms of filial piety or in service to the emperor. In "Station at Sakurai" (Sakurai no shuku, vol. 16),[66] for example, Kusunoki Masashige, who is about to die, takes leave of his eleven-year-old son Masatsura (d. 1348), telling him to remain loyal to his father and his clan even after his father's death. This passage, which appears in textbooks under the shūshin (moral training) curriculum, became widely known as an example of "loyalty and filial piety" (chūkō) and became the text of a popular school song (shōka) called "Of Sakurai, of the Thick Green Leaves" (Aoba shigereru sakurai no), composed by Ochiai Naobumi.[67] But with the discrediting of the emperor system in the postwar period, the *Taiheiki* suddenly became a minor text and has not appeared in high school textbooks during the past ten years.

The *Soga monogatari* (Tale of the Soga Brothers, 1361), a tale of loyalty and revenge in which two brothers pay back the enemy of their father, was popular in prewar textbooks, particularly as a positive example of bravery in war, but after World War II, it too was erased from the canon. Even more striking was the elimination of the *Gikeiki* (Record of Yoshitsune, composed in the early Muromachi period), depicting the youth and tragic end of Yoshitsune, who in the prewar period was a national hero and appeared more than any other figure in Meiji elementary school textbooks.[68] As Karasawa Tomitarō has argued, the narrative of the young Yoshitsune (Ushiwakamaru) appealed not only as a children's story, but also as that of a tragic hero who was hunted down and killed by his brother. In the militarist period of the 1940s, the elementary school textbooks focused in particular on Yoshitsune as a brave soldier, for example, at the battle of Ichi no tani, at Hiyodorigoe, where Yoshitsune, as the leader of the Genji, destroyed the Heike army in a lightning attack from a cliff, an action that, in one wartime textbook, was compared favorably to the Japanese air attack on Pearl Harbor.[69] This kind of association, while a serious distortion of the popular interest in Yoshitsune, contributed to the virtual disappearance of the *Gikeiki* from postwar high school textbooks. As a historical and legendary figure, however, Yoshitsune, who appears in a variety of texts, including *The Tale of the Heike*, continues to be a popular figure, appearing in TV programs and movies.

The only military chronicle (*gunki mono*) to survive in the postwar era is *The Tale of the Heike*. As David Bialock argues in his essay, the continued canonization of *The Tale of the Heike* can be attributed, at least in part, to the fact that the text has been canonized as a tale of tragedy or loss, centered on the theme of impermanence (*mujō*). While a few textbook selections, such as "Shigemori's admonition," in which Shigemori admonishes his father Kiyomori for his lack of respect toward the retired emperor, demonstrate the Confucian ideology of respect and loyalty, the overwhelming majority of the *Heike* textbook selections reflect the theme of impermanence and are heavily lyrical or religious in tone, often dwelling on aristocratic elegance and its loss ("Tadanori," "Moon of the Old Capital") or lamenting, in the fashion of Heian court narratives, the vicissitudes of exile and abandonment (e.g., the Shunkan scenes). The *Heike*, which was considered a form of history in the premodern period, emerges in the postwar period as a tragic epic, reflecting a European notion of literature.[70]

Significantly, the only nō play to appear in Meiji middle school textbooks was *Hachi no ki* (Potted Tree), the story of a disenfranchised warrior who sacrifices his precious potted tree to provide lodging on a snowy night for a traveling priest, who turns out to be Hōjō Tokiyori, the powerful Kamakura military leader, who later repays the poor samurai's earlier devotion by giving him land.[71] In the Taishō and early Shōwa periods, the nō repertoire expanded to include other texts such as *Ataka*, a drama about Yoshitsune and Benkei, *Shunkan*, *Hagoromo* (Feathered Robe), and *Shichiki ochi* (Escape of Seven Mounted Warriors), a drama about two faithful retainers (father and son). Reflecting the postwar shift from samurai virtues to domestic love and family values, *Hachi no ki* and *Shichiki ochi* were dropped in the postwar period, and nō came to be represented by such texts (including a number of women plays) as *Matsukaze* (Wind in the Pines), *Izutsu* (Well-Curb), *Yuya*, and *Tadanori*. By far the most popular nō plays in the postwar period are *Hagoromo*, about separation from a heavenly lover, which appears in thirty different textbooks, and *Sumidagawa* (Sumida River), about the love of a mother for a lost child, which appears in close to ninety textbooks.[72]

The modern canonization of Chikamatsu Monzaemon's (1653–1724) jōruri (puppet theater), texts by Tsubouchi Shōyō (1859–1935), and others as realistic dramatic literature, as described by William Lee in his essay, does not manifest itself at the textbook level until the postwar period. Despite the general popularity of his kabuki and jōruri plays in the prewar period, the only text by Chikamatsu to appear in prewar middle school textbooks was *Kokusenya kassen* (The Battles of Coxinga, 1715), a drama that emphasized samurai virtues (loyalty, sacrifice) and Japanese spirit. In the Taishō period, *The Battles of Coxinga* was joined by the "School House" (Terakoya) scene in *Sugawara denjū tenarai kagami* (Sugawara and the Secrets of Calligraphy, 1746), an eighteenth-century *jōruri* by Takeda Izumo (1691–1756) and others, in which the father sacrifices his son's life to demonstrate his loyalty to his lord—a scene that became particularly prominent in the militaristic era. Not surprisingly, both plays were eliminated from textbooks in the postwar period,[73] when Chikamatsu reemerged as a major dramatist of domestic plays (*sewamono*) about urban commoners (chōnin), represented in particular by *Meido no hikyaku* (Courier for Hell). Other plays used in high school texts include *Tamba Yosaku matsuyo no komurobushi* (Yosaku From Tamba), *Shinjū Ten no amijima* (Love Suicides at Ten no Amijima), *Sonezaki shinjū* (Love Suicides at Sonezaki), and *Onna goroshi abura jigoku* (The Woman-Killer and the Hell of Oil).[74]

Ihara Saikaku (1642–93) was almost completely ignored in the prewar middle school textbooks, but he occupies a major place in the postwar curriculum, one comparable to Bashō, *The Pillow Book*, and *The Tale of Genji*.[75] As noted in the introduction, the fortunes of Saikaku, who had fallen into obscurity by the end of the Edo period, suddenly rose with those of the novel (*shōsetsu*), enjoying a remarkable revival in which his works inspired writers such as Higuchi Ichiyō (1872–1896), those belonging to the Kenyūsha (1885), and the writers of the Naturalist (*shizenshugi*) movement. However, as we have seen, the middle school curriculum in the Meiji period was, like the han and terakoya schools, heavily Confucian in orientation and drew extensively on writings by kangaku and kokugaku scholars, who represented the literary canon, as opposed to Edo fiction and drama, which were thought of as popular entertainment and generally avoided. In their influential history of Japanese literature (*Nihon bungakushi*), Mikami and Takatsu favored the essays of Edo scholars and poets over drama and fiction, especially late Edo *gesaku* (playful writing), which they regarded as "obscene" (*inbi waisetsu*)—an attitude no doubt reflected in the minds of prewar educators when it came to Saikaku and other Edo vernacular fiction writers. Mikami and Takatsu made one important exception: Takizawa Bakin (1767–1848), a Confucian, didactic writer of fiction (*yomihon*), whose *Nansō Satomi hakkenden* (Eight Dog Chronicles, 1814–42), particularly the scene of the Hōryūkaku battle, was frequently used in prewar middle school textbooks. (In a reversal of fortunes, Bakin's *Nansō Satomi hakkenden*, which was immensely popular in the late Edo and Meiji periods, disappeared almost entirely from the postwar curriculum.) No doubt because of their erotic nature, none of Saikaku's *kōshoku mono* (love pieces)—such as *Life of an Amorous Man* (*Kōshoku ichidai otoko*, 1682), *Life of an Amorous Woman* (*Kōshoku ichidai onna*, 1686), *Five Women Who Loved Love* (*Kōshoku gonin onna*, 1686)—appear in postwar high school textbooks,[76] but he is amply represented by extensive selections from *Saikaku shokokubanashi* (Tales from Many Provinces, 1685) and, most of all, by massive use of *Nippon eitaigura* (Japan's Eternal Storehouse, 1688) and *Seken munezanyō* (Worldly Mental Calculations, 1692), which no doubt matched the interest of a consumer-oriented, financially driven postwar era.

Unlike Saikaku or Chikamatsu, Matsuo Bashō (1644–1694) appears repeatedly in Meiji textbooks, both his *hokku* (haiku) and his *haibun* (*haikai* prose), especially *Oku no hosomichi* (Narrow Road to the Interior, 1694), which, as an exemplar of haibun, served as a model for prose writing. In the postwar era his stature is magnified many times over, making him perhaps the most famous literary figure in Japan. Not only has *Narrow Road to the Interior* become an indispensable part of high school curricula, but a number of other haibun texts by Bashō such as *Oi no kobumi* (Backpack Notes, 1687), *Genjūan no ki* (Record of an Unreal Dwelling, 1690), and *Nozarashi kikō* (Skeleton in the Fields, 1684)—almost none of which appear in the prewar period—have become part of the high school canon. The extensive use of *Kyoraishō* (Kyorai's Records) and *Sanzōshi* (Three Booklets), two records of Bashō's teachings kept by his disciples, also attests to the poet's high stature in the postwar canon.[77] Of interest here is the fact that Bashō was canonized both in the "readerly" kokubungaku curriculum and in the "writerly" world of haiku, which has remained immensely popular as a *practiced* genre.

The end of the war marked the return of Heian literature and of *The Tale of Genji* in particular, which had been erased during the war period. *The Tale of Genji* appeared only infrequently in Meiji textbooks—presumably because it served no immediate purpose for moral, political, or historical instruction—and in the Taishō period (1912–26) it disappeared almost entirely from middle school textbooks. By contrast, the space given to military chronicles such as *The Tale of the Heike*, *Gikeiki*, and *Taiheiki* grew by leaps and bounds from mid-Meiji onward, with these texts being used from the lowest levels of middle school kokugo training. In the 1930s, some of *The Tale of Genji* was incorporated into elementary school textbooks—specifically the sparrow episode in "Wakamurasaki" (Young Lavender)—as part of the nationalistic stress on ethnic identity, and middle school texts occasionally included the lonely autumn beach scene in "Suma," but *The Tale of Genji*, like the *Pillow*

Book, played a limited role in prewar textbooks. In the wartime period *The Tale of Genji* was assiduously avoided because of the hero's adultery with the emperor's principal wife Fujitsubo. Today, by contrast, there is probably no high school textbook that does not contain some excerpt from *The Tale of Genji*, widely considered to be not only the ultimate Japanese classic but a great "novel."

Today Heian texts, particularly the *Tale of the Bamboo Cutter*, *The Pillow Book*, *Tales of Ise*, and *The Tale of Genji* form the core of the high school kokugo curriculum, followed by a large number of medieval texts. The Edo texts generally receive the least amount of attention. One reason for the shift toward the Heian period is that Heian grammar is considered the historical basis for classical grammar. Edo popular texts, by contrast, deviate the most from this model and are difficult to read as a result of their frequent use of citations, parody, and allusions. The vastly increased role of Heian literature in the postwar curriculum—due no doubt in part to the shift from military texts to peaceful ones—is reflected in *Tales of Ise*, which appears in the prewar middle school curriculum in a minor, limited role, dwarfed by historical texts such as *Taiheiki* and by Edo period gabun essays by Arai Hakuseki and others. In the postwar period, by contrast, *Tales of Ise* has become one of the most widely used classical texts. As Tomi Suzuki reveals in her essay, Heian women's diaries were first canonized in the 1920s by modern scholars who praised their exploration of the inner self. Ki no Tsurayuki's *Tosa Diary* and *Izayoi nikki*, a medieval diary by Nun Abutsu, were both canonized in the medieval period as a result of their association with waka authority and appear frequently in Meiji textbooks,[78] but Heian women's diaries such as *Sarashina Diary* (1058–64?) and *Gossamer Diary* (late 10th c.) did not make a substantial appearance until after the war,[79] when *Sarashina Diary* became a major classic. Although *The Tale of the Bamboo Cutter*, which contains almost no poetry and consequently was almost forgotten in the medieval period, appears in some prewar textbooks, it too came to play a major role in the postwar period. By contrast, *Wakan rōeishū* (Japanese and Chinese Poems to Sing, 1012), probably the most widely used classical text in the Heian and medieval periods, has faded almost completely from the modern canon.

The rise of Heian texts such as *Bamboo Cutter* and the disappearance of *Wakan rōeishū* reflect the general historical shift in the function of the wagaku canon, from a predominantly writerly curriculum in the premodern period, in which texts such as *Wakan rōeishū* functioned as an important means of learning to read and write, particularly poetry, to a half-readerly and half-writerly curriculum in the Meiji period, and then to an almost totally readerly school curriculum in the postwar period, in which classical texts were meant to be read, not imitated. (At the same time, performative or writerly genres such as haiku and the thirty-one syllable *tanka*, which were practiced outside of public schools and which remain vibrant in the postwar period, still were a major factor in the canonization process, which may reflect popular tastes that run counter to government-controlled curricula.)

The most striking aspect of the postwar kokugo curriculum, however, was the dominance of modern, often European-based notions of literature, particularly the *shōsetsu* (novel), in shaping the canon. The modern disciplinary separation of literature from history, political science, and philosophy, which occurred at the university level in the mid-Meiji period, was not fully institutionalized at the level of secondary education until the postwar period. In contrast to the prewar middle school kokugo curriculum, which, like kokugaku and kangaku before it, had strong historical, philosophical, ethical, political, and linguistic dimensions, the postwar kokugo high school curriculum stressed the "literary" (*bungaku*) and "aesthetic" (*geijutsu*). The word *koten*, used as a translation of the Western term "classic," has come to imply "classical literature" (*koten bungaku*), with literature conceived largely in the modern, highly Western (nineteenth-century European) sense of imaginative literature as a means of expressing the inner self. There has also been a noticeable de-emphasis on histories, which were at the heart of Edo period han school and kokugaku curricula: the *Kojiki* and the *Nihon shoki*, which had been treated as histories or religious texts, are now treated more as "classical literature" or the source of national myths and legends. Likewise, the *Konjaku monogatari*, thought to be a kind of historical record, is now labeled "folk literature" (*setsuwa bungaku*). Various *nikki*, which were public or personal records, have likewise been canonized as "diary literature" (*nikki bungaku*). *The Tale of the Heike*, which previously had been treated as history, has been treated by many scholars as epic literature in the postwar period. This valorization of imaginative literature and its aesthetic dimension—which has created the false impression in the West that Japan produces poets and novelists but not philosophers and historians—coupled with the almost complete elimination of the Chinese kangaku curriculum—which had concentrated on philosophy, politics, and history—brought about a shift away from histories and texts that (in the Confucian manner) dealt with public matters toward an intense focus on the domestic and private, on the lyrical, *and* on the nineteenth-century European genres of prose fiction, drama, and poetry. This phenomenon is perhaps best reflected in the emphasis on the postwar canonization of the Genroku "big three"—Saikaku, Chikamatsu, and

Bashō—as opposed to, for example, someone like Arai Hakuseki, the kangaku historian, who was a central figure in the Meiji canon. Ironically, then, what is now thought to be quintessentially "Japanese" and embodied in Japanese classical literature as we know it today at the beginning of the twenty-first century is, in fact, a modern construction based, at least in significant part, on nineteenth-century European notions of genre and literature.

Notes

Introduction: Issues in Canon Formation

1. Charles-Augustin Sainte-Beuve, "What Is a Classic?" in *The Critical Tradition: Classic Texts and Contemporary Trends*, ed. David Richter (New York: St. Martin's Press, 1989), 1294.

2. John Guillory, *Cultural Capital: The Problem of Literary Canon Formation* (Chicago: University of Chicago Press, 1993), 55.

3. Pierre Bourdieu, *The Field of Cultural Production* (New York: Columbia University Press, 1994), 35.

4. Saeki Shōichi, *Shintō no kokoro* (Nihon kyōbunsha, 1989).

5. *Sagoromo*'s popularity in the Muromachi period was such that it was illustrated in *Sagoromo emaki* (Illustrated Scroll of Sagoromo) and made into a nō play.

6. Fujioka Sakutarō, *Kokubungaku zenshi: Heianchō hen* (reprint, with annotation by Akiyama Ken, Tōyō bunkō series nos. 198 and 247, Heibonsha, 1971), 1: 138.

7. The Latin word *littera* means letter, and *litteratura* originally implied knowledge of reading and writing. The English term "literature" first came into use in the fourteenth century.

8. The emergence of the notion of imaginative literature was closely connected to the rise of aesthetics (a term invented by Alexander Gottlieb Baumgarten in 1735) and of the system of the arts, which had hitherto been indistinguishable from the sciences. In the eighteenth century, a major split emerged between the new humanities, associated with aesthetics, and the new sciences, associated with rationalism. By the nineteenth century a clear distinction had been made between the producers of literature as art, who became the bearers of "imaginative truth," and the philosophers and historians, who made a claim to a literal, objective or "scientific truth." For European views of literature, see René Welleck, "What Is Literature?" in *What Is Literature?* ed. Paul Hernadi (Bloomington and London: Indiana University Press, 1978), 16–23. For more on this topic, see Haruo Shirane, "Constructing 'Japanese' 'Literature': Global and Ethnic Nationalism," in *Japanese Hermeneutics: Current Debates on Aesthetics and Interpretation*, ed. Michele Marra (Honolulu: University of Hawaii Press, forthcoming).

9. *Bungaku*, the word now used for literature, first appeared in Confucius' *Analects*, where it meant "learning," "studies," or "scholars," particularly Confucian scholars. In the early 1870s, Nishi Amane (1829–1897), an early Meiji scholar of Western studies, adapted the term to translate the nineteenth-century European term for "literature" in *Hyakugaku renkan* (Encyclopedia, 1870), using it to mean vaguely humanities or belle lettres.

10. In 1885, the department of Wakan bungaku was split into the Wabun gakka (Japanese literature program) and the Kanbun gakka (Chinese literature program), and in 1889 the Wabun gakka was renamed the Kokubun gakka (national literature program).

11. See Tomi Suzuki, *Narrating the Self: Fictions of Japanese Modernity* (Stanford: Stanford University Press, 1996), 15–32.

12. Takemoto Hirokazu, "Kume Kunitake to nōgaku fukkō," in *Bakumatsu meijiki no kokumin kokka keisei to bunka henyō*, ed. Nishikawa Nagao and Matsumiya Hideharu (Shinyōsha, 1995), 487–510.

13. Satō Dōshin, *"Nihon bijutsu" tanjō* (Kōdansha, 1996).

14. Ellen Friedman, for example, has argued that while modern canonical texts by male authors tend to seek out fathers, or authority, many modern women's works show little nostalgia for the old paternal order, which they find inadequate as a source of identity. "Where Are the Missing Contents? (Post)Modernism, Gender, and the Canon," *PMLA* 108, no. 2 (Mar. 1993), 240–52.

15. Naomi Schor, "Dreaming Dissymmetry: Barthes, Foucault, and Sexual Difference," in *Men in Feminism*, eds. Alice Jardine and Paul Smith (London and New York: Methuen, 1987), 110.

16. Mitamura Masako, "Janru, daihitsu, seitenkan," *Nihon kindai bungaku* 50 (1994). Women did not perform in nō and were largely left out of kabuki. It is only in the modern period, with the rise of the position of women, that we have women cross-dressing, as in Takarazuka, a popular form.

17. Haga Yaichi and Tachibana Senzaburō, "Kokubungaku tokuhon," in *Haga Yaichi senshū*, ed. Haga Yaichi senshū iinkai (Kokugakuin daigaku, 1983), 2: 13–28.

18. In *The Ethnic Origins of Nations* (Cambridge, Mass.: Blackwell, 1986), Anthony D. Smith argues that modern nations—a fusion of premodern ethnic identities and modern "civic" elements—require the symbols, myths, and memories of ethnic cores if they are to generate a sense of solidarity and purpose in a secular era. On the distinctions among *kokka* (nation-state), *kokumin*, and *minzoku*, see Kevin Doak, "What Is a Nation and Who Belongs? National Narratives and Ethnic Imagination in Twentieth-Century Japan," *American Historical Review* (Apr. 1997): 283–309.

19. Benedict Anderson, *Imagined Communities: Reflections on the Origins and Spread of Nationalism*, rev. ed. (London and New York: Verso, 1991).

20. Eric Hobsbawm and Terence Ranger, eds., *The Invention of Tradition* (Cambridge: Cambridge University Press, 1983).

21. Karatani Kōjin, "Japan as Museum: Okakura Tenshin and Ernest Fenollosa,"

trans. Sabu Kohso, in *Japanese Art After 1945: Scream Against the Sky*, ed. Alexandra Munroe (New York: Harry Abrams, 1994), 33–39.

22. As Partha Chatterjee notes, the notion that "language uniquely defines a nation is an invention of nineteenth-century European writers, particularly Herder, Schlegel, Fichte and Schleiermacher, which has been subsequently taken up by nationalist intellectuals of the East." *Nationalist Thought and the Colonial World* (Minneapolis: University of Minnesota Press, 1986), 9.

23. Ueda Kazutoshi, "Kokugo to kokka to" (1894), included in *Ochiai Naobumi, Ueda Kazutoshi, Haga Yaichi, Fujioka Sakutarō shū*, Meiji bungaku zenshū 44 (Chikuma shobō, 1968), 110.

24. Barbara Herrnstein Smith, "Value," in *Canons*, ed. Robert von Hallberg (Chicago and London: University of Chicago Press, 1983), 34.

25. Johann Gottfried von Herder (1744–1803), whose views on the role of the folk had an impact on the Brothers Grimm and other German Romantics, compiled *Volkslieder* (Leipzig) in 1778–79.

Chapter 1: *Man'yōshū*: The Invention of a National Poetry Anthology

1. Emphasis added. Kōno Toshirō, Tsukishima Hiroshi, Kubota Jun, et al., *Seisen shin kokugo 1: Koten hen* (Meiji shoin, 1998), 38.

2. For my use of the word "invention," see Eric Hobsbawm and Terence Ranger, eds., *The Invention of Tradition* (Cambridge: University of Cambridge Press, 1983).

3. At the time, Shiki envisioned the imminent demise of both haiku and tanka after each form had exhausted its creative potential.

4. Yosano Tekkan, "Kokushi kakushin no rekishi," *Kokoro no hana* 3, no. 9 (1900): 7–12.

5. Toyama Masakazu, "Shintai-shi oyobi rōdoku-hō," *Teikoku bungaku* 2 (1896), no. 3: 1–16, no. 4: 1–14.

6. Suematsu Kenchō, "Kagaku-ron," *Tokyo nichinichi shinbun* (Sept. 1884–Feb. 1885), collected in *Meiji geijutsu, bungaku ronshū* (Chikuma shobō, 1975). Suematsu dealt with this same issue in greater detail in his *Kokka shinron*, published in 1897, and it seems that Shiki was influenced by this work. See Koizumi Tōzō, *Kindai tanka-shi: Meiji-hen* (Hakuyōsha, 1955).

7. Inoue Tetsujirō and Nakamura Masanao, *Chokugo engi* (Keigyō-sha, 1891).

8. Inoue Testujirō, "Nihon bungaku no kako oyobi shōrai," *Teikoku bungaku* 1 (1895): 1–14; no. 2: 1–13; no. 3: 18–24.

9. A somewhat imperfect response to these expectations came not in literary forms like tanka and New Style Poetry but from popular ditties and military songs.

10. Letter to Sekine Masanao, in *Haga Yaichi senshū* 7 (Kokugakuin daigaku, 1992). Emphasis added. All subsequent quotations from Haga, with the exception of the one from *Kokubungaku rekidaisen*, are found in this collection.

11. Kaisen [pseud.], "Bungakushi hensan hōhō ni tsukite," *Teikoku bungaku* 1, no. 5 (1895): 12–22.

12. Takemoto Hirokazu, "Kume Kunitake to nōgaku fukkō," in *Bakumatsu Meiji-ki no kokumin kokka keisei to bunka henyō*, eds. Nishikawa Nagao and Matsumiya Shūji (Shin'yō-sha, 1995).

13. In the latter half of the Meiji period there were more than fifty works published with titles like "History of Japanese Literature" (*Nihon bungakushi*) or "History of Our Nation's Literature" (*Kokubungakushi*). Almost half of these were textbooks intended for use at the secondary level. Most of the remaining books were recorded lectures given at universities or at private institutions that later became accredited universities. Of the thirty-six that I have examined, just half (eighteen) contain expressions equivalent to "from emperors to commoners" used in reference to the *Man'yōshū*. A directive from the Ministry of Education stipulated in 1892 that courses in Japanese at the Normal Teachers' Schools (where elementary teachers received their training) were to include Japanese literary history as part of their curriculum. In 1901, a similar directive was made for Middle Schools (belonging to the five-year system). Since the *Man'yōshū* had generally been excluded from materials used for direct readings in Japanese, students came into contact with the work only indirectly during lectures on Japanese literary history, which fostered an unquestioned reverence for the *Man'yōshū* as a national poetry anthology.

14. *Rin'yō ruijinshū*, in *Chōryū zenshū* (Asahi shinbunsha, 1927).

15. Matsumura Yūji, "'Yomibito shirazu'-ron e no kōsō," *Kokugo to kokubungaku* 73, no. 11 (1996): 54–64.

16. See Norinaga's *Isonokami sasamegoto* (published 1816), in vol. 2 of *Motoori Norinaga zenshū* (Chikuma shobō, 1968).

17. See Kamo no Mabuchi's *Niimanabi* (1765), collected in vol. 19 of *Kamo no Mabuchi zenshū*, ed., Zoku gunsho ruijū kanseikai (Zoku gunsho ruijū kanseikai, 1980).

18. Benedict Anderson, *Imagined Communities: Reflections on the Origin and Spread of Nationalism* (London and New York: Verso, 1983).

19. Mori Ōgai, "Girishia no min'yō," *Shigarami zōshi* 35 (1892): 4–5.

20. Ueda Bin, "Gakuwa," *Teikoku bungaku* 10, no. 1 (1904): 47–55.

21. From 1906 to the following year, the poet Maeda Ringai (1864–1946) issued a series of min'yō special editions in his own *Shirayuri* magazine. The issues, which had solicited contributions from readers across the country, ran six times, and each one contained hundreds of examples. These were the first publications in Japan to carry the min'yō label. See Maeda Ringai, *Nihon min'yō zenshū*, 2 vols. (Hongō shoin, 1907).

22. Five years earlier, Ueda had written that the court culture of the Heian period was neither a culture of the populace nor of the ethnos. He had seen it instead as a permutation of foreign (Chinese and Indian) culture. See "Bungei seun no renkan," *Teikoku bungaku* 5, no. 1 (1899): 11–23.

23. *Teikoku bungaku* 1, no. 5 (1895), 12–22, journal reprinted in *Teikoku bungaku* (Nihon tosho sentā, 1981).

24. Shida Gishū, "Haga Hakushi to Nihon shiikagaku," *Kokugo to kokubungaku* 14, no. 4 (1937): 78–87.

25. Shida Gishū, "Nihon min'yō gairon," *Teikoku bungaku* 12, no. 2 (1906): 1–15; no. 3: 32–44; no. 5: 13–27; no. 9: 24–43.

26. Haga Yaichi, *Kokubungaku rekidaisen* (Bunkaidō, 1908), 16.

27. In the same work the number of *Man'yōshū* poets is given as 561. This total comes from Ōwada Takeki's *Wabungakushi* (Hakubunkan, 1892). According to Ōwada, "the total of 561 poets included 120 members of the royal family, 355 officials, 71 women, 13 nuns or priests, and *two commoners*" (emphasis added). This ignores the anonymous poems that constitute almost half of the poems in the *Man'yōshū*.

28. The term *shomin-shi* (people's poetry) was, like Haga's *kokumin-shi* (poetry of the nation's people), another translation for *Volkspoesie*. In "Waka-shi no kenkyū," *shizen-shi* (*Naturpoesie*, another term for *Volkspoesie*) was also used in opposition to *geijutsu-shi* (Kunstpoesie).

29. Shimaki Akahiko, *Kadō shōken* (1924; Iwanami shoten, 1983).

30. Both Itō Sachio (1864–1913) and Masaoka Shiki, leaders of the same school before Akahiko, did not make any similar statements before their deaths (in 1913 and 1902, respectively). Sachio had, in fact, applied the term *minzoku* (ethnos) to the *Man'yōshū*, but as the following passage indicates, he used the term as a vague equivalent for words like "Japanese," "national," and "citizen."

> The *Man'yōshū* should not be viewed simply as a part of our own ancient literature. It is truly the wellspring of the artistic sensibilities of the Japanese race (*minzoku*). Therefore, just as it is necessary for any person to know who his ancestors are, Japanese—of whatever type—must become familiar with the *Man'yōshū*. . . . Though one might be a citizen of a particular country, if one does not know the literature of one's own country and if one does not know the source of one's country's view of things, then one does not deserve to be included among the people [kokumin].

Itō Sachio, "*Man'yō* tsūkai chogen" (Feb. 1904), collected in vol. 5 of *Itō Sachio zenshū* (Iwanami shoten, 1977).

31. For other articles closely related to this chapter, see Shinada Yoshikazu, "Kokumin kashū no hatsumei: josetsu," *Kokugo to kokubungaku* 73, no. 11 (1996): 15–28; Shinada, "'Min'yō' no hatsumei," *Man'yōshū kenkyū* 21 (1997): 205–96; Shinada, "Itō Sachio to *Man'yōshū*," *Kotoba ga hiraku kodai bungakushi*, ed. Suzuki Hideo (Kasama shoin, 1999).

Chapter 2: Constructing Imperial Mythology: *Kojiki* and *Nihon shoki*

1. Whether any of the countries of Korea ever actually entered into a tributary relationship with Japan is not as relevant as the fact that the Japanese imperial

state claimed to have such a relationship so as to justify its standing as a sovereign entity.

2. Mishina Akihide, *Nihon shinwaron*, Mishina Akihide ronbunshū I (Heibonsha, 1970).

3. Yamaguchi Yoshinori and Kōnoshi Takamitsu, eds., *Kojiki*, Shinpen Nihon koten bungaku zenshū I (Shōgakukan, 1997), 28–29.

4. Ibid., 62–67.

5. *Yin* is the feminine principle, and *yang* is the masculine principle, with heaven associated with the male and earth with the female. However, it is customary when referring to the two principles together to place the word *yin* before *yang*.

6. Sakamoto Tarō, Ienaga Saburō, Inoue Mitsusada, Ōno Susumu, eds., *Nihon shoki*, Nihon koten bungaku taikei 67 (Iwanami shoten, 1965), 209.

7. *Jingiryō*, Shintei zōho kokushi taikei 22 (Yoshikawa kōbunkan, 1998), 77.

8. According to *Jingiryō*, the Imbe performed a crucial role in the enthronement ceremony alongside the Nakatomi: "On the day of enthronement (*senso*), the Nakatomi shall recite the *ama tsu kami no yogoto* (blessing of the heavenly deities); the Imbe shall present the mirror and sword of the sacred imperial regalia." *Jingiryō*, 79.

9. Nishimiya Kazutani, ed., *Kogo shūi* (Iwanami shoten, 1985), 26–27, 127–28.

10. The lectures were held in the following years: 812–813, 843–844, 878–881, 904–906, 936–943, 965. In addition, later sources mention a lecture that was supposedly held in 713, the year after the completion of the *Nihon shoki*, but this cannot be confirmed.

11. Sakamoto Tarō, *Rikkokushi* (Yoshikawa kōbunkan, 1970), 135.

12. *Shaku-Nihongi* (Chap. 6, Jutsugi 1), Shintei zōho kokushi taikei 8 (Yoshikawa kōbunkan, 1998), 74.

13. The corresponding section from the *Kojiki* reads:

> The deity that appeared next is named Kuni-no-tokotachi, and the deity after this, Toyokumono. These two were also single deities, and they concealed themselves. Next appeared a deity whose name is Uhizini, and his sister-deity, Suhichini. Next, the deity Tsunoguhi, and his sister-deity, Ikuguhi. Next, the deity Ōtonozi, and his sister-deity, Ōtonobe. Next, the deity Omodaru, and his sister-deity, Ayakashikone. Next, the deity Izanaki, and his sister-deity, Izanami. Of the deities above, those from Kuni-no-tokotachi to Izanami are together known as the "seven generation of deities."

Yamaguchi and Kōnoshi, 28–31.

14. Takeda Yūkichi, ed., *Norito*, Nihon koten bungaku taikei I (Iwanami shoten, 1971), 416–17.

15. The oldest extant catalog of Japanese books, said to have been compiled toward the end of the thirteenth century. It can be used it to identify books that were extant at the time of its compilation.

16. *Sendai kuji hongi*, a text compiled sometime during the tenth century, con-

sists mostly of passages cut and pasted in a patchwork fashion from the *Kojiki* and the *Nihon shoki*. *Tensho*, a late twelfth- or early thirteenth-century chronological listing of events from the Age of the Gods to the reign of Empress Kōgyoku (r. 642–645), conflates accounts from *Kojiki, Nihon shoki,* and *Sendai kuji hongi. Honchō shojaku mokuroku*, a Kamakura period bibliographic catalog, describes *Shunjū reki,* compiled by Fujiwara Chikatsune in the early thirteenth century, as a text in three volumes, but only one volume, covering the beginnings to Emperor Jimmu, is extant today. *Shunjū reki*, which is an example of the "medieval Nihongi" genre, presents the origin of the three imperial regalia and the descent of the Heavenly Grandson using excerpts from the *Nihon shoki* and *Kogo shūi.*

17. The extent of the cut-and-paste process that went into the creation of this text can be seen in Kamata Jun'ichi, *Sendai kuji hongi no kenkyū: Kōhon no bu* (Yoshikawa kōbunkan, 1960), which marks all passages that were copied from the *Kojiki* and the *Nihon shoki.*

18. Ichijō Kanera's *Nihon shoki sanso,* printed in *Tenri toshokan zenpon sōsho* (Tenri daigaku shuppanbu, 1977), 27: 29.

19. *Nihon shoki sanso,* 39.

20. In the *Funbetsu sebon* chapter of *Kusharon*, the universe is described as arising out of the Metal Wheel, which emerges out of the Water Wheel, which in turn comes from the Wind Wheel.

21. *Jinkei shō* (1482), a miscellany that includes items related to Buddhism, Shinto, imperial genealogy, and various theatrical arts. *Jinkei shō,* ed. Ichiko Teiji, Koten bunko 450 (Koten bunko, 1984), 5.

22. *Nihon shoki sanso,* 9.

23. Akinaga Kazue and Tanabe Kayo, eds., *Kokinshū engoki: Tenri toshokan zō* (Kasama shoin, 1978), 8–9.

24. Okada Shōji, ed., *Nihon shoki jindai kan shō,* Yoshida sōsho 5 (Kyoto: Yoshida jinja, 1984), 99.

25. Iwasa Tadashi, ed., *Jinnō shōtōki,* Nihon koten bungaku taikei 87 (Iwanami shoten, 1965), 41.

26. For more detailed descriptions of the "medieval *Nihongi*" texts, see Itō Masayoshi, "Chūsei *Nihongi* no rinkaku," *Bungaku* 40, no. 10 (1974): 28–48, or Abe Yasurō, "*Nihongi* to setsuwa," in *Setsuwa no kōza 3: Setsuwa no ba* (Benseisha, 1993), 199–226.

27. Chap. 1 of Motoori Norinaga's *Kojikiden,* in *Motoori Norinaga zenshū* (Chikuma shobō, 1969), 9: 6.

28. Yamaguchi and Kōnoshi, *Kojiki,* 28–29.

29. *Man'yōshū* (vol. 2, no. 167), in *Man'yōshū,* Shinpen Nihon koten bungaku zenshū 6 (Shōgakukan, 1994), 118–20.

30. *Motoori Norinaga zenshū,* 9: 123.

31. It is interesting to note that Norinaga approved of *Sandaikō* (1791), by his disciple Hattori Nakatsune (1756–1824), as an appendix to his *Kojikiden. Sandaikō*

takes the recently imported cosmology of Western astronomy and incorporates it into the world of *Kojikiden*, explaining the formation of astronomical bodies (sun, moon, and earth) in terms of the *Kojiki* myths. In doing so, it extends the reach of Norinaga's mythology to cover the extent of the known universe.

32. Ueda Kazutoshi, "Kokugo to kokka to," reprinted in *Ochiai Naobumi, Ueda Kazutoshi, Haga Yaichi, Fujioka Sakutarō shū*, ed. Hisamatsu Sen'ichi, Meiji bungaku zenshū 44 (Chikuma shobō, 1968), 110–12.

33. Haga Yaichi, *Kokubungakushi jikkō* (1899; 19th reprint, Fuzanbō, 1922), 7.

34. *Kokutai no hongi* (Monbushō, 1937), 9.

35. See Article 1 of the post-war Japanese Constitution (Nihonkoku kenpō).

36. In the postscript to Yoshida Atsuhiko, *Nihon no shinwa* (Seitosha, 1990).

Chapter 3: Gender and Genre: Modern Literary Histories and Women's Diary Literature

1. Special issues on nikki bungaku or joryū nikki bungaku appear in academic journals almost every year, and a six-volume collection of essays on women's diary literature, Ishihara Shōhei et al., eds., *Joryū nikki bungaku kōza* (Benseisha), appeared in 1990–91.

2. Tomi Suzuki, *Narrating the Self: Fictions of Japanese Modernity* (Stanford, Stanford University Press, 1996).

3. *Gunsho ruijū*, the most extensive collection of texts of its time, with 1,270 works under twenty-five categories, included *Izumi Shikibu nikki, Murasaki Shikibu nikki, Sanuki no Suke nikki, Ben no Naishi nikki, Nakatsukasa Naishi nikki, Gyōkō Hōin nikki, Genkō nikki, Sōchō shuki* (these last three are not considered nikki bungaku today) under the category of nikki, while *Tosa nikki, Sarashina nikki, Utatane*, and *Izayoi nikki* were categorized, together with thirty-one other works written mostly by Kamakura and Muromachi period men, as kikō (travel diaries), an established literary genre in the medieval and Tokugawa periods. Nikki and kikō were thus treated as close but separate genres, with many of the kikō bearing titles with the word nikki. This ambiguous situation lasted until the mid-1920s, when the term nikki bungaku emerged. In his discussion of *Tosa nikki*, Kishimoto Yuzuru (1789–1846), a late Tokugawa kokugaku scholar, stated: "Today people seem to consider nikki as travel diaries, but nikki derive their name from the fact that they record daily events. Nikki, therefore, do not signify only travel diaries. What we now call 'records of the house' (*kaki*) long ago used to be called nikki. In order to refer clearly to travel diaries, we should in fact call them *rojiki* (records of the road) or *tabi nikki* (travel records)." Kishimoto also noted with regard to kikō that: "Starting with *Tosa nikki*, a number of kikō appeared in succession, such as *Sarashina nikki* and *Izayoi nikki*." Cited in Imai Takuji, *Heianchō nikki no kenkyū* (Keibunsha shuppan, 1935), 19; Tamai Kōsuke, *Nikki bungaku gaisetsu* (Kokusho kankōkai, 1945), 183–84. For the history of reception of *Tosa nikki, Kagerō nikki, Izumi Shikibu nikki, Murasaki*

Shikibu nikki, and *Sarashina nikki*, see Akiyama Ken et al., eds., *Heian nikki*, Kokugo kokubungaku kenkyūshi taisei 5 (Sanseidō, 1960).

4. Mikami Sanji and Takatsu Kuwasaburō, *Nihon bungakushi I* (Kinkodō, 1890), 5–6, 23, 29; Haga Yaichi and Tachibana Senzaburō, "Kokubungaku tokuhon shoron," reprinted in *Ochiai Naobumi, Ueda Kazutoshi, Haga Yaichi, Fujioka Sakutarō shū*, ed. Hisamatsu Sen'ichi, Meiji bungaku zenshū 44 (Chikuma Shobō, 1968), 198–99; Ueda Kazutoshi, "Kokubungaku shogen," *Ochiai Naobumi, Ueda Kazutoshi, Haga Yaichi, Fujioka Sakutarō shū*, 107.

5. Taine did not preach the purity or superiority of a race; his "race" is simply the *Volksgeist*, the "genius of a nation." Reflecting the view of the German classical scholar Otfried Muller, Taine believed that every nation is "a moral person." See René Wellek, "Hippolyte Taine's Literary Theory and Criticism," *Criticism* 1 (1959): 1–18, 123–38.

6. Hippolyte A. Taine, "Introduction," *History of English Literature*, vol. 1, trans. H. Van Laun (1883; reprint, New York: Frederick Ungar Publishing Co., 1965), 1–36.

7. Haga and Tachibana, "Kokubungaku tokuhon shoron," 199; Mikami and Takatsu, *Nihon bungakushi I*, 26–27.

8. See Kobori Keiichirō, "'Bungaku' to iu meishō," *Geppō* 82, Meiji bungaku zenshū 79 (Chikuma shobō, 1975), 23–24.

9. Mikami and Takatsu, *Nihon bungakushi I*, 10–12.

10. Mikami and Takatsu, "Shogen," *Nihon bungakushi I*, 3–4.

11. Mikami and Takatsu, *Nihon bungakushi I*, 7–15; Haga and Tachibana, "Kokubungaku tokuhon shoron," 197–98. See also a pioneering study in English by Michael Brownstein on the institutional establishment of kokubungaku and on Mikami and Takatsu's literary history, "From Kokugaku to Kokubungaku: Canon-Formation in the Meiji Period," *Harvard Journal of Asiastic Studies* 47 (Dec. 1987): 435–60.

12. Hasegawa Izumi, *Kindai Nihon bungaku hyōronshi* (Yūseidō, 1966), 30–52.

13. See René Wellek, "What Is Literature?" in *What Is Literature?* ed. Paul Hernadi (Bloomington: Indiana University Press, 1978), 16–23; René Wellek, *The Rise of English Literary History* (Chapel Hill: The University of North Carolina Press, 1966); and Raymond Williams, *Marxism and Literature* (Oxford: Oxford University Press, 1977).

14. Mikami and Takatsu, *Nihon bungakushi I*, 13.

15. Ibid., 23–24.

16. Ibid., 34–36.

17. Ibid., 29.

18. Ibid., 200, 210–11, 221. See also Haga and Tachibana, "Kokubungaku tokuhon shoron," 200.

19. Haga and Tachibana, "Kokubungaku tokuhon shoron," 201.

20. Mikami and Takatsu, *Nihon bungakushi I*, 201–2.

21. Haga and Tachibana, "Kokubungaku tokuhon shoron," 200.

22. Mikami and Takatsu, *Nihon bungakushi II*, 7–11, 27.

23. Ibid., 186–87; Haga and Tachibana, "Kokubungaku tokuhon shoron," 202–5.

24. Mikami and Takatsu, *Nihon bungakushi II*, 430.

25. Mikami and Takatsu, *Nihon bungakushi I*, 262, 265–66.

26. Ibid., 298–99.

27. Ibid., 300, 302–3.

28. Haga Yaichi, *Kokubungakushi jikkō* (Fuzanbō, 1899), 6–8, 14–17.

29. Ibid., 76–77, 89–99, 121–22.

30. Fujioka Sakutarō, *Kokubungaku zenshi: Heianchō hen 1*, ed. Akiyama Ken et al., Tōyō bunko 198 (Heibonsha, 1971), 4.

31. Ibid., 8–9.

32. Ibid., 46–48.

33. Ibid., 164; Fujioka Sakutarō, *Kokubungaku zenshi: Heianchō hen 2*, in Akiyama Ken et al., eds. Tōyō bunko 247 (Heibonsha, 1974), 53, 365.

34. Fujioka, *Kokubungaku zenshi: Heianchō hen 1*, 281.

35. Fujioka, *Kokubungaku zenshi: Heianchō hen 1*, 280–88. Despite his general enthusiasm toward women's nikki, Fujioka did not show much interest in *Izumi Shikibu nikki*: "Izumi Shikibu's true ability was revealed, of course, in her waka poetry, not in the nikki, which does not possess that much literary value." *Kokubungaku zenshi: Heianchō hen 2*, 53.

36. Fujioka, *Kokubungaku zenshi: Heianchō hen 1*, 213. Fujioka extensively refuted all the reasons for the high regard that Tokugawa scholars had for *Tosa nikki*—such as "freedom from *kanbun* styles" and detachment from "the affairs between men and women"—and attributed their views to the "narrow-minded Eastern ethics shared by both Confucian and Nativist Learning scholars." *Kokubungaku zenshi: Heianchō hen 1*, 200–205.

37. After the first volume, *The Age of Aristocratic Literature* (1916), the second volume, *The Age of Warrior Literature* (*Bushi bungaku no jidai*), was published in 1917, and the first and second parts of the three-part *The Age of Commoner Literature* (*Heimin bungaku no jidai*) were published in 1919 and 1921 as the third and the fourth volumes of the series. Due to various reasons, the fifth volume, the last part of *The Age of Commoner Literature*, was not completed.

38. Tsuda Sōkichi, *Bungaku ni arawaretaru waga kokumin shisō no kenkyū: kizoku bungaku no jidai* (Rakuyōdō, 1916), 257. Tsuda inherited Fujioka's respect for the fictional, realistic novel (*shajitsu shōsetsu*) as the most advanced literary form, as well as his emphasis on direct expression, but Tsuda placed yet more emphasis on the "direct depiction of internal emotional life."

39. Ibid., 252.

40. Ibid., 286.

41. Ibid., 317–18, 322, 336. Firmly grounded in the humanistic populism of the Taishō period, Tsuda attempted to show the historical progress of the life of the na-

tion from the "age of aristocratic literature" to the "age of warrior literature" to the "age of commoner literature," implicitly believing in the ultimate achievement of "the age of the nation's people" (*kokumin no jidai*).

42. In *Bungaku josetsu*, which included essays on Thomas Carlyle, Matthew Arnold, and Walter Pater, Doi acknowledged Tsuda's *Bungaku ni arawaretaru waga kokumin shisō no kenkyū* and the instruction of Kaito Matsuzō, who also introduced Richard Green Moulton's genre evolution theory into the study of Japanese literature.

43. Doi Kōchi, *Bungaku josetsu*, in his *Doi Kōchi chosakushū* (Iwanami shoten, 1977), 5: 123. Doi predicted that the "social consciousness of the new period would seek a fairer society that would save the freedom of individual personality (*jinkaku no jiyū*) from the oppressive power of the machine and of capital," and that "their individual consciousness would again long for lyrical poetry" (122–23). Doi's optimistic social outlook reflected the liberal humanistic individualism and idealistic universalism that lay beneath Taishō Democracy.

44. Ibid., 88–89.

45. Ibid., 258.

46. Ibid., 277. Criticizing the narrow canon created by kokubungaku scholars, Doi argued for the value of the philosophical and spiritual works by medieval religious figures such as Hōnen and Shinran as part of Japanese literature.

47. Doi Kōchi and Annie Shepley Omori, trans., *Diaries of Court Ladies of Old Japan* (Boston and New York: Houghton Mifflin Company, 1920).

48. See Kaito Matsuzō, *Kokubungakushi* (Kyōiku shuppan kabushiki gaisha, 1976), 152–62. *Kokubugakushi* consists of notes taken from Kaito's 1922–23 lectures by his student Ishii Shōji.

49. "Jishō bungaku no rekishiteki kōsatsu," in his *Nikki waka bungaku* (Shibundō, 1968), 15, 22. Ikeda applied this genre cycle not only to the history of literature but to the course of a day, the human life cycle, and to the entire history of civilization.

50. Ibid., 15–16. For Ikeda, jishō bungaku was the "precious record of self-cultivation (*kyōyō no kiroku*) . . . realized only when an individual personality seeks the original home of the spirit in its complete wholeness (*zen'itsu na tamashii no genkyō*), after having wandered around" (17, 21).

51. Ibid., 30–31, 44.

52. Ibid., 56–57.

53. See Tomi Suzuki, *Narrating the Self*, 48–58.

54. Fujimura Tsukuru, "Kokubungaku rajio kōza no kaisetsu ni tsuite," in *Nihon bungaku renkō: dai ikki* (Chūkōkan, 1927), 1–10.

55. Ikeda Kikan, *Kyūtei joryū nikki bungaku* (1927; reprint, Shibundō, 1965), 36.

56. Citations from "Jishō bungaku no rekishiteki kōsatsu," 32–33.

57. "Nikki bungaku to josei," in *Kokubungaku renkō: dai ikki*, ed. Fujimura Tsukuru (Chūkōkan, 1927), 239–40.

58. Ibid., 241–49.

262   NOTES TO CHAPTER 3

59. For the emergence of the concept of "women's literature" in the 1920s, see Joan Ericson, "The Origins of the Concept of 'Women's Literature,'" in *The Woman's Hand*, ed. Paul Gordon Schalow and Janet A. Walker (Stanford: Stanford University Press, 1996), 74–115.

60. See Donald Roden, "Taisho Culture and the Problem of Gender Ambivalence," in *Culture and Identity: Japanese Intellectuals during the Interwar Years*, ed. Thomas Rimer (Princeton: Princeton University Press, 1990), 37–55.

61. See Ogata Akiko, "Shakai henkaku to josei bungaku," in *Iwanami kōza Nihon bungakushi XIII: 20 seiki no bungaku* 2 (Iwanami shoten, 1996), 237–55.

62. Enchi Fumiko, "Ōchō josei bungaku to gendai bungaku" (transcript of her public lecture), *Kokubungaku* (Dec. 1965): 209–10.

63. All these aspects were represented by Ikeda Kikan, who became a professor at Tokyo Imperial University. In a short article in 1934, "Nikki bungaku to kikō bungaku," Ikeda discussed the close interrelationship between nikki bungaku and other types of Heian and medieval writings, namely, *kaki* (family record), *kashū* (poetry collection), *zuihitsu* (essay), *kikō* (travelogue), and *monogatari* (narrative fiction). In the following year, 1935, the young Waseda scholar Imai Takuji, published *Heianchō nikki no kenkyū*, which saw the nikki as a "synthetic genre" that provided the key to understanding the "organic development of different contemporary literary forms" such as *kan bungaku* (Chinese literature), waka, *shikashū* (private poetry collection), *shōsoko bumi* (letters), *uta monogatari* (poem tales), monogatari, kikō, *sōshi*, *rekishi monogatari* (historical tales), and *setsuwa*. A similar effort to investigate the larger context of the time also characterizes Tamai Kōsuke's *Nikki bungaku gaisetsu* (1945), which exhaustively examined Chinese and Japanese nikki as the "basic foundation for the study of nikki bungaku."

64. "Kyūtei joryū bungaku no kaika" (the 1949 original title was "Kyūtei joryū bungaku no mondai"), in his *Nihon bungaku no hōhō* (1955; new edition, Miraisha, 1960), especially 161, 176–85.

65. Saigō Nobutsuna, *Nihon kodai bungakushi*, Iwanami zensho 149 (Iwanami shoten, 1951), 163–65.

66. Despite his enthusiastic praise for women's literary achievements, Saigō laments that the high intellectual level, the objective prose, the vigorous comic spirit, and the wide social perspective seen in earlier prose fiction by men (such as *Utsubo monogatari*) were not fully developed in *Genji monogatari*, which, together with other women's works, he saw as marked by emotivity (*shujōsei*), lyricism (*jojōsei*), and mood (*kibunsei*). "Kyūtei joryū bungaku no kaika," 185.

67. Ibid.

68. Ikeda Kikan, "Watakushi shōsetsu to shite no *Kagerō nikki*," in his *Monogatari bungaku* (Shibundō, 1951): 145–55.

69. Ikeda Kikan, "Nikki wa dō shite bungaku tariuru ka," *Kokubungaku kaishaku to kanshō* (Jan. 1954): 69–72.

70. Akiyama Ken, "Nikki bungaku to josei," *Kokubungaku kaishaku to kanshō* (Jan. 1954): 32–35.

71. Akiyama Ken, "Naze onna ga bundan o shihaishita no ka," *Kokubungaku kaishaku to kanshō* (Aug. 1960): 32–37.

72. Akiyama Ken, "Joryū bungaku no seishin to genryū," *Kokubungaku kaishaku to kanshō* (Jan. 1963): 57–66. In the same special issue on "Heian-chō bungaku shi," Kimura Masanori also discussed the "(literary) construction of the self," or the "creation of the second reality," as the essence of nikki bungaku. Kimura, "Nikki bungaku no seiritsu to sono igi," *Kokubungaku kaishaku to kanshō* (Jan. 1963): 51–56. Subsequently, Kimura and Akiyama mutually reinforced this paradigm.

73. Akiyama Ken, "Kodai ni okeru nikki bungaku no tenkai," *Kokubungaku* (Dec. 1965): 25–32.

74. Ibid., 32.

75. Akiyama Ken, "Naze onna ga bundan o shihaishita ka," *Kokubungaku kaishaku to kanshō* (Aug. 1960): 36; "Jijitsu to kyokō," *Kokubungaku* (May 1969): 35. See also Kimura Masanori, "Nikki bungaku no seiritsu to sono igi," *Kokubungaku kaishaku to kanshō* (Jan. 1963), and his "Nikki bungaku no honshitsu to sōsaku shinri," *Kōza Nihon bungaku no sōten* 2 (Meiji Shoin, 1968).

76. Akiyama Ken, "*Kagerō nikki* to *Sarashina nikki*: joryū nikki bungaku no hassei," *Kokubungaku* (Jan. 1981), 8–9.

77. Akiyama Ken, "Joryū nikki bungaku ni tsuite no josetsu," *Ōchō joryū nikki bungaku hikkei*, Bessatsu kokubungaku (Gakutōsha, 1986), 6.

78. See, for example, Rita Felski, *The Gender of Modernity* (Cambridge: Harvard University Press, 1995).

Chapter 4: Modern Constructions of *Tales of Ise*: Gender and Courtliness

1. This topic is treated at greater length in English by Richard Bowring, "The *Ise monogatari*: A Short Cultural History," *Harvard Journal of Asiatic Studies* (winter 1992): 401–80.

2. Imanishi Yūichirō, ed., *Tsūzoku Ise monogatari*, Tōyō bunko 535 (Heibonsha, 1991), 377–79. I am grateful to Lawrence Marceau for drawing this text to my attention.

3. Susan Blakeley Klein, "Allegories of Desire: Kamakura Commentaries and the Noh" (Ph.D. dissertation, Cornell University, 1994), 180–82, 187–209.

4. Ibid., 215–16.

5. Bowring, 450.

6. Ibid., 474.

7. Ibid., 475–76.

8. Fritz Vos, *A Study of the Ise-monogatari with the Text according to the Den-Teika-Hippon and an Annotated Translation* (The Hague: Mouton, 1957), 1: 113.

9. Joshua S. Mostow, *Pictures of the Heart: The Hyakunin Isshu in Word and Image* (Honolulu: University of Hawai'i Press, 1996).

10. Vos, 1: 115.

11. *Gengo ōshi* (The Inner Meaning of *The Tale of Genji*), by Kondō Yoshiki (1876), was the first Meiji period publication on *Genji*.

12. Murasaki Shikibu, *Genji monogatari*, trans. Suyematz Kenchio [Suematsu Kenchō] (London: Trübner, 1882).

13. "*Ise monogatari*," *Jogaku zasshi* 10 (Dec. 20, 1885), 206–7, and "*Ise monogatari* (tsuzuki)," *Jogaku zasshi* 12 (Jan. 15, 1886), 6–7.

14. "Joshi to bunpitsu no gyō: bunpitsu no gyō joryū ni kōtsugō no koto," *Jogakku zasshi* 79 (Oct. 8, 1887), 162–63.

15. Ibid., 163.

16. See chap. 2 of Reina Lewis, *Gendering Orientalism: Race, Femininity, and Representation* (London: Routledge, 1996).

17. Mikami Sanji and Takatsu Kuwasaburō, *Nihon bungakushi* (Kinkōdō, 1890), 1: 201–2.

18. See James Edward Ketelaar, *Of Heretics and Martyrs in Meiji Japan* (Princeton: Princeton University Press, 1990).

19. Mikami and Takatsu, 1: 210.

20. Hagino Yoshiyuki, Ochiai Naobumi, and Konakamura Yoshikata, eds., *Ise monogatari*, Nihon bungaku zensho 1 (Hakubunkan, 1890), 2–3.

21. Fujioka Sakutarō, *Kokubungaku zenshi: Heian chō hen* (Kaiseikan, 1905), 189–90. Perhaps the best-known reference to *Ise* in the first half of the Meiji period is in the title of the short story often thought to be Higuchi Ichiyō's masterpiece, "Take kurabe" ("Growing up"), the first installment of which appeared in the January 1895 issue of *Bungakukai* (The Literary World), the organ for the Japanese romantic movement, which had split off from *Jogaku zasshi* two years previously. Ichiyō apparently studied *Ise* as part of the Kei'en school of waka, under Nakajima Utako, receiving lectures on the text. However, the use of *Ise* in her story goes no farther than the title, and, according to Donald Keene, the "writing of 'Growing up,' under the title 'Hinadori' (Baby Chicks), apparently began in the autumn of 1894." *Dawn to the West* (New York: Holt, Rinehart and Winston, 1984), 179.

22. For more on these concepts and their development, see Tomi Suzuki, *Narrating the Self: Fictions of Japanese Modernity* (Stanford: Stanford University Press, 1996), and Joan E. Ericson, "The Origins of the Concept of 'Women's Literature,'" in *The Woman's Hand: Gender and Theory in Japanese Women's Writing*, ed. Paul Gordon Schalow and Janet A. Walker (Stanford: Stanford University Press, 1996).

23. Kamata Masanori, *Kōshō Ise monogatari shōkai* (Nanboku shuppanbu, 1919).

24. Edo-period popularizations of *Ise* also presented it as one continuous narrative, rather than as a collection of episodes. See *Ise monogatari hirakotoba* (1679), in *Tsūzoku Ise monogatari*, ed. Imanishi Yūichirō.

25. In fact, Kobayashi's repeated suggestion that Narihira's poems were composed for *meisho-e* (pictures of famous places) is the earliest modern appearance of this theory I have found. For a more thorough discussion of the recent popularity

of this theory, see Joshua S. Mostow, "Byōbu-uta to uta-gatari to *Ise monogatari* to," in *Heian bungaku to kaiga*, ed. Nakano Kōichi, Ronshū Heian bungaku 5 (Benseisha, forthcoming).

26. Yoshikawa Hideo, *Shinchū Ise monogatari* (Seibunkan shoten, 1926), 22.

27. Ibid., 19–20.

28. Ibid., 22–24.

29. See the discussion of T. Wakameda's 1922 translation of the *Kokinshū* in Mostow, *Pictures of the Heart*, 71–72.

30. In 1923, the American translator Curtis Hidden Page insisted that the poetry of Emperor Taishō and Crown Prince Hirohito demonstrates that "there certainly is no need to fear from them any unprovoked attack on the peace of the world." Curtis Hidden Page, *Japanese Poetry: An Historical Essay with Two Hundred and Fifty Translations* (1923; reprint, Folcroft, Penn.: Folcroft Library Editions, 1976), 169. See the discussion in Mostow, *Pictures of the Heart*, 72–73.

31. For the best brief survey in English on the term *fūryū*, chiefly in Japan, see Philip Harries, "*Fūryū*, a Concept of Elegance in Pre-Modern Literature," in *Europe Interprets Japan*, ed. Gordon Daniels (Tenterden, Kent, England: Paul Norbury Publications, 1984), 137–44.

32. Iwamoto Yoshiharu, "Fūryū wo ronzu" (On the Elegant Literary Lifestyle), *Jogaku zasshi* 210 (Apr. 26, 1890), collected in *Jogaku zasshi, Bungakkai shū*, Meiji bungaku zenshū 32 (Chikuma shobō, 1973), 29–31.

33. Translations by Donald Keene in *Dawn to the West* and by Chieko Mulhern in her *Kōda Rohan*, TWAS 432 (Boston: Twayne Publishers, 1977).

34. Ikeda Kikan, *Ise monogatari ni tsukite no kenkyū* (Ōokayama shoten, 1933–36), 825.

35. This stance is signaled from the outset, with a xenophobic preface by Nukariya Kaiten (1867–1934), one of the major figures in the post-Russo-Japanese War discourse on the relation between Zen, *bushidō* (way of the warrior), and modern Japanese nationalism. On Zen, the emperor, and nationalism, see Robert H. Sharf, "The Zen of Japanese Nationalism," in *Curators of the Buddha: The Study of Buddhism under Colonialism*, ed. Donald S. Lopez, Jr. (Chicago: University of Chicago Press, 1995), 116. There is not a little irony in the fact that Helen McCullough based her translation of *Ise* largely on Arai's edition.

36. Arai Mujirō, *Hyōshaku Ise monogatari taisei* (Yoyogi shoin, 1939), 13.

37. Ibid., 2–10.

38. On the concept of "national aesthetics," see Leslie Pincus, *Authenticating Culture in Imperial Japan: Kuki Shūzō and the Rise of National Aesthetics* (Berkeley: University of California Press, 1996).

39. Helen Craig McCullough, trans., *Tales of Ise: Lyrical Episodes from Tenth-Century Japan* (Stanford: Stanford University Press, 1968), 69–70.

40. Endō Yoshimoto, "Fūryū kō," *Kokugo kokubun* (Apr. 1940).

41. For more specifically on the postwar history of miyabi, see my "Nihon no bi-

jutsu-shi gensetsu to 'miyabi,'" in *Kataru genzai, katarareta kako: Nihon no bijutsu-shigaku 100–nen*, ed. Tokyo kokuritsu bunkazai kenkyūjo (Heibonsha, 1999), 232–39.

42. Okazaki Yoshie, "Miyabi no dentō," in the "Miyabi no dentō" special edition of *Bungaku* (Nov. 1943), 354–55.

43. *Sōmonka*, translated as both "relationship poems" or "dialogue poems," was one of the three major categories of poems in the *Man'yōshū*.

44. The belief in the importance of women as equal partners of love can be traced back to the Japanese Christians of the 1880s, such as Iwamoto Yoshiharu, and the Japanese romantic movement of the 1890s. Fueled by debates over prostitution (characterized as the opposite of women as equal partners in love), the treatment of women remained for decades a yardstick by which the Western powers, and many Japanese thinkers, measured the country's "progress."

45. Ikeda Tsutomu, "Heian jidai no joryū bungaku to 'miyabi'," *Bungaku* (Nov. 1943), 397.

46. Hasuda Zenmai, "Miyabi," *Bungaku* (Nov. 1943), 378–89.

47. For more on the Japan Romantic School and Japanese nationalism, see Kevin Michael Doak, *Dreams of Difference: The Japan Romantic School and the Crisis of Modernity* (Berkeley: University of California Press, 1994).

48. Ōtsu, 172–73.

49. Ivan Morris's 1964 *The World of the Shining Prince*, which relied heavily on Ikeda's work, would be more properly entitled *The World of the Shining Prince's Women*.

50. Watanabe Minoru, "Minamoto no Tōru to *Ise monogatari*," *Kokugo to kokubungaku* 49 (Nov. 1972), 1–12.

51. Watanabe Minoru, *Ise monogatari*, Shinchō Nihon koten shūsei (Shinchōsa, 1976), 141–42.

52. Ibid., 154.

53. Katagiri Yōichi, *Ise monogatari, Yamato monogatari*, Kanshō Nihon koten bungaku 5 (Kadokawa shoten, 1975), 2.

54. Ibid., 43.

55. Akiyama Ken, "*Ise monogatari*: 'miyabi' no ron," *Kokubungaku kaishaku to kyōzai no kenkyū* (Jan. 1979), 6.

56. Akiyama Ken, "'Miyabi' no kōzō," in *Kōza Nihon shisō 5: Bi*, ed. Sagara Tōru, Bitō Masahide, and Akiyama Ken (Tokyo daigaku shuppankai, 1984).

57. Ibid., 32.

58. For more in English on "overcoming the modern" and the 1942 Kyoto Conference, see H. D. Harootunian, "Visible Discourses/Invisible Ideologies," in *Postmodernism and Japan*, ed. Masao Miyoshi and H. D. Harootunian (Durham: Duke University Press, 1989).

59. This is seen in the appropriation of the work of Okakura Tenshin by Japanese intellectuals in the 1940s. On Japan as museum, see Stefan Tanaka, "Imaging

History: Inscribing Belief in the Nation," *The Journal of Asian Studies* 53, no. 1 (Feb. 1994), 24–44.

60. See Pincus, 209–47.

61. Fukui Teisuke's *Ise monogatari seiseiron* (Yūseidō, 1965) is an exemplary textual study. Scholarship on the premodern exegetical tradition includes Katagiri Yōichi, *Ise monogatari no kenkyū*, 2 vols. (Meiji shoin, 1968), as well as work on *Ise* and nō by Itō Masayoshi.

62. See Ikeda Shinobu, "Chihō fūzoku e no manazashi," in her *Nihon kaiga no josei-zō: jendaa bijutsushi no shiten kara* (Chikuma shobō, 1998), 176–93.

63. See Sharalyn Orbaugh, *Japanese Fiction of the Occupation Period* (Stanford: Stanford University Press, forthcoming).

64. See Marilyn Ivy, *Discourses of the Vanishing: Modernity, Phantasm, Japan* (Chicago: University of Chicago Press, 1995), especially Chap. 1.

65. See Kosaku Yoshino, *Cultural Nationalism in Contemporary Japan* (London: Routledge, 1992).

Chapter 5: *Zuihitsu* and Gender: *Tsurezuregusa* and *The Pillow Book*

1. See such works as William Theodore de Bary and Irene Bloom, eds., *Approaches to the Asian Classics* (New York: Columbia University Press, 1990).

2. A typical example from the illustrated comic or *manga* genre occurs in Sanseidō's *Manga Tsurezuregusa*. The author Kenkō's list of daily events that take time away from the pursuit of our true goals (Section 108) is rendered in small line drawings. For "eating and drinking," we see a medievalish couple at table, with the wife saying "It's been five years since we've dined together this way." To illustrate "walking," the wife carries her shopping basket and says to no one in particular, "We have to have Papa eat well and work hard for us." Papa sits on the "toilet" reading the newspaper, startled at the resignation of the Hōjō cabinet (anachronisms in cultural practice are acceptable in the interest of liveliness, so long as historical names are correct). And under "conversation," we see two women at the river gossiping about another who has left home, her infidelity discovered. Even a fourteenth-century writer could understand the sacrifices of the modern male. The behavior of a medieval salaryman and his wife is unlikely to clarify Kenkō's list for the prepubescent audience (he repeatedly describes the uselessness of conversations between dilettante men, for example, a case that might not occur to youngsters now, and deserves comment), but it surely plays upon and reinforces contemporary gender roles. Takeishi Akio, text, and Watanabe Fukuo, illus., *Manga Tsurezuregusa* (Comic book *Tsurezuregusa*) (Sanseidō, 1989), 98. Takeishi has a number of scholarly books and articles on Kenkō's life and beliefs. Akiyama Kōsaburō's *Tsurezuregusa koroshi no suzuri* (The Murderous Inkstone of *Tsurezuregusa*) (Kadokawa shoten, 1988), is a spy novel concoction laden with biographical details.

3. Donald Keene, whose excellent translation *Essays in Idleness* (New York:

Columbia University Press, 1967) remains in print after thirty years, has written of four principal Japanese aesthetic characteristics, which also happen to be four that he sees as central to *Tsurezuregusa*: suggestion, irregularity, simplicity, and perishability. "Japanese Aesthetics," *Philosophy East and West* 19, no. 3 (July 1969): 293–306. For the most recent version, see *Seeds in the Heart: Japanese Literature from Earliest Times to the Late Sixteenth Century* (New York: Henry Holt and Company, 1993), 857–60.

4. For the colophon on Yūsai, see Yasuraoka Kōsaku, *Tsurezuregusa zenchūshaku* (Kadokawa shoten, 1967–68), 2: 559. Okanishi Ichū says his readings came from a Michikatsu text; Hayashi Dōshun and Kurokawa Yujun quote Michikatsu as well, but such a text no longer exists. Komatsu Misao, "*Tsurezuregusa* chūshakushi," in *Tsurezuregusa kōza 3: Tsurezuregusa to sono kanshō II*, ed. Yūseidō henshūbu (Yūseidō, 1974), 56.

5. See Shimauchi Yūko, *Tsurezuregusa no henbō* (Perikansha, 1992), for an account of readers outside the nobility and warrior class before this period.

6. As in Shimamoto Shōichi, *Matsunaga Teitoku—haikaishi e no michi*, Kyōyō gakkō sōsho 4 (Hōsei daigaku shuppankyoku, 1989), 94. Razan gives his age at the time in *Nozuchi* (Section 238). Hayashi Dōshun, *Tsurezuregusa nozuchi*, collected in *Kokubun chūshaku zensho*, ed. Muromatsu Iwao (Kokugakuin daigaku shuppan, 1909), 229. Most sources set the date for these lectures in the period 1603–1604. Komatsu Misao offers an alternative dating of 1600. Komatsu, "*Tsurezuregusa* chūshakushi," 52.

7. Shimamoto Shōichi, "Kinsei shotō ni okeru *Tsurezuregusa* no kyōju—josetsu, Fujiwara Seika no baai," *Kinsei shoki bungei* 1 (Dec. 1969): 2. Also see Shimamoto Shōichi, *Matsunaga Teitoku*, 99–102.

8. Matsunaga Teitoku, *Taionki*, in *Taionki, Oritaku shiba no ki, Rantō kotohajime*, ed. Odaka Toshio, Nihon koten bungaku taikei 95 (Iwanami shoten, 1964), 60.

9. Drawing on the image in the *Analects* (*Lun-yü*), Section XVII, 4.

10. Hayashi Dōshun, *Tsurezuregusa nozuchi*, 234.

11. Ibid., 1. In a personal communication, Ōsone Shōsuke warned me that the visitor is undoubtedly a fictional device for conveying Razan's own opinion. Also see Ishida Ichirō and Kanaya Osamu, eds., *Fujiwara Seika, Hayashi Razan*, Nihon shisō taikei 23 (Iwanami shoten, 1975), 216–17. Yamagishi Tomoko points out that this preface dates to c. 1648, more than twenty years after the first version of the text. Yamagishi Tomoko, "Kenkyū to kanshō no kiseki," in *Tsurezuregusa hikkei*, ed. Kubota Jun, Bessatsu kokubungaku 10 (Gakutōsha, 1981), 210.

12. Hayashi Dōshun, *Tsurezuregusa nozuchi*, 4.

13. Odaka Toshio, *Kinsei shoki bundan no kenkyū* (Meiji shoin, 1964), 160.

14. Recent scholarly opinion holds that the content of the headnotes resembles less the earlier *Jumyō'in shō* and *Nozuchi* than it does *Tettsui*, which is thus thought to have influenced *Nagusamigusa*. Hinotani Teruhiko, "*Tsurezuregusa* no kyōjushi," in *Tsurezuregusa kōza 4: Gengo, gensen, eikyō*, ed. Yūseidō henshūbu (Yūseidō, 1974), 211–12. Hinotani cites the views of Kōjō Isao and Sekiba Takeshi.

NOTES TO CHAPTER 5

15. Sekiba Takeshi, "*Tsurezuregusa* no eikyō, kyōju to kenkyūshi—kinsei zenki o chūshin ni," *Kokubungaku kaishaku to kanshō* 35, no. 3 (Mar. 1970): 99–102.

16. Donald Keene, *World Within Walls: Japanese Literature of the Pre-Modern Era, 1600–1867* (1976; reprint, New York: Grove Press, 1978), 27.

17. It is remarkable for having been printed while the commentator was still alive, notes Kawase Kazuma in *Zōho kokatsujiban no kenkyū* (The Antiquarian Booksellers Association of Japan, 1967), 1: 526.

18. Yamagishi, "Kenkyū to kanshō no kiseki," 208. The brevity of Jumyō'in's notations probably betray less his scientific mind than the homogeneous nature of his audience. There is some debate as to whether *Jumyō'in shō* itself was based on lectures. Yamagishi believes it could have been used for that purpose, with later teachers borrowing heavily from it. Shigematsu Nobuhiro, by contrast, argues that *Jumyō'in shō* was not based on Jumyō'in's lectures. Shigematsu, "*Tsurezuregusa* kenkyūshi," *Kokugo to kokubungaku* 6, nos. 6–7 (1929).

19. Hinotani, "Kyōjushi," 211. *Tettsui*, also known as *Tetsutsui* or *Kanazuchi*, is a word play on *Nozuchi*. *Tettsui* refers to Section 122 of *Tsurezuregusa*, which points out the usefulness of iron in contemporary life. Aoki's own revision and expansion of his commentary dates to 1649.

20. Komatsu Misao, "Tettsui kōryaku," *Kanazawa bunko kenkyū* 9, nos. 10–11 [95] (Nov. 1963): 30. See Keichū, *Kakiire 2: Tettsui*, in *Keichū zenshū*, ed. Hisamatsu Sen'ichi (Iwanami shoten, 1976), 16: 139–224.

21. Hinotani, "Kyōjushi," 211; Komatsu, "Tettsui kōryaku," 30–31.

22. Shimamoto, "Fujiwara Seika no baai," 3.

23. Odaka Toshio, *Matsunaga Teitoku no kenkyū* (Shibundō, 1953), 126; Keene, *World Within Walls*, 28.

24. Yasuraoka, *Tsurezuregusa zenchūshaku* 1: 272.

25. The other two secret teachings concern *mokō* in Section 28—cloth hung above the blinds—and *hōben no tsukemono* in Section 221—decorations attached to costumes of men freed from prison to participate in the Kamo Festival. The teachings are also ascribed to Ichijō Kanera, although evidence points to a Tokugawa dating. Takei Kazuto, *Ichijō Kanera no shoshiteki kenkyū* (Ōfūsha, 1987), 310–12.

26. The Seven Oral Secrets cover the Three Important Matters plus Sections 64, 66, 100, and 198. Nakamura Yukihiko, "*Tsurezuregusa* juyōshi," *Kokubungaku kaishaku to kanshō* 22 (Dec. 1957): 66.

27. The oldest known is *Mumoregi*, one of the vernacular prose *kanazōshi* genre. Ishida Motosue, "Edo jidai no zuihitsu bungaku," in *Nihon bungaku kōza 5: Zuihitsu, nikki hen*, ed. Yamamoto Mitsuo (Kaizōsha, 1934), 91.

28. *Inu tsurezure* exists in a 1619 manuscript and an expanded 1653 printed edition, with poems. In Asakura Haruhiko, ed., *Kanazōshi shūsei* (Tōkyōdō shuppan, 1983), 4: 3–26; 425–36.

29. Nakamura Yukihiko, "*Hōjōki, Tsurezuregusa* no kinseiteki kyōju," in *Tsurezuregusa, Hōjōki*, Nihon koten kanshō kōza 13 (Kadokawa shoten, 1960), 330.

30. *Nihon zuihitsu zenshū* (Kokumin tosho, 1929), 18: 89–189.
31. Nakamura Yukihiko, "*Hōjōki, Tsurezuregusa* no kinseiteki kyōju," 330–31.
32. Hayakawa Junzaburō, ed., *Kinsei bungei sōsho* (Kokusho kankōkai, 1911), 7: 505.
33. Another take-off on *Tsurezuregusa* is the haikai poet Otokuni's (active c. 1680–1720) *Sorezoregusa* (1704, published 1715), in *Kokkei bungaku zenshū*, ed. Furuya Chishin (Bungei shoin, 1918), 8: 123–80. Fortunately for those who weary of too much faithfulness, it does not open with a variation of the famous preface *tsurezurenaru mama ni* (having nothing in particular to do), but rather a series of wordplays on dream and illusion. Admonitions here are supplemented by satire and humor. One line reads "What tops poverty is wisdom; what tops stupidity is money; what tops a deer is a horn" (131). The unexpected appearance of such a terse dictum recreates the effect of *Tsurezuregusa*'s style.
34. Komatsu, "*Tsurezuregusa* chūshakushi," 53.
35. In Fujii Otoo, ed., *Chikamatsu zenshū* (Shibunkaku, 1930), 7: 703–54. Also *Chikamatsu meisakushū*, Nihon meicho zenshū (Nihon meicho zenshū kankōkai, 1930), 1: 303–16.
36. Nakamura Noakatsu, "*Tsurezuregusa* juyōshi," 65.
37. Ihara Saikaku, *Zoku tsurezure* (1695), in vol. 16 of *Taiyaku Saikaku zenshū*, eds. Asō Isoji and Fuji Akio (Meiji shoin, 1977). *Shin Yoshiwara tsunezunegusa*, in *Teihon Saikaku zenshū*, ed. Ebara Taizō et al. (Chūō kōronsha, 1959), 6: 243–96. Saikaku illustrated the text, and the headnotes by "Ichidai Otoko Yonosuke" are clearly by him, as well. Hinotani Teruhiko, "Kōsei e no eikyō—awasete Saikaku sakuhin to no kanren ni tsuite," in *Shosetsu ichiran Tsurezuregusa*, ed. Ichiko Teiji (Meiji shoin, 1970), 194. In Saikaku's *Nanshoku ōkagami* (1687), Kenkō becomes "a new icon for male love." Ihara Saikaku, *The Great Mirror of Male Love*, trans. Paul Gordon Schalow (Stanford: Stanford University Press, 1990), 11.
38. Bokushiki, *Ressenden* (1763), in *Edo jidai bungei shiryō*, ed. Kokusho kankōkai (Meicho kankōkai, 1964), 1: 1–18.
39. Takarai Kikaku (Tōraku Sanjin), *Irozato Tsurezuregusa*, in vol. 4 of *Sharebon taisei*, ed. Mizuno Minoru (Chūō kōronsha, 1979); Nishiki Bunryū, *Tsurezure imayō sugata*, in *Nishiki Bunryū zenshū, ukiyozōshi hen, ge*, Kinsei bungei shiryō 20, ed. Nagatomo Chiyoji (Koten bunko, 1988), 5–153; *Keisei tsurezuregusa* (Courtesan's Tsurezuregusa), in *Sharebon taisei*, 1: 113–17; *Tsurezure sui ga kawa*, in *Sharebon taisei*, 12: 155–82; *Koinu Tsurezure*, in *Kinsei shomin bunka* 80 (Oct. 1962): 1–16; and Santō Kyōden, *Kaibutsu Tsurezuregusa* (1792), manuscript preserved in Collection of Daitōkyū kinen bunko (Tokyo).
40. Hiraga Gennai, *Shin tsurezuregusa*, collected in *Kinsei bungei sōsho*, ed. Hayakawa Junzaburō (Kokusho kankōkai, 1911), 7: 453–504. Yokoi Yayū (1702–1783), the author of *Uzuragoromo* (Rags and Tatters), the haikai poet Yosa Buson (1716–1783), and the novelist Ueda Akinari (1734–1809) all refer prodigiously to *Tsurezuregusa*. On Yayū, see Nobuhiro Shinji, "*Tsurezuregusa* no eikyō—kinsei bun-

gaku e no eikyō," in *Tsurezuregusa kōza 4: Gengo, gensen, eikyō,* ed. Yūseidō hen-shūba (Yūseidō, 1974), 235–55. For Buson, see Kumasaka Atsuko, "Buson no haiku to *Tsurezuregusa,*" *Renga haikai kenkyū* 17 (1958): 7–15. On Akinari, see Washiyama Jushin, "Akinari bungaku to *Tsurezuregusa*—toku ni sono shisōteki eisei: kankei ni tsuite," *Hanazono daigaku kokubungaku ronkyū* 10 (Nov. 1982): 21–34.

41. John B. Henderson, *Scripture, Canon, and Commentary: A Comparison of Confucian and Western Exegesis* (Princeton: Princeton University Press, 1991), 6, 89, 91, 106, 115, 121.

42. Fujii Ransai, in his *Kansai hikki* (1715), uses this nomenclature. Hayakawa Junsaburō, ed., *Nihon zuihitsu taisei* (Yoshikawa kōbunkan, 1928), 9: 177.

43. Komatsu, "*Tsurezuregusa* chūshakushi," 51. Takeishi Akio, *Tsurezuregusa no bukkyōken* (Ōfūsha, 1971), 198.

44. Saitō Kiyoe, Kishigami Shinji, and Tomikura Tokujirō, eds., *Makura no sōshi, Tsurezuregusa,* Kokugo kokubungaku kenkyūshi taisei 6 (Sanseidō, 1960), 273.

45. In opposition to the *zettai shikan* of the title, he posited a *sōtai shikan* (rela-tive *shikan*) of the text. Saitō Kiyoe et al., *Makura no sōshi, Tsurezuregusa,* 274.

46. Yamagishi, "Kenkyū to kanshō no kiseki," 206. Muraoka Tsunetsugu, *Zoku Nihon shisōshi kenkyū* (Iwanami shoten, 1939), 98. Earlier writers had noted conti-nuity between individual *Tsurezuregusa* segments at various points. Tanaka Jūtarō traces the trend of finding connections back to *Jumyō'in shō.* Tanaka, "Zuihitsu bun-gaku no seikaku to sono keitai," *Geirin* 3, no. 3 (June 1952): 38. But Bansai fixed upon the search for a compositional scheme. He developed a system of eight cate-gories to describe the relations between each section so that he could explain how the units of the text managed to seem independent while still forming a single whole. In his theory of "the meaning carried over" (*rai-i*), whether two adjacent sec-tions were "the same as" each other, "opposites," or some further variation, they were equally bound. See Nishio Minoru, "Zuihitsu no tokusei to kenkyū hōhō no mondai—*Tsurezuregusa Bansai shō* ni okeru rai-i no kōsatsu," *Bungaku* 2, no. 1 (Jan. 1934): 13–14.

47. Saitō et al., *Makura no sōshi, Tsurezuregusa,* 277.

48. *Tsurezuregusa shoshō taisei* (Nihon tosho sentaa, 1978), 5, cited by Shimauchi Yūko, "*Tsurezuregusa* to yōkyoku," *Kaishaku* 33, no. 11 (Nov. 1987): 40; Shimauchi, *Tsurezuregusa no henbō,* 142.

49. The section divisions currently in use originate with the *Tsurezuregusa mondanshō* (1667), in the version found in Asaga Sansei, ed., *Tsurezuregusa shosō taisei* (1688), a compendium of earlier commentaries. Komatsu, "*Tsurezuregusa* chūshakushi," 59.

50. Saitō et al., *Makura no sōshi, Tsurezuregusa,* 275.

51. Ibid., 277.

52. Yoshizawa Sadato, ed., *Tsurezuregusa—Tsurezuregusa Jumyō'in shō* (Nagoya: Chūbu Nihon kyōiku bunkakai, 1982), 1.

53. Saitō et al., *Makura no sōshi, Tsurezuregusa,* 277.

54. Yoshizawa Sadato, "Shimizu Shunryū to *Tsurezuregusa*," *Kinjō gakuin daigaku ronshū* 57 (Dec. 1973): 56–57.

55. Kurokawa Yujun also proposes that the three teachings are at the heart of the text, and suggests that other views do less to explain *Tsurezuregusa* than to provoke arguments. Yoshizawa Yoshinori, ed., *Tsurezuregusa shūishō*, Mikan kokubun kochūshaku taikei 16 (Shibundō, 1969), 8–9.

56. Saitō et al., *Makura no sōshi, Tsurezuregusa*, 279.

57. Cited by Ide Tsuneo, "*Tsurezuregusa* no 'sōshi' teki seikaku," *Bungei to shisō* 29 (Dec. 1966): 1.

58. Komatsu, "*Tsurezuregusa* chūshakushi," 57.

59. Yamagishi, "Kenkyū to kanshō no kiseki," 211.

60. Scroll 29 of Ise Sadatake's *Ansai zuihitsu*, collected in *Kojitsu sōsho* (Kokkai toshokan, 1903), 11: 938. Also Saitō et al., *Makura no sōshi, Tsurezuregusa*, 287.

61. The verses of Matsuo Bashō's (1644–1694) school frequently played on familiar images. Borrowings have been pointed out in Bashō's prose works in praise of reclusion such as *Oi no kobumi* (Backpack Notes), *Oku no hosomichi* (Narrow Road to the Deep North), and *Heikan no setsu* (On Closing the Gate), the last being collected in *Fūzoku monzen* (Popular Literary Selections). On the relationship between Bashō's work and *Tsurezuregusa*, see Hirota Jirō, *Bashō to koten* (Meiji shoin, 1987), 114–17; 142–43; 180–89; 702–7; 786–91; 798–800; 810–13. *Sarashina kikō* (A Journey to Sarashina, 1688) also refers to the didactic biographical poem from *Nozuchi*. Hirota, *Bashō to koten*, 132–33. Hirota notes that the influence of *Mondanshō* can be seen in Bashō. Ibid., 420. Also see Tanaka Shōtarō, "*Heikan no setsu* to *Tsurezuregusa*," *Ritsumeikan bungaku* 140 (1957): 48–53. *Tsurezure no san* itself is an idiosyncratic venture, beginning with explanations of thirteen terms the author will use to make his points, including irony (*fūshi*), criticism (*hōhen*), style (*moyō*), and change (*henka*). Saitō et al., *Makura no sōshi, Tsurezuregusa*, 324–27.

62. Saitō et al., *Makura no sōshi, Tsurezuregusa*, 325, 327–28.

63. *Honchō bunkan*, in Nonaka Jirō, ed., *Kyōbun, haibunshū*, Kindai Nihon bungaku taikei 23 (Kokumin tosho, 1926); *Wakan bunsō*, in Iwatani Sueo, ed., *Haikai bunshū*, Haikai bunko 19 (Haibunkan, 1900).

64. It was one of the "five books" (*gosō*), including *Makura no sōshi*, *Shiki*, *Okazari no ki*, and *Oyudono no ki*, that a bride was supposed to have, along with "ten tales," referring to *Taketori*, *Utsubo*, and various versions of the histories *Ōkagami*, *Masukagami*, and *Eiga monogatari*. Tada Yoshitoshi, *Shūsai kango* (entry number 179), in *Nihon zuihitsu zenshū*, ed. Nakatsukasa Eijirō (Kokumin tosho, 1928), 14: 62.

65. Komatsu, "Shingakusharyū no *Tsurezuregusa* kenkyū," *Kanazawa bunko kenkyū* 81 (July 1962): 6–10. Lectures, which had never completely gone out of fashion (even Chikamatsu is said to have participated), were part of the city scene. Nakamura Yukihiko, "*Hōjōki, Tsurezuregusa* no kinseiteki kyōju," 326. Also see Komatsu, "*Tsurezuregusa* chūshakushi," 52.

66. Manuscript edition. Okanishi Ichū's *Mana Tsurezuregusa* (*Tsurezuregusa* in

Chinese script, 1689) is an early representative of translating *Tsurezuregusa* into Chinese.

67. Yoshida Kōichi, ed., *Tsurezuregusa modoki hyōban*, Koten bunko 418 (Koten bunko, 1981), 170–72. Komatsu links the genesis of this work to farcical lectures (*odoke kōshaku*) that resembled comic *rakugo* monologues. "*Tsurezuregusa* chūshakushi," 53.

68. *Modoki hyōban*, Section 4, 9–10 (woodblock reproduction); 14 (printed edition).

69. Ibid., Sections 5 and 6, 10–11 (woodblock reproduction); 15–16 (printed edition). The Kamo races are the setting for *Tsurezuregusa* Section 41. Tōren appears in Section 188.

70. A more sober textual negation appears in *Tsurezuregusa tekigi* (*Tsurezuregusa* Extracts, published 1688), by the Neo-Confucian Fujii Ransai (1628?–1709), which identifies twenty-seven sections that should not be read by beginners and destroys other peoples' defenses of them on ethical grounds. This text also demonstrates the persistence of didactic readings. *Meikankō Tsurezuregusa ōgishō* of 1725 is the only other primarily negative reading. Takaya Chikabumi (1681–1719) writes that Kenkō is bad at poetry, dim on Confucianism, still barely on the lesser vehicle in Buddhism, only able to write in Japanese on Taoism, and knows just a smattering (one hair from nine oxen) of Shinto. Saitō et al., *Makura no sōshi, Tsurezuregusa*, 282. Nakamura Yukihiko characterizes both *Meikankō* and *Tekigi* as emotional criticism from the point of view of rationalist Neo-Confucianism. "*Tsurezuregusa* juyōshi," 64.

71. Shimamoto Shōichi, *Matsunaga Teitoku*, 111.

72. Vol. 1 of Gotō Tanji and Okami Masao, eds., *Taiheiki*, Nihon koten bungaku taikei 35 (Iwanami shoten, 1960–62), 353–55.

73. Shimauchi Yūko, *Tsurezuregusa no henbō*, 169. *Fusō in'itsuden* is collected in Shimahara Yasuo, ed., *Henchō fukusei*, Fukakusa Gensei shū 3 (Koten bunko, 1977).

74. Shimauchi, *Tsurezuregusa no henbō*, 171–74.

75. Tomikura Tokujirō, *Urabe Kenkō* (Yoshikawa kōbunkan, 1964), 12–13.

76. Nakamura Naokatsu, "*Tsurezuregusa* kenkyū," *Nihon bungaku kōza* 13 (1928), 8.

77. This occurs in *Honchō tonshi* (History of Reclusion in Our Country, 1660, published 1664), by Hayashi Dokkōsai (1624–1661), a Confucian scholar. The biographies of recluses in *Honchō tonshi* are written in Chinese, and there among facts about "Yoshida Kenkō" and what has been introduced as his "book in the vernacular" (*wago no sōshi*) is the line "As a work, Tsurezuregusa is in a class with the *hitsudan* and *zuihitsu* of the Chinese." *Hitsudan*, literally "talks from the brush," is a synonym for *zuihitsu*. Hayashi Dokkōsai, *Honchō tonshi*, collected in *Kanren setsuwashū* (Related Tales), Fukakusa Gensei shū 4, ed. Shimahara Yasuo (Koten bunko, 1978), 435–36.

78. *Nihon zuihitsu taisei*, first series (Nihon zuihitsu taisei kankōkai, 1928; reprint, Yoshikawa kōbunkan, 1976), 21: 16.

79. Ban Kōkei, *Kuni tsu fumi yoyo no ato*, in *Nishio Mitsuo sensei kanreki kinen ronshū Nihon bungaku sōkō*, ed. Nishio Mitsuo (Tōyō hōki shuppan, 1968), 314. An earlier use of zuihitsu to describe *Makura no sōshi* is found in *Shiojiri* (Salt Mounds), Amano Sadakage's (1663–1733) compendium of writings from the period 1697 to 1733. Murase Kentarō, comp., Muromatsu Iwao, ed., *Zuihitsu shiojiri* (Teikoku shoin, 1907), 1: 707.

80. Kansaku Kōichi, "*Makura no sōshi* no chūshakushi," in *Makura no sōshi kōza 4: Gengo, gensen, eikyō, kenkyū* (Yūseidō, 1976), 325–29.

81. Shōtetsu cites *Tsurezuregusa* Section 137 in *Shōtetsu monogatari* (1448–50). "'Are we to look at cherry blossoms only in full bloom, the moon only when it is cloudless?' wrote Kenkō, but apart from him, a person with this kind of sensibility is hardly to be found in the world. Such a temperament is inborn." Robert H. Brower, trans., Steven D. Carter, introduction and notes, *Conversations with Shōtetsu* (*Shōtetsu monogatari*), Michigan Monograph Series in Japanese Studies 7 (Ann Arbor: Center for Japanese Studies, University of Michigan, 1992), 95. Shinkei reacts to the same passage in *Sasamegoto* (Murmurings, 1463): "Priest Kenkō said, 'Are we to look at the moon and flowers only with the eyes? To spend a rainy night lost in thought, to go beneath a tree from which the blossoms have fallen and withered, then one recalls all that is past.' I found what he has written to be deeply beautiful." Kidō Saizō and Imoto Nōichi, eds., *Renga ronshū, haironshū*, Nihon koten bungaku taikei 66 (Iwanami shoten, 1961), 178. Kensai's remarks appear in *Wakakusayama* (before 1497): "It cannot be said that only the full moon is good. The evening moon seen in the night sky is cooling, and the moon that comes up at dawn, among sparse clouds, appearing chill, clears the mind." Cited by Sumita Chihoko, "*Tsurezuregusa* juyōshi no ichikōsatsu," *Chūsei bungaku ronkō* 2 (Apr. 1956): 12, which quotes the *Gunsho ruijū* (17: 9). Tō no Tsuneyori, in *Shinkokin wakashū kikigaki* (Questions and Answers on *Shinkokinshū*, 1470), writes, "In Priest Kenkō's own writing, it says one should not call only the moon at its height good. The mind clears at the moon hesitating to come out from among the clouds after rain, or appearing as dawn spreads. I agree and think this is excellent." Cited by Inada Toshinori, "*Tsurezuregusa* no kyōju wa naze okureta ka?" *Kokubungaku kaishaku to kyōzai no kenkyū* 22, no. 11 (Sept. 1957): 104. This same appreciation for Kenkō's lyric qualities is evident in the mid-fifteenth century tale, *Chōsei no mikado monogatari* (The Tale of Emperor Chōsei). It is the story of an emperor who has his ladies compose fifty seasonal and love poems on their names, in a mock poetry contest. Along the way there are allusions to Kenkō's extended treatment of the seasons and to the infamous line that says "a man who does not enjoy love is disappointing, like a precious wine cup that has no bottom."

82. Imagawa Ryōshun also lists *Makura no sōshi* between *Ise* and *Genji* in his *Ryōshun isshiden*. Cited by Kubota Jun, "Chūseijin no mita *Makura no sōshi*," *Kokubungaku kaishaku to kyōzai no kenkyū* 12, no. 7 (June 1967): 132. *Tsurezuregusa* is cited by warriors only in the fifteenth century.

83. Mary Ellmann, *Thinking About Women* (New York: Harcourt, 1968), 37.

84. Hayashi Razan, *Tsurezuregusa nozuchi*, 30, 36–37. Razan also cites China's Li Po and the priest Ikkyū of Daitokuji.

85. "His *Tsurezuregusa* is similar in form to Sei Shōnagon's *Makura no sōshi*." *Conversations with Shōtetsu* (*Shōtetsu monogatari*), 96.

86. An example of Kigin's defense of the women whom Razan seems to belittle appears in *Tsurezuregusa mondanshō*. See Satō Ninosuke, ed., *Tsurezuregusa mondanshō* (Seizandō shobō, 1926), 49. Kigin spells out precisely what in Kenkō's treatment is new, in order to qualify Razan's contention that Kenkō's writing is not inferior. *Makura no sōshi shunshoshō* (reprint, Iwanami shoten, 1931), 3 vols., gives Sei the same commentarial treatment as Kenkō.

87. *Ruijū meibutsukō* (Kondō shuppan, 1904).

88. Okanishi Ichū (1639–1711) visited *Tsurezuregusa* repeatedly, making his foray into *Makura no sōshi* appear insignificant by contrast. He was a Neo-Confucian and physician by training, but his connection with the *waka* poet Hosokawa Yūsai determined which two works he would approach. He was responsible for *Tsurezuregusa jikige* (*Tsurezuregusa* Explained Directly, 1686); a *mana* transliteration of *Tsurezuregusa* (1689); a compilation of "pure talks" on *Tsurezuregusa*, culled from various commentaries (1701); and *Makura no sōshi bōchū*, an interlinear commentary (1681). The last came from a publisher who was interested in classical parodies and produced Saikaku's *Shin Yoshiwara tsunezunegusa* as well. Hinotani Teruhiko, "Kōsei· e no eikyō—awasete Saikaku sakuhin to no kanren ni tsuite," in *Shosetsu ichiran Tsurezuregusa*, ed. Ichiko Teiji (Meiji shoin, 1970), 193–95. Yamaoka Genrin (1631–1672), although a haikai poet and student of Kigin, chose in his publications to go the didactic route with the two male authors. Even in his *Ta ga mi no ue* (1656, published in Kyoto in 1657), an accessible *kanazōshi* that presents teachings in a colloquial style some say shows the influence of Sei Shōnagon, he finds it necessary to mention only Kenkō. *Kinsei bungei sōsho* (Kokusho kankōkai, 1910), 3: 455–527. Given that this mention is an impassioned defense of morally ambiguous portraits in *Tsurezuregusa*, his avoidance of *Makura no sōshi* seems apt. *Shusho Kamo no Chōmei Hōjōki* (also known as *Hōjōki no shō*, 1657), is Genrin's commentary on the other Buddhist recluse. Ōwada Kigyū's (active mid-seventeenth century) *Tsurezuregusa kokon taii* is a compilation of Jumyō'in, Razan, and Teitoku's comments, and its character suggests it was used for lectures. *Tsurezuregusa kokonshō* and *Hōjōki shisetsu*, his other productions, are also minor. *Shisetsu* was widely read, but it is chiefly Buddhist in interpretation. Nakamura Yukihiko, "*Hōjōki, Tsurezuregusa no kinseiteki kyōju*," 322.

89. Kitamura Kigin, *Makura no sōshi shunshoshō*, 1: 35.

90. Evidence has been presented by Miyauchi Sanjirō for readers of *Tsurezuregusa* prior to Shōtetsu, in the form of lines in their works that he thinks show influence from *Tsurezuregusa*. First is the daughter of Hino Sukena, whose *Takemukigaki* was probably finished in 1349. Second is Ton'a, Kenkō's contemporary, friend, and fellow poet-priest. The lines from *Gumon kenchū* that Miyauchi presents involve popular phrases from Lao-tzu. The third candidate is Nijō Yoshimoto, putative author of *Masukagami*, which has many resemblances to *Tsurezuregusa*. Inada's rebut-

tals to Miyauchi's choices are found in Inada Toshnori, "*Tsurezuregusa* no kyōju wa naze okureta ka," 102–3.

91. Ivan Morris, trans. *The Pillow Book of Sei Shōnagon* (New York: Columbia University Press, 1967), 1: 154. Episode 139.

92. Edward Putzar, trans., "Inu Makura: The Dog Pillow," *Harvard Journal of Asiatic Studies* 28 (1968): 104.

93. "*Makura no sōshi* no kinsei bungaku e no eikyō," *Gekkan bunpō* 3, no. 4 (Feb. 1971), 102–3.

94. See Emori Ichirō, ed., *Edo jidai josei seikatsu ezu daijiten*, 9 vols., (Ōzorasha, 1994) for reproductions of various didactic texts for women, with their obligatory portraits of Sei.

95. See Emori Ichirō, ed., *Edo jidai josei seikatsu kenkyū*, Edo jidai josei seikatsu ezu daijiten bekkan, vol. 10 (Ōzorasha, 1994), 305.

96. Haga Yaichi, *Kokubungakushi jikkō* (Fuzanbō, 1899), 22, 120, 141.

97. Doi Kōchi, *Saitei bungaku josetsu* (1927; reprint, Iwanami shoten, 1949), 87–91, 275.

98. W. G. Aston, *A History of Japanese Literature* (London: William Heinemann, 1908), 184, 54, 65.

99. Naitō Keisuke and Kawashima Shōichirō, eds., *Kōshū yōsho kokugo kyōkasho* (Tanuma shoten, 1902), 2: 71–74.

100. Takada Mizuho, "*Tsurezuregusa* no eikyō—Kindai bungaku," in *Tsurezuregusa kōza*, ed. Yūseidō henshūbu (Yūseidō, 1974), 4: 257–58.

101. Utsumi Kōzō, *Tsurezuregusa shōkai* (Meiji shoin, 1919), 7.

102. Ichikawa Sanki, Introduction to *The Miscellany of a Japanese Priest*, trans. William N. Porter (London: Humphrey Milford, 1914; reprint, Rutland, Vermont: Charles E. Tuttle, 1974), 3, 5.

103. Yosano Akiko, "Koten no kenkyū," (1925), in *Yosano Akiko senshū*, ed. Yosano Hikaru and Shinma Shin'ichi (Shunjūsha, 1967), 4: 140.

104. "Sei Shōnagon no kotodomo" (1911), in Ibid., 4: 96.

105. Sano Yasutarō, *Tsurezuregusa kōgi* (Fujii shoten, 1932), 1: 1–4.

106. L. Adams Beck, Introduction to *The Harvest of Leisure*, trans. Kurata Ryū-kichi (London: John Murray, 1931), 8.

107. An exception is Nakamura Naokatsu's article "*Tsurezuregusa* kenkyū," which portrays Kenkō as a loyalist. Nakamura Naokatsu, "*Tsurezuregusa* kenkyū," *Nihon bungaku kōza* 13 (1928): 1–14; vol. 14: 15–22; vol. 15: 23–34.

108. Satō Haruo, *Tsurezuregusa, Hōjōki*, Gendaigoyaku kokubungaku zenshū 19 (Hibonkaku, 1937), 7–9, 403.

Chapter 6: Nation and Epic: *The Tale of the Heike* as Modern Classic

1. An earlier draft of this essay was written while I was a Mellon fellow at Stanford University in 1996–97. I would like to thank the faculty, graduate students, and

staff of the Asian Languages Department, and also faculty from various other departments, for their gracious hospitality and a stimulating period of scholarly research. Finally, I would like to thank Haruo Shirane and Tomi Suzuki for providing critical help in improving upon earlier drafts of this paper.

2. Komine Kazuaki, "Monogatari ron no naka no *Heike monogatari*," in *Heike monogatari hihyō to bunkashi*, ed. Yamashita Hiroaki (Kyūko shoin, 1998), 49–51.

3. Tsukamoto Yasuhiko, "Yasuda Yojūrō no bungaku to koten," in *Nihon rōman-ha: Yasuda Yojūrō, Ito Shizuo, Kamei Katsuichirō*, ed. Nihon bungaku kenkyū shiryō kankōkai (Yūseidō, 1977), 99.

4. Kobayashi Hideo, "*Heike monogatari*" (originally published in 1942), in *Mujō to iu koto*, in his *Kobayashi Hideo zenshū* (Shinchōsha, 1967), 8: 20–23.

5. The Kakuichi variant refers to those texts that had been in the custody of the guild (*tōdōza*) of blind reciters throughout the medieval period, the most famous being the one dictated in 1371 by the master reciter (*kengyō*) Kakuichi. Most scholars generally recognize two broad categories of *Heike* texts: those of the recited division (*kataribon*), which includes the Kakuichi text, and those of the read division (*yomihon*), which includes among others *Genpei jōsuiki*.

6. The only example of a premodern literary appreciation of *The Tale of the Heike* that I have found is the following stylistic observation by Motoori Norinaga from his *Ashiwake obune*:

> The 'Preface' to *Shinkokinshū* is on the whole a select language written in imitation of the refined style (*gagen*) of ancient times; it was not the current language of its day. That being said, as a further instance of refined language, one could cite the excellence of *The Tale of the Heike*'s prose. After that, around the period of the *Tsurezuregusa*, there are works which imitate the refined language of old, but one observes no [trace of] refined language in the language current at that time. *Taiheiki* appears to be written in an highly select language, but compared to *The Tale of the Heike* it is much inferior. Although it [*Taiheiki*] certainly shows the writer's skill, the evidence of its clumsiness betrays the vulgar language (*zokugen*) of its day.

Ōkubo Tadashi, ed., *Motoori Norinaga zenshū* (Chikuma shobō, 1968), 2: 41.

7. In *Gunsho ichiran*, compiled by Ozaki Masayoshi in 1802, for example, *The Tale of the Heike* is classified as a miscellaneous history (*zasshi*). The literary scholar Sekine Masanao in *Shōsetsu shikō* (1890) and Tsubouchi Shōyō in *Biji ronkō* (1893) referred to *The Tale of the Heike* as "street talk" (*kōdan gaisetsu*), or vulgarized history, and "unofficial history" (*yashi*), respectively. Surveys of the catalogs for the Imperial Library (Teikoku toshokan) in 1900 and for the Ōhashi Library in 1907 show *The Tale of the Heike* being classified as both history (*rekishi*) and literature (*bungaku*). See Takagi Ichinosuke, Ozawa Masao, Atsumi Kaoru, and Kindaichi Haruhiko, eds., *Heike monogatari jō*, Nihon koten bungaku taikei 32 (Iwanami shoten, 1959),

19–20; and Hirata Toshiharu, *Heike monogatari no hihanteki kenkyū* (Kokusho kankōkai, 1990), 1: 5–8.

8. These commentaries include *Heike monogatari shō* and *Heike monogatari kōshō*, both Edo period works, and the modern digest of these and other glosses, *Heike monogatari ryakkai* (1929).

9. The essay, "*Genpei jōsuiki to Taiheiki to*," is collected in *Ochiai Naobumi, Ueda Kazutoshi, Haga Yaichi, Fujioka Sakutarō shū*, Meiji bungaku zenshū 44, ed. Hisamatsu Sen'ichi (Chikuma shobō, 1968), 299–300.

10. See, for example, Hoshino Hisashi's article "*Heike monogatari Genpei jōsuiki wa gobyū ōshi*," *Shigaku zasshi* (Jan. 1898), collected in Takagi Ichinosuke, Nagazumi Yasuaki, Ichiko Teiji, Atsumi Kaoru, eds., *Heike monogatari*, Kokugo kokubungaku kenkyūshi taisei 9 (Sanseidō, 1960), 80–89.

11. Sakakibara Chizuru, "Antoku tennō ibun: kinsei kōki ni miru *Heike monogatari* kyōju no ittan," in *Kokugo to kokubungaku* (Jan. 1997), 29–42.

12. Ibid., 36. In this episode, the otherwise admirable Shigemori, one of the favorite Heike heroes for ideologues of the emperor system, sends large sums of gold to Sung China in order to assure his posthumous fame through the performance of continuous commemorative masses on his behalf.

13. In what follows I am indebted to Hyōdō Hiromi, *Taiheiki "yomi" no kanōsei: rekishi to iu monogatari* (Kōdansha, 1995).

14. Ibid., 39–44. On the influence of Chinese political thought in medieval warrior chronicles, see also Yuge Shigeru, "Gunki monogatari no seidōkan wo megutte," in *Gunki to kanbungaku*, Wakan hikaku bungaku sōsho 15 (Kyūko shoin, 1993), 59–80.

15. Hyōdō, 192–93. The terms Southern and Northern Courts (*Nanbokuchō*) refer to the seats of the two rival imperial lines of the Daikakuji (southern) and Jimyōin (northern), located in Yoshino and Kyōto, respectively. Although the actual split into rival imperial factions occurred earlier, it was exacerbated when GoDaigo moved his court to Yoshino in 1336. The period subsequently known as the Period of the Northern and Southern Courts ended when GoKameyama returned to the capital in 1392. The period was characterized by strained relations between the ruling Ashikaga warlords and the imperial house.

16. See Matsuo Ashie's discussion in *Shintei Genpei seisuiki*, ed. Mizuhara Hajime (Shinjinbutsu ōraisha, 1988), 1: 17–47.

17. Hyōdō, 78–97, especially 78–83.

18. It must be emphasized, however, that imperial ideologues of both the Edo and modern periods appropriated a discourse that, in the medieval period, had functioned as much as a marginal or oppositional discourse to the increasingly hegemonic warrior regime as a justification for absolute imperial rule. See, for example, Amino Yoshihiko's discussion of GoDaigo's affiliation with outcasts (*hinin*) in *Igyō no ōken* (Heibonsha, 1986), 160–212; and Hyōdō on the connection between *Taiheiki* and marginal outcast figures in his *Taiheiki*, 48–72, and 118–26.

19. These views on the Kamakura and Ashikaga shogunates would later be en-shrined in *Kokutai no hongi*, where such periods were written off as a historical anomaly. See Robert King Hall, ed., *Kokutai no hongi: Cardinal Principles of the National Entity of Japan*, trans. John Owen Gauntlet (Cambridge: Harvard University Press, 1949), 113.

20. For a full discussion of this debate, see Hyōdō, *Taiheiki*, 220–33. For a discussion in English concerning the textbook controversy, see Carol Gluck, *Japan's Modern Myths: Ideology in the Late Meiji Period* (Princeton: Princeton University Press, 1985), 92–93.

21. Haga Yaichi, "*Genpei jōsuiki to Taiheiki to*," collected in *Ochiai Naobumi, Ueda Kazutoshi, Haga Yaichi, Fujioka Sakutarō shū*, ed. Hisamatsu Sen'ichi, Meiji bungaku zenshū 44 (Chikuma shobō, 1968), 299–300.

22. Fujioka, *Teikoku bungaku* 13 (May 1907), collected as "Heike monogatari" in *Ochiai Naobumi, Ueda Kazutoshi, Haga Yaichi, Fujioka Sakutarō shū*, 383–88.

23. For a discussion of Takayama's philosophy, see H. D. Harootunian's "Between Politics and Culture: Authority and the Ambiguities of Intellectual Choice in Imperial Japan," in *Japan in Crisis: Essays on Taishō Democracy*, ed. Bernard S. Silberman and H. D. Harootunian (Princeton: Princeton University Press, 1974), 110–55, especially 138–55.

24. Takayama Chogyū, "Taira no Kiyomori ron," collected in *Heike monogatari*, eds. Takagi et al., Kokugo kokubungaku kenkyūshi taisei (Sōgensha, 1957), 89–93.

25. Haga Yaichi, "Chūkun aikoku," in his "Kokuminsei jūron," in *Ochiai Naobumi, Ueda Kazutoshi, Haga Yaichi, Fujioka Sakutarō shū*, 236–39.

26. Haga, of course, was echoing a traditional view on the function of historiography. As late as 1887, the critic Tokutomi Sohō (1863–1957), in remarks aimed at the statesmen of his day, could still invoke *The Tale of the Heike*'s didactic function of "promoting virtue and chastising vice," reflecting a common medieval view of historiography. This didactic function of *The Tale of the Heike* goes back at least to the sixteenth century, as evident in a codicil to the Bunroku variant of *The Tale of the Heike*, dated 1595, which compares *The Tale of the Heike* to the Chinese *Shi ji* in its capacity to "promote virtue and chastise vice (*kanzen chōaku*)." Tokutomi, "*Heike monogatari* wo yomu," *Kokumin no tomo* (June 1887), collected in *Kokumin no tomo*, ed. Fujiwara Masahito (Meiji bunken, 1966), 1: 57–59. The Bunroku codicil is cited by Hirata Toshiharu, *Heike monogatari no hihanteki kenkyū*, 5.

27. Minamoto no Yoshitomo (1123–1160) was a warrior who helped spark the Heiji rebellion by forming an alliance with Fujiwara no Nobuyori (1133–1159) against the Emperor GoShirakawa and his warrior ally Taira no Kiyomori. The warrior Minamoto no Yoshinaka (1154–1184), also known as Kiso no Yoshinaka, fought against the Taira and later against the Emperor GoShirakawa during the Genpei Wars.

28. Haga Yaichi, "Kokuminsei jūron," *Ochiai Naobumi, Ueda Kazutoshi, Haga Yaichi, Fujioka Sakutarō shū*, 237–39.

29. Between 1906 and 1911, for example, state primary school textbooks for ele-

mentary school children were being published that included hymns (*shōka*) aimed at inculcating loyalty to the emperor and love of the nation (*chūkun aikoku*), together with hymns "praising martial valor and beautifying war." Taught to young school children, these same hymns were instrumental in shaping the nostalgic and lyrical view of *The Tale of the Heike*, as in the following verse from "Atsumori to Tadanori": "The warriors of Ichi no Tani are broken, the Heike lords have been struck dead. . . ." Some favorite episodes for hymn-setting included "Nasu no yoichi," "Sanemori," and "Hiyodori goe." See Karasawa Tomitarō, *Kyōkasho no rekishi* (Sōbunsha, 1956), 325–26, and Ichiko Teiji, ed., *Heike monogatari kenkyū jiten* (Meiji shoin, 1976), 523. One of the more extreme expressions of this lyrical view of *The Heike* was Igarashi Chikara's influential book-length study of military chronicles published first in 1920 as *Heike monogatari no shin kenkyū*, and in an expanded form as *Gunki monogatari kenkyū* (Waseda daigaku shuppanbu, 1931). In these works, Igarashi deployed an emotive vocabulary to describe *The Heike* with words that included such adjectives as *amai* (touching), *sabishii* (sad), and *utsukushii* (beautiful), and described the work as "deeply tragic" (*aizetsu no higeki*) and "beautifully pathetic" (*utsukushii hiai*), terms that, for Igarashi, were hallmarks of *The Heike*'s epic style.

30. For a discussion of these works, see Sasaki Hachirō's remarks on *Heike* commentaries in the supplementary essay (*hosetsu*) appended to the end of his *Zōho Heike monogatari no kenkyū*, rev. ed. (Waseda daigaku shuppanbu, 1967), 30–31.

31. Yamada's studies included Yamada Yoshio, *Heike monogatari kō*, ed. Kokugo chōsa iinkai (Kokutei kyōkasho kyōdō hanbai sho, 1911), and *Heike monogatari no gohō* (1914; reprint, Hōbunkan, 1954). In addition to establishing the variant *Heike* texts, both of these studies revealed the interest of Yamada and the agency that sponsored his work—Kokugo chōsa iinkai (Committee for Investigation of the National Language)—in *The Tale of the Heike* as a source for the study of the modern colloquial speech and the establishment of a standard literary style (*hyōjun buntai*). See Yamada's prefaces to both works (*Heike monogatari kō*, 1–9, and *Heike monogatari no gohō*, 1–12), as well as the committee statement (*shogen*) at the very beginning of the former.

32. Yamada Yoshio, *Heike monogatari jo* (Iwanami shoten, 1929), 13–39, especially 25–39.

33. This preference for defeated heroes coincided with the official appropriation of *hōgan biiki*. Episodes from the life of the beautified, and ultimately defeated, hero Yoshitsune became, in fact, one of the staples of prewar textbook selections illustrating martial values (see Karasawa, 694–708).

34. This shift is fully articulated in the work of Fujioka, for whom the literature of the Heian court and warrior-dominated Kamakura and Muromachi periods embodied the contrasting feminine and masculine qualities of *ninjō* (human feelings) and *giri* (obligation) together with corresponding attitudes of submission to and resistance to fate. See Oka Kazuo, *Koten no saihyōka ron: bungei kagaku no juritsu* (Yūseidō, 1968), 547–42, and the essay by Tomi Suzuki in this volume.

35. Yasuda Yojūrō, *Yasuda Yojūrō zenshū* (Kōdansha, 1986), 4: 233–94.

36. Ibid., 238.

37. Ibid., 264.

38. The connection between the prewar slogan "overcoming the modern" (*kindai no chōkoku*) and the quest for an essential Japanese culture uncontaminated by Western influences is discussed by Marilyn Ivy, in *Discourses of the Vanishing: Modernity, Phantasm, Japan* (Chicago: University of Chicago Press, 1995), 19, 73, and 101. For a complete discussion of the prewar usage of the term, see Tanizaki Akio, "Chōkoku no go no ben," in *Nihon rōmanha, Nihon bungaku kenkyū shiryō sōsho*, ed. Nihon bungaku kenkyū shiryō kankō kai (Yūseidō, 1977), 59–74.

39. Yasuda, 4: 274.

40. One signal failure of the canonical view of *The Heike* is its inability to account for, and even to discuss for that matter, the humorous and parodic elements in the work. As a corrective to this entrenched view, Abe Yasurō in a recent essay suggests that the parodic (*oko no monogatari*) may in fact be one of the major sources of *The Heike*'s discourse. See Abe Yasurō, "'Oko' no monogatari toshite no *Heike monogatari*: Tsuzumi hōgan Tomoyasu to 'warai' no geinō," in *Heike monogatari kenkyū to hihyō*, ed. Yamashita Hiroaki (Yūseidō, 1996), 121–43.

41. See Ueki Yukinobu, "Tōdōza no keisei to heikyoku," in *Heike monogatari katari to gentai*, ed. Hyōdō Hiromi (Yūseidō, 1987), 14–16; and Hyōdō Hiromi, "Kakuichibon *Heike monogatari* no denrai wo megutte—Muromachi ōken to geinō," in *Heike biwa: katari to ongaku*, ed. Kamisangō Yūko (Hitsuji shobō, 1993), 66–69; and Sunagawa Hiroshi, *Gunki monogatari no kenkyū* (Ōfūsha, 1990), 50–51.

42. *Tōdōyōshū*, in *Kaitei shiseki shūran*, ed. Kondō Heijō (Kyoto: Rinsen shoten, 1984), 27: 732. Guild books such as *Tōdōyōshū* recorded important traditions, handed down among the blind *biwa hōshi* who recited *The Tale of the Heike*, and were written down with the help of sighted assistants.

43. Hyōdō Hiromi, "Kakuichibon *Heike monogatari* no denrai wo megutte—Muromachi ōken to geinō," 55–65.

44. Noted by Tomikura Tokujirō in "Muromachi jidai no heikyoku," in *Heike monogatari kōza*, ed. Takagi Ichinosuke, Sasaki Hachirō, and Tomikura Tokujirō (Sōgensha, 1957), 2: 31. The performance of *The Tale of the Heike* in its entirety was known as *ichibu heike*.

45. Ogasawara Kyōko, "Chūsei kyōraku ni okeru kanjin kōgyō: Muromachi ki," in *Heike monogatari katari to gentai*, ed. Hyōdō Hiromi (Yūseidō, 1987), 145–53.

46. Cited from the translation of *Sandō* in J. Thomas Rimer and Yamazaki Masakazu, trans., *On the Art of the Nō Drama: The Major Treatises of Zeami* (Princeton: Princeton University Press, 1984), 155.

47. Matsuoka Shinpei, "Nō to ikusa monogatari," in *Anata ga yomu Heike monogatari: juyō to hen'yō*, ed. Yamashita Hiroaki (Yūseidō, 1993), 223–28.

48. Ogasawara, 148, notes that demon-warrior nō (*oni no nō*) was performed together with *kanjin heike* at temples linked to the Buddhist underworld.

49. Discussed in Misawa Yūko, "Monogatari no juyō to hyōgen: kōwaka-maikyoku no baai," in *Anata ga yomu Heike monogatari: juyō to hen'yō*, ed. Yamashita Hiroaki (Yūseidō, 1993), 199–219.

50. *Genpei tōjōroku*, for example, contains many battle narratives concerned with the warrior family of the Chiba; in the Enkyō variant's account of Kiso no Yoshi-naka's initial successes in Kaga and Etchū provinces, there are detailed references to the individual exploits of minor warriors who find no mention in the Kakuichi variant at all. On *Genpei tōjōroku*, see Yamashita Hiroaki, *Heike monogatari kenkyū josetsu* (Meiji shoin, 1972), 79–103; on the Enkyō variant of the Yoshinaka battle narrative, see Kanai Kiyomitsu, "*Heike monogatari* no Yoshinaka setsuwa to Zenkōji hijiri," in *Heike monogatari: katari to gentai*, 98–109, especially 102.

51. The otogi-zōshi are discussed by Sasaki in *Zōho Heike monogatari no kenkyū*, pt. 2, 245–47. As some *Heike* variant texts achieved authoritative status among elite elements of Edo society, gradually attracting the labor of commentators and textual scholars, its oppositional energy lingered on in the margins of Edo urban culture. For example, the earliest jōruri reciters, who probably emerged from the ranks of biwa hōshi that had remained outside the guild (*tōdō*), tended to draw on the more marginal world of kōwaka and nontextual oral traditions for their plots, while kabuki authors relied directly on Gidayū jōruri for plot lines. On *biwa hōshi* and jōruri reciters, see Tomikura, "Muromachi jidai no heikyoku," 27–28. Kabuki's reliance on *Gidayū jōruri* as a source for *Heike* plots is suggested in a passage in *Sekai kōmoku*, cited in Ichiko Teiji, *Heike monogatari kenkyū jiten*, 521.

52. On the popularity of *heikyoku* in the Edo period, see Tomikura Tokujirō, *Heike monogatari kenkyū* (Kadokawa shoten, 1964), 428.

53. In several recent studies, Shimizu Masumi has examined the ties during the late medieval and Edo periods between the blind reciters of *Heike* and elite aristocratic patrons, particularly the Yamashina house. The latter not only provided training and assistance to the reciters but were actively involved in the production of commentaries and the editing of *Heike* texts. Shimizu Masumi, "Biwa hōshi no shūbun: seisha hissui kosha shōgai," *Kokugakuin zasshi* (Jan. 1996), 75–76, and "*Heike monogatari* no juyō kinsei: chūshakushi wo fukumu," in *Heike monogatari hihyō to bunkashi*, ed. Yamashita Hiroaki, (Kyūko shoin, 1998), 135–57.

54. Introduction, *Heike monogatari jō*, Nihon koten bungaku taikei 32, 19.

55. Discussed in Sasaki, *Zōho Heike monogatari no kenkyū*, pt. 2, 652–93, and 726–31, and by Shioda Ryōhei, in "Koten to Meiji igo no bungaku," *Iwanami kōza: Nihon bungakushi* (Iwanami shoten, 1959), 14: 32–33.

56. Discussed in Sasaki, *Zōho Heike monogatari no kenkyū*, pt. 2, 653, 655, 665, 693–96.

57. Kikuchi's *Shunkan* is discussed in Tomihura Tokujiro, *Heike monogatari kenkyū jiten*, 524, and in Sasaki, *Zōho*, pt. 2, 695–96.

58. See Taguchi Ukichi, *Nihon kaika shōshi* (reprint, Kaizōsha, 1929), 121–22.

59. The *Rikkokushi* (Six National Histories) were official histories compiled in Chinese under the direction of the court during the Nara and Heian periods.

60. From Tani's analysis of the famous "Battle at the Bridge" ("Hashi gassen") episode in *The Tale of the Heike*'s fifth scroll, in Tani Hiroshi, *Heike monogatari,* Koten to sono jidai 4 (San'ichi shobō, 1957), 90.

61. As Fujioka, in particular, returned to the problem of *The Tale of the Heike* after his initial 1907 essay, he engaged the epic question more overtly, but always in a slightly distancing tone. See the chapter *"Genpei jōsuiki* to *Heike monogatari* (3): hyōron," in Fujioka Sakutarō, *Kamakura Muromachi jidai bungakushi* (Kokubun shuppansha, 1935), 191–204, especially 191–93, for his remarks on the question of *Heike*'s epic status; see also Chapter 3 of his *Kokubungakushi kōwa* (Iwanami shoten, 1922), 213–21.

62. Chōkō originally published his essay, "Kokuminteki jojishi to shite no *Heike monogatari*," in three installments in *Teikoku bungaku* 12 (Mar., Apr., May 1906). It is collected in *Heike monogatari,* ed. Takagi Ichinosuke et al., Kokugo kokubungaku kenkyūshi taisei (Sanseidō, 1960), 9: 93–112.

63. Anesaki Masaharu, "Jidai no kokuhaku toshite no jojishi," in *Nihon bungaku ronsan* (Meiji shoin, 1932), 529–40. The essay is also collected in *Heike monogatari,* ed. Takagi Ichinosuke et al., Kokugo kokubungaku kenkyūshi taisei (Sanseidō, 1960), 9: 125–34.

64. Iwano Hōmei, "Jojishi toshite no *Heike monogatari*," *Bunshō sekai* (Nov. 1910), reprinted in *Heike monogatari,* ed. Takagi Ichinosuke et al., Kokugo kokubungaku kenkyūshi taisei (Sanseidō, 1960), 9: 134–43.

65. These observations have been made by Kazamaki Keijirō, who has argued that Tsuda's study was an important methodological departure from the work of Haga Yaichi and other classical scholars at Tokyo Imperial University. As heirs of the nativist discourse on origins, which conflated the national essence (*kokutai*) with the narrative of the imperial house, the orthodox scholars did not readily accommodate conflict and class divisions in their narrative of literary history. Kazamaki discusses Tsuda's work in Kazamaki Keijirō, "Koten kenkyū no rekishi," in *Iwanami kōza: Nihon bungakushi,* ed. Iwanami Yūjirō (Iwanami shoten, 1959), 16: 19–27.

66. Tsuda Sōkichi, *Bungaku ni arawaretaru waga kokumin shisō no kenkyū* (Rakuyōdō, 1917) 2: 53–59.

67. See, for example, Takagi's remarks on Haga Yaichi's assessment of *The Tale of the Heike* in Haga's *Kokubungakushi jikkō* (Ten Lectures on Japanese Literature). Takagi Ichinosuke, "Heike monogatari kenkyūshi tsūkan," *Takagi Ichinosuke zenshū* (Kōdansha, 1976), 5: 262–63; in the same essay, Takagi's remarks on Igarashi Chikara's lyrical reading of *The Tale of the Heike,* 271–72.

68. Nagazumi Yasuaki, "Takagi Ichinosuke no *Heike monogatari* ron," in his *Heike monogatari no shisō* (Iwanami shoten, 1989), 131–42.

69. Takagi's early writings cite W. P. Ker's *Epic and Romance,* and in his 1952 essay "Jojishi no dentō," *Takagi Ichinosuke zenshū,* 2: 3, he makes explicit reference not only to Ker, but also to the theories of Aristotle and Herder. In another essay published in 1964, "Eiyū jidai rongi," *Takagi Ichinosuke zenshū,* 2: 131–32, he cites the then recently published work of Albert B. Lord, *The Singer of Tales,* as well as the

work of Maurice Bowra and the Japanese scholar Watsuji Tetsurō's study *Homerosu hihan*, which was published in 1921 and was a thorough exposition of the subject of Homeric criticism up to that time. All of Takagi's major writings on epic and Japanese literature are collected in volumes 1, 2, and 5 of *Takagi Ichinosuke zenshū*.

70. The ideas of Herder had been introduced to Japanese readers by the poet and scholar of English literature Ueda Bin (1874–1916) in the pages of *Teikoku bungaku*. In addition to introducing European theories about the formation of epic and folk poetry, which would have a huge influence on the scholarly reception of the *Man'yōshū* (see the essay by Shinada Yoshikazu in this volume), Bin was possibly the first scholar in Japan to suggest a comparison between Homeric epic reciters and the blind *biwa hōshi* who recited *The Tale of the Heike*. Bin's publications on epic and folk poetry included "Homerosu gaku no shinsetsu," *Teikoku bungaku* (Nov. 1895), included in Ueda Bin zenshū kankōkai, ed., *Teihon Ueda Bin zenshū* (Kyōiku shuppan sentaa, 1978), 3: 388–390; "Minzoku densetsu," *Teihon Ueda Bin zenshū*, 9 (1978): 94–117; and a two-part essay entitled "Min'yō" (1906, 1907), in vol. 9 of *Teihon Ueda Bin zenshū*. In this latter essay, p. 138, Bin compares the *biwa hōshi* to a Homeric rhapsode. For a discussion of Herder's ideas, see Theodore M. Andersson, "Oral Tradition in the Chanson de Geste and Saga," *Scandinavian Studies* 34, no. 4 (Nov. 1962): 225.

71. For a thorough discussion of Wolf's theories, see the introduction to F. A. Wolf, *Prolegomena to Homer, 1795*, trans. with an introduction and notes by Anthony Grafton, Glenn W. Most, and James E. G. Zetzel (Princeton: Princeton University Press, 1985), 3–35; John L. Myres, *Homer and his Critics*, ed. Dorothea Gray (London: Routledge and Kegan Paul, 1958), 69–93, especially 75–76; and Andersson, "Oral Tradition," 225–26.

72. See Ikuta Chōkō, "Kokuminteki jojishi toshite no *Heike monogatari*," 108–9.

73. Kwame Appiah, "Race," in *Critical Terms for Literary Study*, ed. Frank Lentricchia and Thomas McLaughlin (Chicago and London: University of Chicago Press, 1990), 284.

74. See David Quint, "Ossian, Medieval 'Epic,' and Eisenstein's Alexander Nevsky," in *Epic and Empire* (Princeton: Princeton University Press, 1993), 343–61.

75. Ironically, even as the theory of the folk epic was being embraced by Japanese scholars in the early years of the century, European scholars were beginning to attack it as a product of romantic ideology. See Hans Aarsleff, "Scholarship and Ideology: Joseph Bédier's Critique of Romantic Medievalism," in *Historical Studies and Literary Criticism*, ed. Jerome J. McGann (Madison: University of Wisconsin Press, 1985), 93–113. The same essay (pp. 105–6) also notes the close connection between national ideology and such products of romance philology as Karl Lachmann's "genealogical method of stemmatic reconstruction," which aimed at recovering "the ultimate archetype" of a text. It was this method, studied in Europe by Haga Yaichi and other scholars, that would later become enshrined in the *gentairon* (ur-text theory) so pervasive in *Heike* scholarship. On Haga Yaichi's study of European textual scholarship while in Germany, see Kazamaki, "Koten kenkyū no rekishi," 3–6; Tak-

agi Ichinosuke discusses the application of stemmatic theory to the *Heike* in "*Heike monogatari* kenkyūshi tsūkan," *Takagi Ichinosuke zenshū*, 5: 263–65. In the only contribution in English to this methodological approach, Kenneth Dean Butler proposed an original text in Chinese (*kanbun*), *Shibu kassen jō* (*Four Part Battle Account*), which was supposed to have been revised for recitation by generations of reciters, resulting in the Kakuichi dictated text of 1371. Although scholars now believe that the Shibu variant was in fact a much later work, Butler's lucid presentation still makes his essay a valuable introduction to *Heike* textual problems. Kenneth Dean Butler, "The Textual Evolution of *The Tale of the Heike*," *Harvard Journal of Asiatic Studies* 26 (1966): 5–51; for recent discussions of the *Shibubon*, see the two articles by Saeki Shin'ichi, "*Shibubon Heike monogatari* no saishūteki kaisaku wo megutte," *Kokugo to kokubungaku* 64 (Mar. 1987): 30–42, and "*Shibubon Heike monogatari* no Yoritomo kyoheitan wo megutte," *Nihon bungaku kenkyū* 21 (Feb. 1990): 69–82.

76. See also Takagi Ichinosuke's 1927 essay "Gunki mono no honshitsu II," in *Takagi Ichinosuke zenshū*, 5: 13–24.

77. *Takagi Ichinosuke zenshū*, 1: 76–100.

78. Scholars have characterized this as a bow to the reigning ideology of the times. See the *kaisetsu* to *Takagi Ichinosuke zenshū*, 2: 487.

79. Takagi, "Gunki mono no honshitsu II," in *Takagi Ichinosuke Zenshū*, 5: 16–19. In this passage, Takagi surely echoes the nativist (*kokugaku*) attack on Chinese; but he is also drawing on W. P. Ker's distinction between the epic and the more artificial romance, with its weakening foreign influences. See, for example, Ker's *Epic and Romance* (New York: Dover Publications, 1957), 20–21, and Takagi in "Nihon bungaku ni okeru jojishi jidai," *Takagi Ichinosuke zenshū*, 1: 84. For an excellent review of Ker's work, see Theodore M. Andersson, "A Glance Back at W. P. Ker's *Epic and Romance*," in *Envoi: A Review Journal of Medieval Literature* 3 (1995): 277–91.

80. Takagi, "Gunki mono no honshitsu II," *Takagi Ichinosuke Zenshū*, 5: 19–20.

81. Minamoto no Tametomo (1139–1170) was the eighth son of Minamoto no Tameyoshi who fought on the losing side in the Hōgen rebellion. On Takagi's pedagogical view of warrior literature, see his 1934 essay "Senkimono to kokugo kyōiku," in *Takagi Ichinosuke zenshū*, 5: 81–107.

82. See Yoshida Seiichi, *Gendai bungaku to koten*, in his *Yoshida Seiichi chosakushū* (Ōfūsha, 1981), 23: 74, and Kazamaki, 44.

83. Takagi's praise of Tametomo, who along with Masakado was one of the most overtly anti-imperial warrior-rebels in the literature, could hardly have been looked on favorably by the guardians of imperial ideology.

84. Ishimoda's principal studies dealing with *Heike* include *Chūseiteki sekai no keisei* (Itō shoten, 1946) and *Heike monogatari* (Iwanami shoten, 1957); Nagazumi's theory of medieval literature is set forth magisterially in his *Chūsei bungaku no tenbō* (Tokyo daigaku shuppankai, 1956); for Tani Hiroshi's views, see his *Heike monogatari*, Koten to sono jidai (San'ichi Shobo, 1957), 4.

85. It was also in 1946 that Ishimoda initiated the debate over the existence of a

heroic past (*eiyūteki jidai*) in Japan's ancient period. This was followed by the publication in 1948 of Egami Namio's horserider theory, which attacked the foundations of the imperial ideology by arguing that the line of Japanese emperors was not indigenous and immemorial but the creation of foreign conquerors who invaded Japan sometime in the fourth century A.D. For a full discussion of the debate on Japan's heroic past, see Saeki Arikiyo, "Eiyū jidai no ronsō," in *Kōza: Nihon bungaku no sōten 1: jōdai hen* (Meiji shoin, 1969), 113–40. For Egami Namio's horserider theory, see *Kiba minzoku kokka: Nihon kodaishi e no apurōchi* (Chūō kōronsha, 1967). See also Gary Ledyard's contribution to the debate, "Galloping Along with the Horseriders: Looking for the Founders of Japan," *Journal of Japanese Studies* 1 (1975): 217–54.

86. Ishimoda, *Chūseiteki sekai no keisei*, 239–56. On the medieval period (*chūsei*) as a dialectical critique of the ancient period (*kodai*), see 239–44.

87. Ibid., 250. Despite the Marxist methodology, Ishimoda's view of the *biwa hōshi* betrays an essentialist view of orality as somehow closer to origins and authenticity, and in this regard, his views are remarkably close to those of Yanagita Kunio. Yanagita's study of oral narrative *Monogatari to katarimono* (published in 1938) contained an essay on the Ariō narrative ("Ariō to Shunkan sōzu") in *The Tale of the Heike* that would later have a huge influence on folkloric approaches to the study of *Heike*. In that essay, Yanagita argued that the Ariō story in *The Tale of the Heike*, traces of which he discovered all over Japan, actually belonged to an originary world of oral narrative that predated any written texts, and was hence outside history. Wandering storytellers were both the sign and vehicle of this displaced and placeless narrative. In Ishimoda's Marxist vision, orality sublates written narrative into a higher synthesis, a synthesis that also conflates orality with a warrior peasantry rooted in the soil, and writing with an urban aristocracy. The Marxist discourse on *Heike*, then, is a kind of reharmonizing of all previous elements in the various discourses analyzed so far. For Yanagita's discussion of the Ariō narrative, see Yanagita Kunio, *Yanagita Kunio zenshū* (Chikuma shobō, 1990), 9: 93–111.

88. Ishimoda, *Chūseiteki sekai no keisei*, 248. This emphasis on a popular as opposed to an aristocratic origin for the *Heike*'s Buddhism coincided with the view of the Kamakura New Buddhism (*Kamakura shin bukkyō*) as an expression of a more purely indigenous, national religious sensibility as opposed to the so-called "old Buddhism" (*kyū bukkyō*) of the aristocratic class. It has resulted in an oversimplified and sentimental view of *The Heike*'s Buddhism, which, in addition to a variety of Pure Land influences, also includes elements of *hongaku* (original awakening) and, in some variants, Zen. One of the earliest proponents of the Kamakura New Buddhism influence in *The Heike*, in the form of Hōnen's Pure Land teaching, was Watsuji Tetsurō in "Nihon bungaku to gairai shisō I: bukkyō shisō," in *Iwanami kōza Nihon bungaku* (Iwanami shoten, 1933), cited by Imanari Genshō, "*Heike monogatari* to bukkyō," in *Shosetsu ichiran Heike monogatari*, ed. Ichiko Teiji (Meiji shoin, 1970), 215.

89. See Nagazumi Yasuaki, *Chūsei bungaku no tenbō*, 131–44.

90. For Nagazumi's analysis of the mixed-style, see *Chūsei bungaku no tenbō*, 25–46. Ever since Yamada Yoshio's pioneering work on *The Heike* textual variants and language forms, Heike studies have been inextricably linked to the discourse on the "national language" (*kokugo*). For a thorough discussion of *The Tale of the Heike* and the emergence of Japanese language study (*kokugogaku*), see Nishida Naotoshi, "*Heike monogatari* to kokugogaku: Kamakura jidai kōgo shiryō kara buntai/bunshō kenkyū no kōtaishō e," *Musashino bungaku* 30 (Nov. 1982): 27–31, and more recently by the same author, *Heike monogatari no kokugogakuteki kenkyū* (Izumi shoin, 1990), especially 12–42, and 262–83. On the dissemination of language standards and Western canon formation, see John Guillory, "Canon," *Critical Terms for Literary Study*, 233–49.

91. Cited, from remarks made by Masamune in a *Yomiuri shinbun* editorial (July 1, 1952), in Ozaki Hotsuki, "*Heike monogatari* to kindai sakka: Yoshikawa Eiji no baai," *Kokubungaku kaishaku to kanshō* (Feb. 1971), 111.

Chapter 7: Chikamatsu and Dramatic Literature in the Meiji Period

1. Milan V. Dimic, "Why Study Canonization?" *Canadian Review of Comparative Literature* 20, nos. 1–2 (1993): 182. I wish to express a debt of gratitude to Professor C. Andrew Gerstle, who read an early version of this paper and provided many valuable suggestions for its improvement.

2. These include the kabuki plays *Keisei hotoke no hara* (1699) and *Keisei mibu dainembutsu* (1702); jōruri jidaimono such as *Yōmei tennō shokunin kagami* (1705), *Komochi yamauba* (1712), and *Kokusenya kassen* (1715); and jōruri sewamono such as *Sonezaki shinjū*, the success of which is said to have reversed the fortunes of the theater at which it was first performed.

3. Kabuki hyōbanki kenkyūkai, ed., *Kabuki hyōbanki shūsei* (Iwanami shoten, 1972), 1: 244.

4. Mori Shū, *Chikamatsu Monzaemon* (San'ichi shobō, 1959), 91–98.

5. The passage from *Ima mukashi ayatsuri nendaiki* is quoted in Shuzui Kenji, Kondō Tadayoshi, and Otoba Hiroshi, eds., *Chikamatsu*, Kokugo kokubungaku kenkyūshi taisei 10 (Sanseidō, 1964), 82; for the *Sekai kōmoku*, see *Kyōgen sakusha shiryō shū 1: Sekai kōmoku, shibai nenjū gyōji* (Kokuritsu gekijō, 1974), 7–84.

6. See, for example, *Gidayūbon kōso ikken* (1833), the records of a dispute among publishers over the rights to publish jōruribon. The records show that among the works in question were many plays by Chikamatsu. The *Gidayūbon kōso ikken* can be found in Geinōshi kenkyūkai, ed., *Nihon shomin bunkashi shiryō shūsei* 7 (San'ichi shobō, 1977), 79–121. I am grateful to Professor Gerstle for pointing out this source.

7. Shuzui et al., 33–36; an English translation of a slightly shorter passage from *Naniwa miyage* can be found in Donald Keene, *Anthology of Japanese Literature* (New York: Holt, Rinehart and Winston, 1984), 386–90.

8. For *Zokuji kosui*, see Nihon zuihitsu taisei henshūbu, ed., *Nihon zuihitsu tai-*

sei, 3d series (Yoshikawa kōbunkan, 1977), 4: 133–78. The relevant passage is found in 145–48. Ryūtei Tanehiko's *Jōruribon mokuroku* is described in Shuzui et al., 376, and an excerpt is provided in the same work, 121–25.

9. This is clearly shown by the list of performances of Chikamatsu's plays (including later adaptions) found in Shuzui et al., 542–60. To take, for example, the last twenty years of the Edo period (1848–1867), the list indicates a total of 442 performances. Of these, 303 took place in the Kyoto/Osaka area, compared to only 92 in Edo. The contrast is even more striking when the figures for jōruri alone are compared. Of the total of 104 jōruri performances, most took place in Osaka (85), a much smaller number in Kyoto (12) and regional theaters (6), and only 1 in Edo.

10. Shuzui et al., 22. On the activities of Hayashi Tamiji and the Musashiya, see also Uemura Seiji and Kimura Takeshi, *Maruzen hyakunenshi* (Maruzen, 1980), 1: 208–18.

11. Michael C. Brownstein, "From *Kokugaku* to *Kokubungaku*: Canon-Formation in the Meiji Period," *Harvard Journal of Asiatic Studies* 47 (Dec. 1987): 446.

12. Related to this is the importance of the theater reform movement for the reform of prose fiction. As Karatani points out, the Meiji period privileging of the novel was in fact born out of this movement, especially of the efforts by the actor Ichikawa Danjūrō IX to express the inner reality of the characters he portrayed by doing away with the conventions of exaggerated makeup and grandiose gestures and presenting to the audience instead the simple naked face. See Karatani Kōjin, *Origins of Modern Japanese Literature*, ed. Brett de Bary (Durham: Duke University Press, 1993), 54–56. Such a conception of the theater, which, as Karatani notes, was soon accepted by the Meiji intelligentsia (55), no doubt also played a role in Chikamatsu's canonization. To see Chikamatsu's plays in terms of the psychological reality of the characters, however, required a de-emphasis of performance, especially in the case of jōruri, where it is difficult to associate the disparate elements of performance (puppets, chanted narration, and shamisen music) with the concept of the autonomous individual. Needless to say, this downplaying of the performance features of Chikamatsu's plays only reinforced the tendency to accept them as literature.

13. On amateur chanting and the phenomenon of *onna gidayū* in the late Edo and Meiji periods, see C. Andrew Gerstle, "Amateurs and the Theater: The So-called Demented Art of Gidayū," *Senri Ethnological Studies* 40 (1995): 37–57. One might speculate that a perception of immorality in the popular appeal of women chanters was a further reason why jōruri was not given serious consideration by the elite. In any case, the fact that Chikamatsu's plays were praised while the performance genre for which he wrote (jōruri) was not taken seriously is only another example of how the canonization of Chikamatsu's work involved the separation of text from performance.

14. Komiya Toyotaka, ed., *Japanese Music and Drama in the Meiji Era*, trans. Donald Keene (Tōyō bunko, 1956), 13–14, 87.

15. Hijikata Teiichi, ed., *Meiji geijutsu bungaku ronshū*, Meiji bungaku zenshū 79 (Chikuma shobō, 1975), 407.

16. Suematsu Kenchō, "Engeki kairyō iken," in Hijikata, 108–9, 105, 110.

17. Toyama Shōichi [Masakazu], "Engeki kairyōron shikō," in Hijikata, 146–48.

18. Toyama, 144–45.

19. Suematsu, 107.

20. Tsubouchi Shōyō, "Engeki kairyōkai no sōritsu," reprint in Meiji bunka zenshū 12 (Nihon hyōronsha, 1928), 252.

21. Tsubouchi Shōyō, "Makubesu hyōshaku no chogen," in *Bungaku no shisō*, Nihon shisō taikei 13, ed. Nakamura Mitsuo (Chikuma shobō, 1965), 86–87.

22. Tsubouchi, "Makubesu hyōshaku no chogen," 87.

23. In 1899, Hakubunkan published a third volume of Chikamatsu's plays, the *Zoku Chikamatsu jōrurishū*. The editing and republication of Chikamatsu's works continued throughout the late Meiji and Taishō eras, culminating in a burst of activity on the 200th anniversary of Chikamatsu's death in 1924, at which time no less than three different "complete works" were published: *Chikamatsu Monzaemon zenshū*, edited by Takano Tatsuyuki; *Dai Chikamatsu zenshū*, edited by Kitani Hōgin; and Fuji Otoo's *Chikamatsu zenshū*. For a comprehensive (though not exhaustive) list of modern editions of Chikamatsu's work, see the Appendix.

24. Kitamura Tōkoku, "*Uta nembutsu o yomite*," *Jogaku zasshi* 321 (1892); Uchida Roan, *Bungaku ippan* (Hakubunkan, 1892); Takayama Chogyū, "Chikamatsu Sōrinshi ga jinseikan," *Teikoku bungaku* 2 (1895); Takayama Chogyū, "Sōrinshi no josei ni tsuite," *Teikoku Bungaku* 4 (1895); and Takayama Chogyū, "Gikyokuteki jinbutsu to Chikamatsu Sōrinshi," *Taiyō* 4 (1895).

25. Tsubouchi Shōyō and Tsunashima Ryōsen, eds., *Chikamatsu no kenkyū* (Shun'yōdō, 1900).

26. Due to the fact that there are many plays of doubtful or uncertain authorship, the actual number of Chikamatsu's extant plays is impossible to determine. However, if we can take as a rough guide the five "complete" editions that have appeared since 1922, then the total number of Chikamatsu's jōruri plays could be said to lie somewhere between 104 and 147. This would mean that the twenty-four sewamono represent only one-sixth to one-quarter of the total. It should also be noted that of the five so-called "complete" editions, only the most recent, Iwanami shoten's *Chikamatsu zenshū*, also contains all of Chikamatsu's extant kabuki plays, which are at least as numerous as the sewamono. See the Appendix for more detail.

27. Tsubouchi Shōyō, "Waga kuni no shigeki," *Tsubouchi Shōyō shū*, Meiji bungaku zenshū 16 (Chikuma Shobō, 1969), 287; English translation from Donald Keene, *Dawn to the West: Japanese Literature of the Modern Era* (New York: Holt, Rinehart and Winston, 1984), 2: 411; emphasis added.

28. Tsubouchi, "Waga kuni no shigeki," 411.

29. Shuzui et al., 142. The section of *Bungaku ippan* dealing with Chikamatsu is reprinted in 142–53.

30. Ibid., 143. For the pertinent passage in *Naniwa miyage*, see Keene, *Anthology*, 388.

31. Tsubouchi and Tsunashima, 116.

32. Shuzui et al., 142.

33. Karatani, 82.

34. Brownstein, 445.

35. Earl Miner, *Comparative Poetics: An Intercultural Essay on Theories of Literature* (Princeton: Princeton University Press, 1990), 22–23.

36. Haga Yaichi and Tachibana Senzaburō, eds., *Kokubungaku tokuhon* (Fuzanbō, 1890), 202–24, 244–49.

37. Mikami Sanji and Takatsu Kuwasaburō, *Nihon bungakushi* (Kinkōdō, 1890), 2: 151–66, 429–58.

38. All the articles connected with the debate are reprinted in Shuzui et al., 205–11.

39. Hirosue Tamotsu, *Chikamatsu josetsu* (1957; rev. ed., Miraisha, 1963).

40. For the criticism of the literary method in the study of kabuki, see for example Gunji Masakatsu, *Kabuki no hassō* (1959; Nishizawa shoten, 1978), 3–5; Imao Tetsuya, *Henshin no shisō* (Hōsei daigaku shuppankyoku, 1970), 1–12, 261–98; on jōruri, see Tsuchida Mamoru, "Sewa higeki no seiritsu to hembō," *Kokubungaku: kaishaku to kanshō* 39, no. 11 (1974), 33; Gunji Masakatsu, "Genroku, Chikamatsu, gendai," *Kokubungaku: kaishaku to kanshō* 35, no. 10 (1970), 10–16. As for attempts to analyze jōruri and Chikamatsu's plays from a nonliterary point of view, mention should be made above all of the work of Yūda Yoshio, especially his *Jōrurishi ronkō* (Chūō kōronsha, 1975). By focusing on, among other things, the musical structure of jōruri, Yūda reveals many aspects of the genre and of the plays he deals with that escape traditional literary analysis. A similar approach is taken by C. Andrew Gerstle in his *Circles of Fantasy: Convention in the Plays of Chikamatsu* (Cambridge, Mass.: Council on East Asian Studies, Harvard University, 1986), which has the great merit for Western readers not only of introducing the musical structure of jōruri, but also of dealing at length with representative jidaimono in addition to the more familiar sewamono.

41. For a more detailed treatment of this problem, see William Lee, *Genroku Kabuki: Cultural Production and Ideology in Early Modern Japan* (Ph.D. dissertation, McGill University, 1996), 1: 22–42.

Chapter 8: *Kangaku*: Writing and Institutional Authority

1. Momo Hiroyuki, "Jōdai shisō, bunka" (Sept. 1939), in his *Jōdai gakusei ronkō*, Momo Hiroyuki chosakushū 2 (Shibunkaku shuppan, 1993), 14.

2. Yamaguchi Keiji, *Sakoku to kaikoku* (Iwanami shoten, 1993), 60.

3. The use of *magana* given here as an example employs the method of writing that Ō no Yasumaro refers to in the *Kojiki* preface as "spelling out entirely with *on*." Yasumaro also mentions two other methods of writing: "mixed use of *on* and *kun*" and "inscription entirely with *kun*." These latter two methods are used in most of the *Kojiki*. In Yasumaro's preface "on" refers to transcribing the syllables of words by

means of the original sounds of kanji, while "kun" refers to writing words with kanji used for their meanings. At any rate, in the *Kojiki* there is a conscious attempt to preserve the naturalness of Japanese. Nakata Norio argues that the writing of the *Kojiki* relied on the kundoku reading technique. Nakata Norio, *Nihon no kanji*, Nihongo no sekai 4 (Chūō kōronsha, 1982).

4. The practice of silent reading did not appear until texts were used in great numbers and did not become widespread until printing. It is likely that most people in ancient Japan read their highly valued texts out loud.

5. See the second series of national language textbooks, which were adopted in 1910 (Meiji 43), in *Nihon kyōkashō taikei Kindai hen 7 Kokugo 4* (Kōdansha, 1963).

6. Yata Tsutomu's commentary on the illustrations in Motoori Norinaga's *Kojikiden*, in *Rekishi no moji—kisai, katsuji, kappan*, Tōkyō daigaku collection III, ed. Nishino Yoshiaki (Tōkyō daigaku shuppankai, 1996).

7. Tsukishima Hiroshi, *Kana*, Nihongo no sekai 5 (Chūō kōronsha, 1981), 154. Even though the cursivization (*sōshoka*) of man'yōgana led to *onnade*, artistic cursivization developed in another, separate current of calligraphic practice. Ōno Susumu, *Nihongo no seiritsu*, Nihongo no sekai 1 (Chūō kōronsha, 1980), 301.

8. Tsukishima, *Kana*, 94, 67.

9. I use the term *wago* to refer to so-called *Yamato-kotoba*: the native language that does not include words derived from kanji (i.e., *kango*). However, there are cases where that which is thought to be "Japanese" includes Chinese words or words that have been influenced by Chinese; moreover, the regional and historical nature of *Yamato-kotoba* is difficult to determine, so that it is merely a concept of convenience. Since the term "native language" (*koyūgo*) refers to words that predate other, newer words introduced through linguistic contact, it goes without saying that it is also a historically formed object. Even imported Chinese words become fixed as Japanese when they are contrasted with European loan words, and then function as part of the "native language."

10. Miyazaki Michisaburō, "Kanji no bekkun ryūyō to kodai ni okeru wagahō seidojō no yōgo," *Hōgaku kyōkai zasshi* 28, no. 5 (1910), reprinted in *Miyazaki hakushi hōseishi ronshū* (Iwanami shoten, 1929).

11. This kind of dynamic is not limited to the general relationship between *on* and *kun* readings; it is also at work in the variety of readings for the many characters that have multilayered sets of *go-on* and *kan-on* readings rather than a single *on* reading. For *kun* readings as well, there are frequently multiple words assigned to each character. For example, the character with the *on* reading *jō* (Ch. *shang*) has several *kun* readings, including *ue* (upper side), *agaru* (elevate), and *noboru* (climb). The assigning of multiple pronunciations to an individual kanji has increased along with the development of the Japanese language. Nakata, *Nihon no kanji*, 95, 374.

12. The scripts of the Liao state (Khitan) in the tenth century, of Hsi Hsia in the eleventh century, and of the Chin dynasty (the Jurchens) in the twelfth century are all examples of such systems, with Japan's kana syllabary a comparatively early exam-

ple. This phenomenon of writing or reading Chinese into another language existed in the Liao state, and possibly also among the Jurchens and the Uighurs. The situation in Japan was different in that *kun* was made into a system, the *kundoku* techniques based on that system were continually practiced, and the kanbun lineage of style and locution born from kundoku became part of the Japanese language. On the formation of writing among peoples on the Chinese periphery, see Nishida Tatsuo, *Kanji bunmeiken no shikō chizu* (PHP, 1984). Moreover, kun readings and kundoku also occurred in other countries. In the Silla period in Korea, *hyangch'al* was used as a character-based inscription for *hyangga* poetry in the seventh century; it is also said that Sol-chong created *t'o*, a notation for reading Chinese in the language of Silla. Among the lower classes of officials, the *idu* system (Chinese read or written out in accordance with Korean syntax, using some graphs for words of the native language) was used until the Choson period. Kim Moonkyung, "Kanji bunkaken no kundoku genshō," in *Wakan hikaku bungaku kenkyū no shomondai*, Wakan hikaku bungaku sōsho 8 (Kyūko shoin, 1988). Lee Kimoon, *Kankokugo no keisei* (Seikō shobō, 1983).

13. See Kim, "Kanji bunkaken no kundoku genshō," and Nakata, *Nihon no kanji*, 95, 395.

14. Nakata, *Nihon no kanji*, 96. Another interesting phenomenon is the persistence, due to "distance" from the original cultural and linguistic influence, of things that have been lost through historical change in the source country. Some examples of vanished or outdated linguistic or cultural elements that persisted in the periphery include the *on* readings of Japanese kanji, the preservation of texts that were lost in China, and the continued existence of Zen Buddhism, which in China was absorbed by Neo-Confucianism and ceased to be practiced.

15. Even in the Tang period, which saw the establishment of the examination system, the literary leanings that had been part of the Chinese tradition from the Six Dynasties on were hardly absent. Moreover, the classical studies that were recognized by the examination system became a fixed, empty, and overcomplicated framework, which eventually led to a reaction against them. See Togawa Yoshirō, *Jukyōshi* (Yamakawa shuppansha, 1987), Section 4.

16. On this topic, and on the issues discussed below, see Chapter 1 of Wajima Yoshio, *Chūsei no jugaku* (Yoshikawa kōbunkan, 1965).

17. The demands of these rites of the kami are clearly indicated by the governmental organization of the ritsuryō state. Although it was based on the Tang system, it did not reproduce the unitary Chinese imperial monarchy, but had the dual structure of a dyarchy, in which the Daijōkan (Council of State; the political system) and the Jingikan (Council of *Kami* Affairs; the ritual system) were arranged alongside each other.

18. This period was later called the "Engi (901–923) and Tenryaku (947–957) reigns" and idealized as a period of a government preceding the oppression of the Fujiwara regency.

19. For a reevaluation of Heian nobility, see Takahashi Masaaki, "Jōshikiteki ki-

zokuzō, bushizō no sōshutsu katei," in *Nihonshi ni okeru kō to shi*, ed. Rekishi to hōhō henshū iinkai (Aoki shoten, 1996).

20. Matsunaga Sekigo's *Irinshō* (1640), in *Fujiwara Seika, Hayashi Razan*, Nihon shisō taikei 28 (Iwanami shoten, 1975).

21. Maruyama Masao, *Nihon seijishisōshi kenkyū* (Tōkyō daigaku shuppankai, 1951), translated into English by Mikiso Hane as *Studies in the Intellectual History of Tokugawa Japan* (Princeton: Princeton University Press, 1974).

22. On the currents of Confucianism and their place in the varied thought of the Edo period, see Kurozumi Makoto, "Jugaku to kinsei Nihon shakai," *Nihon tsūshi: kinsei 3* (Iwanami shoten, 1994), and "Kinsei Nihon shisōshi ni okeru bukkyō no ichi," *Nihon no bukkyō* 1 (Hōzōkan, 1994). On Maruyama, see Kurozumi, "Nihon shisō to sono kenkyū—Chūgoku ninshiki o megutte," in *Chūgoku—shakai to bunka* 11 (June 1996).

23. It is thought that the reasons woodblock rather than moveable-type printing became widespread during the Edo period were the use of hiragana, ease of adding kunten to kanji, and the prevalence of illustrations. Had only kanji been used, or if, on the other hand, katakana had been the only system, then movable type would have been much easier to use, and it is likely that it would have been adopted much sooner.

24. Kurozumi Makoto, "Jukyō no Nihonka o megutte," *Nihongaku* 12 (Nov. 1988).

25. On nationalism and the composite nature of Japanese Confucianism, see Kurozumi Makoto, "Tokugawa zenki jukyō no seikaku," *Shisō* 792 (June 1990), translated by Herman Ooms as "The Nature of Early Tokugawa Confucianism," *Journal of Japanese Studies* 20, no. 2 (autumn 1994).

26. See Kurozumi, "Jugaku to kinsei Nihon shakai."

27. Preface to the first section of Sorai's *Yakubun sentei*, in *Ogyū Sorai zenshū* (Misuzu shobō, 1974), 2: 4.

28. On the positivistic, methodological aspect of kangaku, see Kurozumi Makoto, "Yakubun sentei o megutte (1)," *Jinbun kagakuka kiyō* 102 (Tōkyō daigaku kyōyōgakubu, March 1995).

29. On the appearance of a general awareness of an imperial nation (*kōkoku*) after the middle of the Edo period, see Watanabe Hiroshi, "Yasuhira to kōkoku," in vol. 2 of *Kokka to shimin*, ed. Kokka gakkai (Yūhikaku, 1987).

30. Ishikawa Matsutarō, *Hankō to terakoya* (Kyōikusha rekishi shinsho, 1978); Tsujimoto Masashi, *Kinsei kyōiku shisōshi no kenkyū* (Shibunkaku shuppan, 1990).

31. As described in vol. 2, pt. 5, chap. 8 of Watsuji Tetsurō, *Nihon rinri shisōshi* (Iwanami shoten, 1952).

32. Makino Kenjirō, *Nihon kangakushi* (Sekaidō Shoten, 1938), chap. 1, especially 245.

33. On the modern establishment of *kokubungaku*, see Fujii Sadakazu, "Kokubungaku no tanjō," *Shisō* 745 (Nov. 1994), and Momokawa Takahito, "Kokugaku kara kokubungaku e," in *Iwanami kōza Nihon bungakushi* 11 (Iwanami shoten,

1996). On *kokushi*, see Hyōdō Hiromi, "Rekishi to iu monogatari," in *Taiheiki yomi no kanōsei*, Kōdansha sensho mechie 61 (Kōdansha, 1995).

34. On the circumstances surrounding *kango* (Chinese words) in the early Meiji period, see Yamamoto Masahide, *Kindai buntai keisei shiryō shūsei: hasseihen* (Ōfūsha, 1978), and Katō Shūichi and Maeda Ai, eds., *Buntai*, Nihon kindai shisō taikei 16 (Iwanami shoten, 1989). On the general situation of kangaku in the Meiji period, see Miura Kanō, *Meiji no kangaku* (1981, privately published, held by the Literature Department of Tokyo University; rev. ed., Kyūko shoin, 1998).

35. "Barber" (*kamidoko*) became a "hair-dresser" (*rihatsuten*), "getting into the bath" (*furo ni hairu*) was termed "immersion" (*nyūtō*), one apologized for inappropriate behavior by saying, "rudeness" (*shikkei*). Miura Kanō, "Kangakuron," in his *Meiji no kangaku*, 18.

36. Makino, *Nihon kangakushi*, 231.

37. The publication of Inoue Tetsujirō's famous three volume study of Japanese Confucianism—*Nihon yōmeigakuha no tetsugaku* (1900), *Nihon kogakuha no tetsugaku* (1902), and *Nihon shushigakuha no tetsugaku* (1905)—took place at this time, toward the end of the Meiji period.

38. Taoka Reiun's *Seinenbun* (1896), and Endō Ryūkichi, *Kangaku no kakumei* (1910), cited by Miura Kanō, *Meiji no kangaku* (1981; rev. ed., Kyūko shoin, 1998), 46, 48.

39. Cited by Togawa Yoshirō, "Kangaku Shinagaku no enkaku to sono mondaiten," *Risō* 387 (June 1996), 19.

40. The word "Shina," a phonetic transcription of the word "China," was first used by scholars of Western studies in the middle of the Edo period, and then spread to kokugaku nativists and others. Because it is phonographic, it can be seen as a more neutral label, but it was probably chosen as a word that would reverse and deny the term "chūka" ("central blossom"), as the *shi* of Shina clearly had the meaning of "branch." On the changes in cultural perception involved in the Edo period use of "Chūgoku" and "Shina," see Kurozumi, "Nihon shisō to sono kenkyū."

41. Koyasu Nobukuni, "Kindaichi to Chūgoku ishiki," in *Kindaichi no aruke-orojii* (Iwanami shoten, 1996), 65, 67.

Chapter 9: Curriculum and Competing Canons

1. Much gratitude to Fujiwara Mariko for introducing me to important resources in Japan. Thanks also to Tomi Suzuki, David Lurie, Shang Wei, Martin Kern, and Lewis Cook, for their comments.

2. Terry Eagleton, *Literary Theory* (Minneapolis: University of Minnesota Press, 1983), 17.

3. Benedict Anderson, *Imagined Communities: Reflections on the Origins and Spread of Nationalism*, rev. ed. (London and New York: Verso, 1991).

4. The use of the terms "readerly" and "writerly" are not to be confused with the terms Roland Barthes uses in *S/Z*.

5. John Guillory, "Canon," in *Critical Terms for Literary Study*, 2d ed., eds. Frank Lentricchia and Thomas McLaughlin (Chicago: University of Chicago Press, 1995), 240.

6. Students chose from two of the following three sets of texts: (1) *Collection of Rituals* (*Li-chi, Raiki*) and the *Tso-chuan* (*Saden*) commentary on the *Spring and Autumn Annals* (*Ch'un-ch'iu, Shunjū*); (2) *Classic of Songs* (*Shih-ching, Shikyō*), *Ritual of the Chou Dynasty* (*Chou-li, Shurai*), and *Ceremony and Ritual* (*I-li, Girai*); or (3) *Book of Changes* (*Chou-i, Shūeki*, also called *I-ching*, or *Ekikyō*) and *Book of Documents* (*Shang-shu, Shōsho*, also called *Shu-ching*, or *Shokyō*).

7. The text, the original of which was lost in China, is otherwise known as *Rikyō zatsuei* (*Li-chiao tsa-yung*, Li Chiao's Various Poems), *Rikyō hyakunijūei*, and *Rikyō hyakuei* (Rikyō's Hundred Poems). Evidence for the pedagogic use of this and other texts mentioned here is found in early histories such as *Nihon sandai jitsuroku* (858–87, a *Rikkokushi*, Kokushi taikei), *Nihonkiryaku* (1036, Kokushi taikei), *Gōke shidai* (late Heian, edited by Ōe Masafusa, Shintei zōho kojitsu sōsho), *Fusō ryakki* (late twelfth century, by Bishop Kōen of Enryakuji, Kokushi taikei), *Goyuigō* (last testament) by Retired Emperor GoUda (1267–1324), and textbooks such as *Kuchizusami* (Humming Lines, 970, *Zoku gunsho ruijū*), an encyclopedic textbook written by Minamoto Tamenori to teach the children of nobility astronomy, geography, history, etc. Momo Hiroyuki, *Jōdai gakusei no kenkyū* (Shibunkaku shuppan, 1994), 401–5. Takeuchi Akira, ed., *Nihon kyōikushi* (Bukkyō daigaku tsūshin kyōikubu, 1989), 86–94.

8. *Gunsho ruijū*. The *ōraimono*, which took the form of exchanged letters, became popular from the late Heian period.

9. Shibukawa Hisako, "Heian kizoku no joshi kyōiku," in Kōza Nihon kyōikushi henshū iinkai, ed., *Kōza Nihon kyōikushi 1: Genshi, kodai, chūsei* (Daiichi hōki shuppan, 1984), 123; Momo Hiroyuki, *Jōdai gakusei no kenkyū* (Shibunkaku shuppan, 1994), 394–400.

10. The four fields of Confucian studies, law, literature, and mathematics were confined to eleven family houses. Ishikawa Ken, *Nihon gakkōshi no kenkyū* (Shōgakukan, 1968), 75–76.

11. Haga Kōshirō, *Higashiyama bunka no kenkyū* (Kyoto: Shibunkaku shuppan, 1981), 381–82.

12. Other texts include Fujiwara Mototoshi's (d. 1142) *Shinsen rōeishū* (New Selection of Poems to Sing), *Taketori monogatari, Utsubo monogatari*, and *Kokonchomonjū*. Ibid., 97–130.

13. *Kogo shūi*, which was written to validate the role of the Imbe family, supplements the histories found in the *Nihon shoki* and the *Kojiki*.

14. Both *Great Learning* and *Middle Way*, which were originally parts of the *Collection of Rituals* (*Li-chi*), were read along with the new Sung commentaries, reflecting the Sung Neo-Confucian emphasis on the Four Books—*Analects, Mencius, Great Learning, Middle Way*—over the Five Classics (*Gokyō*)—*Classic of Divination* (*I-ching, Ekikyō*), *Classic of Documents* (*Shu-ching, Shokyō*), *Classic of Songs* (*Shih-ching*,

Shikyō), *Classic of Ritual* (*Li-ching, Raiki*, which included the *Collection of Rituals*, or *Li-chi*), and the *Spring and Autumn Annals* (*Ch'un-ch'iu, Shunjū*)—a shift transmitted to Japan from the late Kamakura period particularly by Zen priests. The typical curriculum began with the *Classic of Filial Piety*, then proceeded to *Analects, Great Learning, Middle Way*, and then to *Mencius*, which was by far the least popular of the Four Books, before going to the Five Classics, of which the most appealing to the nobility were the *Classic of Documents* and *Classic of Poetry*. Haga Kōshirō, *Higashiyama bunka no kenkyū*, I, 285–87.

15. There were three commentaries on the *Yung-shih-shih* (*Eishishi*, Poems on Historical Events), *Ch'ien-tzu-wen* (*Senjimon*), and *Meng-ch'iu* (*Mōgyū*), respectively. Wajima Yoshio, *Chūsei no jugaku* (Yoshikawa kōbunkan, 1965), 240. Ishikawa Ken, *Nihon gakkōshi no kenkyū*, 148.

16. Yūki Rikurō, "Sengoku jidai no Ashikaga gakkō," Kōza Nihon kyōikushi henshū iinkai, ed., *Kōza Nihon kyōikushi* (Daiichi hōki shuppan, 1984), 1: 362, 364.

17. The Christian missionary Francis Xavier described the school in 1549 as the largest and most famous university in Japan. The average student was about 19 or 20 years of age and studied from anywhere from 4 to 8 years. Nakai Yoshihiro, "Chūsei shakai no kyōiku," in *Nihon kyōikushi*, eds. Tsuchiya Tadao, Yoshida Noboru, Saitō Shōji (Gakubunsha, 1993), 263.

18. Kawai Masayoshi, "Sengoku bushi no kyōyō to shūkyō," in his *Chūsei buke shakai no kenkyū* (Yoshikawa kōbunkan, 1973), 262–90.

19. Yonehara Masayoshi, *Sengoku bushi to bungei no kenkyū* (Ōfūsha, 1976), 930–31.

20. Records show that a number of late-Muromachi military leaders—such as Takeda Shingen, Uesugi Kenshin, Oda Nobunaga, Tokugawa Ieyasu—received their elementary education in temple schools. Ishikawa Ken, *Nihon gakkōshi no kenkyū*, 122–23.

21. The curriculum for *chigo*, child acolytes, as opposed to those who returned to secular life, was slightly different. The *Uki* (Right Record, 1265), written by Shūkaku Hōshinnō in 1185–89, shows that the chigo recited sutras such as *Hannya shinkyō, Jumyōkyō, Fumonbon* (*Kannonkyō*), and studied four areas—reading, calligraphy, Chinese poetry and prose composition, and *waka*—in addition to music. Ibid., 114–18.

22. A typical example from the *Dōjikyō* (Nihon kyōkasho taikei) is "The mouth is the gate to disaster, the tongue is the root of disaster" (*Kuchi wa kore wazawai no mon, shita wa kore wazawai no ne*) or "A person dies and leaves behind a name, a tiger dies and leaves behind a skin" (*Hito wa shishite na wo todome, tora wa shishite kawa wo todomu*). *Jitsugokyō* (*Zoku gunsho ruijū*) has phrases such as "A mountain is not respected because it is tall, it is respected because it has trees. A person is not respected because s/he is rich, a person is respected because s/he has wisdom" (*Yama takaki ga ue ni tōtokarazu ki aru wo motte tōtoshi to nasu. Hito koetaru ga yue ni tōtokarazu, chi aru wo motte tōtoshi to nasu.*). Karasawa Tomitarō, *Kyōkasho no rekishi* (Sōbunsha, 1956), 33.

23. From the printed text of "Mijikagami" in *Kokushigaku* 69 (Sept. 1957), 66–88, and *Kokushigaku* 70 (Oct. 1958): 49–78. The curriculum is unusual only in that Chinese poetry and prose, a standard part of kangaku, is missing, as are Japanese histories and court records (*yūsoku kojitsu*), which were usually a part of wagaku. Other records show that temple schools also taught mathematics. Yonehara Masayoshi, *Sengoku bushi to bungei no kenkyū*, 931. Mid-fourteenth century *ōraimono* such as *Isei teikin ōrai* (1356–75, Nihon kyōkasho taikei), and *Shinsen yūgaku ōrai* show that temple school education typically had nine subjects: (1) games and performance arts, (2) tea, (3) incense, (4) reading of non-Buddhist texts, (5) calligraphy, (6) waka, (7) renga, (8) music, and (9) Buddhist ritual (*hōji*). In the late Muromachi period, the first three subjects—games, tea, and incense—were downgraded and replaced by more practical subjects such as clothing and martial instruments. Ishikawa Ken, *Nihon gakkōshi no kenkyū*, 120–27.

24. *Zoku gunsho ruijū*. Ishikawa Ken, *Nihon gakkōshi no kenkyū*, 128–29.

25. Yonehara, *Sengoku bushi to bungei no kenkyū*, 934–35.

26. Ibid., 936.

27. The terakoya placed emphasis on arithmetic, a subject lightly regarded in the han schools.

28. According to one count of 199 terakoya administrators in the mid-eighteenth century, 22 percent were samurai, 36 percent commoners, 11 percent Buddhist priests, 14 percent Shinto priests, and 16 percent doctors. Tone Keizaburō, "Minshū no kyōiku juyō no zōdai to terakoya," in *Kōza Nihon no kyōikushi 2: kinsei I, kinsei II, kindai I*, ed. Kōza Nihon kyōikushi henshū iinkai (Daiichi hōki shuppan, 1984), 181.

29. Ibid., 180. According to one count, in 1752, there were more than 2,500 terakoya in Osaka alone, with some 75,000 students. Taga Akigorō, *Gakkō no rekishi* (Chūō daigaku seikyō shuppan, 1974), 44.

30. *Shōbai ōrai* (published 1693, available in Nihon kyōkasho taikei) was written in kana and differed from earlier ōraimono such as *Teikin ōrai* (1350, available in Tōyō bunko) that were written in kanbun or semi-kanbun.

31. Tone Keizaburō, "Minshū no kyōiku juyō no zōdai to terakoya," 200–201.

32. Karasawa Tomitarō, *Kyōkasho no rekishi*, 34–35, based on documents in *Ehime ken kyōikushi*, 454.

33. *Onna imagawa*, which, together with the *Onna daigaku*, was the most important moral training book for women, had a list of prohibitions such as do not "make light of one's husband, place oneself in the limelight, and fail to understand the way of heaven" (*otto o karoshime, ware o tate, tendō o wakimaezaru koto*). A typical curriculum for women consisted of *Onna imagawa*, *Hyakunin isshu*, *Onna shōgaku*, *Onna daigaku*, and *Yamato shōgaku*. Karasawa Tomitarō, *Kyōkasho no rekishi*, 35–36.

34. Taga Akigorō, *Gakkō no rekishi*, 45.

35. *Menoto no fumi* (Letters of a Wet Nurse, also called *Niwa no oshie*, attributed to Nun Abutsu, d. 1283, Nihon kyōiku bunko) states that women should be conversant with *The Tale of Genji*, *Kokinshū*, and *Shinkokinshū*. A number of other me-

dieval texts—such as *Menoto no sōshi* (Writings of a Wet Nurse), *Mi no katami* (Remembrance of Life, Muromachi women's handbook, available in Nihon kyōiku bunko), and *Chikubashō* (Hobbyhorse Collection, 1383, a moral text for warriors, attributed to Shiba Yoshiyuki, included in *Gunsho ruijū*)—use characters in the *Genji* as examples of how a woman should behave and suggest that knowledge of the text was considered a significant part of a young woman's education.

36. Nihon kyōkasho taikei. Karasawa Tomitarō, *Kyōkasho no rekishi*, 31.

37. Odaka Michiko, "Wagaku," in *Genroku bungaku no nagare* (Benseisha, 1992), 207–21.

38. In 1710, there were only 10 han schools, but by the 1780s they had spread throughout the country and multiplied to a total of 78.

39. Ishikawa Ken, *Nihon gakkōshi no kenkyū*, 444–45.

40. Karasawa Tomitarō, *Kyōkasho no rekishi*, 19.

41. From a record of a student at the Gakushūkan. *Ryō no gige* is an early commentary on the ritsuryō (legal) codes of the Yōrō period (717–24). Document cited in Karasawa, *Kyōkasho no rekishi*, 24.

42. The main data for the prewar middle school curriculum was found in Tasaka Fumiho, ed., *Kyūsei chūtō kyōiku, Kokugoka kyōkasho naiyō sakuin* (Kyōkasho kenkyū sentaa, 1983), and that for the postwar high school kokugo curriculum was taken from "Kōtō gakkō kokugoka kyōkasho dētabēsuran," an unpublished presentation by Abu Izumi, Yokohama Fujimigaoka Chūkōtōgakkō, at the 89th Zenkoku daigaku kokugo kyōiku gakka, Nov. 1995.

43. In 1887, there were 48 *jinjō chūgakkō* (43 public, 5 private), with about one for each prefecture. There were only five *kōtō chūgakkō* in the country, with programs in law, medicine, engineering, humanities, science, agriculture, and business.

44. Between 1886 and 1918, nine Teikoku daigaku were established, in Tokyo, Kyoto, Tōhoku, Kyūshū, Hokkaidō, Osaka, Nagoya, Taibei (Taihoku), and Seoul (Keijō).

45. Tobita Takio and Inoue Toshio, in *Kyūsei chūtō gakkō kyōka naiyō no hensen*, ed. Kyōkasho kenkyū sentaa (Gyōsei, 1984), 116–17.

46. Mikami Sanji and Takatsu Kuwasaburō, *Nihon bungakushi* I (Kinkōdō, 1890), 338.

47. Ochiai Naobumi was also the editor of the influential *Nihon bungaku zensho*, the 24-volume anthology of Japanese literature published in 1890–92.

48. *Kyūsei chūtō gakkō kyōka naiyō no hensen*, 125.

49. *Jinnō shōtōki, Yoshino shūi* (Collection of Tales at Yoshino, 1384), and *Taiheiki* in volume 7; *Hōgen monogatari, Heiji monogatari, Genpei jōsuiki, Konjaku monogatari,* and *Uji shūi monogatari* in volume 8; *Tsurezuregusa, Hōjōki, Izayoi nikki,* and *Tosa nikki* in volume 9, and *Masukagami, Ōkagami,* and *Eiga monogatari* in volume 10.

50. *Kokubungaku tokuhon,* in *Haga Yaichi senshū* 2: *kokubungakushi hen* (Kokugakuin daigaku, 1983), 73.

51. Tasaka Fumiho, *Meiji jidai no kokugoka kyōiku*, 107–8.

52. *Kokubungaku tokuhon*, in *Haga Yaichi senshū* 2, 23–24.

53. Fujiwara Mariko, *Koten kyōiku igiron* (unpublished Master's thesis, Waseda University, 1996), 41–42.

54. Ibid., 42.

55. Ueda Kazutoshi, "Kokugo to kokka to" (1894), *Ochiai Naobumi, Ueda Kazutoshi, Haga Yaichi, Fujioka Sakutarō shū*, Meiji bungaku zenshū 44 (Chikuma shobō, 1968), 110.

56. Tasaka Fumiho, *Meiji jidai no kokugoka kyōiku*, 4.

57. Karasawa, 280–81.

58. Yamamura Yoshiaki, *Nihonjin to haha* (Tōyōkan, 1971), 228.

59. Sakata Fumiho, *Meiji jidai no kokugoka kyōkasho*, 97.

60. *Kyūsei chūtō gakkō kyōka naiyō no hensen*, 154–55.

61. Takamori Kuniaki, *Kindai kokugo kyōikushi* (Hato no mori shobō, 1979), 328.

62. *Hōgen monogatari* and *Heiji monogatari*, while prominent in the prewar period, faded away in the postwar period, with *Hōgen* appearing only several times and *Heiji* disappearing completely.

63. Interestingly, the postwar high school kokugo curriculum includes Buddhist texts written in the vernacular (*kana hōgo*)—such as Dōgen's *Shōbōgenzō* (and *Shōbōgenzō suimonki*) and *Tan'nishō*, Shinran's teachings—which never appeared in Meiji textbooks.

64. *Jinnō shōtōki* appears from as early as the very first middle school textbook (*Kintai kokubun kyōkasho*) in 1888, as well as in Haga Yaichi's *Kokubungaku tokuhon* (1893), but today it is not even included in the Nihon koten bungaku zenshū series (Shogakukan) or the Shinchō Nihon koten shūsei series (Shinchōsha).

65. Hyōdo Hiromi argues that the word *chūshin* (loyal retainer) in the title of *Kandehon chūshingura* (1748), the jōruri drama of revenge that uses *Taiheiki* as its *sekai* (world), implied the notion of loyalty and revenge found in the story of Kusunoki Masashige. *Taiheiki yomi no kanōsei* (Kōdansha, 1995).

66. In "Kusunoki Masashige Brothers Retreat to Hyōgo" ("Kusunoki Masashige kyōdai Hyōgo gekō no koto"), also known as "Last Testament at Sakurai" ("Sakurai no ikai"), *Taiheiki* 2, Shinpen Nihon koten bungaku zenshū, 55: 302–9.

67. *Nihon kakū denshō jinmei jiten*, 186.

68. There is only one example of the *Gikeiki* in the postwar period, in a 1956 high school textbook.

69. Karasawa, *Kyōkasho no rekishi*, 698.

70. Both the *Genpei jōsuiki*, which can be considered a version of the *Heike monogatari*, and the *Heike monogatari* appear in prewar textbooks as a form of history, but in the postwar period, the *Genpei jōsuiki* disappears completely and is replaced by the Kakuichi version of the *Heike monogatari*, which is treated as a form of literature and which becomes the canonical *Heike monogatari*.

71. *Hachi no ki*, which draws on a story from the *Taiheiki*, also appears in Haga Yaichi's *Kokubungaku tokuhon* (1890).

72. Kyōgen, which rarely appears in the prewar curriculum (except for limited instances of *Hagi daimyō*, 1536) but becomes significant in the postwar period, is represented by *Hagi daimyō*, *Buaku*, *Kaminari* (Lightning), and *Kitsunezuka* (Fox Grave), with *Busu* and *Uri nusubito* (Melon Thief) being the most popular.

73. In the postwar period, *Kokusenya kassen* appears in only two special drama textbooks, *Kotengeki no sekai* (1963, 1970) and *Kinsei no engeki* (1957).

74. Further evidence of Chikamatsu's high stature in the postwar period is the widespread inclusion of *Naniwa miyage* by Hozumi Ikkan, a record of Chikamatsu's views on drama. The one exception to the postwar emphasis on Chikamatsu's sewamono is *Keisei hangonkō*, a Chikamatsu *jidaimono* (history play), which appears twice in 1956.

75. The only Saikaku text in a prewar textbook is "Nezumi no fumizukai" (Mouse Courier), a short story in *Seken munezanyo*, which appears in several early Shōwa textbooks.

76. *Kōshoku ichidai otoko* appears only once, in a 1957 high school textbook.

77. Also prominent in the postwar period are Yosa Buson (1716–1783) and Kobayashi Issa (1763–1827), whose haiku appear repeatedly. Issa is also represented by two haibun texts, *Chichi no shūen nikki* (Record of My Father's Last Days) and *Oraga haru* (My Spring), neither of which appear in prewar middle school textbooks.

78. Nun Abutsu was the wife of Fujiwara no Tameie (1198–1275), Teika's son, and the mother of Reizei Tametsuke (1263–1328), the founder of the Reizei poetry family.

79. *Izumi Shikibu Diary* does not appear in prewar textbooks, *Gossamer Diary* emerges only once (in 1893), and *Murasaki Shikibu Diary*, which was recognized early as a result of its association with *The Tale of Genji*, can be seen only three times. Both *Gossamer Diary* and *Murasaki Shikibu Diary*, however, appear frequently after the war, and *Izumi Shikibu Diary* emerges often to a lesser extent. *Tosa Diary* appears in the postwar period far more often than any of the women's diaries except for *Sarashina Diary*.

Works Cited

Aarsleff, Hans. "Scholarship and Ideology: Joseph Bédier's Critique of Romantic Medievalism." In *Historical Studies and Literary Criticism*, edited by Jerome J. McGann. Madison: University of Wisconsin Press, 1985, 93–113.

Abe Yasurō. "*Nihongi* to setsuwa." *Setsuwa no kōza 3: Setsuwa no ba*. Benseisha, 1993.

——. "'Oko' no monogatari toshite no *Heike monogatari*: Tsuzumi hōgan Tomoyasu to 'warai' no geinō." In *Heike monogatari kenkyū to hihyō*, edited by Yamashita Hiroaki. Yūseidō, 1996, 121–43.

Aeba Kōson, ed. *Chikamatsu jidai jōruri*. Hakubunkan, 1896.

——, ed. *Chikamatsu sewa jōruri*. Hakubunkan, 1897.

Akinaga Kazue and Tanabe Kayo, eds. *Kokinshū engoki: Tenri toshokan zō*. Kasama shoin, 1978.

Akiyama Ken. "*Ise monogatari*: 'miyabi' no ron." *Kokubungaku kaishaku to kyōzai no kenkyū* (Jan. 1979).

——. "Jijitsu to kyokō." *Kokubungaku* (May 1969).

——. "Joryū bungaku no seishin to genryū." *Kokubungaku kaishaku to kanshō* (Jan. 1963): 57–66.

——. "Joryū nikki bungaku ni tsuite no josetsu." *Ōchō joryū nikki bungaku hikkei*. Bessatsu kokubungaku. Gakutōsha, 1986.

——. "*Kagerō nikki* to *Sarashina nikki*: joryū nikki bungaku no hassei." *Kokubungaku* (Jan. 1981).

——. "Kodai ni okeru nikki bungaku no tenkai." *Kokubungaku* (Dec. 1965): 25–32.

——. "'Miyabi' no kōzō." In *Kōza Nihon shisō 5: Bi*, edited by Sagara Tōru, Bitō Masahide, and Akiyama Ken. Tokyo daigaku shuppankai, 1984.

——. "Naze onna ga bundan o shihaishita no ka." *Kokubungaku kaishaku to kanshō* (Aug. 1960): 32–37.

——. "Nikki bungaku to josei." *Kokubungaku kaishaku to kanshō* (Jan. 1954).

Akiyama Ken et al., eds. *Heian nikki*. Kokugo kokubungaku kenkyūshi taisei 5. Sanseidō, 1960.

Akiyama Kōsaburō. *Tsurezuregusa koroshi no suzuri*. Kadokawa shoten, 1988.

Amano Sadakage. *Zuihitsu shiojiri* 1. Compiled by Murase Kentarō, edited by Muromatsu Iwao. Teikoku shoin, 1907.

Amino Yoshihiko. *Igyō no ōken*. Heibonsha, 1986.

Anderson, Benedict. *Imagined Communities: Reflections on the Origins and Spread of Nationalism*. Rev. ed. London and New York: Verso, 1991.

Andersson, Theodore M. "A Glance Back at W. P. Ker's *Epic and Romance*." *Envoi: A Review Journal of Medieval Literature* 3 (1995): 277–91.

———. "Oral Tradition in the Chanson de Geste and Saga." *Scandinavian Studies* 34, no. 4 (Nov. 1962).

Anesaki Masaharu. "Jidai no kokuhaku toshite no jojishi." *Nihon bungaku ronsan*. Meiji shoin, 1932, 529–40. Collected in *Heike monogatari*, edited by Takagi Ichinosuke et al. Kokugo kokubungaku kenkyūshi taisei 9. Sanseidō, 1960, 125–34.

Appiah, Kwame. "Race." In *Critical Terms for Literary Study*, edited by Frank Lentricchia and Thomas McLaughlin. Chicago and London: University of Chicago Press, 1990.

Arai Mujirō. *Hyōshaku Ise monogatari taisei*. Yoyogi shoin, 1939.

Asakura Haruhiko, ed. *Kanazōshi shūsei*. Tōkyōdō shuppan, 1983.

Aston, W. G. *A History of Japanese Literature*. London: William Heinemann, 1908.

Ban Kōkei. *Kuni tsu fumi yoyo no ato*. In *Nishio Mitsuo sensei kanreki kinen ronshū Nihon bungaku sōkō*, edited by Nishio Mitsuo. Tōyō hōki shuppan, 1968.

Bokushiki. *Ressenden* (1763). *Edo jidai bungei shiryō* 1. Edited by Kokusho kankōkai. Meicho kankōkai, 1964: 1–18.

Bourdieu, Pierre. *The Field of Cultural Production*. New York: Columbia University Press, 1994.

Bowring, Richard. "The *Ise monogatari*: A Short Cultural History." *Harvard Journal of Asiatic Studies* (winter 1992): 401–80.

Brower, Robert H., trans., Steven D. Carter, introduction and notes. *Conversations with Shōtetsu* (*Shōtetsu monogatari*). Michigan Monograph Series in Japanese Studies 7. Ann Arbor: Center for Japanese Studies, University of Michigan, 1992.

Brownstein, Michael C. "From *Kokugaku* to *Kokubungaku*: Canon-Formation in the Meiji Period." *Harvard Journal of Asiastic Studies* 47 (Dec. 1987): 435–60.

Butler, Kenneth Dean. "The Textual Evolution of *The Tale of the Heike*." *Harvard Journal of Asiatic Studies* 26 (1966): 5–51.

Chatterjee, Partha. *Nationalist Thought and the Colonial World*. Minneapolis: University of Minnesota Press, 1986.

Chikamatsu meisakushū. Nihon meicho zenshū 1. Nihon meicho zenshū kankōkai, 1930.

Chikamatsu shoshi kenkyūkai, ed. *Shōhon Chikamatsu zenshū*. 36 vols. Benseisha, 1977–89.

Chikamatsu zenshū kankōkai, ed. *Chikamatsu zenshū*. 17 vols. Iwanami shoten, 1985–92.

de Bary, William Theodore, and Irene Bloom, eds. *Approaches to the Asian Classics.* New York: Columbia University Press, 1990.

Dimic, Milan V. "Why Study Canonization?" *Canadian Review of Comparative Literature* 20, nos. 1–2 (1993): 182.

Doak, Kevin Michael. *Dreams of Difference: The Japan Romantic School and the Crisis of Modernity.* Berkeley: University of California Press, 1994.

———. "What Is a Nation and Who Belongs? National Narratives and Ethnic Imagination in Twentieth-Century Japan." *American Historical Review* (Apr. 1997): 283–309.

Doi Kōchi. *Bungaku josetsu. Doi Kōchi chosakushū* 5. Iwanami shoten, 1977.

———. *Saitei bungaku josetsu.* 1927. Reprint, Iwanami shoten, 1949.

Doi Kōchi and Annie Shepley Omori, trans. *Diaries of Court Ladies of Old Japan.* Boston and New York: Houghton Mifflin Company, 1920.

Eagleton, Terry. *Literary Theory.* Minneapolis: University of Minnesota Press, 1983.

Ebara Taizō et al., eds. *Shin Yoshiwara tsunezunegusa. Teihon Saikaku zenshū* 6. Chūō kōronsha, 1959, 243–96.

Egami Namio. *Kiba minzoku kokka: Nihon kodaishi e no apurōchi.* Chūō kōronsha, 1967.

Ellmann, Mary. *Thinking About Women.* New York: Harcourt, 1968.

Emori Ichirō, ed. *Edo jidai josei seikatsu ezu daijiten.* 9 vols. Ōzorasha, 1994.

———. *Edo jidai josei seikatsu kenkyū.* Ōzorasha, 1994.

Enchi Fumiko. "Ōchō josei bungaku to gendai bungaku." *Kokubungaku* (Dec. 1965).

Endō Yoshimoto. "Fūryū kō." *Kokugo kokubun* (Apr. 1940).

Ericson, Joan. "The Origins of the Concept of 'Women's Literature.'" In *The Woman's Hand: Gender and Theory in Japanese Women's Writing,* edited by Paul Gordon Schalow and Janet A. Walker. Stanford: Stanford University Press, 1996, 74–115.

Felski, Rita. *The Gender of Modernity.* Cambridge: Harvard University Press, 1995.

Friedman, Ellen. "Where Are the Missing Contents? (Post)Modernism, Gender, and the Canon." *PMLA* 108, no. 2 (Mar. 1993).

Fuji Otoo, ed. *Chikamatsu zenshū.* 12 vols. Osaka Asahi shimbunsha, 1925–28.

Fujii Ransai. *Kansai hikki* (1715). *Nihon zuihitsu taisei.* Edited by Hayakawa Junzaburō. Yoshikawa kōbunkan, 1928.

Fujii Sadakazu. "Kokubungaku no tanjō." *Shisō* 745 (Nov. 1994).

Fujimura Tsukuru. "Kokubungaku rajio kōza no kaisetsu ni tsuite." *Nihon bungaku renkō: dai ikki.* Chūkōkan, 1927, 1–10.

Fujioka Sakutarō. "Heike monogatari." Reprinted in *Teikoku bungaku* 13 (May 1907). *Ochiai Naobumi, Ueda Kazutoshi, Haga Yaichi, Fujioka Sakutarō shū,* edited by Hisamatsu Sen'ichi. Meiji bungaku zenshū 44. Chikuma shobō, 1968, 383–88.

———. *Kamakura Muromachi jidai bungakushi.* Kokubun shuppansha, 1935.

———. *Kokubungakushi kōwa.* Iwanami shoten, 1922.

———. *Kokubungaku zenshi: Heianchō hen.* 2 vols.(Kaiseikan, 1905). Reprinted in Akiyama Ken et al., eds., Tōyō bunko 198, 247, Heibonsha, 1971, 1974.

Fujiwara Mariko. *Koten kyōiku igiron.* Unpublished Master's thesis, Waseda University, 1996.

Fukui Teisuke. *Ise monogatari seiseiron.* Yūseidō, 1965.

Geinōshi kenkyūkai, ed. *Gidayūbon kōso ikken.* Nihon shomin bunkashi shiryō shūsei 7. San'ichi shobō, 1977, 79–121.

Gerstle, C. Andrew. "Amateurs and the Theater: The So-called Demented Art of Gidayū." *Senri Ethnological Studies* 40 (1995): 37–57.

———. *Circles of Fantasy: Convention in the Plays of Chikamatsu.* Cambridge, Mass.: Council on East Asian Studies, Harvard University, 1986.

Gluck, Carol. *Japan's Modern Myths: Ideology in the Late Meiji Period.* Princeton: Princeton University Press, 1985.

Gotō Tanji and Okami Masao, eds. *Taiheiki,* vol 1. Nihon koten bungaku taikei 35. Iwanami shoten, 1960–62.

Guillory, John. "Canon." In *Critical Terms for Literary Study,* 2d ed., edited by Frank Lentricchia and Thomas McLaughlin. Chicago: University of Chicago Press, 1995, 233–49.

———. *Cultural Capital: The Problem of Literary Canon Formation.* Chicago: University of Chicago Press, 1993.

Gunji Masakatsu. "Genroku, Chikamatsu, gendai." *Kokubungaku: kaishaku to kanshō* 35, no. 10 (1970).

———. *Kabuki no hassō.* 1959. Nishizawa shoten, 1978.

Haga Kōshirō. *Higashiyama bunka no kenkyū.* Kyoto: Shibunkaku shuppan, 1981.

Haga Yaichi. "*Genpei jōsuiki* to *Taiheiki* to." In *Ochiai Naobumi, Ueda Kazutoshi, Haga Yaichi, Fujioka Sakutarō shū,* edited by Hisamatsu Sen'ichi. Meiji bungaku zenshū 44. Chikuma shobō, 1968, 299–300.

———. *Kokubungaku rekidaisen.* Bunkaidō, 1908.

———. *Kokubungakushi jikkō.* Fuzanbō, 1899.

———. "Kokuminsei jūron." In *Ochiai Naobumi, Ueda Kazutoshi, Haga Yaichi, Fujioka Sakutarō shū,* edited by Hisamatsu Sen'ichi. Meiji bungaku zenshū 44. Chikuma shobō, 1968, 235–80.

Haga Yaichi senshū iinkai, ed. *Haga Yaichi senshū* 7. Kokugakuin daigaku, 1992.

Haga Yaichi and Tachibana Senzaburō. "Kokubungaku tokuhon." In *Haga Yaichi senshū* 2, edited by Haga Yaichi senshū iinkai. Kokugakuin daigaku, 1983, 13–28.

———. "Kokubungaku tokuhon shoron." Reprinted in *Ochiai Naobumi, Ueda Kazutoshi, Haga Yaichi, Fujioka Sakutarō shū,* edited by Hisamatsu Sen'ichi. Meiji bungaku zenshū 44. Chikuma Shobō, 1968.

Hagino Yoshiyuki, Ochiai Naobumi, and Konakamura Yoshikata, eds. *Ise monogatari.* Nihon bungaku zensho 1. Hakubunkan, 1890.

Hall, Robert King, ed. *Kokutai no hongi: Cardinal Principles of the National Entity of Japan*. Translated by John Owen Gauntlet. Cambridge: Harvard University Press, 1949.

Harootunian, H.D. "Between Politics and Culture: Authority and the Ambiguities of Intellectual Choice in Imperial Japan." In *Japan in Crisis: Essays on Taishō Democracy*, edited by Bernard S. Silberman and H. D. Harootunian. Princeton: Princeton University Press, 1974, 110–155.

———. "Visible Discourses/Invisible Ideologies." In *Postmodernism and Japan*, edited by Masao Miyoshi and H. D. Harootunian. Durham: Duke University Press, 1989.

Harries, Philip. "*Fūryū*, a Concept of Elegance in Pre-Modern Literature." In *Europe Interprets Japan*, edited by Gordon Daniels. Tenterden, Kent, England: Paul Norbury Publications, 1984, 137–44.

Hasegawa Izumi. *Kindai Nihon bungaku hyōronshi*. Yūseidō, 1966.

Hayakawa Junzaburō, ed. *Kinsei bungei sōsho*. Kokusho kankōkai, 1911.

Hayashi Dokkōsai. *Honchō tonshi*. Collected in *Kanren setsuwashū*. Fukakusa Gensei shu 4. Edited by Shimahara Yasuo. Koten bunko, 1978.

Hayashi Dōshun. *Tsurezuregusa nozuchi*. Kokubun chūshaku zensho. Edited by Muromatsu Iwao. Kokugakuin daigaku shuppan, 1909.

Hayashi Tamiji, ed. *Chikamatsu chosaku zensho*. 2 vols. Maruzen, 1881–82.

———. *Chikamatsu jidai jōruri*. Musashiya sōshokaku, 1892.

———. *Chikamatsu sewa jōruri*. Musashiya sōshokaku, 1892.

Henderson, John B. *Scripture, Canon, and Commentary: A Comparison of Confucian and Western Exegesis*. Princeton: Princeton University Press, 1991.

Herrnstein Smith, Barbara. "Value." In *Canons*, edited by Robert von Hallberg. Chicago and London: University of Chicago Press, 1983.

Hinotani Teruhiko. "Kōsei e no eikyō—awasete Saikaku sakuhin to no kanren ni tsuite." In *Shosetsu ichiran Tsurezuregusa*, edited by Ichiko Teiji. Meiji Shoin, 1970.

———. "*Tsurezuregusa* no kyōjushi." In *Tsurezuregusa kōza 4: Gengo, gensen, eikyō*, edited by Yūseidō henshūbu. Yūseidō, 1974.

Hiraga Gennai. *Shin Tsurezuregusa*. Kinsei bungei sōsho 7. Edited by Hayakawa Junzaburō. Kokusho kankōkai, 1911.

Hirata Toshiharu. *Heike monogatari no hihanteki kenkyū*. 3 vols. Kokusho kankōkai, 1990.

Hirosue Tamotsu. *Chikamatsu josetsu*. 1957. Rev. ed. Miraisha, 1963.

Hirota Jirō. *Bashō to koten*. Meiji shoin, 1987.

Hisamatsu Sen'ichi. "Nikki bungaku to josei." In *Kokubungaku renkō: dai ikki*, edited by Fujimura Tsukuru. Chūkōkan, 1927.

Hisamatsu Sen'ichi, ed. *Keichū zenshū* 16. Iwanami shoin, 1976.

Hobsbawm, Eric, and Terence Ranger, eds. *The Invention of Tradition*. Cambridge: Cambridge University Press, 1983.

Hoshino Hisashi. "*Heike monogatari Genpei jōsuiki* wa gobyū ōshi." *Shigaku*

zasshi, Jan. 1898. In *Heike monogatari*, edited by Takagi Ichinosuke, Nagazumi
  Yasuaki, Ichiko Teiji, Atsumi Kaoru. Kokugo kokubungaku kenkyūshi taisei 9.
  Sanseidō, 1960.
Hyōdō Hiromi. "Kakuichibon *Heike monogatari* no denrai wo megutte—
  Muromachi ōken to geinō." In *Heike biwa: katari to ongaku*, edited by
  Kamisangō Yūkō. Hitsuji shobō, 1993, 55–82.
———. *Taiheiki "yomi" no kanōsei: rekishi to iu monogatari*. Kōdansha, 1995.
Ichijō Kanera. *Nihon shoki sanso*. Tenri toshokan zenpon sōsho 27. Tenri daigaku
  shuppanbu, 1977.
Ichiko Teiji, ed. *Heike monogatari kenkyū jiten*. Meiji shoin, 1976.
———. *Jinkei shō*. Koten bunko 450. Koten bunko, 1984.
Ide Tsuneo. "*Tsurezuregusa* no 'sōshi' teki seikaku." *Bungei to shisō* 29 (Dec.
  1966).
Igarashi Chikara. *Gunki monogatari kenkyū*. Waseda daigaku shuppanbu, 1931.
Ihara Saikaku. *The Great Mirror of Male Love*. Translated by Paul Gordon
  Schalow. Stanford: Stanford University Press, 1990.
———. *Zoku Tsurezure* (1695). *Taiyaku Saikaku zenshū* 16. Edited by Asō Isoji and
  Fuji Akio. Meiji shoin, 1977.
Ikeda Kikan. *Ise monogatari ni tsukite no kenkyū*. Ōokayama shoten, 1933–36.
———. "Jishō bungaku no rekishiteki kōsatsu." Reprinted in *Nikki waka bungaku*.
  Shibundō, 1968.
———. *Kyūtei joryū nikki bungaku*. 1927. Reprint, Shibundō, 1965.
———. "Nikki bungaku to kikō bungaku." In *Nihon bungaku kōza 5: zuihitsu,
  nikki*. Kaizōsha, 1934.
———. "Nikki wa dō shite bungaku tariuru ka." *Kokubungaku kaishaku to kanshō*
  (Jan. 1954): 69–72.
———. "Watakushi shōsetsu to shite no *Kagerō nikki*." *Monogatari bungaku*.
  Shibundō, 1951, 145–55.
Ikeda Shinobu. "Chihō fūzoku e no manazashi." *Nihon kaiga no josei-zō: jendaa,
  bijutsushi no shiten kara*. Chikuma shobō, 1998, 176–93.
Ikuta Chōkō. "Kokuminteki jojishi to shite no *Heike monogatari*." *Teikoku
  bungaku* 12 (Mar., Apr., May 1906). Collected in *Heike monogatari*. Edited by
  Takagi Ichinosuke, Nagazumi Yasuaki, Ichiko Teiji, Atsumi Kaoru. Kokugo
  kokubungaku kenkyūshi taisei 9. Sanseidō, 1960, 93–112.
Imai Takuji. *Heianchō nikki no kenkyū*. Keibunsha shuppan, 1935.
Imanari Genshō. "*Heike monogatari* to bukkyō." In *Shosetsu ichiran Heike
  monogatari*, edited by Ichiko Teiji. Meiji shoin, 1970, 204–37.
Imanishi Yūichirō, ed. *Tsūzoku Ise monogatari*. Tōyō bunko 535. Heibonsha,
  1991.
Imao Tetsuya. *Henshin no shisō*. Hōsei daigaku shuppankyoku, 1970.
Inada Toshinori. "*Tsurezuregusa* no kyōju wa naze okureta ka." *Kokubungaku
  kaishaku to kyōzai no kenkyū* 22, no. 11 (Sept. 1957).

Inoue Minoru. "*Makura no sōshi* no kinsei bungaku e no eikyō." *Gekkan bunpō* 3, no. 4 (Feb. 1971).

Inoue Tetsujirō. "Nihon bungaku no kako oyobi shōrai." *Teikoku bungaku* 1 (1895); pt. 1: 1–14; pt. 2: 1–13; pt. 3: 18–24.

———. *Nihon kogakuha no tetsugaku* (1902).

———. *Nihon shushigakuha no tetsugaku* (1905).

———. *Nihon yōmeigakuha no tetsugaku* (1900).

Inoue Tetsujirō and Nakamura Masanao. *Chokugo engi*. Keigyō-sha, 1891.

"Ise monogatari." *Jogaku zasshi* 10 (Dec. 20, 1885).

"Ise monogatari (tsuzuki)." *Jogaku zasshi* 12 (Jan. 15, 1886).

Ise Sadatake. *Ansai zuihitsu*. Collected in *Kojitsu sōsho* 11. Kokkai toshokan, 1903.

Ishida Ichirō and Kanaya Osamu, eds. *Fujiwara Seika, Hayashi Razan*. Nihon shisō taikei 23. Iwanami shoten, 1975.

Ishida Motosue. "Edo jidai no zuihitsu bungaku." In *Nihon bungaku kōza 5: zuihitsu, nikki hen*, edited by Yamamoto Mitsuo. Kaizōsha, 1934.

Ishihara Shōhei et al., eds. *Joryū nikki bungaku kōza*. 6 vols. Benseisha, 1990–91.

Ishikawa Ken. *Nihon gakkōshi no kenkyū*. Shōgakukan, 1968.

Ishikawa Matsutarō. *Hankō to terakoya*. Kyōikusha rekishi shinsho, 1978.

Ishimoda Shō. *Chūseiteki sekai no keisei*. Itō shoten, 1946.

———. *Heike monogatari*. Iwanami shoten, 1957.

Itō Masayoshi. "Chūsei *Nihongi* no rinkaku." *Bungaku* 40, no. 10 (1974).

Itō Sachio. "*Man'yō* tsūkai chogen." (Feb. 1904), *Itō Sachio zenshū* 5, Iwanami shoten, 1977.

Ivy Marilyn. *Discourses of the Vanishing: Modernity, Phantasm, Japan*. Chicago: University of Chicago Press, 1995.

Iwamoto Yoshiharu. "Fūryū wo ronzu." *Jogaku zasshi* 210 (Apr. 26, 1890).

Iwano Hōmei. "Jojishi toshite no *Heike monogatari*." *Bunshō sekai* (Nov. 1910). Reprinted in *Heike monogatari*, edited by Takagi Ichinosuke, Nagazumi Yasuaki, Ichiko Teiji, Atsumi Kaoru. Kokugo kokubungaku kenkyūshi taisei 9. Sanseidō, 1960, 134–43.

Iwasa Tadashi, ed. *Jinnō shōtōki*. Nihon koten bungaku taikei 87. Iwanami shoten, 1965.

Jingiryō. Shintei zōho kokushi taikei 22. Yoshikawa kōbunkan, 1998.

"Joshi to bunpitsu no gyō: bunpitsu no gyō joryū ni kōtsugō no koto." *Jogakku zasshi* 79 (Oct. 8, 1887).

Kabuki hyōbanki kenkyūkai, ed. *Kabuki hyōbanki shūsei* 1. Iwanami shoten, 1972.

Kaisen [pseud.]. "Bungakushi hensan hōhō ni tsukite." *Teikoku bungaku* 1, no. 5 (1895): 12–22.

Kaito Matsuzō. *Kokubungakushi*. Kyōiku shuppan kabushiki gaisha, 1976.

Kamata Jun'ichi. *Sendai kuji hongi no kenkyū: kōhon no bu*. Yoshikawa kōbunkan, 1960.

Kamata Masanori. *Kōshō Ise monogatari shōkai*. Nanboku shuppanbu, 1919.

Kanai Kiyomitsu. "*Heike monogatari* no Yoshinaka setsuwa to Zenkōji hijiri." In *Heike monogatari: katari to gentai*, edited by Hyōdo Hiromi. Yūseido, 1987, 98–109.

Kansaku Kōichi. "*Makura no sōshi* no chūshakushi." In *Makura no sōshi kōza 4: gengo, gensen, eikyō, kenkyū*. Yūseidō, 1976, 325–39.

Karasawa Tomitarō. *Kyōkasho no rekishi*. Sōbunsha, 1956.

Karatani Kōjin. "Japan as Museum: Okakura Tenshin and Ernest Fenollosa." Translated by Sabu Kohso. In *Japanese Art After 1945: Scream Against the Sky*, edited by Alexandra Munroe. New York: Harry Abrams, 1994.

———. *Origins of Modern Japanese Literature*. Edited by Brett de Bary. Durham: Duke University Press, 1993.

Katagiri Yōichi. *Ise monogatari no kenkyū*. 2 vols. Meiji shoin, 1968.

———. *Ise monogatari, Yamato monogatari*. Kanshō Nihon koten bungaku 5. Kadokawa shoten, 1975.

Katō Shūichi and Maeda Ai, eds. *Buntai*. Nihon kindai shisō taikei 16. Iwanami shoten, 1989.

Kawai Masayoshi. "Sengoku bushi no kyōyō to shūkyō." *Chūsei buke shakai no kenkyū*. Yoshikawa kōbunkan, 1973.

Kawase Kazuma. *Zōho kokatsujiban no kenkyū* 1. The Antiquarian Booksellers Association of Japan, 1967.

Kazamaki Keijirō. "Koten kenkyū no rekishi." *Iwanami kōza: Nihon bungakushi* 16. Edited by Iwanami Yūjirō. Iwanami shoten, 1959, 19–27.

Keene, Donald. *Anthology of Japanese Literature*. New York: Holt, Rinehart and Winston, 1984.

———. *Dawn to the West*. New York: Holt, Rinehart and Winston, 1984.

———. *Essays in Idleness*. New York: Columbia University Press, 1967.

———. "Japanese Aesthetics." *Philosophy East and West* 19, no. 3 (July 1969): 293–306.

———. *Seeds in the Heart: Japanese Literature from Earliest Times to the Late Sixteenth Century*. New York: Henry Holt and Company, 1993.

———. *World Within Walls: Japanese Literature of the Pre-Modern Era, 1600–1867*. 1976. Reprint, New York: Grove Press, 1978.

Keene, Donald, trans. *Major Plays of Chikamatsu*. New York: Columbia University Press, 1961.

Ker, W. P. *Epic and Romance*. New York: Dover, 1957.

Ketelaar, James Edward. *Of Heretics and Martyrs in Meiji Japan*. Princeton: Princeton University Press, 1990.

Kidō Saizō and Imoto Nōichi, eds. *Renga ronshū, haironshū*. Nihon koten bungaku taikei 66. Iwanami shoten, 1961.

Kim Moonkyung. "Kanji bunkaken no kundoku genshō." In *Wakan hikaku bungaku kenkyū no shomondai*. Wakan hikaku bungaku sōsho 8. Kyūko shoin, 1988.

Kimura Masanori. "Nikki bungaku no honshitsu to sōsaku shinri." *Kōza Nihon bungaku no sōten* 2. Meiji shoin, 1968.

———. "Nikki bungaku no seiritsu to sono igi." *Kokubungaku kaishaku to kanshō* (Jan. 1963): 51–56.

Kitamura Kigin. *Makura no sōshi shunshoshō* 1. 3 vols. Reprint, Iwanami shoten, 1931.

Kitamura Tōkoku. "*Uta nembutsu o yomite.*" *Jogaku zasshi* 321 (1892).

Kitani Hōgin, ed. *Dai Chikamatsu zenshū*. 16 vols. Dai Chikamatsu zenshū kankōkai, 1922–25.

Klein, Susan Blakeley. "Allegories of Desire: Kamakura Commentaries and the Noh." Ph.D. dissertation, Cornell University, 1994.

Kobayashi Hideo. "*Heike monogatari*" (originally published in 1942). *Mujō to iu koto. Kobayashi Hideo zenshū* 8. Shinchōsha, 1967.

Kobori Keiichiro. "'Bungaku' to iu meishō." *Geppō* 82. *Meiji geijutsu, bungaku ronshū*. Meiji bungaku zenshū 79. Chikuma shobō, 1975.

Koizumi Tōzō. *Kindai tanka-shi: Meiji-hen*. Hakuyōsha, 1955.

Kojima Noriyuki et al., eds. *Man'yōshū*. Shinpen Nihon koten bungaku zenshū 6. Shōgakukan, 1994.

Kokutai no hongi. Monbushō, 1937.

Komatsu Misao. "Shingakusharyū no *Tsurezuregusa* kenkyū." *Kanazawa bunko kenkyū* 81 (July 1962): 6–10.

———. "Tettsui kōryaku." *Kanazawa bunko kenkyū* 9, nos. 10–11 [95] (Nov. 1963).

———. "*Tsurezuregusa* chūshakushi." In *Tsurezuregusa kōza 3: Tsurezuregusa to sono kanshō II*, edited by Yūseidō henshūbu. Yūseidō, 1974.

Komine Kazuaki. "Monogatari ron no naka no *Heike monogatari*." In *Heike monogatari hihyō to bunkashi*, edited by Yamashita Hiroaki. Kyūko shoin, 1998.

Komiya Toyotaka, ed. *Japanese Music and Drama in the Meiji Era*. Translated by Donald Keene. Tōyō bunko, 1956.

Kōno Toshirō et al. *Seisen shin kokugo 1: Koten hen*. Meiji shoin, 1998.

Koyasu Nobukuni. "Kindaichi to Chūgoku ishiki." *Kindaichi no arukeorojii*. Iwanami shoten, 1996.

Kubota Jun. "Chūseijin no mita *Makura no sōshi*." *Kokubungaku kaishaku to kyōzai no kenkyū* 12, no. 7 (June 1967).

Kumasaka Atsuko. "Buson no haiku to *Tsurezuregusa*." *Renga haikai kenkyū* 17 (1958): 7–15.

Kurata Ryūkichi, trans., L. Adams Beck, Introduction. *The Harvest of Leisure*. London: John Murray, 1931.

Kurozumi Makoto. "Jugaku to kinsei Nihon shakai." *Nihon tsūshi: kinsei 3*. Iwanami shoten, 1994.

———. "Jukyō no Nihonka o megutte." *Nihongaku* 12 (Nov. 1988).

———. "Kinsei Nihon shisōshi ni okeru bukkyō no ichi." *Nihon no bukkyō* 1. Hōzōkan, 1994.

——. "Nihon shisō to sono kenkyū—Chūgoku ninshiki o megutte." *Chūgoku—shakai to bunka* II (June 1996).

——. "Tokugawa zenki jukyō no seikaku." *Shisō* 792 (June 1990).

——. "Yakubun sentei o megutte (1)." *Jinbun kagakuka kiyō* 102. Tōkyō daigaku kyōyōgakubu, March 1995.

Kyōgen sakusha shiryō shū 1: Sekai kōmoku, shibai nenjū gyōji. Kokuritsu gekijō, 1974.

Ledyard, Gary. "Galloping Along with the Horseriders: Looking for the Founders of Japan." *Journal of Japanese Studies* 1 (1975): 217–54.

Lee Kimoon. *Kankokugo no keisei.* Seikō shobō, 1983.

Lee, William. "Genroku Kabuki: Cultural Production and Ideology in Early Modern Japan." Ph.D. dissertation, McGill University, 1996.

Lewis, Reina. *Gendering Orientalism: Race, Femininity, and Representation.* London: Routledge, 1996.

Maeda Ringai. *Nihon min'yō zenshū.* 2 vols. Hongō shoin, 1907.

Makino Kenjirō. *Nihon kangakushi.* Sekaidō shoten, 1938.

Maruyama Masao. *Nihon seijishisōshi kenkyū.* Tōkyō daigaku shuppankai, 1951. Translated by Mikiso Hane, *Studies in the Intellectual History of Tokugawa Japan.* Princeton: Princeton University Press, 1974.

Matsumura Yūji. "'Yomibito shirazu'-ron e no kōsō." *Kokugo to kokubungaku* 73, no. 11 (1996): 54–64.

Matsunaga Sekigo. *Irinshō* (1640). *Fujiwara Seika, Hayashi Razan.* Nihon shisō taikei 28. Iwanami shoten, 1975.

Matsunaga Teitoku. *Taionki. Taionki, Oritaku shiba no ki, Rantō kotohajime.* Edited by Odaka Toshio. Nihon koten bungaku taikei 95. Iwanami shoten, 1964.

Matsuo Ashie. "*Sankō Genpei seisuiki* ni tsuite." In *Shintei Genpei seisuiki* 1, edited by Mizuhara Hajime. Shinjinbutsu ōraisha, 1988.

Matsuoka Shinpei. "Nō to ikusa monogatari." *Anata ga yomu Heike monogatari: juyō to hen'yō.* Edited by Yamashita Hiroaki. Yūseidō, 1993, 223–28.

McCullough, Helen Craig, trans. *Tales of Ise: Lyrical Episodes from Tenth-Century Japan.* Stanford: Stanford University Press, 1968.

Mikami Sanji and Takatsu Kuwasaburō. *Nihon bungakushi.* 2 vols. Kinkōdō, 1890.

Miner, Earl. *Comparative Poetics: An Intercultural Essay on Theories of Literature.* Princeton: Princeton University Press, 1990.

Misawa Yūko. "Monogatari no juyō to hyōgen: kōwakamaikyoku no baai." In *Anata ga yomu Heike monogatari: juyō to hen'yō,* edited by Yamashita Hiroaki. Yūseidō, 1993, 199–219.

Mishina Akihide. *Nihon shinwaron.* Mishina Akihide ronbunshū 1. Heibonsha, 1970.

Mitamura Masako. "Janru, daihitsu, seitenkan." *Nihon kindai bungaku* 50 (1994).

Miura Kanō. *Meiji no kangaku.* (1981, privately published, held by Literature Department of Tokyo University). Rev. ed., Kyūko shoin, 1998.

Miyazaki Michisaburō. "Kanji no bekkun ryūyō to kodai ni okeru wagahō seidojō no yōgo." *Hōgaku kyōkai zasshi* 28, no. 5 (1910). Reprinted in *Miyazaki hakushi hōseishi ronshū*. Iwanami shoten, 1929.

Mizuhara Hajime, ed. *Shintei Genpei seisuiki*. 6 vols. Shinjinbutsu ōraisha, 1988–91.

Mizutani Futō, ed. *Chikamatsu kessaku zenshū*. Waseda daigaku shuppanbu. 1910.

——. *Zoku Chikamatsu jōrurishū*. Hakubunkan, 1899.

Momo Hiroyuki. *Jōdai gakusei no kenkyū*. Shibunkaku shuppan, 1994.

——. *Jōdai gakusei ronkō*. Momo Hiroyuki chosakushū 2. Shibunkaku shuppan, 1993.

Momokawa Takahito. "Kokugaku kara kokubungaku e." *Iwanami kōza Nihon bungakushi* 11. Iwanami shoten, 1996.

Mori Ōgai. "Girishia no min'yō." *Shigarami zōshi* 35 (1892).

Mori Shū. *Chikamatsu Monzaemon*. San'ichi shobō, 1959.

Mori Shū, Torigoe Bunzō, and Nagatomo Chiyoji, eds. *Chikamatsu Monzaemon shū*. 2 vols. Nihon koten bungaku zenshū 43–44. Shōgakukan, 1972–75.

Morris, Ivan, trans. *The Pillow Book of Sei Shōnagon*. 2 vols. New York: Columbia University Press, 1967.

Mostow, Joshua S. "Byōbu-uta to uta-gatari to *Ise monogatari* to." In *Heian bungaku to kaiga*, edited by Nakano Kōichi. Ronshū Heian bungaku 5. Benseisha, forthcoming.

——. "Nihon no bijutsu-shi gensetsu to 'miyabi.'" In *Kataru genzai, katarareta kako: Nihon no bijutsu-shigaku 100-nen*, edited by Tokyo kokuritsu bunkazai kenkyūjo. Heibonsha, 1999, 232–39.

——. *Pictures of the Heart: The Hyakunin Isshu in Word and Image*. Honolulu: University of Hawai'i Press, 1996.

Motoori Norinaga. *Motoori Norinaga zenshū*. 23 vols. Edited by Ōno Susumu and Ōkubo Tadashi. Chikuma shobō, 1968–93.

Mulhern, Chieko. *Kōda Rohan*. TWAS 432. Boston: Twayne Publishers, 1977.

Muraoka Tsunetsugu. *Zoku Nihon shisōshi kenkyū*. Iwanami shoten, 1939.

Myres, John L. *Homer and His Critics*. Edited by Dorothea Gray. London: Routledge and Kegan Paul, 1958.

Nagazumi Yasuaki. *Chūsei bungaku no tenbō*. Tokyo daigaku shuppankai, 1956.

——. *Heike monogatari no shisō*. Iwanami shoten, 1989.

Naitō Keisuke and Kawashima Shōichi, eds. *Kōshū yōsho kokugo kyōkasho*. Tanuma shoten, 1902.

Nakai Yoshihiro. "Chūsei shakai no kyōiku." In *Nihon kyōikushi*, edited by Tsuchiya Tadao, Yoshida Noboru, and Saitō Shōji. Gakubunsha, 1993.

Nakamura Naokatsu. "*Tsurezuregusa* kenkyū." *Nihon bungaku kōza* 13 (1928).

Nakamura Yukihiko. "*Hōjōki*, *Tsurezuregusa* no kinseiteki kyōju." *Tsurezuregusa, Hōjōki*. Nihon koten kanshō kōza 13. Kadokawa shoten, 1960.

——. "*Tsurezuregusa* juyōshi." *Kokubungaku kaishaku to kanshō* 22 (Dec. 1957).

Nakata Norio. *Nihon no kanji.* Nihongo no sekai 4. Chūō kōronsha, 1982.

Nihon kyōkashō taikei: Kindai hen 7 Kokugo 4. Kōdansha, 1963.

Nihon zuihitsu taisei henshūbu, ed. *Nihon zuihitsu taisei* 4, 3d series. Yoshikawa kōbunkan, 1977.

Nishi Amane. *Hyakugaku renkan.* Lectures, 1870.

Nishio Minoru. "Zuihitsu no tokusei to kenkyū hōhō no mondai— *Tsurezuregusa Bansai shō* ni okeru rai-i no kōsatsu." *Bungaku* 2, no. 1 (Jan. 1934).

Nishida Naotoshi. *Heike monogatari no kokugogakuteki kenkyū.* Izumi shoin, 1990.

———. "*Heike monogatari* to kokugogaku: Kamakura jidai kōgo shiryō kara buntai/bunshō kenkyū no kōtaishō e." *Musashino bungaku* 30 (Nov. 1982): 27–31.

Nishida Tatsuo. *Kanji bunmeiken no shikō chizu.* PHP, 1984.

Nishiki Bunryū. *Keisei tsurezuregusa. Sharebon taisei* 1. Chūō kōronsha, 1978, 113–17.

———. *Koinu tsurezure. Kinsei shomin bunka* 80 (Oct. 1962): 1–16.

———. *Tsurezure imayō sugata. Nishiki Bunryū zenshū, ukiyozōshi hen, ge.* Edited by Nagatomo Chiyoji. Kinsei bungei shiryō 20. Koten bunko, 1988, 5–153.

———. *Tsurezure suigakawa. Sharebon taisei* 12. Chūō kōronsha, 1978, 155–82.

Nishimiya Kazutani, ed. *Kogo shūi.* Iwanami shoten, 1985.

Nishino Yoshiaki, ed. *Rekishi no moji—kisai, katsuji, kappan.* Tōkyō daigaku collection III. Tōkyō daigaku shuppan, 1996.

Nobuhiro Shinji. "*Tsurezuregusa* no eikyō—kinsei bungaku e no eikyō." In *Tsurezuregusa kōza 4: gengo, gensen, eikyō,* edited by Yūseidō henshūbu. Yūseidō, 1974, 235–55.

Odaka Michiko. "Wagaku." In *Genroku bungaku no nagare.* Benseisha, 1992.

Odaka Toshio. *Kinsei shoki bundan no kenkyū.* Meiji shoin, 1964.

———. *Matsunaga Teitoku no kenkyū.* Shibundō, 1953.

Ogasawara Kyōko. "Chūsei kyōraku ni okeru kanjin kōgyō: Muromachi ki." In *Heike monogatari katari to gentai,* edited by Hyōdō Hiromi. Yūseidō, 1987, 145–53.

Ogata Akiko. "Shakai henkaku to josei bungaku." In *Iwanami kōza Nihon bungakushi XIII: 20 seiki no bungaku 2.* Iwanami shoten, 1996, 237–55.

Ogyū Sorai. *Yakubun sentei. Ogyū Sorai zenshū.* Misuzu shobō, 1974.

Oka Kazuo. *Koten no saihyōka ron: bungei kagaku no juritsu.* Yūseidō, 1968.

Okada Shōji, ed. *Nihon shoki jindai kan shō.* Yoshida sōsho 5. Kyoto: Yoshida jinja, 1984.

Okazaki Yoshie. "Miyabi no dentō." *Bungaku* (Nov. 1943): 354–55.

Ōno Susumu. *Nihongo no seiritsu.* Nihongo no sekai 1. Chūō kōronsha, 1980.

Ooms, Herman, trans. "The Nature of Early Tokugawa Confucianism." *Journal of Japanese Studies* 20, no. 2 (autumn 1994).

Orbaugh, Sharalyn. *Japanese Fiction of the Occupation Period.* Stanford: Stanford University Press, forthcoming.

Otokuni. *Sorezoregusa.* (1704, published 1715). *Kokkei bungaku zenshū* 8. Edited by Furuya Chishin. Bungei shoin, 1918.

Ōwada Takeki. *Wabungakushi*. Hakubunkan, 1892.

Ozaki Hotsuki. "*Heike monogatari* to kindai sakka: Yoshikawa Eiji no baai." *Kokubungaku kaishaku to kanshō* (Feb. 1971), 110–15.

Page, Curtis Hidden. *Japanese Poetry: An Historical Essay with Two Hundred and Fifty Translations*. 1923. Reprint, Folcroft, Penn.: Folcroft Library Editions, 1976.

Pincus, Leslie. *Authenticating Culture in Japan: Kuki Shūzō and the Rise of National Aesthetics*. Berkeley: University of California Press, 1996.

Porter, William N., trans., Ichikawa Sanki, Introduction. *The Miscellany of a Japanese Priest*. London: Humphrey Milford, 1914; reprint, Rutland, Vermont: Charles E. Tuttle, 1974.

Putzar, Edward, trans. "Inu Makura: The Dog Pillow." *Harvard Journal of Asiatic Studies* 28 (1968).

Quint, David. "Ossian, Medieval 'Epic,' and Eisentsein's Alexander Nevsky." In *Epic and Empire*. Princeton: Princeton University Press, 1993, 343–61.

Rimer, J. Thomas and Yamazaki Masakazu, trans. *On the Art of the Nō Drama: The Major Treatises of Zeami*. Princeton: Princeton University Press, 1984.

Roden, Donald. "Taisho Culture and the Problem of Gender Ambivalence." In *Culture and Identity: Japanese Intellectuals during the Interwar Years*, edited by Thomas Rimer. Princeton: Princeton University Press, 1990, 37–55.

Saeki Arikiyo. "Eiyū jidai no ronsō." *Kōza: Nihon bungaku no sōten 1: jōdai hen*. Meiji shoin, 1969, 113–40.

Saeki Shin'ichi. "*Shibubon Heike monogatari* no saishūteki kaisaku wo megutte." *Kokugo to kokubungaku* 64 (Mar. 1987): 30–42.

———. "*Shibubon Heike monogatari* no Yoritomo kyoheitan wo megutte." *Nihon bungaku kenkyū* 21 (Feb. 1990): 69–82.

Saeki Shōichi. *Shintō no kokoro*. Nihon kyōbunsha, 1989.

Saigō Nobutsuna. "Kyūtei joryū bungaku no kaika." (The 1949 original title was "Kyūtei joryū bungaku no mondai.") *Nihon bungaku no hōhō*. 1955. New edition, Miraisha, 1960.

———. *Nihon kodai bungakushi*. Iwanami zensho 149. Iwanami shoten, 1951.

Sainte-Beuve, Charles-Augustin. "What Is a Classic?" In *The Critical Tradition: Classic Texts and Contemporary Trends*, edited by David Richter. New York: St. Martin's Press, 1989.

Saitō Kiyoe, Kishigami Shinji, and Tomikura Tokujiro, eds. *Makura no sōshi, Tsurezuregusa*. Kokugo kokubungaku kenkyūshi taisei 6. Sanseidō, 1960.

Sakaguchi Genshō. *Heike monogatari hyōshaku*. Chūkōkan, 1931.

Sakakibara Chizuru. "Antoku tennō ibun: kinsei kōki ni miru *Heike monogatari* kyōju no ittan." *Kokugo to kokubungaku* (Jan. 1997): 29–42.

Sakamoto Tarō. *Rikkokushi*. Yoshikawa kōbunkan, 1970.

Sakamoto Tarō, Ienaga Saburō, Inoue Mitsusada, Ōno Susumu, eds. *Nihon shoki*. Nihon koten bungaku taikei 67. Iwanami shoten, 1965.

Sano Yasutarō. *Tsurezuregusa kōgi* 1. Fujii shoten, 1932.

Santō Kyōden. *Kaibutsu Tsurezuregusa* (1792). Manuscript preserved in Collection of Daitōkyū kinen bunko (Tokyo).

Sasaki Hachirō. *Zōho Heike monogatari no kenkyū*. Waseda daigaku shuppanbu. Rev. ed. 1967.

Satō Dōshin. *"Nihon bijutsu" tanjō*. Kōdansha, 1996.

Satō Haruo. *Tsurezuregusa, Hōjōki*. Gendaigoyaku kokubungaku zenshū 19. Hibonkaku, 1937.

Satō Ninosuke, ed. *Tsurezuregusa mondanshō*. Seizandō shobō, 1926.

Schor, Naomi. "Dreaming Dissymmetry: Barthes, Foucault, and Sexual Difference." In *Men in Feminism*, edited by Alice Jardine and Paul Smith. London and New York: Methuen, 1987.

Sekiba Takeshi. "*Tsurezuregusa* no eikyō, kyōju to kenkyūshi—kinsei zenki o chūshin ni." *Kokubungaku kaishaku to kanshō* 35, no. 3 (Mar. 1970): 99–102.

Shaku-Nihongi. Shintei zōho kokushi taikei 8. Yoshikawa kōbunkan, 1998.

Sharf, Robert H. "The Zen of Japanese Nationalism." In *Curators of the Buddha: The Study of Buddhism under Colonialism*, edited by Donald S. Lopez, Jr. Chicago: University of Chicago Press, 1995.

Shibukawa Hisako. "Heian kizoku no joshi kyōiku." In *Kōza Nihon kyōikushi 1: Genshi, kodai, chūsei*, edited by Kōza Nihon kyōikushi henshū iinkai. Daiichi hōki shuppan, 1984.

Shida Gishū. "Haga Hakushi to Nihon shiikagaku." *Kokugo to kokubungaku* 14, no. 4 (1937): 78–87.

———. "Nihon min'yō gairon." *Teikoku bungaku* 12, no. 2 (1906): 1–15; no. 3, 32–44; no. 5, 13–27; no. 9, 24–43.

Shigematsu Nobuhiro. "*Tsurezuregusa* kenkyūshi." *Kokugo to kokubungaku* 6, nos. 6–7 (1929).

Shigetomo Ki, Shuzui Ki, and Ōtomo Tadakuni, eds. *Chikamatsu jōrurishū*. 2 vols. Nihon koten bungaku taikei 49–50. Iwanami shoten, 1958–59.

Shimahara Yasuo, ed. *Fusō in'itsuden*. In *Hencho fukusei*. Fukakusa Gensei shū 3. Koten bunko, 1977.

Shimaki Akahiko. *Kadō shōken*. 1924. Iwanami shoten, 1983.

Shimamoto Shōichi. "Kinsei shotō ni okeru *Tsurezuregusa* no kyōju—josetsu, Fujiwara Seika no baai." *Kinsei shoki bungei* 1 (Dec. 1969).

———. *Matsunaga Teitoku—haikaishi e no michi*. Kyōyō gakkō sōsho 4. Hōsei daigaku shuppankyoku, 1989.

Shimauchi Yūko. *Tsurezuregusa no henbō*. Perikansha, 1992.

———. "*Tsurezuregusa* to yōkyoku." *Kaishaku* 33, no. 11 (Nov. 1987).

Shimizu Masami. "Biwa hōshi no shūbun: seisha hissui kosha shōgai." *Kokugakuin zasshi* (Jan. 1996).

———. "*Heike monogatari* no juyō kinsei: chūshakushi wo fukumu." In *Heike monogatari hihyō to bunkashi*, edited by Yamashita Hiroaki. Gunki bungaku kenkyū sōsho 7. Kyūko shoin, 1998, 135–57.

Shinada Yoshikazu. "Kokumin kashū no hatsumei: josetsu." *Kokugo to kokubungaku* 73, no. 11 (1996): 15–28.

———. "'Min'yō' no hatsumei." *Man'yōshū kenkyū* 21 (1997): 205–96.

———. "Itō Sachio to *Man'yōshū*." In *Kotoba ga hiraku kodai bungakushi*, edited by Suzuki Hideo. Kasama shoin, 1999.

Shioda Ryōhei. "Koten to Meiji igo no bungaku." *Iwanami kōza: Nihon bungakushi* 14. Iwanami shoten, 1959.

Shirane, Haruo. *The Bridge of Dreams: A Poetics of 'The Tale of Genji.'* Stanford: Stanford University Press, 1987.

———. *Traces of Dreams: Landscape, Cultural Memory, and the Poetry of Bashō.* Stanford: Stanford University Press, 1998.

Shirane, Haruo, and Tomi Suzuki, eds. *Sōzōsareta koten: kanon keisei, kokumin kokka, Nihon bungaku.* Shin'yōsha, 1999.

Shuzui Kenji, Kondō Tadayoshi, Otoba Hiroshi, eds. *Chikamatsu.* Kokugo kokubungaku kenkyūshi taisei 10. Sanseidō, 1964.

Smith, Anthony D. *The Ethnic Origins of Nations.* Cambridge, Mass.: Blackwell, 1986.

Sōrinshi gikyoku. 2 vols. Minyūsha, 1896.

Suematsu Kenchō. "Engeki kairyō iken." In *Meiji geijutsu bungaku ronshū*, edited by Hijikata Teiichi. Meiji bungaku zenshū 79. Chikuma shobō, 1975.

———. "Kagaku-ron." *Meiji geijutsu, bungaku ronshū.* Meiji bungaku zenshū 79. Chikuma shobō, 1975. (First published in *Tokyo nichinichi shinbun.* Sept. 1884–Feb. 1885).

———. *Kokka shinron.* Tetsugaku shoin, 1897.

Sumita Chihoko. "*Tsurezuregusa* juyōshi no ichikōsatsu." *Chūsei bungaku ronkō* 2 (Apr. 1956).

Sunagawa, Hiroshi. *Gunki monogatari no kenkyū.* Ōfūsha, 1990.

Suyematz, Kenchio [Suematsu Kenchō], trans. *Genji monogatari.* London: Trübner, 1882.

Suzuki, Tomi. *Narrating the Self: Fictions of Japanese Modernity.* Stanford: Stanford University Press, 1996.

Tada Yoshitoshi. *Shūsai kango* (entry number 179). In *Nihon zuihitsu zenshū* 14, edited by Nakatsukasa Eijirō. Kokumin tosho, 1928.

Tadami Keizō, ed. *Chikamatsu jōrurishū.* 3 vols. Yūmeidō, 1910–14.

Taga Akigorō. *Gakkō no rekishi.* Chūō daigaku seikyō shuppan, 1974.

Taguchi Ukichi. *Nihon kaika shōshi.* Kaizōsha, 1929.

Taine, Hippolyte A. *History of English Literature*, vol. 1. Translated by H. Van Laun. 1883. Reprint, New York: Frederick Ungar Publishing Co., 1965.

Takada Mizuho. "*Tsurezuregusa* no eikyō—Kindai bungaku." In *Tsurezuregusa kōza* 4, edited by Yūseidō henshūbu. Yūseidō, 1974.

Takagi Ichinosuke. *Takagi Ichinosuke zenshū.* 10 vols. Kōdansha, 1976–77.

Takaki Ichinosuke, Ozawa Masao, Atsumi Kaoru, and Kindaichi Haruhiko, eds.

Heike monogatari. 2 vols. Nohon Koten bungaku taikei 32–3. Iwanami shoten, 1959–60.

Takagi Ichinosuke, Sasaki Hachirō, Tomikura Tokujirō, eds. *Heike monogatari: kōza.* 2 vols. Sōgensha, 1957.

Takahashi Masaaki. "Jōshikiteki kizokuzō, bushizō no sōshutsu katei." In *Nihonshi ni okeru kō to shi,* edited by Rekishi to hōhō henshū iinkai. Aoki shoten, 1996.

Takamori Kuniaki. *Kindai kokugo kyōikushi.* Hato no mori shobō, 1979.

Takano Tatsuyuki, ed. *Chikamatsu kabuki kyōgenshū.* 2 vols. Rokugōkan, 1927.

Takano Tatsuyuki and Kuroki Kanzō, eds. *Chikamatsu Monzaemon zenshū.* 10 vols. Shunyōdō, 1922–24.

Takarai Kikaku (Tōraku Sanjin). *Irozato Tsurezuregusa. Sharebon taisei* 4. Edited by Mizuno Minoru. Chūō kōronsha, 1979.

Takayama Chogyū. "Chikamatsu Sōrinshi ga jinseikan." *Teikoku bungaku* 2 (1895).

———. "Gikyoku-teki jinbutsu to Chikamatsu Sōrinshi." *Taiyō* 4 (1895).

———. "Sōrinshi no josei ni tsuite." *Teikoku bungaku* 4 (1895).

———. "Taira no Kiyomori ron." Collected in *Heike monogatari.* Edited by Takagi Ichinosuke et al. Kokugo kokubungaku kenkyūshi taisei, 89–93.

Takeda Yūkichi, ed. *Norito.* Nihon koten bungaku taikei 1. Iwanami shoten, 1971.

Takei Kazuto. *Ichijō Kanera no shoshiteki kenkyū.* Ōfūsha, 1987.

Takeishi Akio. *Tsurezuregusa no bukkyōken.* Ōfūsha, 1971.

Takeishi Akio, text, and Watanabe Fukuo, illus. *Manga Tsurezuregusa.* Sanseidō, 1989.

Takemoto Hirokazu. "Kume Kunitake to nōgaku fukkō." In *Bakumatsu Meiji-ki no kokumin kokka keisei to bunka henyō,* edited by Nishikawa Nagao and Matsumiya Hideharu. Shinyōsha, 1995.

Takeuchi Akira, ed. *Nihon kyōikushi.* Bukkyō daigaku tsūshin kyōikubu, 1989.

Tamai Kōsuke. *Nikki bungaku gaisetsu.* Kokusho kankōkai, 1945.

Tanaka Jūtarō. "Zuihitsu bungaku no seikaku to sono keitai." *Geirin* 3, no. 3 (June 1952).

Tanaka Shōtarō. "*Heikan no setsu* to *Tsurezuregusa.*" *Ritsumeikan bungaku* 140 (1957): 48–53.

Tanaka, Stefan. "Imaging History: Inscribing Belief in the Nation." *Journal of Asian Studies* 53, no. 1 (Feb. 1994): 24–44.

Tani Hiroshi. *Heike monogatari.* Koten to sono jidai 4. San'ichi shobō, 1957.

Tanizaki Akio. "Chōkoku no go no ben." In *Nihon rōmanha.* Nihon bungaku kenkyū shiryō sōsho, edited by Nihon bungaku kenkyū shiryō kankō kai. Yūseidō, 1977.

Taoka Reiun. *Seinenbun* (1896).

Tasaka Fumiho. *Meiji jidai no kokugoka kyōiku.* Tōyō shuppansha, 1969.

Tasaka Fumiho, ed. *Kyūsei chūtō kyōiku, Kokugoka kyōkasho naiyō sakuin.* Kyōkasho kenkyū sentaa, 1983.

Tobita Takio and Inoue Toshi. *Kyūsei chūtō gakkō kyōka naiyō no hensen.* Edited by Kyōkasho kenkyū sentaa. Gyōsei, 1984.

Tōdōyōshū. In *Kaitei shiseki shūran,* edited by Kondō Heijō. Kyoto: Rinsen shoten, 1984, 27: 705–36.

Togawa Yoshirō. *Jukyōshi.* Yamakawa shuppansha, 1987.

———. "Kangaku Shinagaku no enkaku to sono mondaiten." *Risō* 387 (June 1996).

Tokutomi Sohō. "*Heike monogatari* wo yomu." *Kokumin no tomo* (June 1887). Collected in *Kokumin no tomo* 1, edited by Fujiwara Masahito. Meiji bunken, 1966.

Tomikura Tokujirō. *Heike monogatari kenkyū.* Kadokawa shoten, 1964.

———. "Muromachi jidai no heikyoku." In *Heike monogatari kōza* 2, edited by Takagi Ichinosuke, Sasaki Hachirō, and Tomikura Tokujirō. Sōgensha, 1957.

———. *Urabe Kenkō.* Yoshikawa kōbunkan, 1964.

Tone Keizaburō. "Minshū no kyōiku juyō no zōdai to terakoya." In *Kōza Nihon no kyōikushi 2: kinsei I, kinsei II, kindai I,* edited by Kōza Nihon kyōikushi henshū iinkai. Daiichi hōki shuppan, 1984.

Toyama Masakazu. "Shintai-shi oyobi rōdoku-hō." *Teikoku bungaku* 2, nos. 3–4 (1896): 1–16, 1–14.

———. "Engeki kairyōron shikō." In *Meiji geijutsu bungaku ronshū,* edited by Hijikata Teiichi. Meiji bungaku zenshū 79. Chikuma shobō, 1975.

Tsubouchi Shōyō. "Engeki kairyōkai no sōritsu." In *Bungaku geijutsu hen. Meiji bunka zenshū* 12. Nihon hyōronsha, 1928.

———. "Makubesu hyōshaku no chogen." In *Bungaku no shisō.* Edited by Nakamura Mitsuo. Nihon shisō taikei 13. Chikuma shobō, 1965.

———. "Waga kuni no shigeki." *Tsubouchi Shōyō shū.* Edited by Inagaki Tatsurō. Meiji bungaku zenshū 16. Chikuma shobō, 1969.

Tsubouchi Shōyō and Tsunashima Ryōsen, eds. *Chikamatsu no kenkyū.* Shun'yōdō, 1900.

Tsuchida Mamoru. "Sewa higeki no seiritsu to hembō." *Kokubungaku: kaishaku to kanshō* 39, no. 11 (1974).

Tsuda Sōkichi. *Bungaku ni arawaretaru waga kokumin shisō no kenkyū.* 4 vols. Rakuyōdō, 1916–21.

Tsujimoto Masashi. *Kinsei kyōiku shisōshi no kenkyū.* Shibunkaku shuppan, 1990.

Tsukamoto Yasuhiko. "Yasuda Yojūrō no bungaku to koten." In *Nihon rōman-ha: Yasuda Yojūrō, Ito Shizuo, Kamei Katsuichirō,* edited by Nihon bungaku kenkyū shiryō kankōkai. Yūseidō, 1977.

Tsukishima Hiroshi. *Kana.* Nihongo no sekai 5. Chūō kōronsha, 1981.

Tsurezuregusa shoshō taisei 5. Nihon tosho sentaa, 1978.

Uchida Roan. *Bungaku ippan.* Hakubunkan, 1892.

Ueda Bin. "Bungei seun no renkan." *Teikoku bungaku* 5, no. 1 (1899): 11–23.

———. "Gakuwa." *Teikoku bungaku* 10, no. 1 (1904): 47–55.

———. *Teihon Ueda Bin zenshū,* edited by Ueda Bin zenshū kankōkai. 11 vols. Kyōiku shuppan sentaa, 1978.

Ueda Kazutoshi. "Kokubungaku shogen." In *Ochiai Naobumi, Ueda Kazutoshi, Haga Yaichi, Fujioka Sakutarō shū,* edited by Hisamatsu Sen'ichi. Meiji bungaku zenshū 44. Chikuma shobō, 1968.

———. "Kokugo to kokka to" (1894). In *Ochiai Naobumi, Ueda Kazutoshi, Haga Yaichi, Fujioka Sakutarō shū*, edited by Hisamatsu Sen'ichi. Meiji bungaku zenshū 44. Chikuma shobō, 1968.

Ueki Yukinobu. "Tōdōza no keisei to heikyoku." In *Heike monogatari: katari to gentai*, edited by Hyōdō Hiromi. Yūseidō, 1987.

Uemura Seiji and Kimura Takeshi. *Maruzen hyakunenshi* 1. Maruzen, 1980.

Utsumi Kōzō. *Tsurezuregusa shōkai*. Meiji shoin, 1919.

von Herder, Johann Gottfried. *Volkslieder*. Leipzig, 1778–79.

Vos, Fritz. *A Study of the Ise-monogatari with the Text according to the Den-Teika-Hippon and an Annotated Translation*. The Hague: Mouton, 1957.

Wajima Yoshio. *Chūsei no jugaku*. Yoshikawa kōbunkan, 1965.

Washiyama Jushin. "Akinari bungaku to *Tsurezuregusa*—toku ni sono shisōteki eisei ni tsuite." *Hanazono daigaku kokubungaku ronkyū* 10 (Nov. 1982): 21–34.

Watanabe Hiroshi. "Yasuhira to kōkoku." In *Kokka to shimin* 2, edited by Kokka gakkai. Yūhikaku, 1987.

Watanabe Minoru, ed. *Ise monogatari*. Shinchō Nihon koten shūsei. Shinchōsha, 1976.

———. "Minamoto no Tōru to *Ise monogatari*." *Kokugo to kokubungaku* 49 (Nov. 1972): 1–12.

Watsuji Tetsurō. "Nihon bungaku to gairai shisō I: bukkyō shisō." *Iwanami kōza Nihon bungaku*. Iwanami shoten, 1933.

———. *Nihon rinri shisōshi*. 2 vols. Iwanami shoten, 1952.

Wellek, René. "Hippolyte Taine's Literary Theory and Criticism." *Criticism* 1 (1959): 1–18, 123–38.

———. *The Rise of English Literary History*. Chapel Hill: University of North Carolina Press, 1966.

———. "What Is Literature?" In *What Is Literature?*, edited by Paul Hernadi. Bloomington and London: Indiana University Press, 1978.

Williams, Raymond. *Marxism and Literature*. Oxford: Oxford University Press, 1977.

Wolf, F. A. *Prolegomena to Homer*. 1795. Translated with introduction and notes by Anthony Grafton, Glenn W. Most, and James E. G. Zetzel. Princeton: Princeton University Press, 1985.

Yamada Yoshio. *Heike monogatari*. 2 vols. 1914. Reprint, Iwanami shoten, 1929.

———. *Heike monogatari kō*. Edited by Kokugo chōsa iinkai. Kokutei kyōkasho kyōdō hanbai sho, 1911.

———. *Heike monogatari no gohō*. 1914. Reprint, Hōbunkan, 1954.

Yamagishi Tomoko. "Kenkyū to kanshō no kiseki." In *Tsurezuregusa hikkei*, edited by Kubota Jun. Bessatsu kokubungaku 10. Gakutōsha, 1981.

Yamaguchi Keiji. *Sakoku to kaikoku*. Iwanami shoten, 1993.

Yamaguchi Yoshinori and Kōnoshi Takamitsu, eds. *Kojiki*. Shinpen Nihon koten bungaku zenshū 1. Shōgakukan, 1997.

Yamamoto Masahide. *Kindai buntai keisei shiryō shūsei: hasseihen.* Ōfūsha, 1978.

Yamamura Yoshiaki. *Nihonjin to haha.* Tōyōkan, 1971.

Yamashita Hiroaki. *Heike monogatari kenkyū josetsu.* Meiji shoin, 1972, 79–103.

Yanagita Kunio. *Yanagita Kunio zenshū.* 32 vols. Chikuma shobō, 1989–91.

Yasuda Yojūrō. *Yasuda Yojūrō zenshū* 4. Kōdansha, 1986.

Yasuraoka Kōsaku. *Tsurezuregusa zenchūshaku* 2. Kadokawa shoten, 1967–68.

Yonehara Masayoshi. *Sengoku bushi to bungei no kenkyū.* Ōfūsha, 1976.

Yosano Akiko. "Koten no kenkyū" (1925). In *Yosano Akiko senshū* 4, edited by Yosano Hikaru and Shinma Shin'ichi. Shunjūsha, 1967.

———. "Sei Shōnagon no kotodomo" (1911). In *Yosano Akiko senshū* 4, edited by Yosano Hikaru and Shinma Shin'ichi. Shunjūsha, 1967.

Yosano Tekkan. "Kokushi kakushin no rekishi." *Kokoro no hana* 3, no. 9 (1900): 7–12.

Yoshida Atsuhiko. *Nihon no shinwa.* Seitosha, 1990.

Yoshida Kōichi, ed. *Tsurezuregusa modoki hyōban.* Koten bunko 418. Koten bunko, 1981.

Yoshida Seiichi. *Gendai bungaku to koten. Yoshida Seiichi chosakushū* 23. Ōfūsha, 1981.

Yoshikawa Hideo. *Shinchū Ise monogatari.* Seibunkan shoten, 1926.

Yoshino Kosaku. *Cultural Nationalism in Contemporary Japan.* London: Routledge, 1992.

Yoshizawa Sadato. "Shimizu Shunryū to *Tsurezuregusa.*" *Kinjō gakuin daigaku ronshū* 57 (Dec. 1973).

———, ed. *Tsurezuregusa—Tsurezuregusa Jumyō'in shō.* Nagoya: Chūbu Nihon kyōiku bunkakai, 1982.

Yoshizawa Yoshinori, ed. *Tsurezuregusa shūishō.* Mikan kokubun kochūshaku taikei 16. Shibundō, 1969.

Yūda Yoshio. *Jōrurishi ronkō.* Chūō kōronsha, 1975.

Yuge Shigeru. "Gunki monogatari no seidōkan wo megutte." *Gunki to kanbungaku.* Wakan hikaku bungaku sōsho 15. Kyūko shoin, 1993, 59–80.

Yūki Rikurō. "Sengoku jidai no Ashikaga gakkō." *Kōza Nihon kyōikushi 1*, edited by Kōza Nihon kyōikushi henshū iinkai. Daiichi hōki shuppan, 1984.

Index

In this index an "f" after a number indicates a separate reference on the next page, and an "ff" indicates separate references on the next two pages. A continuous discussion over two or more pages is indicated by a span of page numbers, e.g., "57–59." *Passim* is used for a cluster of references in close but not consecutive sequence.

Age of the Gods, 17–18, 39, 63–64, 226
Akahito (court poet), 16
Akiyama Ken, 91–95, 114, 116, 119
Akutagawa Ryūnosuke, 146
Amaterasu, 17–18, 53–54, 56–57, 61, 111
Ame-no-tomi, 57
Analects, 123, 125, 222, 227, 233
Ancient period, 51, 173–77. *See also* Nara period
Anderson, Benedict, 11–12, 41, 221
Anesaki Masaharu, 171–72
The Anthology of Literature, see Wen-hsüan (Monzen)
Antoku, Emperor, 155
Aoki Sōko, 126
Appiah, Kwame, 174
Arai Hakuseki, 78, 239
Arai Mujirō, 108f
Araragi school, 34
Aristocracy, 47–49, 59, 63, 98, 151, 171, 176–77, 223–24, 226, 230, 282n53. *See also* Social class
Ariwara no Narihira, 97
Art, 8–9, 13, 251n8
Asaga Sansei, 133
Asai Ryōi, 127
Ashikaga gakkō, 227–28, 229
Ashikaga Takauji, 156–57, 162, 166

Ashikaga Yoshimasa, 166
Aston, W.G., 144
Autobiographical novels, 88–89. *See also* Diary literature; I-novels
Azuma kagami (Mirror of the East), 209, 228
Azuma-uta, 17, 19, 39, 46–47, 49

Baishōron, 156
Bakufu, see Shogunate
Ban Kōkei, 138, 239
The Battles of Coxinga, see Kokusenya Kassen
Beck, L. Adam, 145
Belles lettres, 134, 252n9
Bibungaku, 6, 75ff
Bijutsu, 9
"Bitextuality," 9
Biwa hōshi, 176, 281n42, 282n53, 284n70, 286n87. *See also* Tale of Heike
Book of Songs, see Shih ching
Bourdieu, Pierre, 2
Bowring, Richard, 98
Brownstein, Michael, 183, 191
Buddhism, 78; canon of, 4, 22, 220, 226f, 229f, 234; in *Genpei jōsuiki*, 157–58, 159; and *kangaku*, 25, 208–12, 216; separation from Shinto, 101; in *Tale of the Heike*, 153, 166f, 176, 286n88; in *Tsurezuregusa*, 128,

321

and cultural identity, 78; curricula during,
230–35, 238–40, 247; folk songs of, 47;
historical documents of, 23; and imperial
ideologues, 278n18; *kangaku* and Confucianism during, 25, 211, 213–17; and
kokubungaku, 191–93; literature of, 14,
127, 171; *Tale of the Heike* in, 168, 282n51;
and *Tales of Ise* editions, 99, 103; theater in,
9, 180–82; writers and commentators of,
7, 10
Education, 26, 100, 116f, 123–34, 175, 183,
207, 215, 223–25, 232, 235–36, 297n33,
297–98n35. *See also* Curricula; Schools
Ekū, 130
Ellmann, Mary, 139
Emotion, 81–83, 163–64, 190–91, 195f, 242
Emperor: allegiance to, 21, 58, 64, 66–67,
119, 240; dismantling of system, 176; and
miyabi, 112, 116–17; mythology of system,
51f, 55. *See also* Imperial system
Enchi Fumiko, 89
Endō Ryūkichi, 218
Endō Yoshimoto, 110
Engi shiki, 56, 58
Epics, national, 37–38, 170–78
Erhya (*Jiga*), 222
Ethnicity, 45, 49–50
European influence, 6–9, 13–14, 16, 23, 27,
35, 37, 42–44, 74–75, 174, 237, 248–49,
284n70. *See also* Western influence

Families, and education, 224–25, 232
Family values, 100, 240, 244
Femininity, 75, 83, 115, 118; of Heian period,
10–11, 20, 90, 97, 100–104, 113, 205, 209–
10; of *Man'yōshū*, 40–41; of writing styles,
207. *See also* Gender; Women
Festivals, 55, 208, 216
Fiction, 4, 78–79, 82, 93, 242
Filial piety, 240, 243
First Eight Imperial Poetry Anthologies, see
Hachidaishū, 229
Five Mountains (Gozan), 203, 227
Folk literature, 16–19. *See also* Min'yō
Folklore studies, *see Minzokugaku*
Folk songs, 42f, 46. *See also Minyō*
Fujii Otoo, 45

Fujii Takanao, 105
Fujimura Tsukuru, 86–87
Fujioka Sakutarō, 6, 10, 80–83, 103–4; on
epic literature, 171f; on *Tale of the Heike*,
152, 154, 158–62
Fujita Tōko, 157
Fujita Yūkoku, 157
Fujiwara Akihira, 223
Fujiwara Kintō, 5, 223
Fujiwara no Nobuyori, 279n27
Fujiwara no Tokihira, 207
Fujiwara Shunzei, 225, 234
Fujiwara Teika, 11, 73, 97f, 105, 108, 125, 225,
228, 231f, 234
Fukakusa Gensei, 136
Fukuzawa Yukichi, 216
Furukoto, 19, 52, 62–64, 66
Furuta Oribe, 125
Fūryū, 106f, 110
Futabatei Shimei, 186, 239
Futodama, 56–57. *See also* National language

Gabun, 239, 242
Gagaku, 44
Gakumon, 5, 75, 209, 222
Gakusei edict, 235–36
Gakushūkan, curriculum at, 235
Genbun-itchi, 14, 72, 83, 239–40
Gender: and book marketing, 99; and canon
formation, 9–11, 22, 252n14; and genre,
71–95, 137–43; and Heian period, 10–11,
20, 90, 97, 100–104, 113, 205, 209–10; and
historical periods, 88, 162–63, 164; and
Tales of Ise, 21–22, 113–14; and *Tsurezure-
gusa*, 124. *See also* Femininity; Masculinity
Genealogy, 3–4, 89
Genji ippon kyō (Genji One Volume Sutra), 4,
226
Genji monogatari, see The Tale of Genji
Genji warrior clan, 166f
Genkai, 211–12
Genpei jōsuiki, 152, 154f, 157–59, 165, 167f,
236, 238, 299n70
Genpei Wars, 171–72
Genre, 4–9, 22, 71–95, 102, 137–43, 226
Genroku period, 15, 192, 194, 248. *See also*
Edo period